The Great
NO-HITTERS

ALSO BY GLENN DICKEY:
The Jock Empire

The
Great
NO-HITTERS

Glenn Dickey

Chilton Book Company
Radnor, Pennsylvania

Library of Congress Cataloging in Publication Data
Dickey, Glenn.
  The great no-hitters.
  Bibliography: p.
  Includes index.
  1. No-hitter (Baseball) I. Title.
GV871.D52   1976   796.357'78   75-28136
ISBN 0-8019-6251-X

*To my father,
who made me a baseball fan,
and my mother,
who had to endure it.*

Acknowledgments

I owe special thanks to Clifford Kachline, historian for the National Baseball Hall of Fame at Cooperstown, New York, who was of great assistance in providing me with material on no-hit games, particularly statistics from the game's early days which are unavailable from other sources.

Charles S. (Chub) Feeney, president of the National League, graciously allowed me access to his office library and files.

My editor at Chilton, Benton Arnovitz, conceived this project.

There is a complete bibliography in the back of the book and I mention the names of books I have used in the text as well, but I must make special mention here of two invaluable reference books: Macmillan's *The Baseball Encyclopedia* and Grosset & Dunlap's *The Sports Encyclopedia: Baseball*. These two books supplied me with important statistics and also first names, which were frequently left out of early newspaper accounts of games.

Last but not least, I must thank my wife, Nancy, who endured numerous dinner table conversations about no-hitters, and my son, Scott, who wanted me to play with him instead of write and could not understand why it took so long to finish this book. Neither could I.

Contents

Introduction

A no-hitter is an almost mystical feat, causing otherwise rational people to act very strangely indeed. In progress, it usually is not mentioned by anybody concerned lest the pitcher be jinxed, though some pitchers have been relaxed enough to mention it themselves. Ballplayers are reduced to whispers in the dugout and announcers are often forced to torturous circumlocutions to indicate to listeners that something important is happening without being able to tell them what.

Some sportswriters will inevitably write of a no-hitter that "Joe Doakes pitched his way into the Hall of Fame today with a no-hitter . . .", although no such thing happens. There is a listing in the Hall of Fame of every no-hit game pitched, but a lot of no-hit pitchers have not made the Hall; don't look for Bobo Holloman there.

It is a tribute to the power of the no-hitter that it can make men act this way, when other important achievements are treated with much more diffidence. The feat of hitting four home runs in a game, for instance, is much rarer than a no-hit game, yet no announcer would omit mentioning that a batter had already hit three home runs when he came up with a chance to hit his fourth.

The regard in which a no-hitter is held is not easy to explain. It is an unusual feat, but hardly unique. In two years, 1908 and 1969, there were six no-hitters thrown: In the first of those years, there was another no-hitter halted by rain after six innings.

There have been two occasions when pitchers have thrown no-hitters in consecutive games in the same park, and another game when two pitchers each had a no-hitter for nine innings.

Only three times in baseball history since 1901 have two seasons gone by without a no-hitter. With 24 teams now playing major league baseball, the average number of no-hitters in a season approximates four.

Even for pitchers, there are game feats that are more unusual. Striking out 17 or more batters in a game, for instance, has happened less frequently than no-hit games. And yet, there is no question that a fan, given the choice between seeing a no-hitter thrown or seeing an 18-strikeout game, would prefer to see the no-hitter. And the pitcher would prefer to pitch it.

Pitching a no-hitter is not necessarily an indication of ability. Try these names on: George Culver, Bill Kietrich, Bill McCahan. All pitched no-hitters but did little else of note. On the other hand, there have been some Hall of Fame pitchers who never threw a no-hitter, as we shall see.

Yet, there's something about a no-hitter. It represents perfection, because the pitcher cannot allow one ball to fall safely. Sometimes, it seems impossible that a pitcher could ever throw a no-hit game. The law of averages must be suspended for nine innings. Consider that an average team might hit about .250; that means that one in every four hitters should get a hit. In an average game, that means somewhere between seven and nine hits. Yet, in a no-hitter, there are obviously none.

Even if the pitcher is overpowering, as Sandy Koufax was in his prime, there is still the matter of luck. In any game you see, there will be at least one ball hit off the handle of the bat that somehow bloops in past an infielder, or a ball not hit particularly well that goes into exactly the right spot between fielders. Not in this game.

The no-hitter lends itself well to drama. The tension builds, inning after inning. Each batter counts, each pitch. When a ball is hit, there is that moment when nobody knows exactly where it is going. Will it be caught or will it fall in just beyond the reach of an infielder or outfielder? If it is a ground ball, will the throw get the runner or be a fraction of a second late? When a pitcher reaches the ninth inning of a no-hitter, even the moments between pitches have an excruciating excitement. Pitchers have lost no-hitters with one or two outs in the ninth inning and everybody is aware of that.

There are other participants in the drama. The official scorer, for instance. No-hitters have been gained or lost on controversial decisions, as we shall see, and there have been occasions when a call had to be changed later in the game.

For the scorer, who is one of the sportswriters covering the game, some prior planning is involved. "I never went to the bathroom when I was scoring," says Harry Jupiter, who scored the first no-hitter in San Francisco's Candlestick Park, by Juan Marichal on June 15, 1963, when he was with the *San Francisco Examiner.* "I didn't want to get in the situation of getting heat for a play that I missed and that had to be explained to me."

Jupiter had an unusual situation in the no-hitter he scored. There were no controversial calls to be made when Marichal was pitching, but there was for a time a controversial one on the other side. In the first inning, Willie Mays hit a ball into the hole and shortstop Bob Lillis bounced his throw to first, with Mays beating it out. Jupiter immediately called it a hit.

"Nobody said anything about it at the time," says Jupiter, "but then Dick Drott didn't give up another hit until the eighth inning [when he gave up two and the only run of the game]. About the sixth, one of the other writers asked me about the Mays' call. 'Could you reconsider that?' he said. 'If it wasn't for that call, we'd have a double no-hitter going.'"

In the broadcast booth, announcers have debated with themselves for years whether to say the pitcher has a no-hitter going.

Red Barber always believed he was in the booth to report what was happening: That included no-hitters. In the 1947 World Series, Bill Bevens nearly pitched a no-hitter for the Yankees and Barber made frequent references to it, including one just before Cookie Lavagetto broke it up with a double with two outs in the ninth.

"A lot of people wanted to string me up on the nearest tree," said Barber, "but I always felt I had no right to ignore the absence of hits, just as I had no right to ignore errors or runs. I consider that to be the single broadcast I'm proudest of because right then, I feel I matured as a broadcaster."

Other broadcasters have preferred not to mention the no-hitter. Mel Allen, for instance, never did. "I always believed in simply following the tradition of the dugout," he said. "The tradition of not mentioning a no-hitter was not started by broadcasters, but was carried over from the dugout."

Waite Hoyt, a Hall of Fame pitcher who never had a no-hitter, was another who refused to mention a no-hitter in progress. Bob Wolff, who broadcast Don Larsen's perfect game in the 1956 World Series, takes the middle road. "Whether people should or should not be superstitious was hardly the question," Wolff noted in Maury Allen's *Voices in Sports,* while talking of Larsen's game. "The fact is that some were, and they were entitled to their rights as well as anyone else. If I could inform everyone without offending this group, I'd be fulfilling my broadcast role in the broadest possible manner.

"But the key I knew was not just the choice of words—it was when they were used. A broadcaster, I felt, could make any reference he wanted to the no-hitter in progress, including the actual words 'no-hitter' if he desired, as long as he avoided using them just before the pitch was made that could end it all."

In his 1956 broadcast, however, Wolff usually referred obliquely to Larsen's perfect game. ". . . Larsen has retired 21 straight men. The Yankees have four hits. That's all there are in the game . . . Larsen has retired 24 straight Dodgers. . . . Listen to that crowd. One question consumes them all. Is it possible? Can it happen?"

There is one significant difference between that game and the normal no-hitter: Very often during the season, people will tune in and out of a game and not be aware of something unusual unless the announcer tells them; in the World Series, people listen or watch TV in groups and everybody knows exactly what is happening.

Vince Scully, the excellent Dodger announcer, started his career working with Barber and he has always believed, as Red did, that people should know a no-hitter is being pitched. He carries it even further. Before the ninth inning of a no-hitter, he will call his studio and tell them to tape the rest of the broadcast. If the game then ends as a no-hitter, he will give the tape to the pitcher as a memento.

Despite the broadcaster's gyrations on the issue, the obvious fact remains: It is the pitcher who determines whether a no-hitter will be pitched, not the announcer. With Scully mentioning it all the way, Sandy Koufax pitched no-hitters in four consecutive years, and so much for a hex.

A no-hit game always comes as a surprise, because there can be no way of predicting it. Watching Koufax pitch, it seemed he was always capable of throwing a no-hitter; yet, his 4 came in 314 starts during his major league career. That means he failed to pitch a no-hitter 310 times, or nearly 99 per cent of the time.

If a pitcher as talented and successful as Koufax could throw a no-hitter only slightly more than one per cent of the time, who could ever predict that less-talented pitchers would do it? Who, for instance, would have wanted to bet that Larsen would do it in the World Series?

No-hitters come in all sizes and shapes. There are those pitched by great pitchers and those by mediocre ones; there are those in which the pitcher had great stuff and there are those in which every ball was hit right at somebody; there are those pitched in important games and those in meaningless ones; there are those pitched by fastball pitchers and those by curveball specialists.

There is even a question of what constitutes a no-hitter. A no-hitter is usually defined as a game wherein pitchers do not allow a hit for nine innings and their teams win the game. But what of those games that are halted short of nine innings because of rain; should a pitcher get credit for a no-hitter even if he hasn't pitched nine innings? And what of those games in which a pitcher had nine innings of no-hit ball and then gave up a hit, or more, in extra innings?

For the purpose of this book, I am using the generally recognized baseball formula: Any game when a pitcher had a no-hitter for nine innings is a legitimate no-hitter, even if he lost the no-hitter in later innings.

This, then, is a look at the great no-hitters and the men who pitched them and, in some instances, those who didn't.

Foreword

by Jim "Catfish" Hunter

Catfish Hunter is the richest player in baseball history. After the 1974 season, during which he won 25 games and subsequently the Cy Young Award for pitching excellence, Hunter claimed that Oakland A's owner Charlie Finley had breached his contract. His position was upheld in arbitration and he was declared a free agent. Twenty-two clubs bid for his services, with the New York Yankees finally signing him for a package estimated at $3.7 million. Six years before that, Hunter had first let the baseball world know he would be a pitcher to be reckoned with as he pitched a perfect game, 27 men up and 27 men down, for the first time in regular season play since 1922. Here, he describes his feelings about that game and about no-hitters.

Pitching a perfect game in 1968 has to be one of my biggest thrills in baseball, right up there with winning a World Series. A no-hitter is every pitcher's dream, and to pitch a perfect game, well, that's beyond dreaming.

I've thought a lot about what it takes to pitch a no-hit game. I think it's easier for a curveball pitcher than a fastball pitcher because he's usually going to have better control.

Still, Nolan Ryan has pitched four no-hitters. He just has that overwhelming fastball, and when he's on, guys just can't do anything with him.

Everything has to be going for you when you pitch a no-hitter. You have to have your best stuff and you have to be lucky, too, because sometimes balls are hit hard off you but go right to a fielder.

Some pitchers who haven't done much have pitched no-hitters, pitchers like Bobo Holloman and Bo Belinsky. I remember when Dick Bosman of Cleveland pitched a no-hitter against us [the A's] just before the All-Star break in 1974. I wasn't with the club then; I had gone home to North Carolina for a couple of days. My brother told me, "Hey, your club got a no-hitter thrown against it." I said it must have been Gaylord Perry, and he said, "No, it was Dick Bosman." I said, "You've got to be kidding." But he wasn't.

How does that happen? Well, you just have to say that for that one game, those pitchers had everything going for them.

I remember the night I pitched my no-hitter. I just felt great that night. I'm not a fastball pitcher, but I felt like I could throw the ball past anyone that night—Tony Oliva, Harmon Killebrew, anybody.

Nothing bothered me. I remember once I was 3–0 on Oliva, and then I threw three straight strikes. My control was just great. I don't even remember any great plays that had to be made behind me.

I had two strikes on the last hitter and threw a curve I thought got the outside corner. The umpire didn't agree with me. He called it a ball, but that didn't bother me. I just came back and threw another strike and got the hitter out of there.

In the fourth inning that night, Mike Hershberger (then an Oakland outfielder) was talking on the bench with another player about whether there had been a baserunner. Mike said, "I think there was one guy who got to first."

Well, I didn't want to hear them talking about it, so I went into the toilet, but I knew there hadn't been a hit. I couldn't remember whether I had walked anybody. So, at the end of the game, until somebody told me, I wasn't sure whether I'd pitched a no-hitter or a perfect game.

I don't go out there to pitch a no-hit game every time. Winning the game is the most important thing, and so you try to keep the other team from scoring runs because you can't get beat if they don't score any runs. But, sure, I'd like to pitch another no-hitter.

I've had some games I thought I had the stuff and control to pitch a no-hitter, but I wound up giving up two or three hits. I remember one game in particular just before the end of the 1973 season. We had clinched the divisional title and I was just supposed to pitch part of the game and then come out. But I hadn't given up a hit until the seventh, and so [manager] Dick Williams left me in.

In the seventh, there was a ball hit just wide of first base. [Second baseman] Dick Green was there and waiting for it, and I was covering first to take the throw, but [first baseman] Gene Tenace tried for it and the ball went off his glove. Well, you couldn't give Gino an error for trying for the ball, so the batter got a hit and I came out of the game.

I had another game against Kansas City, I think it was in 1972, when I really felt sharp, as sharp as I had since I pitched my perfect game. But we had a 7–0 lead that night, and it's hard to concentrate on a no-hitter when you've got that kind of lead. I wound up giving up three hits that night.

I can't believe that Johnny Vander Meer pitched two straight no-hitters. I remember the game I pitched after my perfect game; I didn't have anything. This was against Minnesota again, this time in Minnesota. They got six runs off me and hit three home runs. The first batter up, Rod Carew, hit a home run to dead center field, and he's not even a power hitter. But I was lucky; the team got eight runs for me and I wound up winning the game.

Knowing what a thrill it is to pitch a no-hitter, I've even secretly rooted for other pitchers when they've had a no-hitter going against my team in the late innings. When I was with the A's, we had a couple thrown against us, by Jim Bibby and Clyde Wright, in addition to the Bosman one I didn't see, and I was rooting for them. I mean, when it got down to two outs in the ninth inning, I knew we weren't going to win the game, and I'd have hated to see one hit break it up.

When I was with the A's, there was another game I remember, when Blue Moon Odom was pitching for us and I thought he should have had a no-hitter. I was charting the game that night and he threw 205 pitches! I thought I was going to run out of paper. I think he walked 10–11 guys that night.

But he really had his stuff. He had one ball that was hit to third base and Sal Bando overthrew first base when the guy was still five feet from the base. I thought it was an error, but the scorer gave the guy a hit. Then, there was another ball that was hit to Blue Moon and he threw wildly to first when he should have had it, and that was called a hit, too. Two hits, but I thought they both should have been errors. A lot of people said, well, it was such a sloppy game, he didn't deserve a no-hitter, but I don't buy that. A no-hitter is a no-hitter.

In this book, Glenn Dickey has covered the history of the no-hit game from its very beginnings. It's the most comprehensive look at the no-hitter that I've seen.

The
Great
NO-HITTERS

1

In the beginning

Joe Borden, George Washington Bradley, John Lee Richmond, Ted Breitenstein and Charles Leander (Bumpus) Jones are names that would mean nothing to any but most devoted of baseball historians, but in one way or another, they can all claim to have been pioneers in pitching no-hit games.

Borden is the father of the no-hitter, having pitched the first recorded no-hit game for Philadelphia against Chicago in the old National Association, his team winning 4–0. The account in the records of the Baseball Hall of Fame at Cooperstown, New York, puts it this way: "Joseph E. Borden, who played professionally as 'Josephs,' was the first big league no-hit pitcher. On July 28, 1875, on the grounds at Twenty-Fifth and Jefferson Sts., Philadelphia, Borden tossed the Chicago team up and down in a blanket, so to speak."

They don't write sports like that any more, for which we can all be grateful.

But Borden's feat, because it was recorded in the ragtag National Association, gets little recognition. Indeed, his record in the National Association is not even included in his career performances, which are listed in *The Baseball Encyclopedia* published by Macmillan.

Thus, controversy surrounds the very origin of the no-hitter. The aptly named George Washington Bradley is considered by some to be the father of the major league no-hitter because he threw his in the National League, for St. Louis against Hartford, in a home game on July 15, 1876.

1

Yet, Borden's name crops up here, too, because the late Lee Allen, former historian for the Hall of Fame, has always maintained that Borden threw the first no-hitter in the National League. The game he cites was an 8–0 win for Boston on May 23, 1876, over Cincinnati, though the box score shows two hits for Cincinnati.

"Although the game was played at Boston," wrote Allen in *100 Years of Baseball*, "the score was sent to the league office by Oliver Perry Caylor, a writer for *The Cincinnati Enquirer*, and during the season Caylor, at variance with contemporary scorers, counted bases on balls as hits . . . Borden granted passes to two Cincinnati batters, passes which appeared as hits in the box score."

Allen has never received any support for his position, though, and the Hall of Fame records do not include Borden's National League game among the no-hitters. That kind of luck was typical of Borden's career: He was only 11–12 in his one year in the National League and finished the season with a sore arm, never again to pitch in the National League.

A sore arm is still the No. 1 occupational hazard for pitchers, who throw with a motion nature never intended, but the infirmity was even more rampant in the early days of baseball when pitchers were expected to work much more frequently than they do now. In his no-hit year of 1876, for instance, Bradley pitched 64 games, all of which he completed for a total of 573 innings! That was quite a year for George Washington, who won 45 games and had a 1.23 earned run average (ERA).

Yet only two years later, Bradley lost 40 games, winning only 13. Understandably, his 40 losses were a league high that season; not so understandably, his 45 wins the two years before were not.

Unless you count Borden's game, Bradley's no-hitter was the first and only in the National League for four years. Then on June 12, 1880, Worcester beat Cleveland 1–0 in a game at Worcester, Massachusetts. The account of the game read like this: "The most wonderful game on record, and one of the shortest, was played this afternoon between the Clevelands and the Worcesters. The Worcesters played without an error and, for nine straight innings, retired their opponents in one two three order, not a man getting a base hit or reaching first base. . . ."

The story goes on in that vein at some length, telling the reader about double plays and fly balls and attendance and even the fact that rain stopped the game for eight minutes in the eighth inning. What the story does not tell is the score of the game (1–0) or the pitcher (John Lee Richmond). Athletes were not over-publicized in those days.

So, Richmond became the first pitcher to throw a perfect game. Information about the early pitchers is sparse, and we do not know whether Richmond celebrated by getting drunk or with female companionship, or both. Chances are, he went home early and rested, because he was another of the workhorse pitchers. In 1880, he started a league high 74 games and split 64 decisions down the middle.

It was 11 years before another no-hit precedent was set. On October 4, 1891, at St Louis, rookie St. Louis lefthander Ted Breitenstein pitched a no-hit game against Louisville in his first major league game. The headline writer proclaimed: "He's a $10,000 Beauty; Breitenstein Pitches a Remarkable Game; Only One Man Reached First Base, and He Got There on Balls." It was an unusual display of enthusiasm in an era when no-hit games were often greeted rather casually.

Breitenstein later pitched another, better no-hitter, this time for Cincinnati against Pittsburgh on April 22, 1898, when he faced only 27 men: He walked one batter, who was then cut down on a double play. This was hardly typical of his career, since he finished with 168 wins and 169 losses in 11 years. But Breitenstein was a Hall-of-Famer compared to Bumpus Jones, who duplicated Breitenstein's feat by pitching a no-hitter in his first big league game, giving Cincinnati a 7–1 win over Pittsburgh on October 15, 1892. The next year, Jones won a more routine game and that was it for his big league career—two wins, four losses, and the tag of the first and best of the flukes.

In a sense, a lot of the no-hitters pitched before 1901, when baseball took the form it retains to the present with American and National Leagues, could be considered flukes. The game was in its infancy and changes were plentiful. The distance between pitcher and batter changed, as well as the method of pitching. Scoring rules changed back and forth. We have already seen how one recalcitrant scorer took a no-hitter away from Joe Borden; some years later, that style of scoring—considering walks as hits—became the norm and we cannot know whether that cost one pitcher or several a no-hit game. Because of the newness of the game, scoring differed greatly from community to community; no doubt, some pitchers benefited from this and others suffered. Even the official records were imprecise, hard as that is to believe of a sport which has since become so enmeshed in numerical data that it has been described as an island of activity in a sea of statistics. The records at the Hall of Fame are studded with names like Worcester and Providence and even Allegheny in the early days; one is forced to think that some pitchers lost no-hitters and others received credit for no-hitters that were not really thrown.

Thus, there can only be an estimate—somewhere between 50 and 60—of no-hitters thrown before 1901.

The game only superficially resembled the one which is played today. The pitching distance, for instance, started at 45 feet, was increased to 50 feet in 1881 and, finally, to its present distance of 60 feet, 6 inches in 1893.

Until 1883 the pitcher threw underhanded and it was not until 1889 that four balls became a walk; before that, it took anywhere from nine, in 1879, to five, in 1887. The three-strike rule was not adopted until 1888. In 1895, a foul tip also became a strike and in 1903, a foul tip caught after two strikes resulted in an out. And a final, whimsical rule of baseball's infancy: Before 1887, a batter could call for either a high or low pitch.

Scoring rules affected the pitchers, too. In 1887, for instance, walks were counted as hits and an 1876 rule charged the batter with a time at bat on a walk. For a time, walks, wild pitches, hit batters and balks were all lumped together under the heading of "error." That rule was first established in 1883, reversed in 1887, reestablished in 1888 and finally abolished for good in 1889.

The level of competition ebbed and flowed with the formation and dropping of new leagues, another factor which makes it difficult to judge the quality of the early no-hitters. After the demise of the National Associations, usually considered a professional but not "major" league because of its erratic scheduling, the National League started in 1876. It was joined in 1882 by the American Association and that league lasted until 1891. Other leagues weren't so successful. Both the Union Association and the Players' League (which was, as the name indicates, a league formed by the players themselves) lasted only one year each: 1884 for the Union Association; 1890 for the Players' League.

Finally, the National League expanded to twelve clubs after the American Association folded in 1891. It lasted in that form until 1899, when four teams were dropped. In turn, that led to the creation of the American League two years later and the stabilizing of professional baseball.

It was a far different game in those days, and that applied to pitchers as much as anybody. Although Candy Cummings is given credit for inventing the curveball as far back as 1867, before organized league play, many good pitchers of the pre-1901 era disdained the pitch, relying instead on speed and control. As mentioned earlier, pitchers were expected to work much more frequently than they do now, and they often hit in spots in the batting order other than the ninth place slot that later became traditional.

Probably because there was little interest in the game, compared to what was to come later, and so much confusion about leagues and teams, no-hit games were often treated casually in the newspaper stories of the day. As we've seen, stories often didn't even mention the pitcher's name; those which did mentioned him by last name only.

Typical was a no-hitter thrown by Ledell (Cannonball) Titcomb for Rochester, 7–0 over Syracuse on September 15, 1890. Here is the story of the game in its entirety: "The Rochesters kept hitting the ball, and Syracuse couldn't. That tells the story." Indeed it does.

Other stories were just as succinct. When William H. (Adonis) Terry pitched a no-hitter, 1–0 for Brooklyn over St. Louis on July 24, 1886, it was described thusly: "The game today was a fine one, and there was an excellent attendance." Exactly what the attendance was, the writer didn't get around to saying, even in the box score.

Bradley's 1876 no-hitter, the first recorded in the National League, was described: "The game played here today between the Hartfords and the home club [St. Louis] resulted in a whitewash for the visitors." And when Lawrence J. Corcoran pitched a 5–0 no-hitter for Chicago over Worcester on September 20, 1882, the writer noted that "Corcoran's pitching was a stumbling block to the visitors."

Only occasionally did a writer truly get excited about a no-hitter. Such an occasion was June 6, 1888, when Henry Porter threw a 4–0 no-hitter for Kansas City over Baltimore.

The headline over the story read: "Thank You, Mr. Porter; All Admire You for the Good Record That You Made," and the anonymous writer continued:

> The happiest man in Baltimore last night was Porter, the pitcher of the Kansas City Club. The cause of this happiness was that in the afternoon, in one hour and twenty-five minutes, he had not only shut out the home club but had prevented them from making a single hit. It was the greatest record made so far by any pitcher in the American Association or the [National] League, and the worst defeat of any club in either.
>
> Porter is to be congratulated for his work, and it eclipsed his record against the Brooklyns last month. In that game, he shut out the team, but they made four hits. He was in excellent form, and had great command of the ball. In no instance was he wild, and he was continually putting balls over the plate. The Baltimores either became afraid of him, or else his delivery was so peculiar that they were bewildered. . . .

And so much for the Baltimores.

Whatever the playing conditions, there were some great no-hitters thrown in the early days of baseball. Corcoran and James F. Galvin, later named to the Hall of Fame, pitched back-to-back no-hitters in August of 1880—which perhaps influenced the rulemakers to move the pitchers back from 45 feet to 50—and Corcoran became the first pitcher to throw three no-hitters, the other two coming in 1882 and 1884. Later, Cy Young and then Bob Feller threw three no-hitters, and Jim Maloney threw two that everybody recognizes and one that some don't; after pitching ten no-hit innings, he gave up a hit in the eleventh. Not until Sandy Koufax came along did a pitcher throw four no-hitters.

Three pitchers who were later elected to the Hall of Fame —Galvin, Young and Charles (Old Hoss) Radbourn—pitched no-hitters in the pre-1901 era. Young was the only one of the three whose career extended past the turn of the century.

Galvin, also known as "Gentle Jeems" or "Pud," pitched two no-hitters in the National League, both for Buffalo, against Worcester in 1880 and Detroit in 1884.

He also pitched two no-hit games that were not recorded. According to Lee Allen and Tom Meany in *Kings of the Diamond,* the explanation is that they were thrown for the St. Louis Reds, a team that was not a National League member.

Galvin, a fastball pitcher with control, pitched 5959 innings in 14 years, an average of 425 each season, more than any pitcher in baseball history except Young. He won 365 games, including back-to-back years of 46 wins in 1883 and 1884 for Buffalo. Only Young, Walter Johnson, Christy Mathewson and Grover Cleveland Alexander have won more. Yet he did not win election to the Hall of Fame until 1965.

Galvin's success on the baseball field, however, was not matched by success off it. When he retired, he opened the largest cafe in Pittsburgh, employing nine bartenders, but could not make it financially. "As a commentary on human nature," noted Allen and Meany wryly, "it can be observed that while Galvin was going broke, each of his bartenders opened a place of his own."

Galvin, who moved into a roominghouse on the lower north side of Pittsburgh after going out of the cafe business, died at age 47 on March 7, 1902. His passing was almost unnoticed because the Ohio River was flooding a nearby area, leaving thousands homeless.

Radbourn pitched his only no-hitter on July 25, 1883, an 8–0 victory for Providence over Cleveland, and the story of the day hinted that it was with a bit of good fortune on his side.

"Providence caught Cleveland today with Dunlap and McCor-

mick on the sick list and gave them their worst defeat of the
season. Radbourn pitched a wonderful game, not a hit being made
on him and only one getting to first base . . ."

Radbourn won 49 games the year of his no-hitter, but his best
season came a year later; indeed, it is the best season any pitcher
has ever had or is likely to have. He won 60 games and lost 12,
pitched complete games in all the 73 he started, (one game was
stopped by darkness while tied), worked 678⅔ innings and had an
earned run average of 1.38. He pitched 11 shutouts and at one
time, won 18 consecutive games.

The first World Series was held that year and, naturally, Radbourn's Providence team was in it. It was supposed to be a best-of-
five series, but Radbourn shortened it by winning the first three
games on successive afternoons 6–0, 3–1 and 12–2.

Perhaps because of his iron-man performance that season—Allen and Meany noted that some mornings his arm
would be so sore he could not raise it to comb his hair—Radbourn
never won as many as half of his 60 wins in 1884 again, but he still
won 20 games or more in five of his remaining seven seasons, and
he finished his career with 308 wins.

Like Galvin, Radbourne died at an early age, 43, long before
his selection to the Hall of Fame in 1939. Happily, that was not
Young's fate. The winningest pitcher in baseball history, with 511
wins, Young lived nearly as long as Galvin and Radbourn combined; when he died at 88, he had been in the Hall of Fame for 18
years.

Cy Young started life as Denton True Young. There are con-
flicting stories about how he got his nickname, but the accepted
version is that reported by Allen and Meany.

Young had started his career in 1890 with Canton of the Tri-
State League, a minor league. Owner George Moreland was not at
first impressed with the 6 foot, 2 inch, 210-pound, hulking farm
boy.

"I thought I had to show all my stuff," said Young later. "I
threw the ball so hard I tore a couple of boards off the grandstand.
One of the fellows said the stand looked like a cyclone struck it.
That's how I got the name that was shortened to Cy."

As the story indicates, Young had a fearsome fastball in his
youth. Later, he acquired a curve and more guile, but virtually
from the start of his career he was a great pitcher. In his second
season with Cleveland of the National League, he won 27, starting
an incredible string of 14 straight years in each of which he won at
least 20 games.

Nothing stopped Young. He pitched for five teams in two

major leagues and until his final two years, when he was 43 and 44, he was a winner for all of them. He started his career when the pitching distance was 50 feet, but when another 10½ feet were added on, it didn't stop him; he won 36 games the year before the change, 32 games the next.

His durability was amazing. He pitched for 22 years and won 511 games, 95 more than Walter Johnson, the second-biggest winner in baseball history. That's one record that's safe. It seems unlikely it will ever even be approached, because only extraordinary pitchers win more than half that total these days; since 1930, Warren Spahn's 363 victories are high.

Besides his record for wins, Young is also the career pace-setter in losses, games started, games completed, innings pitched and hits allowed. For most if his 22 years he was a machine, pitching at least 295 innings in 18 of those sessions. He never seemed to get sick, and he never had a sore arm. Years after his retirement, Young said:

> You have to have good legs to pitch and I always took care of them. When I would go to spring training, I would never touch a ball for the first three weeks. Just would do a lot of walking and running. I never did any unnecessary throwing. I figured the old arm just had so many throws in it and there wasn't any use wasting them.
>
> Like, for instance, I never warmed up ten, fifteen minutes before a game like most pitchers do. I'd loosen up for maybe three, four minutes. Five at the outside. And I never went to the bullpen. Oh, I'd relieve all right, plenty of times, but I went right from the bench to the box and I'd take a few warm-up pitches there and I'd be ready.
>
> Then, I had good control. I aimed to make the batter hit the ball, and I made as few pitches as possible. That's why I was able to work every other day. That and having good legs and keeping them good.

Young, of course, pitched before the advent of Babe Ruth and the lively ball. Probably, he couldn't have pitched as often and as easily in the lively ball era as he did in his time. Yet other pitchers of his day had the same advantage, but none approached his record.

Like others in the pre-1901 era, Young pitched one no-hitter for which he got no credit, in his first and last minor league season. Pitching his final game for Canton in the Tri-State League, Young not only threw a no-hitter against McKeesport (Pennsylvania), but also struck out 18 batters. Shortly after that, he was sold to Cleveland of the National League.

His first major league no-hitter came on September 19, 1897, when Cleveland beat the Cincinnati Reds 6–0. The account of the game read:

> Young performed a feat today which is said not to have been accomplished since Hawk performed it for Baltimore in 1893—shutting the Reds out without a hit in the first game this afternoon. Four of the visitors reached first base during the game. Young gave one base on balls, a wild throw by McKean on an easy chance gave Corcoran a life, and Holliday was twice safe on errors by Wallace. One was a fumble of an easy grounder, and the other a wild throw after a fine stop of a sharp hit drive. The last named was the only approach to a hit the visitors got, and it was by no means close enough to mar Young's record.

The story illustrates one of the problems with measuring no-hitters: There had been one thrown since 1893, a June 2, 1894, game in which Edward Stein of Brooklyn had shut out Chicago 1–0. But that game had been shortened to six innings because of rain, so Young's was the first nine-inning no-hitter since 1893. Obviously, the change in pitching distance had made a difference to most pitchers, if not to Young.

Cy did not pitch another no-hitter until May 5, 1904, by which time he was with the Boston Red Sox, but this one was a beauty. Connie Mack, who probably saw more games in his lifetime than anybody else, called it the best-pitched game he had ever seen.

Although the game was played at Boston, the pregame odds would certainly have favored Philadelphia because the A's great though goofy lefthander, Rube Waddell, was pitching against Young. Mack, asked once by Grantland Rice which pitcher had the best combination of speed and a curveball, instantly answered Waddell.

"Now, Johnson had the best speed," said Mack, "but Walter had only a fair curve ball. His speed was enough. Matty [Christy Mathewson] and Alexander depended largely on control and smartness. [Lefty] Grove and [Bob] Feller had fine speed . . . but Waddell had terrific speed. He was a big, loose, lanky fellow who was almost as fast as Johnson. And his curve was even better than his speed. The Rube had the fastest and deepest curve I've ever seen."

Waddell, ten years younger than Cy, was at the peak of his game in 1904. He won 25 games that year and struck out 349 batters. (Waddell was originally credited with 343 strikeouts, but later the historians put the figure at 349, a figure only Nolan Ryan and Sandy Koufax have surpassed.) Just four days before, on May

1, he had pitched a one-hitter against this same Boston club. He had given up a bunt single to the first batter, Patsy Dougherty, then retired the next 27 men in a row.

But that game and Waddell were upstaged by Young on May 5. Cy retired 27 straight batters for the first perfect game in American League history; he allowed only six balls to be hit out of the infield in the 1-hour, 25-minute contest. Connie Mack had a point.

Years later, Young told Francis J. Powers, in *My Greatest Day in Baseball*, the obvious:

> It's no job for me to pick out my greatest day. It was May 5, 1904 . . . of all the 879 games I pitched in the big leagues, that one stands clearest in my mind.
>
> . . . the Athletics . . . were building up to win the 1905 pennant, and Rube Waddell was their pitcher. And I'd like to say that beating Rube anytime was a big job.
>
> I was real fast in those days but what very few batters knew was that I had two curves. One of them sailed in there as hard as my fast ball and broke in reverse. And the other was a wide break.
>
> I don't think I ever had more stuff, and I fanned eight, getting [Harry] Davis and Monte Cross twice.

The closest the Athletics came to a hit was in the third, when Cross hit a pop fly behind the infield that Buck Freeman caught on a dead run. Boston center fielder Chick Stahl made a similar catch back of second on a pop fly by Ollie Pickering, and Pickering also nearly beat out a slow roller to short on another time at bat.

The game ended in a strange note. With two outs in the ninth, it was Waddell's turn to bat. Instead of pinch-hitting for Rube, Mack let him bat; Waddell hit a fly to Stahl to end the game. A crowd of 10,267, a big one for the time, watched the first perfect game since 1880, when both Richmond and John Montgomery Ward had done it.

In human terms, though, Young's most impressive no-hitter was probably his last, an 8–0 win for the Red Sox over the New York Highlanders, later to become the Yankees. By this time Cy was 41 years old and nearly halfway through what would be his last 20-win season. The June 30, 1908, game was almost another perfect one for him. Only one batter reached first, Harry Niles on a walk, and he was cut down trying to steal second. To top it off, Cy got three hits himself and knocked in four of Boston's runs.

Three years later, Young retired. His arm was still sound, but he had gotten fat and teams were beating him by bunting. "The boys are taking an unfair advantage of the old man," he said. "They know this big stomach of mine makes it difficult to field bunts."

He won only seven games that final year, but he was still capable of pitching very well on occasion. One of his last games was a 1–0 loss to Grover Cleveland Alexander, then a rookie with the Philadelphia Phillies.

2

Larsen and his miracle

It was the unlikeliest of pairings: Toots Shor, the famed New York restauranteur, and Earl Warren, Chief Justice of the Supreme Court. The two men, tied together by a common love of sports, were friends for many years and Shor told Hearst columnist Bob Considine about it in the aftermath of Warren's death in 1974. Part of the story appeared in Considine's syndicated column:

The first time I saw the Chief, he was governor of California. He came into my place when it was on 51st Street, years ago, and he had some of his kids with him. He had been touted onto my place by a California bodyguard who was traveling with him.

We hit it off right away because we both were interested in sports. I don't think there was ever a man in public life, like he was, who ever knew more about sports than the Chief. The only time he ever made a mistake was the night he came in to have dinner during the World Series of 1956. He never missed a World Series, wherever it was, or a Super Bowl or anything else like that. He was such a fan that he used to watch the Washington Senators . . . That took guts.

Anyway, this night he came into the place and saw me having a few quiet drinks with Don Larsen in the back of the dining room. Don was scheduled to pitch the next day for the Yankees against the Dodgers.

I went over to say hello to him and was surprised to hear the Chief say, "I'm going back to work tonight."

12

"But the game tomorrow, Chief. You won't want to miss that."

"Why should I stay over another day to see Larsen pitch, if he's going to stay up all night drinking with you?" said the Chief.

It was indeed a mistake. The next day, Larsen pitched the first, and to this writing *only*, perfect game in World Series history. Though everybody who has seen a lot of baseball games has his own candidate for the best-pitched one, it is hard to argue with a perfect game in the World Series. Sixteen years after the feat, a *Police Gazette* panel of sportswriters and broadcasters picked Larsen's game as the greatest feat in World Series history, beating out Babe Ruth's called-shot home run in the 1932 World Series.

The Chief Justice could be forgiven for not expecting a great performance from Larsen. Probably more than any other no-hit game, Larsen's illustrates the mystery that surrounds no-hitters. For all of his career, Larsen was an in-and-out pitcher: good one day, terrible the next, causing baseball people to shake their heads and mutter about his potential. His night in Toots Shor's—which Larsen characterized as a "couple of beers" after the game the next day—was typical; he was dedicated to the pursuit of happiness, which meant women and liquor and not necessarily baseball.

There were certainly better pitchers than Larsen in that Series. Don Newcombe had won 27 games for the Dodgers that season and Whitey Ford had won 19 for the Yankees; of the eight starters in that Series, five of them had won more games during the season than Larsen. And yet, it was Larsen who pitched the perfect game, shattering all laws of probability.

There was nothing in Larsen's background to indicate that he was capable of such a feat. In his youth, in high school in San Diego, he was known more for his hitting than his pitching; he often played the outfield, though he preferred to pitch.

He showed enough potential as a pitcher to be signed by the old St. Louis Browns (now the Baltimore Orioles) in 1947, but in four years in the minor leagues, his only outstanding year was 1948, when he was 17–11. After those four years, he went into the service for two years and was discharged in 1953. Despite his mediocre minor league record, he stuck with the inept Browns (they finished last that year) and had a 7–12 record.

The next year, the Browns moved to Baltimore and Larsen responded by leading the league in losses with 21, while winning only 3. Nevertheless, he was included in a 16-player deal with the Yankees after that season. The Yankees got Larsen, pitcher Bob

Turley and shortstop Billy Hunter from the Orioles for outfielder Gene Woodling, pitchers Harry Byrd and Jim McDonald, catchers Gus Triandos and Hal Smith and shortstop Willie Miranda. Baltimore later sent four minor leaguers to the Yankees and the Yankees sent three minor league players to Baltimore.

The key man in the deal was Turley, the fastest pitcher in the American League since Bob Feller had been in his prime. However, Larsen was also important to the Yankees, who had insisted he be included in the deal. "When we got Turley and Larsen," said New York general manager George Weiss, "we plugged the major weakness of the Yankee club. They are two of the finest and fastest young righthanders in the game. Both of them figure to get better and they are young. Turley is only 24 and Larsen 25."

Weiss had a well-deserved reputation as a shrewd judge of talent, but he was fooled in this one. Turley showed flashes of greatness, winning 21 games one season, but had only 82 wins in eight years with the Yankees, hardly an outstanding record on a team which won seven of eight pennants in that stretch. Larsen was even less effective, winning only 45 games in five years before the Yankees gave up on him and traded him away.

His first year with the club, he was only 1–1 in early season and had showed so little that the Yankees sent him down to the minors. When he came back, he won eight of nine decisions to finish at 9–2 and the Yankees thought he was on his way at last. Combined with a 9–1 minor league record at Denver of the American Association, he had had a remarkable 18–3 year.

"See that big feller out there: He can throw, he can hit, he can field, he can run. He can be a big man in this business—any time he puts his mind to it."

The speaker was Yankee manager Casey Stengel in spring training in 1956, off on one of his nonstop monologues. The subject, of course, was Larsen.

Stengel had some other words to say, none of them pleasant, a few days after that. This was to have been the year of Larsen's "new attitude." He was in before curfew every night, and concentrating on baseball, for a change—until one night when he crashed into a telephone pole at 5 a.m. Somehow, he escaped uninjured. "Not only did I get the telephone pole," said Larsen later, "but you should have seen what I did to the mail box." Neither the St. Petersburg police nor Stengel shared Larsen's amusement. Stengel had a long talk with Larsen, no doubt much straighter than Casey's rambling discourses with sportswriters; showing remarkable patience, Stengel announced he would not fine Larsen.

But if Stengel thought the gentle approach would work with

Larsen, he was disappointed in the early season in 1956. Don was his old erratic self; he was knocked out in five of his first seven starts and by September he was only 7–5.

Then, he seemed to find himself at last. He won his last four games, to finish at 11–5, and the wins were impressive—one three-hitter and three four-hitters. That earned him a start in the second game of the Series and the Yankees badly needed a win after losing the opener to Brooklyn. Stengel, shrugging off the fact that Larsen had been knocked out in the fifth inning of the one World Series game he had started the previous year, gave big Don another chance.

And again, Larsen wasn't up to it. It seemed he would breeze to a win when the Yankees scored one run in the top of the first and five more in the top of the second to take a 6–0 lead. But then Larsen walked four batters in the bottom of the second and out came Stengel. Johnny Kucks came on to relieve Larsen, but it did no good. The Dodgers scored six runs in the inning and went on to win the game, 13–8.

"When Casey came to take the ball away from me, he was mad," said Don later. "That made two of us because I was mad, too. I was mad at myself, Casey, the Dodgers—everybody in the world. I was still boiling in the clubhouse. I figured I had blown my chance. I was sure I'd never get another chance to start in that Series."

Larsen's failure to come through had put the Yankees in a serious hole. It seemed that the Dodgers, who had won their first World Series in history the year before, might now put two championships back to back. Not yet, though; the Yankees won the next two games at Yankee Stadium and Stengel, who made decisions that sometimes seemed to have come from reading tea leaves, surprised everybody by announcing that Larsen would start the pivotal fifth game. It was a game the Yankees almost had to win, because the Series would shift to tiny Ebbets Field for the final two games and it was very unlikely the Dodgers would lose two straight there.

Why Larsen? "He wasn't throwing in Brooklyn, he was just pushing the ball up there," said Stengel. "Maybe he was worried about the fences. He can pitch better."

Larsen's opponent was Sal (The Barber) Maglie, who had been the scourge of Brooklyn when he was with the New York Giants. Maglie's prime was behind him, but he had enough to be 13–5 for the Dodgers in the regular season and to win the first game of the Series—and he was always at his best in the big games.

Unknown to almost everybody, there was a secondary drama

going on: Ralph (Babe) Pinelli was umpiring his last game behind the plate. Pinelli, who had played eight years as a third baseman in the major leagues, twice hitting .300 and finishing with a .276 career average, had umpired in the National League since 1935 without missing a game. "I had told the National League office before the Series that I was retiring," says Pinelli, now living in Boyes Hot Springs, 40 miles north of San Francisco, "but I hadn't announced it."

He almost missed this game. On Sunday, he had been hit just below the chest by a foul line drive hit by Yankee Gil McDougald, who was, ironically, Babe's wife's second cousin. But he had recovered in time for what he now calls "one of the easiest games I ever worked."

Larsen came to his job more grouchy than nervous. His preference was to sleep till noon, but he had no choice this time. He had to be in the Yankee clubhouse by 10 a.m.: Stengel's orders. So he got up about 8 a.m. and, fortified only with a cup of tea, he took a taxi to Yankee Stadium. In the clubhouse, still not hungry, he declined a can of fruit juice offered to him by Pete Previte, one of the Yankees' clubhouse men.

A capacity crowd of 64,519 was on hand at Yankee Stadium and the fans soon realized they were seeing something special. Through the first three innings, neither Larsen nor Maglie gave up a hit. The closest to a hit was a smash by Jackie Robinson in the second which caromed off the glove of Yankee third baseman Andy Carey, directly to McDougald at shortstop. Gil threw Robinson, no longer the fleet runner he had been in his early career, out at first by an eyelash.

Behind the plate, Pinelli realized he was seeing something special, too. He had worked four no-hitters before—all of them by Dodger pitchers—and he recognized the signs early. "The atmosphere carries you right along," he says. "You can tell by the way the players act and the noises from the fans when you've got a no-hitter going."

Almost 40 years before, Fred Toney of the Cincinnati Reds and Jim (Hippo) Vaughn of the Chicago Cubs had tangled in a double no-hitter, which Vaughn finally lost in the tenth. For the first three innings at Yankee Stadium on this gray day, it seemed the fans might see a repeat of that feat. If not, it seemed more likely that Maglie would throw a no-hitter than Larsen; the crafty Barber had thrown his only no-hitter just 13 days before.

But then, in the fourth, Mickey Mantle ended Maglie's dream of a no-hitter and put the Yankees on the scoreboard with one swing. With two outs, Maglie worked the count to two-and-two on

Mantle, coming off a .353, 52 home run, 130-RBI year that was the best of his career. Then, Sal put a pitch just a trifle high and Mantle whipped it down the right field line and into the seats.

After doing it at the plate, Mantle did it in the field the next inning, Larsen's shakiest. With one out, Gil Hodges lashed a long drive to left center that seemed to be going through for an extra-base hit until Mantle, running at full speed, made a lunging back-handed stab of the ball.

Sandy Amoros, the next man up, lashed a line drive into the right field seats, but it curved foul by no more than a few feet. Larsen wiped his forehead, hitched up his pants and got Amoros to ground out. From then on, he was in control—literally.

"He was a master of control that day," remembers Pinelli. "His change of pace, particularly to the righthanded hitters, was great, because it kept curving away from them, but the biggest thing is the way he was pin-pointing his pitches. He wasn't an overpowering pitcher that day, but he was making them hit his pitch."

Larsen figured in the scoring of the Yankees' second, and last, run in the sixth. Carey opened with a single to center, only the second off Maglie, and Larsen sacrificed him along with a two-strike bunt. Hank Bauer followed with a single to left to score Carey, then Dodger manager Walt Alston came to the mound to talk to Maglie.

Alston left Maglie in and Sal got out of trouble quickly. Mantle ripped a one-hopper to Hodges at first, and Gil stepped on first to get one out and then threw home to enable catcher Roy Campanella and third baseman Robinson to run down Bauer for the second out of the inning-ending double play.

After that, Maglie allowed only one more hit—a two-out single to Billy Martin in the seventh—and even struck out the side in the eighth. He ended with a five-hitter on a very good day, but he had no chance on this one because Larsen was more than great.

Baseball is a different game; nobody has ever explained it better than Roger Angell in *The Summer Game*. "The last dimension is time," wrote Angell:

Within the ballpark, time moves differently, marked by no clock except the events of the game. This is the unique, unchangeable feature of baseball, and perhaps explains why this sport, for all the enormous changes it has undergone in the past decade or two, remains somehow rustic, unviolent and intro-spective. Baseball's time is seamless and invisible, a bubble within which players move at exactly the same pace and rhythms as all their predecessors. This is the way the game was played in our youth and in our fathers' youth, and even back then—back in the country days—there must have been the same feeling that time could be stopped.

On a warm day in early August, particularly in one of the older parks which encourages intimacy between players and fans, there is nothing more relaxing than watching a baseball game. The moments between pitches, between plays, is a time when a fan can call for a beer, talk to a friend or just sit there.

But when the game assumes an unusual importance, as in a World Series or a no-hitter, it becomes a different game. Then, the moments between pitches are moments of high drama, as fans and players alike wonder if the next pitch will be the one that breaks the bubble or decides the game.

Larsen's game was like that. Inning by inning, as he set the Dodgers down 1–2–3, the pressure mounted. He not only had his perfect game to worry about; with a 2–0 lead, he knew he had also to be concerned with simply winning the game.

By the ninth inning, the pressure was almost unbearable. "I'm not what you call a real praying man," said Larsen later, "but once out there, in the eighth or ninth, I said to myself, 'Help me out somebody.'" But there was nobody else out there to help him; in a game like that, the pitcher's mound is the loneliest spot in the world.

Carl Furillo, the first man up for Brooklyn in the ninth, fouled off Larsen's first two pitches, took a ball and then fouled two more, the crowd collectively taking a deep breath each time he swung and then letting it out. Finally, Furillo flied to Bauer in right field, a few feet in front of the fence. Now, Larsen was just two outs away. He took off his cap for a moment and shook his head, then he went back to work.

Campanella, still dangerous in his next-to-last year, was next. Roy had hit 20 home runs during the season and he pulled a Larsen pitch down the left field line, safely foul, before grounding out to Martin at second. One out away.

And then Dale Mitchell came to the plate as a pinchhitter. Mitchell was exactly the worst kind of hitter for Larsen to have to face in that situation. Never a power hitter, Mitchell had always tried just to hit the ball where it was pitched and he had succeeded admirably: in a 11-year career, he averaged .312 and struck out only 119 times, fewer than some sluggers do in a single season.

The first pitch to Mitchell was a ball and Larsen thought, "Oh, no. All day I've been getting ahead of the hitters and now I have to get behind on the last batter."

Larsen threw two strikes, then Mitchell fouled a pitch back to the backstop, with the crowd roaring on each pitch. And then Larsen put a fastball low and outside. Mitchell started to swing and then held up, and Pinelli shot his right arm in the air. Mitchell was out and Larsen had his perfect game.

Mitchell turned around angrily to argue with Pinelli. "He thought it was a lousy call," says Pinelli now, "but he was crazy to take it. Pictures later proved that it was a strike."

Oblivious to Mitchell's futile protest, Yankee catcher Yogi Berra ran to the mound and leaped into the arms of Larsen, who was perhaps eight inches taller. It made a strange and memorable picture. Players and fans were soon swarming around Larsen; the hero of the day then spent 90 minutes in the dressing room, explaining over and over to the writers how nervous he had been, especially in the ninth inning.

Yankee owners Dan Topping and Del Webb came by to shake Larsen's hand, as did baseball commissioner Ford Frick. From the Dodgers' dressing room, Robinson and Maglie also came over. "I felt sorry for you in the ninth, Don," said Maglie, "because I knew what was going through your mind. You were the best and there was nothing we could do about it."

And one writer supposedly asked Stengel, "Is that the best game you've ever seen Larsen pitch?"—though nobody ever identified that writer.

Thousands of congratulatory telegrams were received by Larsen, including one from the President of the United States, Dwight D. Eisenhower. A later President would make phone calls and telegrams to winning coaches and players a routine thing, but Ike was more sparing in his praise:

Dear Mr. Larsen:

It is a noteworthy event when anybody achieves perfection in anything. It has been so long since anyone pitched a perfect big-league game that I have to go back to my generation of ballplayers to recall such a thing—and that is truly a long time ago.

This note brings you my very sincere congratulations on a memorable feat, one that will inspire pitchers for a long time to come. With best wishes,

Sincerely,
Dwight D. Eisenhower
President of the United States

Larsen was pleased, and he quickly replied:

Dear Mr. President:

I can't begin to tell you how much I appreciate your recent letter. And if anyone were to ask me now what is the greatest thrill I've ever experienced, I'd certainly find it difficult trying to decide between the no-hitter and the congratulatory note I re ceived from you . . .

Then Larsen started to get the treatment that has become standard for sports heroes since. First, there was a television appearance with Bob Hope, for which he got $7500. That was a lot of money in those days, though an athlete of today would probably reject it out of hand.

Larsen flew from New York out to Hollywood shortly after the Series—which the Yankees won in seven games—and was rushed to the NBC studio. He was introduced to Hope and to Diana Dors, one of the many Marilyn Monroe imitations of the day. Given a little dialogue for the show, he looked as nervous as when he had been on the mound for the ninth inning at Yankee Stadium.

There were other television appearances, personal appearances, parties, magazine interviews and awards. It would be nice to think that Larsen went on from there to become the pitcher Stengel, and others, always thought he could be.

But it was not to be. Larsen won only 30 games in his next three seasons with the Yankees and was eventually traded to Kansas City; Stengel had finally given up on him.

Then on July 8, 1960, a story moved out of Kansas City on the Associated Press wire: "Don Larsen, who once did the incredible by pitching the only perfect game in World Series history but now just a righthander who has lost 11 in a row, was sent to the minors today by the Kansas City A's. Larsen was optioned to Dallas-Fort Worth of the American Association . . ."

It was not even four full years from the day he had pitched a perfect game in the World Series.

Larsen's career after that was a series of anticlimaxes. He came back up to Kansas City in 1961, then was traded to the Chicago White Sox. The White Sox, in turn, traded him to the San Francisco Giants in 1962. It was a trade that helped the Giants win the National League pennant—but because they got Billy Pierce in the deal, not Larsen; Don won only five games. The Giants traded him to Houston in 1965 and he went to Baltimore later that year. In 1967, he was traded to the Chicago Cubs and he ended his career with them.

In 14 years in the major leagues, Don Larsen won only 81

games and lost 91. Some theorized that he felt added pressure because of his perfect game, a game he could never hope to duplicate. More likely, he lacked the self-discipline and mental toughness of the great athletes and his perfect game kept him in the majors longer than he deserved on his ability.

Waste no tears for Don Larsen. Many other pitchers have won more games, but nobody else has done what he did. On October 8, 1956, for two hours and six minutes and 97 pitches, nobody was ever as good.

3

Johnny Vander Meer: It couldn't be done

It takes a suspension of the law of averages for a pitcher to throw a no-hitter, which is one reason no-hit pitchers often have trouble the next time they throw. To pitch no-hitters in succession, then, would seem to be impossible, but it didn't seem that way to Johnny Vander Meer. In June of 1938, he pitched a no-hitter against Boston on June 11, then came back four days later to no-hit Brooklyn. Perhaps the fact that Vander Meer was virtually a rookie made it possible; he didn't realize it couldn't be done until he had done it.

As often happens with no-hitters, there was irony connected with Vander Meer's great feat. The bombastic Larry MacPhail had twice bought Vander Meer's contract in the pitcher's early career, yet it was against MacPhail's team that Vander Meer pitched the second of his no-hitters. Making it worse, the Cincinnati left-hander upstaged one of MacPhail's innovations and the most famous player of all time, George Herman (Babe) Ruth.

There is a traditional baseball legend that lefthanded pitchers take longer to mature, that they are wilder in their youth than righthanders. As proof, baseball people point to such examples as Lefty Grove and Sandy Koufax, conveniently ignoring such wild righthanders as Rex Barney and Joe Shipley, a San Francisco Giant farmhand who once hit a player in the on-deck circle!

Vander Meer fit that baseball tradition perfectly. He was fast but so wild in his early career that it seemed he would never get a chance to make it in the major leagues. He was signed first by

Brooklyn but released after an 11–10 year at Dayton because manager Ducky Holmes thought he was too wild.

Then, MacPhail entered the picture for the first time. General manager of Cincinnati at the time, he bought Vander Meer's contract for $4000, then sold the young lefthander to Boston after one year.

MacPhail, though, agreed with Samuel Johnson: Consistency is an overrated virtue. When Vander Meer struck out 295 batters at Durham and was named minor league of the year in 1936, MacPhail bought him back, this time for $10,000.

Vander Meer was still troubled by wildness and he lost 11, winning only 5, at Syracuse in 1937. Brought up to Cincinnati at the end of the season, he was 3–5. Nothing remarkable, but in spring training of 1938, Cincinnati manager Bill McKechnie altered his delivery slightly and it seemed to help. For the first time in his career, Vander Meer seemed to have an idea where the ball was going when he let it loose.

Johnny won 5 of his first 7 decisions in 1938 and was on his way to a 15–10 record in his first full year in the majors when he faced the Boston Bees on June 11 and pitched his first no-hitter. Predictably (*see* Introduction), the Associated Press dispatch of the day said Vander Meer "pitched himself into baseball's Hall of Fame today . . ."

The story went on to say:

. . . the six-foot, 190-pounder hurled as fine a game as any veteran could have. Only 28 men faced him, and only three reached first base, all on walks. None got past first as Vander Meer came in with a 3–0 victory, the first National League no-hit nine-inning job since Paul Dean turned the trick back in 1934. Vander Meer is the first southpaw to accomplish the stunt in the majors since Bob Burke did it for the Senators in 1931.

After the game team-mates and fans carried the fastball strikeout artist from the field on their shoulders. Vander Meer himself was surprised when it was all over.

"Gee, I had no idea of pitching a no-hitter," he told his mates. "My arm felt better as I went along and I bore down harder, particularly in the late innings."

. . . Today he was in control of the situation from start to finish. . . . He retired the first nine men to face him, lost momentary control of his fast ball in the fourth and fifth, then breezed in by retiring the last 13 Boston batters. He fanned four.

The Reds fielded perfectly behind him, but his mainstay was Ernie Lombardi, who hit a homer with one aboard in the sixth inning. In addition, after Johnny walked Gene Moore to open the fourth, Lombardi took Johnny Cooney's foul and fired the ball to first to double Moore off the bag.

Again in the fifth, when Tony Cuccinello, first up, was passed, Lombardi tossed to first and caught Tony napping. With two out in the same frame, Vander Meer issued his third walk, to Gilly English, who was left on first as Johnny Riddle grounded weakly to the box.

Vander Meer's no-hitter is the only one in the major league books this season. Bill Dietrich, White Sox right-hander, hurled the last one, on June 1 of last year against the Browns in the American League . . ."

Though Vander Meer seemed in control in the late innings, McKechnie was taking no chances. He had a good club that he thought could win the pennant—ultimately, it finished third, six games back, but then won in 1939 and 1940—and he was far less concerned with a no-hitter than simply winning the game. Thus, he had two pitchers warming up in the ninth inning in case Vander Meer faltered.

Since 1938, whenever a pitcher throws a no-hitter, his next start is awaited anxiously to see if he can do it again. When Vander Meer made his next start, however, nobody was thinking in those terms. In the modern era (1901 on), no pitcher had ever thrown two no-hitters in one season, let alone in consecutive games. Walter Johnson, Christy Mathewson and Cy Young, all in the Hall of Fame by then, had never pitched two no-hitters in a single season; if they couldn't do it, who could expect it of Vander Meer?

Johnny's second start came in Brooklyn; by this time, MacPhail was executive vice-president of the Dodgers. He had quite an evening planned. In Cincinnati, in 1935, he had introduced night baseball, but it has been less than an instant success. He had not given up on the idea, however, and on June 15, 1938, he scheduled the first night game in New York City. Some 40,000 people, 38,748 paid, crowded into Ebbets Field, no doubt while the fire marshals looked the other way.

Before the lights were on, two fife and drum corps and a band provided music, and flag-lowering ceremonies were held. At 8:35 p.m., the lights were turned on and the crowd roared.

The game, though, was a long time coming. First, MacPhail had arranged for exhibitions by Olympic sprint and broad jump champion Jesse Owens. Owens first ran a 100-yard dash against ballplayers Ernie Koy of the Dodgers and Lee Gamble of the Reds, who each had a 10-yard head start. Koy finished a yard ahead of Owens, who covered the distance in 9.7 seconds.

After jumping 23 feet, 6 inches in a broad jump exhibition, Owens then ran a novel 120-yard race with the Dodgers' Gibby Brack. He had ten low hurdles to clear while Brack sprinted on the flat. Brack won by 10 yards.

And then, Babe Ruth made an appearance. Robert Creamer, in his biography *Babe,* told the circumstances:

> In June, 1938, Babe and Claire went to Ebbets Field for the first major league night game ever played in New York City and saw Johnny Vander Meer pitch his second straight no-hit no-run game for Cincinnati. Vander Meer's feat was front-page news, but earlier in the evening, the biggest excitement in the ballpark was the arrival of Babe. A stir ran through the crowd, and fans swarmed around him. Larry MacPhail . . . was doing everything he could to pump life into the then-moribund franchise. He remembered the Babe Ruth Day he put on in Cincinnati three years earlier, and the crowd the Babe attracted. Ruth, who in 1936 was one of the five original players elected to the Cooperstown Hall of Fame . . . was still the biggest name in baseball . . .

The game that night didn't start until 9:45, but once it did, Ruth and Owens and the lights were upstaged as Vander Meer pitched his second straight no-hitter.

The game was not as artistic a one as his first no-hitter. Johnny's wildness was back and he walked eight, while striking out seven. This game, too, was not in doubt as the first no-hitter had been; the Reds scored four times in the third inning and went on to win 6–0. That big lead was a mixed blessing for Vander Meer. He had no worry about winning the game, but it is difficult for a pitcher to bear down in a lopsided game as he knows he must in a close one.

Frank McCormick gave Vander Meer all the working margin he needed with a home run into the left field stands in the fourth inning, with Wally Berger and Ival Goodman on base; then a walk to Ernie Lombardi, and singles by Harry Craft and Lew Riggs added the fourth run of the inning.

Craft's third straight single knocked in Goodman in the seventh for the fifth Cincinnati run. Earlier, Goodman's hit had caromed off the right kneecap of Brooklyn pitcher Tot Pressnell, knocking him out of the camp, quite literally; Pressnell had to be carried off on a stretcher.

Vander Meer himself scored the last Cincinnati run, in the eighth, coming in on Luke Hamlin's triple.

But the runs, after that Cincinnati outburst in the fourth, were incidental. The crowd wanted to know if Vander Meer could pitch another no-hitter and the Cincinnati southpaw certainly seemed capable of it. His speed, though often out of control, was too much for the Dodgers. His only bad inning until the last one was the seventh, when he walked both Cookie Lavagetto and Dolf Camilli before pitching out of the jam; that was the only time before the ninth that the Dodgers got a runner as far as second.

Vander Meer seemed in perfect control as he breezed through the eighth in 1–2–3 order, striking out Woody English and Johnny Hudson, and he got the first out in the ninth easily. Brooklyn first baseman Buddy Hassett hit the first pitch to the first-base side of the pitcher's mound and Vander Meer grabbed it and tagged Hassett out.

Then his control deserted him again and he walked Babe Phelps, Lavagetto and Camilli in order to fill the bases. While Camilli was in the process of walking, Brooklyn manager Burleigh Grimes sent in Goody Rosen as a runner for Phelps. Most likely, Grimes was feeling the tension and felt he had to do something; the run that Phelps-Rosen represented was meaningless.

After Vander Meer walked Camilli, manager McKechnie came to the mound to talk to him and settle him down. Unlike the first no-hitter, McKechnie had nobody warming up in the ninth inning of this game. McKechnie's strategy seemed to work. Vander Meer threw a ball and a strike to Koy, then Koy grounded to third baseman Lew Riggs. Brooklyn writer Roscoe McGowen noted that Riggs was so careful in making the throw to Lombardi at the plate—and who could blame him?—that a double play was not possible. Lombardi did not even attempt a throw to first to double Koy.

One batter was left, the weak-hitting Durocher, but Leo scared everybody—by now, even the Brooklyn fans were rooting for Vander Meer—by lashing a ball down the right field line. At the last moment the ball curved foul, then Durocher ended the suspense by flying to Craft in center field for the final out.

Reported McGowen:

> . . . the putout . . . brought unique distinction to the young hurler.
>
> It brought, also, a horde of admiring fans onto the field, with Vandy's team-mates ahead of them to hug and slap Johnny on the back and then to protect him from the mob as they struggled toward the Red dugout.
>
> The fans couldn't get Johnny, but a few moments later they got his father and mother, who had accompanied a group of 500 citizens from Vandy's home town of Midland Park, N.J. The

elder Vander Meers were completely surrounded and it required nearly fifteen minutes before they could escape.

The feat ran the youngster's remarkable pitching record to
18⅓ hitless and scoreless innings and a string of 26 scoreless
frames. This includes a game against the Giants, his no-hitter
against the Bees and last night's game . . .

Vander Meer still wasn't through, either. For 3⅓ innings in
his next start against the Boston Bees, who were his first no-hit
victims, it seemed he might pitch still another no-hitter. Nervous
at the start of the June 19 game in Boston, he walked Elbie
Fletcher, the first man up, on four straight pitches but then settled
down and allowed no hits until one man was out in the fourth.
Only one ball was even hit out of the infield during that time.

Then, Bees' third baseman Debs Garms lined a single to short
left center on a 2–1 pitch in the fourth inning to end the string.
"I'm glad that's over," said Johnny after the game. "I only wish
the first man up could have hit and ended the strain."

Ironically, Garms—a lefthanded hitter—had been kept out of
Vander Meer's first no-hitter because the Boston manager thought
he couldn't hit a fast lefthander. The Boston manager was Casey
Stengel, platooning even then.

Vander Meer was wild in this game but effective, giving up
only three more hits after Garms' single and winning the game
14–1 for his seventh straight victory. He was to go on to win nine
in a row before being beaten.

It was quite a streak for Vander Meer. Since he had pitched a
three-hitter before his double no-hitters, he set a record for least
hits in three consecutive games. His 21⅔ consecutive scoreless innings also set a National League record, though Cy Young's 23
consecutive hitless innings remained the major league record.
Young watched Vander Meer's attempt at a third no-hitter.

Like Larsen, Vander Meer's subsequent career was an anticlimax—he finished with 119 wins and 121 losses in a 13-year
career. There is a temptation to dismiss him as a fluke; however, it
wasn't quite that simple. Throughout the rest of his career, Vander
Meer was bothered by arm problems and wildness, McKechnie's
altered motion not to the contrary. The wildness he probably
could have lived with, but the arm problems hit him almost immediately, greatly curtailing his pitching in the two years following
his double no-hit year. In all likelihood, if he hadn't been plagued
by arm problems, Vander Meer would have had an outstanding
career.

From time to time, he showed what he could do. After winning only eight games combined in 1939 and 1940, the Reds' pen-

nant years, he came back with a string of three straight years in which he won 16, 18 and 15, with earned run averages of 2.82, 2.43 and 2.87. Again, after two subpar years, he bounced back with a 17–14 record in 1948 for a Cincinnati team which finished seventh in an eight-team league. For his career, he had a solid enough ERA of 3.44, and there was one more indication that Johnny Vander Meer was quite a pitcher when his arm was sound: He allowed only 1799 hits in 2104 career innings.

When his arm and control allowed it, Vander Meer was a good pitcher. For one two-game stretch in June, 1938, he was a great one.

4

Sandy throws four

The date was September 9, 1965. The Chicago Cubs were in Los Angeles for one game against the Dodgers, a weird bit of scheduling even by modern baseball standards. The National League had one of its tightest races in history; the San Francisco Giants led by a half game over the Dodgers and Cincinnati Reds, and by a game over the Milwaukee Braves. Only 18 days before, the pennant race tension had provoked an ugly incident in a Giants-Dodgers game, with Giant pitcher Juan Marichal hitting Dodger catcher John Roseboro on the head with his bat.

But for 1 hour and 43 minutes on that warm September evening, everybody forgot about the tension of the pennant race: Dodger Sandy Koufax became the first pitcher in baseball history to pitch four no-hitters. To cap it off, his fourth no-hitter was a perfect game.

It was a remarkable feat, made more so by the fact that it had seemed in spring training that Koufax's career might be over. He had traumatic arthritis in his left elbow, which caused the elbow to swell to the size of his knee when he pitched. But he found that by soaking the joint in ice water immediately after the game and throwing between starts, he was able to pitch, though often in pain. He did not miss a start in 1965 and Mel Durslag, sports columnist for the *Los Angeles Herald-Examiner,* called him the "pin-up boy of the Arthritis and Rheumatism Foundation."

Despite his 1965 success—he was 21–7 going into the game that night—it hardly seemed that night would be the one he would pitch a no-hitter, let alone a perfect game. He had lost three

29

games in a row and had not won in the last five starts, mostly because the Dodgers were not scoring behind him. In his previous start, against Houston, he had been taken out for a pinchhitter in the eighth inning, trailing 2–1.

In the dressing room that night, he was so angry he threw a rubbing table against the wall. Then, two good things happened. First, Jim Gilliam won the game for the Dodgers with a two-out triple in the ninth; then, Sandy's elbow felt as good the next day as it had all year. Maybe it was the exercise he got throwing the table.

Still, though his elbow felt fine, Koufax had no premonition that he would have an exceptional game. Warming up and during the first few innings, he felt he had no better than average stuff. The Cubs were not a good team to face with average stuff. Though they finished a distant eighth, they had some hitters. Billy Williams hit .315, with 34 home runs, 39 doubles and 108 RBIs that year. Ron Santo had 33 home runs and 101 RBIs. Ernie Banks had 28 home runs and 106 RBIs.

Koufax got by in the early innings on his curve, then something happened to his fastball. ". . . my fastball really came alive, as good a fastball as I'd had all year."

The crowd of 29,139 also came alive. The fans realized they were seeing something special, as Koufax went 1–2–3 inning after inning. The Chicago pitcher, Bob Hendley, was nearly as good. Not until the fifth did he allow a run and it came without a hit. Lou Johnson walked for the Dodgers, was sacrificed to second, stole third and came home when Cub catcher Chris Krug threw the ball into left field.

Not until two men were out in the seventh did the Dodgers get a hit, as Johnson blooped a double down the right field line, and they never got another. Hendley, who had been in the minors earlier in the year, pitched the game of his life but had the misfortune to run into the game of Koufax's life.

Koufax could never relax because the Dodgers got only the one run, but on this night that worked to his advantage. With a bigger lead, he might have relaxed and lost his perfect game.

With two outs in the seventh, Sandy fell behind at 3–0 to the dangerous Williams before getting him out. "I tried to throw as hard as I could down the pike," he said, "because if Williams walked, Ron Santo was up next and he could put it out of the park."

Santo, though, was no worry in the eighth as he struck out to lead off the inning. Koufax, grunting with each pitch and throwing with so much effort his cap was falling off his head, also struck out

Banks and Bryon Browne in the eighth. He began the ninth with strikeouts against Krug and pinchhitter Joey Amalfitano.

And then, it all came down to one man: Harvey Kuenn, traded with Hendley to the Cubs from the Giants before the start of the season. Kuenn was near the end of his career, but he was still dangerous. A .303 lifetime hitter, he had always hit the ball where it was pitched instead of trying for a home run, which made him the hardest kind of batter to strike out. He struck out only 16 times in 1965, but this was one of them; Koufax set him down with three pitches.

"I gave Kuenn all fastballs," he said. "I have great respect for Harvey as a hitter, and I gave it everything I had."

Sandy had ended the game with 6 straight strikeouts—7 of the last 9, 14 for the game—which was significant: He always felt that when he had his best stuff, his strikeout total reflected that. The strikeouts ran his seasonal total to 332; he was to add 50 more to that to set a major league seasonal record, since broken by Nolan Ryan.

"I wasn't necessarily trying to strike out those fellows," Koufax said after the game, "but I was trying to keep the ball low and away because Chicago is a good hitting team. I was afraid I would lose the game—let alone the no-hitter."

Koufax sympathized with losing pitcher Hendley after the game, but not during it. "I was sitting there rooting for us to score six more times and knock him out of the box," he said. "I sympathized with him only as a fellow pitcher, only in retrospect, and—most of all—only when we were in the locker room with the game safely won."

He had been aware that he was pitching a no-hitter, but not because his teammates told him. "For the first time," he said, "nobody on either bench said anything about the no-hitter. Usually, you hear a lot, especially from the other dugout. But this time, Chicago didn't say anything."

"We didn't talk to Sandy about it," said Dodger captain and shortstop Maury Wills, "but we didn't stay away from him. Not talking to him at all would have been worse than anything."

In a sense, this final no-hitter of Koufax's career may have made the old sportswriting cliche come true: It did put him in the Hall of Fame. When he was elected to the Hall in 1971, it was a controversial election because he had won only 165 games in his injury-shortened career, but he had some impressive arguments for his admittance. His manager, Walt Alston, had said he couldn't imagine a pitcher being better. In one four-year stretch, he was incredible. Pitching with a ball so lively some pitchers claimed they could hear the rabbit's heart beating, he had three seasons with an earned run average under two runs and a fourth at 2.04. He won 25, 19, 26 and 27 games in succession and he had three seasons of 300 or more strikeouts, including the record-setting 382.

And, most of all, he had four no-hitters. Nobody—not Cy Young, not Walter Johnson, not Warren Spahn, not Bob Feller—had ever done that before. He belongs in the Hall of Fame.

During Koufax's career, a myth formed about him, that he had become a ballplayer by accident and it was not a career he wanted. That myth bothered Koufax more than anybody. He talked about it in his autobiography, *Koufax*, done with Ed Linn: ". . . the way this fantasy goes, I am really a sort of dreamy intellectual who was lured out of college by a bonus in the flush of my youth and have forever after regretted—and even resented—the life of fame and fortune that has been forced upon me. . . . But far from being a non-athlete before I signed with the Dodgers, I had no interest as a boy in anything except sports . . . As a student, I was—to give myself the best of it—indifferent. . ."

The only honor Koufax got in high school was Boy Athlete of the Year. It is, thus, no surprise that he became a professional athlete. The surprise is that his career came in baseball. Basketball was his first love and, indeed, in his one year of college at the University of Cincinnati, he was on a basketball scholarship.

Sandy played baseball as a youngster, simply because everybody else was playing. He sometimes pitched, sometimes played the outfield, sometimes played first base. At all three positions, he displayed a strong arm—naturally—and little hitting ability.

It was a man named Milt Laurie who first saw Sandy's pitching potential. Laurie had once played semipro baseball and he had signed a contract with the Boston Braves. He never played professionally. Just before spring training the year he had signed with Boston, the delivery truck he was driving overturned and his whole right side was crushed. By the time he came into Koufax's life, Laurie was managing a sandlot team called the Parkviews. "You've got a big league arm," he told Koufax.

Koufax pitched for the Parkviews and learned that he liked being in the middle of the action. He also learned he could do it well—at least, on that level—when he pitched a no-hitter in what he remembers as his first or second game with the club. He looked good enough to attract the attention of some major league scouts, but he scared them off by saying he wanted enough bonus money so that if he didn't make it playing baseball, he could af-

ford to pay his way through college. And so, he went to Cincinnati—on the basketball scholarship.

He played baseball at Cincinnati, too, with mixed results. He
had a 3–1 record and struck out 51 batters in 31 innings, including
a school-record 18 in one game. He also walked 30 batters.

Koufax never pitched again for the University of Cincinnati.
He got tryouts with three clubs: the Giants, Dodgers and Pittsburgh Pirates. He finally signed with the Dodgers for $26,000, a
figure which represented a $14,000 bonus and two years at the
major league minimum salary of $6000.

Because of the bonus rule then in effect, which made a team
keep any player signed for a $4000 bonus or more for two full
years, Koufax had to stay with the Dodgers in 1955, though he
would have been better off in the minors. The Dodgers were on
the way to their fifth pennant in nine years and their first World
Series victory, and Koufax obviously could not help them. They
had plenty of pitching, with Don Newcombe, Carl Erskine,
Johnny Podres, Clem Labine, Billy Loes and Russ Meyer.

But by July, the Dodgers had nothing but sore-armed pitchers. Pitching in cozy Ebbetts Field could do that. The fences were
all close and the field actually sloped down from home plate to
center, so the top of the center field fence was approximately on
the same level as home plate.

So Koufax got a chance to start. The results were mixed. In the
first game, he walked eight men and threw 105 pitches before
being relieved in the fifth, in a game the Dodgers lost. Years later,
a woman who had seen that game in Pittsburgh wrote that she had
been so sorry for Koufax she had almost cried. "If it was that sad
from up there," noted Koufax wryly, "think of how it must have
felt down on the field."

In his next start, though, Koufax pitched a one-hitter against
Cincinnati, striking out 14. He was a phenom—for a time. It didn't
last. He finished 2–2 that year and followed with seasons of 2–4,
5–4, 11–11, 8–6 and 8–13. Hall of Fame material he wasn't. The
pattern seemed set. He would pitch a brilliant game, then two bad
ones. He was in and out, either striking out batters or walking
them. He was the kind of pitcher most managers hate because he
always seemed on the verge of doing something big, but then he
didn't do it—or didn't do it consistently, which is what counts in
the big leagues. It seemed he would always be the kind of pitcher
who would be talked about in terms of potential, rather than performance.

Koufax, then and later, didn't think it was quite that simple.
Part of the problem, he felt, was that Alston resented having to

carry him on the roster originally and that resentment colored his appraisal of Koufax later. Koufax needed work to ease his wildness, but because he was wild when he pitched, he got little work. It was a vicious circle.

Even in his early career, Koufax had his moments. In 1959, for instance, he struck out 16 Philadelphia batters in what turned out to be a record for a night game. He won three in a row for the first time. He struck out 18 Giants to tie Bob Feller's major league record and beat Dizzy Dean's National League mark of 17—and he did it by striking out 15 of the last 17 men he got out. But for the year, he was only 8–6; the next year, he was 8–13.

Then, in 1961, he became a pitcher. His 18–13 record reflected it; more important was the fact that he knew where the ball was going and why. He dared for the first time to throw a curve when he had three balls on a hitter. Before, he had always bowed his back and tried to throw a fastball past the hitter.

What made the difference? Alston gives credit to former Dodger pitching coach Joe Becker. "Joe would have Koufax pitching with a windup and without a windup, trying to discover some method that would put rhythm into his delivery," said Alston in *Alston and the Dodgers*, with Si Burick. "And just like that, they found it one day—all at once—just a little rocking motion on the pitching mound. Suddenly, he was a pitcher, not a thrower."

It would be nice to think that life was that simple, that one little adjustment could make a man a great pitcher, a great writer, a great architect. It isn't that simple, of course, and it wasn't for Koufax, either. In the end, it was probably Koufax's intelligence that turned him into a great pitcher. He was smart enough to listen. He listened to Becker and he tightened his pitching windup. He listened to Wally Moon, who had been traded from St. Louis to the Dodgers, when Moon said that the way Koufax put his arms when he went into a stretch tipped off his pitches; he changed that motion.

He listened to club statistician Allan Roth, who broke down statistics into scores of categories to help players who were smart enough to learn. He told Koufax that lefthanded batters hit him for a higher average than righthanders; Sandy knew immediately that it was because his curve broke down and actually tailed in slightly to lefthanders. So he changed his grip and made his curve break out, and he did much better against lefthanders. Roth showed him that one year, batters had hit his first pitch for a whopping .349 average, so Koufax concentrated on making that first pitch a better one instead of just trying to get it over the plate. Roth showed

Koufax just how important control was: When Koufax had been ahead on the count at the time the ball was hit, batters averaged only .146; when he was behind, they averaged .286. The lesson was clear: With average control, Koufax could be a big winner.

And, most important of all, Koufax listened to catcher Norm Sherry in spring training of 1961, when they were on their way to a B squad game against the Minnesota Twins in Sarasota, Florida. Sherry convinced Koufax not to try to force his fastball, which usually went high, when he got behind a batter, but to throw curves instead and try to hit spots. Koufax tried it and the strategy worked; in seven innings, he did not allow the Twins a hit. And they had an outstanding hitting lineup with Harmon Killebrew, Jim Lemon, Bob Allison, Earl Battey and Rich Rollins all playing that day.

"There is nothing like instantaneous success to convince you that you are on the right course," said Koufax later.

He was on his way. While winning 18, he struck out 269 batters to break Christy Mathewson's National League record of 267 for a season.

The next season, he started on his remarkable no-hitter run, one a year for four consecutive years, with a 5–0 win over the New York Mets. There were some qualifications to the no-hitter. For openers, it was pitched against the Mets, who lost a record 120 games that season. For another, though the Dodgers' new stadium in Chavez Ravine had just been opened that year, Bo Belinsky of the Angels and Earl Wilson of the Red Sox had already pitched no-hitters there, Wilson's coming just in the previous week.

But none of that mattered to Koufax, whose best previous game had been a one-hitter against Pittsburgh in 1960. "This has to be my greatest thrill in baseball," he said after the game. "Every pitcher wants at least one no-hitter. Once you have it, it feels great—no one can take it away from you."

Koufax started the game with what he later called the best inning of his life, striking out the side on nine pitches. Every pitch went exactly where he wanted it to go. Against Rod Kanehl, the second hitter, he threw a fastball, change and curve: all right where he intended.

After the first inning, his control wasn't so sharp and he walked 5 men—"because I was really trying to hit those corners"—and he struck out 13. He got at least one strikeout against every Met except Frank Thomas and pinchhitter Gene Woodling.

The Dodgers made it easy for him to win by scoring four times in the first inning, a welcome change from the previous 34 innings, when they had scored only three runs for Sandy. With two outs, the Dodgers reached Bob Miller for a walk and five hits, knocking out Miller. Willie Davis got a triple and John Roseboro a two-RBI double in the rally.

Only twice did the Mets come close to getting a hit. In the second, Frank Thomas hit a grounder into the hole at shortstop but Maury Wills moved over quickly to make the play and throw Thomas out. In the sixth, Richie Ashburn hit a sinking line drive to left field, but Tommy Davis made a fine running catch.

The no-hitter was in Koufax's mind all the way, largely because of Solly Hemus, who was coaching at third for the Mets. Hemus kidded Koufax after the first inning. "You know something? You've got a no-hitter."

After the fifth inning, Hemus passed Koufax and said, "You know something? You still got a no-hitter."

"Hell," said Koufax, "I've had 'em later than this and lost them."

After each subsequent inning, Hemus again reminded Koufax that he had a no-hitter going and Sandy laughed it off. Inside, though, he didn't feel like laughing. "Anyone who says there's no pressure in a no-hitter is out of his mind," said Koufax. "I kept thinking to myself, somebody's going to do it. The pressure really got me in the eighth. I almost expected to lose it. I've had no-hitters going before for seven or eight innings—and I've lost them."

He didn't lose this one. In the late innings, he went more and more to his fastball, using his curve less and his change not at all. "I was tempted to throw change-ups a few times," he said, "but I didn't. I'd never forgive myself if I lost a no-hitter because some guy hit a change-up."

In the ninth, he was throwing nothing but fastballs, challenging the Mets on every pitch, daring them to hit his best. He wanted the no-hitter badly. Pressing a little, he walked Gene Woodling to open the inning and Richie Ashburn lined a ball to left field, but it went foul by ten feet and then Koufax got Ashburn out.

Now, he was only two outs away—Kanehl and Mantilla. He remembered a game in spring training that year when Kanehl and Mantilla had gotten consecutive hits in the ninth inning to beat him. It wasn't going to happen this time.

Kanehl tried to bunt his way on and the crowd of 29,797 groaned before the bunt went foul. Then Kanehl grounded to third, Mantilla hit a high hopper to short that Wills handled and Koufax had his first no-hitter.

The no-hitter on June 30 was Koufax's eleventh win that year and he seemed certain to get his first 20-game season. It didn't happen that way. A problem with the blood circulation in his index finger curtailed his season, limiting him to 14 wins, but he came back stronger than ever in 1963. This time, he pitched his no-hitter even earlier in the season—on May 11 against the hated Giants. Again, his no-hitter came at Los Angeles, in only his sixth start of the year, as the Dodgers buried the Giants 8–0.

Koufax later called this no-hitter more satisfying than his first one, because it was against a tough team (the Giants were leading the league at the time and had won the pennant the year before) and because he felt he had finally conquered his wildness. He did not have overpowering stuff—he struck out only four, an unusually low total for a man who averaged slightly more than a strikeout per inning for his career—but he walked only two. He had felt in his previous start that he had finally become a control pitcher when he had thrown only 87 pitches to beat St. Louis; even more remarkably, the St. Louis hitters had taken only five pitches in the final three innings. The no-hitter against San Francisco proved that was no fluke and control became an asset for Koufax for the rest of his career.

The first batter, Harvey Kuenn, hit a hard line drive that went right to center fielder Willie Davis. Twenty feet to either side, and the no-hitter would not have lasted one out, but a pitcher—even one as talented as Koufax—needs some luck to pitch a no-hitter.

There were few hard chances, though, behind Koufax. In the fifth, Orlando Cepeda dribbled a ball just past the pitching mound and shortstop Dick Tracewski came in fast to shovel it up and throw out Cepeda.

In the seventh, Felipe Alou crashed one deep to left and Koufax sucked in his breath. He thought the ball was out, but it wasn't; Tommy Davis caught it up against the fence. Koufax was worried about the game as well as the no-hitter at that point, because he thought the score was only 1–0, as a result of Wally Moon's home run in the second. Actually, it was 4–0 because the Dodgers had scored three runs in the sixth, but the rally had not registered with Koufax. Probably it was conditioning: One run was about as many as he could expect from the Dodgers at that time.

Right after Alou's drive, Willie Mays crashed a line drive down third base, face high at Jim Gilliam, and Gilliam caught it almost in self-defense. "I had no idea Mays had hit the ball so hard until I heard it slam into Gilliam's glove," said Koufax later.

The Dodgers made it a rout with four runs in the eighth, but again Koufax admitted the runs did not register in his mind. In the ninth, he tired and started to aim the ball. He went to 2–0 on Joey Amalfitano and then got him to pop out to first baseman Ron Fairly. Jose Pagan flied out to deep center and then Koufax walked McCovey on four straight pitches. Not until then did he realize the score. "I looked at the scoreboard," he said, "and it relaxed me."

He still had to face Kuenn, who had hit the ball hard off him as the first man up. Kuenn took a strike, then hit a fastball on one hop back to Sandy. Koufax, taking no chances on throwing the ball away, started to run it to first and then flipped to Fairly for the final out. "I decided it would be easier than to try to run to first base and beat Harvey."

And thus, for trivia fans, if you're asked who was the last out in each of Koufax's four no-hitters, just remember Harvey Kuenn's name and you're halfway there.

Again, Koufax knew he was working on a no-hitter. "Every time I go to the mound, I'm thinking of a no-hitter," he said. "Nobody on my bench reminded me I was working one, but a couple of times when I came off the hill, I could hear some of the Giants making sure I was aware of it."

Koufax went on to accumulate 25 victories that year, as he made his first 20-win season a big one, and he was awesome. To one who had the pleasure of seeing him several times, as I did, the experience was unforgettable. The fastball would come rocketing down, the curve would come almost as fast and then drop sharply, and he seemed to be able to put the ball precisely where he wanted it to go. He was so overpowering, one almost expected him to pitch a no-hitter any time he went out there. His no-hitters were no once in a lifetime shot, for a pitcher who had everything going for him on one day, but a logical culmination. He was easily the best pitcher of his day.

In 1964, he pitched his third no-hitter and the only one on the road. This one came in Philadelphia, as he blanked the Phils 3–0 on June 4, and it couldn't have come at a more opportune time for Sandy. He had been struggling, with a 5–4 record, and couldn't understand it until, looking at pictures of his delivery in an old *Sport* magazine, he realized he was stepping too far to his left with his right foot when he came forward with the pitch. That meant he had to throw across his body instead of with it, robbing him of both power and control.

His next turn to pitch was against the Phils and he knew when he was warming up that he had solved his problem. The game confirmed it as he completely handcuffed the Phillies. Though Philadelphia manager Gene Mauch started a predominantly righthanded hitting lineup, the Phils could hit only four balls out of the infield.

This one was almost a perfect game. Richie Allen went to a 3–2 count in the fourth, fouled off a pitch, then walked. Five pitches later, he tried to steal second and was thrown out; he was the only Phil to reach base. Koufax thus faced the minimum of 27 men. "On the other hand," he said, "I had really got only 26 men out myself, hadn't I? When you're talking about a no-hitter, that's cheating a little, isn't it? But I'll take it."

The game was scoreless until the top of the seventh. Then Jim Gilliam and Tommy Davis singled and Frank Howard hit a home run, and it was all but over.

Koufax got stronger as he went along and struck out 4 of the last 5 men he faced, for a total of 12 in the game. It was the fifty-fourth time he had struck out 10 or more in a game, which tied the record owned by Bob Feller and Rube Waddell; before he quit, Koufax put that record virtually out of sight at 97.

Later that season, Koufax injured his elbow, diving back into second base as Milwaukee pitcher Tony Cloninger tried to pick him off. He pitched two more games, both wins, making his record 19–5, but then the elbow swelled up to impossible size. Dr. Robert Kerlan diagnosed the injury as traumatic arthritis and recommended that Koufax take the rest of the year off.

The off-season rest helped and Koufax went on to win 26 games in 1965, including the perfect game described earlier, and 27 the next season. But by 1966, he was pitching in pain most of the time; the elbow was so stiff that he had to bend his body at a 90-degree angle so he could shave, unable to bring his hand up to his face otherwise.

After the 1966 season, Koufax retired. He was turning his back on a $100,000-plus baseball contract, but he feared that one more year of pitching might render his left arm useless the rest of his life. "If you had one good arm and one bad arm," he told Dick Young, "and somebody said you could buy back the use of your bad arm, I think you'd do it. In a sense, that's what I'm doing."

Koufax's retirement was a blow to the Dodgers, of course. To the rest of the league, it was a mixed blessing. His loss meant the temporary end of the Dodgers as contenders—they immediately dropped to eighth in a ten-team league the next season—but Koufax had been a great draw around the circuit. At home, the Dodgers had figured that Koufax pitching meant an additional 10,000 fans. On the road, it wasn't quite as much, but he meant a substantial difference and all the clubs he faced benefited from that.

But Koufax could hardly be blamed for his decision. Given the condition of his arm, he had no choice. Just short of his thirty-first birthday when he retired, Koufax could undoubtedly have set more records if he had continued, but he already had a bunch. He set a record by leading the National League in earned run average for four straight seasons and he is mentioned 13 times in the various strikeout record categories.

His team had twice won the World Series and he had a 4–2 record in three World Series. And, most of all, he pitched four no-hitters. Nobody had ever done that.

5

Harvey Haddix: The best game ever lost

Just as Don Larsen stands alone in World Series history with his perfect game, Harvey Haddix can claim to have pitched the best game in regular season play. On May 26, 1959, Haddix pitched 12 innings of perfect baseball: no runs, no hits, no errors, no walks. Nobody had ever done that before. There had been no-hitters that lasted more than nine innings—the longest being a 10⅔-inning effort by Harry McIntire of Brooklyn on August 1, 1906—but there is no record of another perfect game lasting longer than nine innings.

There was only one thing wrong with Haddix's feat: At the end of those 12 innings, his Pittsburgh team hadn't scored any runs. In the bottom of the thirteenth, Milwaukee scored a run and beat him.

Harvey Haddix was called "The Kitten" by a nickname-happy sporting press because he resembled Harry Brecheen, a St. Louis Cardinal pitcher best known for winning three games in the 1946 World Series, who was nicknamed "The Cat."

There was a lot of resemblance between Haddix and Brecheen. They were both lefthanded pitchers who depended more on guile and quick-breaking curves than on fastballs; they were about the same size, 5 feet, 10 inches and 160 pounds for Brecheen, 5 feet, 9½ inches and 170 for Haddix; they both came up with St. Louis; and they finished their careers with almost identical major league win totals, 136 for Haddix, 132 for Brecheen.

Haddix was what baseball men considered an unusual lefthander: He had good control from the start. He also had obvious

41

ability: in one game with Columbus of the International League, he retired 28 consecutive batters from the second to the eleventh innings, after giving up a hit in the first.

But Haddix was starting his career during a time in the late '40s when the minor league system was much more extensive than it is now and it took players, even good ones, much longer to reach the big leagues. The Cardinals had one of the most extensive, and best, farm systems of the day; Haddix was almost 27 before he was finally brought up to stay in the big leagues at the end of the 1952 season.

He was an immediate success with the Cardinals, winning 20 games in his first full season, 1953, for a team which finished tied for third. He led the Cardinal starters in virtually every important category: games won, earned run average, complete games, innings pitched.

He also came close to pitching a no-hitter that year. On August 6, 1953, he had a no-hitter for eight innings against the Philadelphia Phillies. Richie Ashburn, leading off the ninth, tried to bunt his way on but was unsuccessful, as the St. Louis crowd of 9073 booed.

Then, St. Louis catcher Del Rice signaled for a fastball. Haddix shook him off; he wanted to throw a curve. Ashburn lined the curve into right field for the first Philadelphia hit.

'I'd throw the same pitch again," Haddix said after the game. "I still feel that was the pitch to throw in that spot."

Haddix got Earl Torgeson, the next man up for the Phillies, but then gave up another single to Del Ennis. He realized he could lose the game as well as the no-hitter; his lead was only 2–0. So, he settled down and got Granny Hamner to ground into a double play which ended the game and preserved his shutout.

Haddix came back with an 18-win season in 1954, but then his pitching fell off and he was traded around the league: to Philadelphia in 1956, to Cincinnati in 1958 and, finally, to Pittsburgh in 1959. It was with the Pirates that he made baseball history on May 26, 1959.

Years later, Haddix remembered what he always refers to as "that game" at Milwaukee's County Stadium, a park that had always been known as a good one for hitters. Not that night.

"There was lightning and strong winds in County Stadium that night," he remembered, almost 15 years to the day after the game. "I remember telling my teammates in the clubhouse just how I planned to pitch. I would pitch high to this batter, low and away to another . . . and so on.

"Don Hoak, our third baseman, said, 'Harv, if you pitch the

way you say you will, you'll have a no-hitter.' Everybody laughed, and we headed for the field."

Nobody was laughing, though, after Haddix retired the first 27 men to face him.

"When Harvey came to the bench after nine innings," said Pirate Manager Danny Murtaugh years later, "we mobbed him. And for the next three innings, there was no one seated on the bench. We were all on our toes, cheering him on."

Haddix was as good as a pitcher could be over those first nine innings. Not only did no Braves get on base, only two balls were hit out of the infield in that time and Haddix struck out eight batters. To show that the pressure wasn't getting to him, in the ninth inning he struck out two of the three Braves to face him.

All this was done against a very strong hitting team, too. The Braves, after winning consecutive pennants in 1957 and 1958, finished two games back of the Dodgers in 1959, but not because of a lack of hitting. Hank Aaron hit .355 with 39 home runs and 123 RBIs that season. Eddie Mathews hit 46 home runs, with 114 RBIs to go with a .306 average. Joe Adcock hit 25 home runs and Del Crandall 21 that year: This was the team Haddix was cutting down 1–2–3 in every inning.

Unfortunately for Haddix, Lew Burdette was pitching just as effectively, if not as artistically, for the Braves. Burdette, who was to go on to set a career high with 21 wins that season, allowed eight hits over the first nine innings, but none of them produced a run. Burdette did not walk a man the entire game.

"Oh, we had several chances to win," Haddix remembered later. "Roman Mejias made a base running mistake. My roomie, Bob Skinner, belted the ball over the fence, but the high winds blew the ball back and Hank Aaron just reached up in right field and caught it."

The base running error by Mejias to which Haddix aluded came in the third inning, when the Pirates could have wrapped up the game, and, oddly, it came on a hit by Haddix.

Mejias had led off with a single and, with one out, Haddix rapped a line drive off Burdette's leg. The ball rolled a few feet toward second base but shortstop Johnny Logan grabbed it and made a fine throw to nail Mejias, who was trying to go to third on the play.

Dick Schofield, who singled three times off Burdette, then followed with one of those singles which would have scored Mejias had he stayed on second. Instead, Haddix and Schofield were left on base when Bill Virdon flied out.

The Pirates had other opportunities. Rocky Nelson had singled in the second inning but was then wiped out on Skinner's double-play ball. Mejias singled in the fifth; this time, it was Haddix who hit into a double play.

Burdette then retired the Pirates in 1–2–3 order until, with one out in the ninth, the Pirates had another chance to score—and win. Virdon singled to center and then, after Smoky Burgess had flied out, went to third on Nelson's single to right. But Skinner grounded out to Adcock unassisted at first base and the Pirate rally was over. When Haddix again set the Braves down in order in the bottom of the ninth, the game went into extra innings.

For the first three extra innings, the pattern remained: The Pirates threatened sporadically but could not score, and the Braves did nothing with Haddix's pitches.

With one out in the tenth, Hoak singled, but the Pirates could not advance him. Schofield scratched a single off Burdette's hand to open the eleventh but Virdon, trying to advance him to second, forced him instead and Burgess then hit into a double play.

With two outs in the twelfth, Bill Mazeroski singled, but Hoak forced him. In the thirteenth, Schofield got his third hit with two outs, but Virdon grounded out.

If Haddix felt frustrated by this time, he had reason. He had been pitching perfect ball in every sense. Though he had not come close to yielding a hit—there were few hard-hit balls all night by the Braves and no tough chances for the Pirates in the field—he still had only a draw.

He knew he was pitching a no-hitter, though he was not aware it was a perfect game as well. "I thought perhaps I might have walked somebody in the early innings," he said immediately after the game, "but going down the stretch, my main idea was to win. We needed this one badly to keep going."

Then, the spell was broken in the bottom of the thirteenth by leadoff hitter Felix Mantilla. Pittsburgh third baseman Hoak fielded Mantilla's grounder and threw in the dirt to first baseman Nelson. The ball eluded Nelson and Mantilla was safe. The Pirates argued that Mantilla had turned toward second and was tagged out, but they were overruled.

Mathews sacrificed Mantilla to second, then Aaron was intentionally walked; the potential run that Aaron represented meant nothing because Mantilla's run would be enough for the Braves to win, and Hank was the Braves' most dangerous hitter.

Haddix, unaware that he had lost a perfect game on Hoak's throwing error, was still concerned with preserving his no-hitter and winning the game. The crowd of 19,194 that had been rooting for Haddix to pitch his perfect game now realized that its team had a chance to win the game and turned back to rooting for the Braves.

Haddix tried to throw a slider down and away to the next hitter, Adcock, but he got it high instead. Adcock fattened his average on mistakes like that and he hit this one deep to right center field. Virdon in center and Joe Christopher in right raced to the spot, and Virdon made a frantic leap for the ball, but it went over his glove and barely cleared the fence about 375 feet away. The fans roared. Haddix, as soon as he saw the ball had cleared the fence, turned and walked quickly into his dugout.

There was still some excitement and confusion. Mantilla scored easily for the only run that Milwaukee needed, but Aaron rounded second base and then cut across the pitchers' mound for the Braves' dugout.

Adcock, seeing the umpire's signal for a home run, kept running and passed Aaron between second and third. The umpires stayed on the field as Milwaukee manager Fred Haney and his coaches tried to regroup their runners.

Aaron and Adcock eventually retraced their steps from third to second, but it made no difference: Adcock was out when he passed Aaron. The score was announced as 2–0, but the next day National League President Warren Giles ruled that Adcock would be given credit for a double but that only Mantilla's run would count, making the final score 1–0. None of that, of course, made any difference to Haddix. He had pitched a remarkable game, but he had lost.

In the immediate aftermath of the game, Haddix was very disappointed. As reporters told him what he had accomplished, however, his gloom lifted. A loss, after all, was only another loss; he had 113 of them in his major league career. A game that nobody else had pitched before, and nobody else was likely to do again, was something else.

Haddix and Hoak, who had ended his perfect string with the throwing error on Mantilla's grounder, left the park together because they were the last to leave the clubhouse. Haddix had taken longer because he was talking to writers; Hoak because, no doubt, he was upset that it was his error that had broken up the perfect game and led to the loss.

In the cab, Hoak turned to Haddix and said, "Harv, I've made a lot of errors and I'll make more. But I also will make good plays for you."

"It was not an apology," said Haddix later. "That was not necessary."

In his next start, Haddix was luckier. This time, he gave up eight hits to his old team the St. Louis Cardinals, but he won 3–0. The Pittsburgh crowd of 28,644 gave him a standing ovation at the start of the game and also cheered when Bob Skinner caught Hal Smith's fly for the final out.

One of the runs in that game was knocked in by Haddix with a single. He should have done it a game earlier.

The May 26 game got Haddix into the record books in two places: most perfect innings and longest one-hit game. He also got something else to remember the game by—a silver tray and a dozen sterling goblets, gifts that were presented later during that Pittsburgh home stand in which Haddix had beaten the Cardinals.

Giles, who made the decision about the gift and also the presentation, told Haddix he was welcome to any other memento he might prefer.

"That will be a perfect rememberance," Haddix told Giles. "I couldn't think of anything I'd rather have to recall the occasion." The tray was inscribed:

> To Harvey Haddix—in recognition of his outstanding performance—unprecedented in baseball history—pitching 12 consecutive perfect innings—game of May 26, 1959.

Pittsburgh   000 000 000 000 0—0 12 0
Milwaukee   000 000 000 000 1—1 1 0

Presented by National League Professional Baseball Clubs.

Haddix went on to pitch for six more seasons before finally retiring at 40, but nothing he did later ever blurred the memory of that one incredible night. "I've never had a chance to forget that night," said Haddix in a telephone interview from his farm home in South Vienna, Ohio, almost 15 years to the day after that game. "I get four or five letters a week from fans commenting on that game."

No wonder.

6

Bo and Bobo, the immortal flukes

It was the night of July 20, 1974, in Cleveland and the Oakland A's were laughing in the clubhouse after the game, kidding each other with comments like "Nice hitting, Sal," and "Nice hitting, Larry." They had just run into a 2–0 no-hitter thrown by Dick Bosman of the Indians, but they were surprisingly unruffled.

"I'm glad for the guy," said Reggie Jackson. It takes far more than a no-hitter to shut up Reggie. "If we're going to lose a game, it might as well be to a no-hitter, and I'm glad it's to a guy like that. He's a nice guy."

Bosman's no-hitter had been an impressive one. He had thrown only 79 pitches, 60 of them strikes. He had faced only 28 men, one more than the minimum, and only then because Sal Bando had reached base on an error. "The man pitched a no-hitter and he didn't pitch it scared," said A's pitcher Ken Holtzman who, as a two-time no-hit pitcher, knew the feeling. "He didn't pitch around Reggie; he didn't pitch around anyone. He came right at you."

The error came in the fourth with two outs and it was Bosman's. He picked up Bando's topper to the right of the mound and threw it wildly past first. Bando ended up on second, but he remained there as Bosman struck out Jackson for one of his four strikeouts of the night. There was no question about the error call. "The ball beat me to the bag and I would have been out if it had been a good throw," said Bando.

Bosman redeemed himself with a good play on another Bando

47

grounder in the seventh, this one much harder hit, and there were only four other balls hit by the A's all night that came close to being hits.

The best defensive play came in the fifth, when Cleveland shortstop Frank Duffy went into the hole to throw out Joe Rudi. Right after that, left fielder John Lowenstein made a long run to catch Claudell Washington's drive in left center.

In the seventh, second baseman Buddy Bell made a good play to his left to throw out Campy Campaneris, and first baseman Pat Bourque of Oakland sent right fielder Charlie Spikes to the warning track to catch a drive in the eighth, the A's best hit ball of the night.

Aside from that, it was routine up and down for the A's, an impressive effort by Bosman. Why, then, weren't the A's discouraged and silent in the dressing room after the game? Part of the reason was that they had just won 6 in a row and led their division by 5½ games.

More than that, however, they couldn't believe that Dick Bosman had done it to them. Bosman's no-hitter was one of those that really defied the odds because there was nothing in his immediate past to suggest he would ever throw one. In eight major league seasons, he had won only 60 games and lost 72, and he had been on the Indians' junk pile earlier in 1974.

Until the training deadline of June 15, the Indians had tried to deal him away. He got a chance only when Steve Kline went on the disabled list with a sore elbow. He hadn't won a game in April or in May or in June. Two weeks before his no-hitter, he had finally won a game, but he needed 2⅓ innings of relief to get it. He hadn't beaten the A's since a shutout on the opening day of the 1971 season, when he was with the Washington Senators. This was the pitcher who had no-hit a team which was to go on to become a three-time world champion. (Ironically, Bosman was traded to Oakland in 1975.)

"I've got a quote for you," said Pat Bourque to *Oakland Tribune* baseball writer Ron Bergman. "If Dick Bosman can throw a no-hitter, anyone can."

By fluke standards, though, Bosman was better than average. Far worse pitchers have thrown no-hitters. Some strange names are squeezed in between ones like Feller and Koufax and Young. There was, for instance, a pitcher in the early part of the century named George Davis who had a lifetime record of 7–10; one of those seven was a no-hitter. Bill McCahan won only 16 games, but one was a no-hitter. Ernie Koob, Don Black, Neal Eason, Bob

Burke and Cliff Chambers all won less than 50 games in their careers and lost more games than they won, but all pitched no-hitters.

The all-time modern fluke, though, is unquestionably Bobo Holloman, who pitched one year for the St. Louis Browns (now the Baltimore Orioles), had a 3–7 record with a 5.23 earned run average and yet threw a no-hitter. Better yet, he did it in his first major league start, the first pitcher in modern baseball history to do that.

The Holloman story, even in retrospect, is incredible. There was nothing in his past, present or future to suggest such drama as a no-hitter in his first start, but it happened. Baseball is not an exact science.

Holloman, whose given name was Alva Lee (he had been nicknamed Bobo because of a physical resemblance to Bobo Newsome, which included the workings of his mouth), did not lack confidence. He had been knocking on Browns' manager Marty Marion's door for a chance to pitch. That remark is meant literally. When he didn't pitch early in the season, he would come by Marion's door at night and pound on it, asking for a chance to pitch.

He made such a pest of himself that Marion gave him a chance in relief. He showed nothing. In 5⅓ innings, he gave up 10 hits, 3 walks and 5 runs.

"I'm not a relief pitcher," said Holloman, unabashed. "I'm a starter."

"What's the difference?" asked Marion. "You pitch just the same way, no matter whether you start or relieve, don't you?"

"Not me," Holloman insisted. "I gotta start."

So, finally, Marion gave Holloman his chance to start, against the then-Philadelphia A's, the night of May 6, 1953. Those who cared—and there weren't many—figured Marion was just giving Holloman a chance to show he couldn't do it and would then let him go; the cutdown date to 25 players was only 9 days away. Marion had little to lose. The Browns finished last that year, strictly on their merits, as owner Bill Veeck noted.

The night did not start auspiciously. There were only 2473 fans in the stands in St. Louis; it was "crowds" like that which sent the Browns to Baltimore the next year. It had rained intermittently all afternoon and it was damp and chilly at game time.

In the second inning, Gus Zernial, who hit 42 home runs that season, powered a drive to left field. The Browns' Jim Dyck made a great, leaping, twisting catch to end the inning, but nobody thought much about it. In the fifth inning, Zernial hit a hopper back to the mound which Holloman misplayed. He still had a no-hitter, but nobody was getting excited yet.

In the press box, Veeck confided, "He's getting by because the hitters are giving him credit for having more stuff than he really has." Veeck looked around at the sparse crowd and decided that any fans who would come out on a night like that deserved a reward, so he had public relations director Bob Fishel announce: "We appreciate your attendance on such a bad night. We'd like to have you as our guests on a nicer night or day. So, your rain checks are good for any other game played here this season."

The fans let out a roar, but they'd have cheered even louder had they realized what was coming. It is not, after all, very often a fan gets a chance to see history made and then come back for another game at the club's expense.

Holloman was almost the entire show on this historic evening, because he brought his bat along with him, too, knocking in three runs. The biggest was the first, a bloop single that scored catcher Les Moss with the first run of the game in the second.

That run would have been enough for Holloman that night, but the Browns added five more, to make the final score 6–0. In the third, Bill Hunter doubled and Dyck singled through the middle for the second run. Another run was scored in the fifth on two walks and a double by Vic Wertz. A hit batter, Holloman's sacrifice and Johnny Groth's single scored the fourth run; with two outs in the seventh, Holloman doubled in two runs to end the scoring.

With that many runs behind him, the only question was whether Holloman would get the no-hitter. It didn't seem possible that he was getting as far with it as he was. Though his curve and slider were sharp, his fastball was as mediocre as it always had been and his control was not particularly good; he walked five and struck out only three.

Yet he went into the eighth with a no-hitter. He came out with it intact only because of a great play by shortstop Hunter. Joe Astroth hit a hard grounder up the middle and Hunter had to make a diving stop. Fortunately, Astroth was a slow runner and Hunter threw him out at first by a step.

The fans sat almost completely silent as Bobo came out for the ninth; the strain was beginning to tell on him as he walked pinch-hitter Elmer Valo on four pitches. He threw three more balls to Eddie Joost and St. Louis pitching coach Harry Brecheen came out to try to settle Holloman down.

Brecheen's talk didn't work immediately—Joost walked on

the next pitch—but then Holloman got Dave Philley to hit into a double play and the fans came roaring to their feet.

It wasn't over yet, however. Holloman walked Loren Babe to put runners at first and third and Eddie Robinson came to the plate. Robinson was a very dangerous hitter. He hit 172 homers in his major league career and 22 of them, plus 102 RBIs, were to come in that 1953 season. He missed the first pitch and foul tipped the second. The third was lined down the right field line, but foul. Finally, he hit the fourth pitch high and deep to right field—but Wertz was there to grab it and end the game.

Holloman, a superstitious man who had scratched the initials of his wife, Nan, and son, Gary, in the dirt at the third base line each time he went out to the mound, had his no-hitter. In addition to being the first to throw a no-hitter in his first major league start since Ted Breitenstein in 1891 and Charles (Bumpus) Jones in 1892 had done it, in the days of a pitching mound only 50 feet from home plate, Holloman was also the first St. Louis Browns' pitcher to do it since Newsom had done it for $9^2/_3$ innings on September 18, 1934. Newsom, though, had lost his no-hitter in the tenth. The last completed Brown no-hitter was by Bob Groom, 36 years before to the day.

It would have given a nice touch to that story if Holloman had gone on to a solid major league career, but it was not to be. He never again pitched a complete game for the Browns and he dropped out of the majors after that one season.

If Holloman was the biggest no-hit fluke, though, Bo Belinsky was the most publicized. If there was ever a case of a man being in the right place at the right time, it was Bo.

Robert Belinsky came to the Los Angeles (now California) Angels in 1962, at a time when the writers covering the team badly needed somebody who could provide some excitement. The Angels had been added to the American League as an expansion franchise the previous year and, with the usual culls that an expansion team gets, had finished eighth. It had been a dreary year and the writers covering the team were expecting little better in 1962. And then, along came Bo.

Belinsky had been around for awhile. He had signed on May 15, 1956, seven months short of his twentieth birthday, with the Pittsburgh Pirates. Unlike most players, it had not been his high school record that recommended him but his pitching on the sandlots. Pirate scout Rex Bowen had seen him a couple of games, in one of which Belinsky had struck out 15, and signed him. There was no bonus. All Bo got was a salary of $185 a month with the

Pittsburgh farm club in Brunswick, Georgia, and a bus ticket from his home in Trenton, New Jersey, to Brunswick.

He didn't last in Brunswick. Two months later, he jumped the club and, after a detour through Jacksonville, Florida, and New York, went home. The next year he got a letter from Fred Davis, who was starting an independent club in Pensacola. Davis had seen Bo pitch at Brunswick and offered him $300 a month. Bo took it.

Belinsky seemed to mature at Pensacola. He was 13–6 with 202 strikeouts in 195 innings and he had a good fastball for the first time. More important to Bo, there were beaches and plenty of girls in bikinis in Pensacola, and the bars were live.

Pensacola had a working agreement with the Baltimore Orioles; Belinsky was marked down as a "prospect" by the Orioles after that season. It didn't help, Bo learned. He found out about life in towns named Knoxville, Aberdeen, Amarillo, Stockton and Vancouver, not to mention a stretch in the Army Reserve.

"My career wasn't going anywhere," he said. "The Orioles had two young left-handers they liked a lot more, Steve Barber and Steve Dalkowski." Barber went on to have a successful major league career. Dalkowski, often considered the fastest pitcher ever by those who saw him in the minor leagues, never did learn to control his wildness and never pitched a game in the major leagues.

By 1961, Belinsky was in Little Rock and he had a fair year there, 9–10 with a bad team; he also led the league in strikeouts. Pitching winter ball in the off-season, he learned how to throw a screwball, a most appropriate pitch for Belinsky. He was also drafted by the Angels, who knew exactly what they were getting. "We knew he was flaky and we knew he had been around and would be good copy," said Irv Kaze, then the Angels' publicity man and now public relations director for the National League. "We were in direct competition with the Dodgers for tickets and we knew Bo would sell us some."

The Angels, though, weren't quite prepared for what was about to happen. They sent Bo the normal rookie contract, for the minimum $6000. Bo sent it back. He reasoned that, after six years in the minors, he was worth $8500. Before he had even thrown a ball in a major league game, he was a holdout.

So Belinsky stayed home in Trenton. The writers loved it and thousands of words were written daily for a week on the case of Bo Belinsky. "He was the most heavily covered player we ever had before he ever set foot in our camp," said Kaze.

Finally, the Angels persuaded Belinsky to come to camp to talk contract. Bo liked it in Palm Springs, where the Angels trained, because there were plenty of what he called "broadies" around. He finally settled for the original $6000 the Angels offered, but not until there was another spate of stories on him in camp. "I was certain to get a chance," he said. "No ball club builds a guy up the way the Angels built me up and then doesn't give him a chance."

A chance, though, was about all Belinsky could expect, but he made the most of it by getting off at 3–0. The girls and writers loved him, in about that order. "There's no problem meeting girls in baseball," said Bo. "They come to your room and knock on the door . . ."

And then came the day that turned Bo's life around: May 5, 1962. He talked about the day, and the night preceding, to Maury Allen in *Bo Pitching and Wooing:*

> I can't ever forget that date. . . . It [the night before] was some sort of a Mexican holiday and the strip was jammed with tourists. I see this one doll and we strike up a conversation. . . . I can hardly hear what she's saying because I'm too busy eyeing her. . . . She was tall and really built.
>
> I figured it was time to move. She figured the same thing. "My pad or yours?" She said hers was nearby and very private so we made it to hers. She was fabulous, those long legs and all, that long black hair. Fantastic. Now it's four o'clock in the morning and I have to pitch the next night so I figured I'd better blast off. She wishes me good luck. . . ."

Good luck indeed. Some hours later, Belinsky pitched a no-hitter, the first ever at the newly opened Dodger Stadium in Chavez Ravine. To make it sweeter, it was against his old team, the Baltimore Orioles. The pitcher was Steve Barber, his old minor league friend.

Belinsky had a couple of things going for him in that game. One was that the Orioles, who had finished third the year before, were in a season-long slump that would send them into seventh place. The other was that Dodger Stadium, known only as Chavez Ravine when the Angels played in it, was definitely a pitcher's park. The fences were far away and there was a curious deadness to the air; balls that seemed on their way to home runs when they left the bat most often settled into fielders' gloves. That can be a very comforting feeling for a pitcher.

But Bo being Bo, he felt his biggest advantage going in was his eventful evening. He later told writers he had started thinking about a no-hitter at 4 a.m., which only confused them since they didn't know where he had been at 4 a.m. After he had gone home, he had slept for 12 hours.

It was the kind of soft spring night that Los Angeles often gets, temperature in the low 70s, as Belinsky went out to pitch against his old team. "I guess I was as high for that game as any I had every pitched," he said. "I really wanted to show them I could pitch."

A crowd of 15,886 was on hand, an indication that Bo's fast start and his publicity had people interested. The Angels had not been drawing anywhere near that well. Los Angeles is a town which supports the best very well and the almost-best not at all. The Angels were off to a good start and were in the pennant race, but the Los Angeles fans were interested only in the Dodgers, who seemed on their way to the National League pennant (they eventually lost it to the Giants in a playoff). The night before, the Orioles and Angels had drawn only 5341.

Belinsky felt good as he warmed up, the ball moving as it should. He told catcher Bob Rodgers he'd like to use the screwball a lot in the early innings and save the fastball for later.

The Angels got him single runs in both the first and second innings, as Bo retired the Orioles 1–2–3. In the third, he got two outs and then walked Barber—the kind of thing that turns managers' hair gray—before getting the third out.

In the fourth, he got into real trouble. Jim Gentile walked to lead off the inning, Jackie Brandt got on base on an error and Gus Triandos walked. Angels' manager Bill Rigney signaled to the bullpen for Ryne Duren and Eli Grba to start throwing.

That upset Belinsky, because he felt Rigney should have more confidence in him after his fast start and his three hitless innings. He shouldn't have taken it personally. Throughout Rigney's managerial career, he has been known as a man with a quick hook. He didn't get a chance to exercise it on this night, thought, as Bo struck out Dave Nicholson on a high fastball and Hansen on a screwball and then got Barber to fly out to center to end the inning without scoring.

Belinsky set the Orioles down without a hit through the seventh inning. He had realized after the fifth inning that he was pitching a no-hitter, but it was not until after the seventh that the fans really got excited. "That's when it started," he said, "the noise, the excitement, the cheering, everybody pulling for me. It sounded like a hundred thousand people were in that park."

True to his word, Belinsky was going more and more to the fastball as the game went on. Just before going out for the ninth, having retired the last seven men in order, he told catcher Rodgers that he would throw nothing but fastballs in that inning. Like many other pitchers, he didn't want to lose the no-hitter on an off-speed pitch that would have him second-guessing himself.

As he walked to the mound, Jackie Brandt of the Orioles, the leadoff hitter in the ninth, said, "Nice game, Bob, but it's over. I'm going to lead off with a bunt single."

Brandt's words didn't disturb Belinsky's concentration and Jackie failed to make good on his promise: He didn't try to bunt and he flied out. Two outs to go.

Triandos was next, and he grounded out to second baseman Joe Koppe. Now, Belinsky needed only one out and the batter was Nicholson. Unlike Bo, Nicholson had gotten a large bonus because of his great potential. He was a tremendously strong man—there was a story that he had once turned the shower faucets off in the clubhouse and the Orioles had had to hire a plumber to turn them back on—and he could hit the ball great distances. His problem was that he didn't hit the ball with any frequency. "If you could throw a fastball up and in on him," said Bo, "you'd have him." Nicholson went on in 1963 to set what was then a major league record by striking out 175 times.

Nevertheless, Belinsky was acutely aware that it wouldn't take much to lose the no-hitter. A hit off the handle could do it, or a pitch that was a few inches from where he had intended it to go. He worked very carefully to Nicholson, getting a ball and a strike, then threw his tenth pitch of the inning, another fastball. It was up and in, exactly where he wanted it, and Nicholson lifted a foul just off third base.

Third baseman Felix Torres moved under it and, said Bo, "The ball went up like a balloon and seemed to hang there like some little kid's bubble. It was if the whole world stood still . . . I goddam nearly got goose bumps until the thing came down."

Come down it did and Belinsky had his no-hitter, the first by a rookie since Bobo Holloman had done it nine years before. He talked to the sportswriters after the game for more than an hour before going to a champagne party in his honor.

The no-hitter made Belinsky a national celebrity. More important to Bo, it made him a Hollywood celebrity. As plentiful as girls had been before, they were even more so now. He met Walter Winchell, the famed gossip columnist, and whatever women Bo couldn't get, Winchell could. Bo went out with Mamie Van Doren and later became engaged; he dated Tina Louise, Ann-Margaret and other lovelies. And though it didn't seem possible, he got

credit for even more than he did, because starlets learned the easiest way to get their names in the gossip columns was to fabricate a
date with Bo Belinsky.

After he had pitched his no-hitter, Bo seemed to have everything going for him, but that didn't last long. He got into a much-
publicized incident where a woman was hurt and he was fined;
there was another incident in which he and sportswriter Braven
Dyer got into a fight, for which Belinsky was fined and suspended.

His freewheeling lifestyle caught up with him on the field.
Probably, Belinsky could have been a better pitcher if he had
trained better or been more serious about the game, but then he
wouldn't have been Bo Belinsky, the original. He lived life to the
fullest, exactly as he wanted to, and he had no regrets when his
career was over. If he had it to do all over again, he would probably change very little.

Belinsky's career took a plunge in 1963, when he won only
two and lost nine. His lifestyle took an even bigger plunge in
1965, when he was traded to Philadelphia. The Phillies traded
him two years later to Houston, and he pitched for Pittsburgh and
Cincinnati before retiring after the 1970 season.

In his eight years in the majors, Belinsky won only 28 games
and lost 51. He was in double figures only once, his rookie year,
when he won 10 and lost 11. He never earned more than $18,000
in a season.

And yet, he was a celebrity because he threw a no-hitter. He
even had an explanation for why he never threw another: He
never again saw the girl he had balled the morning of his great
game. "After the game," he said, "I went back to look for her. I
couldn't find her. She was my good luck charm. When I lost her, I
lost all my pitching luck."

7

Some went extra innings

Harvey Haddix has no monopoly on misfortune among no-hit pitchers. Though nobody else in baseball history has pitched as good a game as Haddix did and lost, several pitchers have discovered that pitching a no-hit game for nine or more innings is no guarantee of success. Counting Haddix's great effort, in the first 75 years of this century, pitchers carried a no-hitter into extra innings 13 times; astonishingly, only four of those pitchers won their games!

The extra-inning no-hit string was started, in fact, with a loss. On May 9, 1901, Earl Moore, pitching for Cleveland against Chicago in the American League, lost a no-hitter in the tenth inning. Moore had allowed two unearned runs in the fourth inning, Cleveland having scored twice in the third, and the score was 2–2 going into the tenth. Chicago finally broke through for two hits in that inning to beat Moore and Cleveland.

That year was Moore's rookie year—he finished with a 16–14 record—and he must have thought he would get another chance at a no-hitter, this time a winning one, in the years to come. But though he pitched 14 years in the majors, he never pitched another no-hitter.

The next extra-inning no-hitter was a remarkable one on several counts, not the least of which was that it was won by the man who pitched the no-hitter, Bob Wicker of the Chicago Cubs.

The date was June 11, 1904, at the Polo Grounds and the Cubs and Giants were in a pennant race that eventually turned into a runaway for the Giants, who won by 13 games. A crowd of

38,505 fans, a record to that date, was there for the game; most of them were there to see Joe (Iron Man) McGinnity of the Giants. Wicker, a good but not great pitcher (two men on his own staff won more than his 17 wins in the 1904 season) was a minor attraction.

McGinnity was quite a pitcher and eventually he was elected to the Baseball Hall of Fame. He had originally gained his nickname because he worked in an iron foundry during the off season, and the name later came to be applied to his pitching habits as well. Five times during his career he pitched a doubleheader. Three of those came in one month, August of the 1904 season, and McGinnity won all three!

On this June day, he was still undefeated and on his way to his best record, 35 wins against only 8 losses, an earned run average of 1.61 and a whopping 408 innings pitched. But none of that mattered, because this game belonged to Wicker.

For nine innings, Wicker held the Giants hitless, but his teammates, though they were hitting McGinnity with some frequency, could not score.

Wicker lost his no-hitter, though not his composure, on a one-out single in the tenth by Sam Mertes. Finally, in the top of the twelfth, Johnny Evers singled, moved to second on an out and, with two outs, scored on Frank Chance's third hit of the game.

In the bottom of the inning, Wicker set the Giants down 1–2–3 for his win, a richly deserved one. He had allowed only Mertes' single in 12 innings, which was the longest one-hitter on record until Haddix came along; McGinnity had allowed 10 hits. Wicker had walked only one batter and struck out 10.

Harry McIntire of Brooklyn went Wicker four outs better in a game against Pittsburgh on August 1, 1906, when he went 10²/₃ innings without yielding a hit, a record which stood until Haddix's game. McIntire, however, had the same luck as Haddix. After giving up one hit in the eleventh, he gave up three hits and a run in the thirteenth and lost the game 1–0, just as Haddix had done.

That was typical of the kind of luck McIntire had throughout his career. Losing was something he became quite accustomed to. He pitched nine years in the major leagues and won 71 games, but he lost 117; in three of those seasons, he lost at least 20 games.

George (Hooks) Wiltse of New York carved himself a niche in the baseball record book when he became the first pitcher in modern times to pitch a no-hitter for ten innings and win. He picked a good day for it, too—the morning game of a morning–afternoon doubleheader on July 4, 1908, against Philadelphia.

Wiltse was named "Hooks" for the obvious reason: He threw

a good curve, or hook. The Wiltse family was given to colorful nicknames; his brother, also a major league pitcher, was nicknamed "Snake."

The next extra-inning no-hitter came on the opening day of the 1909 season, April 15 in New York, when Leon (Red) Ames of the Giants held Brooklyn without a hit for 9⅓ innings. It was Ames' second brush with no-hit fame. On September 14, 1903, he had thrown a no-hitter against St. Louis, but the game—the second of a doubleheader—had been called at the end of five innings, so he is not generally given credit for a no-hitter in that game.

He did, however, win that shortened game 5–0, which was better than he could do against Brooklyn in 1909. He pitched a remarkable game against Brooklyn, facing only the minimum of 27 batters in the first nine innings.

The Giants, weakened by the loss of star second baseman Larry Doyle, who had not signed his contract and was told by manager John McGraw that he could not play, did little better. Their one chance to score was stopped in the eighth when Brooklyn center fielder Jimmy Sebring made an excellent throw to cut down a runner at the plate. Ironically, Sebring had been traded from Cincinnati to Brooklyn between the 1908 and 1909 seasons.

In the game, which eventually went 13 innings, the Giants got only three singles off winning pitcher Irvin Wilhelm (saddled with the nickname of Kaiser), and the first one didn't come until that eighth inning.

Ames began to weaken in the extra innings, giving up three hits in the first three extra innings, but he held Brooklyn scoreless until the thirteenth. Unfortunately for him, Wilhelm was doing the same for New York.

Finally, in the top of the thirteenth, Brooklyn broke through. Manager Harry Lumley—starting what was to be the first and last year of his major league managerial career—tripled with one out. Tim Jordan was intentionally walked by Ames to set up a double play possibility, but then Ed Lennox singled in Lumley. Two more runs were scored on hits by Bill Bergen and Al Burch and an error by catcher George (Admiral) Schlei before Ames retired the side.

In the bottom of the thirteenth, the Giants sent up two pinch-hitters, Harry (Moose) McCormick and John Myers, the latter for Ames, but Wilhelm got the side out easily to win the game 3–0, leaving Ames with nothing but frustration to show for his efforts.

In a remarkably similar game, Tom Hughes of the New York

Highlanders pitched an extra-inning no-hitter against Cleveland on August 30, 1910, and had nothing to show for it but a marker in the loss column.

Hughes held the Indians hitless for the first 9⅓ innings, before giving up two hits in the tenth. In the eleventh, he weakened and allowed five hits and a walk, and Cleveland scored five runs. New York could not score in the bottom of the inning, and Hughes lost 5–0. Like the Ames' loss, Hughes came out for a pinchhitter in the eleventh, and the winning pitcher, George Kahler, ended up allowing fewer hits, three to Hughes' seven.

Most of the extra-inning no-hitters—9 of the first 13—were thrown before 1920, when Babe Ruth showed everybody how much fun home runs could be and the ball got its first injection of rabbit, though surely not its last.

The reason for the relative frequency of these games is obvious: Fewer runs were scored than in later years, so the chance of both teams being scoreless after nine innings was correspondingly greater.

The seventh of the extra-inning no-hitters came in 1914, a year otherwise noteworthy because a third "major" league—the Federal League—competed with the established American and National Leagues.

Chicago businessman James A. Gilmore became president of the Federal League, then a minor league, in 1913 and tried to turn a sectional (midwest) league into a major one. He lined up backing for most of the eight teams, with leading industrialists Phil Ball, Charles Weeghman and Robert Ward in on the planning.

Starting in 1914 as a major league, Gilmore said his teams would not honor the "monopolistic" reserve clause. Big money, for those days, was waved around and the Federal league signed star Chicago Cub shortstop Joe Tinker (of Tinker-Evers-Chance fame) to play and manage the Chicago Whales.

The league also signed some players who had been big names in the past but whose skills were fading, including Three Finger Brown, Chicago Cubs; George Mullin, Detroit Tigers; Danny Murphy, Philadelphia Athletics; and Hal Chase, Chicago White Sox.

The next year, the Federal League got two star pitchers, Eddie Plank and Chief Bender from Philadelphia, but the chief beneficiaries of the Federal League's loose money policy were established superstars like Ty Cobb, Tris Speaker and Walter Johnson, who had their salaries boosted considerably by worried club owners.

After the 1915 season, the Federal League sued for peace because of mounting losses and the likelihood that most of the available players would soon be marching off to war in Europe, a possibility which did not really materialize. Ball was allowed to buy the St. Louis Browns and Weegham the Chicago Cubs; they also kept the players from their St. Louis and Chicago franchises in the Federal League. Otherwise, all the Federal League players were sold to the highest bidder in the established leagues.

It was against this background that Jim Scott of the Chicago White Sox took a no-hitter into the tenth inning against the Washington Senators on May 14, 1914. Naturally, he lost.

While Scott was holding Washington without a hit in the first nine innings, his teammates were nearly as helpless, getting only three hits off Doc Ayers, two singles and a triple by Chase, who had not yet jumped to the Federal League.

In the bottom of the tenth, Scott lost his no-hitter and the game almost before he knew what was happening. Chick Gandil, first up, singled and then scored when Howard Shanks doubled.

The pitchers who have carried no-hitters into a tenth inning have been a mixed bag: some good, some bad, some indifferent, proving once again that no-hit lightning can strike anybody. Of the pitchers who turned the feat, for instance, there have been good ones like Ames (181 wins) and Jim Vaughn (176 wins) and mediocre ones like Wicker (64 wins) and Tom Hughes (58).

But there was only one pitcher who was a mixed bag in himself, Louis (Bobo) Newsom of the Brooklyn Dodgers, Chicago Cubs, St. Louis Browns, Washington Senators, Boston Red Sox, Detroit Tigers and Philadelphia Athletics.

Newsom's career was an incredible one, spanning 20 years. He moved back and forth from team to team and league to league. There have been players who played with as many teams—seven— as Newsom, but none who kept returning so much. He had two tours of duty, for instance, with the Athletics and Brooklyn, three with the Browns and an incredible five with Washington.

Newsom won more than 200 games, which few pitchers do. Unfortunately, he also lost more than 200, which even fewer do. His lifetime record was 211–222.

Unquestionably, he was better than his career record would indicate; he played for a lot of bad teams. But nobody could quite figure out just how good Newsom was. There were no doubts in his mind: He kept telling everybody how good he was and he convinced enough owners and managers to keep coming back and back and back.

Newsom, who was also known as "Buck," never gave up on

himself. He led the league four times in most games lost, which would discourage most men. Not Newsom. The last time that happened, he came back the next year to post a 14–13 record with a 2.93 earned run average. In 1949, approaching his forty-second birthday, nobody in either league wanted him, but by 1952, he had talked his way back into the league—with Washington, of course—and pitched that year and the next before finally retiring at 46.

It was probably inevitable, given his career, that when Newsom pitched a no-hitter he would lose it. It came in his first full season, 1934, when he was pitching for the Browns for the first time and, yes, leading the league in losses with 20.

The most disappointing of the losses came on September 18 against the Boston Red Sox at old Sportsmans Park in St. Louis. The day before, the Red Sox had hit safely in every inning while beating the Browns, but on this day Bobo held them hitless for 9²/₃ innings—and then lost the game in the tenth.

It was a weird game, which figured since Newsom pitched it. Though Boston was hitless through the first nine, the Red Sox had a run, scored in the second inning on two walks, an error and a ground ball. The Browns, who had not scored for 26 straight innings, equaled that with a run in the sixth on a single by Rollie Hemsley, an error by Boston third baseman Billy Werber and a single by Alan Strange.

Newsom was in frequent trouble because he was wild, issuing seven walks in the game. The Browns, too, had several chances to score, with ten hits, but could only do it once.

To add to the bizarre aspects of the game, Boston pitcher Wes Ferrell was called out on strikes in the second inning and complained so strenuously that he was thrown out of the game by plate umpire Kouls, with Rube Walberg taking over on the mound. It may sound strange that a pitcher would argue so long over a strikeout that he was thrown out of the game, but Ferrell was a good hitter and proud of it. In his 15-year career, he averaged .280. He was used as a pinchhitter and had even played 13 games as an outfielder in 1933.

Newsom was at his peak in the third and fourth innings, retiring the Red Sox in order and striking out four of them. He also had a 1–2–3 inning in the first, but otherwise did not retire the Red Sox in order in any other innings.

In the tenth, Newsom started by retiring Walberg on a grounder, but then walked Max Bishop and Werber. Mel Almada followed by flying out to left field, but then Johnson hit a hard ground ball which hopped past shortstop Strange into center field. Strange, racing to his left, made a desperate lunge for it with his glove, but the ball bounced high and missed his outstretched glove by a couple of inches. Bishop came home with the run that put the Red Sox in front to stay at 2–1.

Newsom then struck out Arthur Graham, his ninth strikeout of the game, but the damage had been done.

There was a lot more pitching ahead for Bobo, who won his last major league game when he was 46. His best year was 1940, when he won 21 games and lost only 5 for Detroit as the Tigers beat out Cleveland by a game for the pennant.

Newsom got the starting assignment for the first World Series game and beat Cincinnati 7–2, the tenth straight win for American League teams in World Series competition. His father watched the game, but that night had a heart attack and died the next morning. Though grieving, Newsom shut out the Reds 8–0 in the fifth game for his second win of the Series.

But the Series went down to the seventh game and Detroit manager Del Baker called on Newsom again. Baker had little choice. Schoolboy Rowe, who had won 16 regular season games as the second starter, had pitched the day before; the third starter was Tommy Bridges, who had won only 12 in the regular season. Baker wanted his best out there for the final game, and his best was Newsom.

Bobo gave it a good shot. He held the Reds scoreless for the first six innings and yielded only seven hits and two runs for the game. Unfortunately, Detroit got only one run off Paul Derringer and Newsom lost the game. It was only fitting for a man who could lose a no-hit game.

There are two other outstanding feats in the annals of extra-inning no-hit games. The first involves one game and two pitchers; the second, one pitcher and two games.

When the Chicago Cubs and Cincinnati Reds met in Chicago on May 2, 1917, the game was hardly of overriding importance; Cincinnati was to finish fourth, 20 games out, that year and Chicago was 4 games further back in fifth place.

Still, it was an attractive matchup because of the starting pitchers, Fred Toney for Cincinnati and Jim (Hippo) Vaughn for Chicago. Both were good pitchers on the way to their best winning seasons. Toney would finish 1917 with a 24–16 record and a 2.20 ERA; Vaughn compiled a 23–13 record with a 2.01 ERA.

They were both 29 that season and at their peaks, but in other ways they differed. Vaughn was a lefthander who depended on a fastball that got him a lot of strikeouts; Toney was a righthander with less speed who was more dependent on guile.

And on this spring day in 1917, they were to pitch a game

unique in baseball history, a double no-hitter. The odds for a single no-hitter are high; for a double no-hitter, they are astronomical.

For his career, Vaughn was the better pitcher. Toney had two 20-win seasons and 137 career wins; Vaughn had four 20-win seasons and 176 career wins. Vaughn was starting a four-season stretch in which he would win 85 games, lead the league twice in strikeouts and twice compile earned run averages of under two runs a game.

If anything, he looked like the better pitcher in this game, too. Cincinnati manager Christy Mathewson, the great pitcher, started an all righthanded hitting lineup against Vaughn, but it made little difference. With some remarkable fielding behind him, Vaughn retired the Reds without a hit for the first nine innings. Two men walked, neither getting beyond first base, and he struck out ten.

Meanwhile, Toney was matching him nearly pitch for pitch. He struck out only three in that spell and one Cub runner got to second, though no further, but no Cub got a base hit; the game went into the tenth tied at 0–0. The nearest thing to a hit was a drive by Fred Merkle that was pulled down just in front of the left field fence by Manuel Cueto.

Then, the Reds struck in the top of the tenth. Larry Kopf broke Vaughn's no-hit spell with a single and advanced to third when Cy Williams, the Chicago center fielder, dropped a fly ball hit by the ubiquitous Hal Chase.

The next batter was Jim Thorpe, the famed Indian athlete from Carlisle, Pennsylvania. Thorpe was considered the best all-round athlete of his day and beyond, but his fame rested more on his football and track and field exploits than baseball; he hit only .237 in 1917 and .252 lifetime. This time, though, he hit a slow grounder to Vaughn's left that had the effect of a drag bunt. Vaughn had to field it, but his throw to first was too late to catch the speedy Thorpe, who got credit for a single and a run batted in.

In the bottom of the inning, Toney retired the Cubs without a hit to get the win. Vaughn got only a loss, and a spot in the baseball record book.

But Vaughn had little to complain about compared to Jim Maloney of Cincinnati. In 1965, Maloney became the only pitcher to throw two extra-inning no-hit games, and he tied a strikeout record in one of them; yet, he got only one win out of that, and just barely.

Maloney was a hard-throwing righthander who had hardly pitched in his younger days. Playing for Fresno High in the late '50s, Maloney played shortstop most of the time because his team had almost more pitching than it could use. One starter on that team was Dick Ellsworth, a lefthander who went on to win 115 games in the major leagues. A righthanded starter, Lynn Rube, was good enough to sign a $30,000 bonus contract with the St. Louis Cardinals, though he never got out of their minor league system.

Ellsworth also signed a bonus contract out of high school, for a reported $75,000, but Maloney didn't; he went on to Fresno City College and the decision paid for itself. At Fresno CC, he was made a pitcher and often used in the second game of double-headers, when the light was fading and his whooshing fastball was that much more effective. He looked so good that he signed a bonus contract with Cincinnati for a reported $100,000.

Like most fastball pitchers, Maloney had control problems early in his career, but by 1963 he was an accomplished pitcher, winning 23 games and losing only 7, striking out 265 batters in 250¹/₃ innings. He fell off to 15 wins the next year, but in 1965 he had what was probably his best all-round season, winning 20 games, pitching more innings (255) than ever before, more complete games (14) and posting his best earned run average (2.54) while striking out 244.

And 1965 was also the year he made throwing no-hit games look easy. He started relatively slowly, with a 2–0 win in his first start on April 19, in which he pitched no-hit ball for the first seven innings.

It turned out that Maloney was only warming up. On June 14, pitching in old and tiny Crosley Field in Cincinnati, known always as a hitter's park, Maloney no-hit the New York Mets for ten innings, while setting one strikeout record and tying another. His 18 strikeouts were a club record and tied the National League record first set by Warren Spahn (in a 15-inning game) and later tied twice by Sandy Koufax. (The record has since been broken by Steve Carlton and then Tom Seaver, both with 19.)

Maloney was overpowering through the first ten innings. The Mets didn't come close to a hit and the only walk was to Ed Kranepool in the second inning. Kranepool got to second on an infield out but was left there when Maloney whistled a third strike past Roy McMillan.

In the fourth, Charley Smith got to first when Cincinnati catcher Johnny Edwards missed the ball on which he was struck out, but then Kranepool hit into a double play. That started a streak of 19 straight batters retired by Maloney.

New York pitchers Frank Lary, who started and went the first eight, and Larry Bearnarth, who later got the win in relief, weren't as spectacular as they scattered seven singles, but they were just as effective as Maloney when it came to keeping the opposition scoreless. Only two Reds reached third base.

The Reds nearly won it in the tenth, after Edwards led off with a single and was sacrificed to second, pinchhitter Chico Ruiz replacing him. Maloney bounced out, with Ruiz going to third.

Tommy Harper swung at Bearnarth's first pitch and tapped a grounder to Smith at third. It was an easy play, but Smith fired into the dirt to first base and only a fine save by Kranepool got Harper out and sent the game into the eleventh inning.

The leadoff hitter in the eleventh was Johnny Lewis, hitting only .250 for the season and a strikeout victim for three straight times. With a count of two balls and one strike, Lewis swung at a belt-high fastball and sent it on a line to deep center field. The ball crashed against the wall, five feet above a yellow line painted on it, for a home run under the ground rules.

Maloney then struck out Ron Swoboda for his eighteenth strikeout, gave up a single to McMillan and got Jesse Gonder to ground into a double play to end the inning. The Reds could not score in the bottom of the inning and Maloney lost the game 1–0.

"That's baseball, I guess," he said to sportswriters after the game. "I can't compare this game to any other. It's by far the best I've ever pitched.

"I felt good and the low fastball was the best I've ever had, but I mixed it up with good control and a crackling curve. The ball that Lewis hit was a fastball. I tried to jam him, but failed. He hit the same kind of pitch for a homer off me the last time the Mets were here."

Maloney, who had thrown two one-hitters in previous seasons in preparation for this year, was so overpowering at this stage of his career that—like other power pitchers such as Bob Feller, Sandy Koufax and Nolan Ryan—it was only a matter of time until he threw another no-hitter. That time came on August 19. Like his first no-hitter, this one went ten innings, but there was a significant difference: This time he won, beating the Cubs 1–0.

Artistically, this game did not equal Maloney's first no-hitter because he was very wild. He seemed to be working from a stretch for half the game, as he walked ten batters and hit another. In only five of the ten innings could he retire the Cubs in 1–2–3 order. Thirteen times he worked to a full 3–2 count, and he threw 187 pitches, half again what most pitchers would have thrown in that time.

Yet in a way, this game was much more satisfying to the hard-throwing righthander because he had to show the ability—and temperament—of a great pitcher when it counted. Three times the Cubs got a runner to third base, and three times they had the bases loaded in Wrigley Park, where pop flies become home runs when the wind is blowing out. Yet, Maloney turned them back every time. There was nothing resembling a hit and only three Cubs—Doug Clemens in the eighth, pinchhitter Jim Stewart in the ninth and Billy Williams in the tenth—could even hit the ball out of the infield. All three of those balls were routine fly balls, easily handled by the Cincinnati outfielders. In the game, the Cubs stranded ten runners.

As usual, Maloney's best pitch was the fastball: He was to strike out 244 hitters in 255 innings that season. In this game he struck out 12, all of them in the first nine innings. He struck out the side in the fifth and had at least one strikeout in each of the first nine innings.

Maloney was in trouble as early as the third inning, walking the bases full with two outs; Williams, the Cubs' leading hitter with a .297 average and 20 homers at that stage, was the next batter. But he got Williams to ground out to second baseman Pete Rose to end the inning.

He walked two more in the fourth, ending the threat with his fifth strikeout. In the eighth, he walked pitcher Larry Jackson leading off. Jackson went to second on a sacrifice and, after the second out, Williams was up again.

Cincinnati manager Dick Sisler came out to talk to Maloney and then ordered an intentional walk to Williams. That brought up Ernie Banks, who had 19 homers and 85 RBIs. Maloney worked to a full count against Banks and then, in a devastating display of power against power, threw a fastball past Banks for his eleventh strikeout, ending the Cubs' threat.

Again in the ninth, Maloney got himself into trouble, first hitting Ron Santo and then walking Ed Bailey. Glen Beckert tried to bunt along the runners and failed before striking out. Stewart flied to short center, but then Maloney again walked pitcher Jackson, an indication of how wild he was on this day, before getting Don Landrum to pop up to shortstop to end the inning and send the game into extra innings.

Meanwhile, the Reds had twice gotten a runner to third base off Jackson, who gave up nine hits in the game, without being able to score. In the seventh, Frank Robinson tripled high off the left field fence with one out, but was stranded there.

In the ninth, the Reds got the first two men on when Banks bobbled Rose's grounder and Vada Pinson singled. Robinson—whose triple was stopped short of a home run by a brisk wind blowing in from left—hit another shot to deep left, but this time Clemens was able to gather it in for the first out. Gordy Coleman lashed a drive to deep right, but again the wind caught the ball and held it up just enough to enable Williams to catch it against the ivy-covered wall. The Reds still had Deron Johnson, leading the majors in RBIs at that point with 97, but Johnson could only bounce to the infield for the inning-ending out.

Maloney must have wondered if this game was going to be a repeat of his loss to the Mets, but that thought disappeared when, with out one in the tenth, 155-pound Cincinnati shortstop Leo Cardenas did what the Cincinnati musclemen couldn't do in earlier innings, crashing a home run to give Maloney the run he needed.

It wasn't over yet. Maloney, seemingly uncomfortable if he didn't have a runner on base, opened the bottom of the tenth by walking Clemens. But Williams then flied out and Banks hit the first pitch to him to Cardenas, who started a game-ending double play with his flip to Rose.

Maloney pitched a third no-hitter in 1969, becoming only the fourth pitcher to do that (Cy Young, Bob Feller, and Sandy Koufax with four, beating him to it). Miraculously, he did not have to pitch an extra-inning game this time, winning the game in nine innings, 10–0 over the Houston Astros on April 30 at Crosley Field in Cincinnati.

By this time, Maloney was already on the way downhill, arm trouble cutting his career prematurely short. In 1969, he was to win only 12 games and strike out only 102 batters, and he was never again to win in double figures for a season. But on this day, he was as good as he ever was. He walked 5, but struck out 13.

The Astros, who lost their eighth straight game in this one, hit just two balls to the outfield and there were only two tough fielding plays. In the sixth, rookie shortstop Darrel Chaney saved the no-hitter when he made a diving catch of Johnny Edwards' pop fly in short left; Edwards, interestingly, had been Maloney's catcher in his first two no-hitters.

"I told myself," said Chaney later, "that Jim had a no-hitter and I had to get to the ball. If I got there and dropped it, it would have been an error, not a hit."

Tommy Helms made the other tough play, racing in on a softly hit roller by Norm Miller and throwing him out on a close play at first base in the fifth inning.

Maloney remained cool throughout the game. "He was as cool as anyone I've ever see," said reserve first baseman Fred Whitfield.

Maloney said later he was concerned first with winning, and secondly with pitching a no-hitter. The Reds made the first point academic with a seven-run fourth inning that pushed their lead to 8–0; Maloney could concentrate on the no-hitter after that.

In the ninth inning, Maloney faced the top of the Houston batting order but said he wasn't nervous. "I'm beyond the point of getting scared," he said. "I felt good and was making the right pitches at the right time. As you learn more about pitching and learn more about hitters, you learn to mix your pitches up better. I was mixing my pitches up very well."

In that ninth, he got the Astros out with a minimum of trouble. Joe Morgan flied to Rose, by now playing center field, and Helms threw out Jesus Alou for the first two outs. Maloney then walked Jimmy Wynn, but struck out Doug Rader to end the game.

His first thought was, "I pitched another no-hitter. It's hard to believe those things."

Even when a pitcher throws three, a no-hitter is not commonplace.

8

The cream of the crop

If pitching a no-hitter is a remarkable feat, allowing no runners to reach base on either a hit, walk or error is a stunning one, which is why it is called a perfect game. A pitcher must indeed be perfect to pitch such a game, because he must have both control and ability on that day. He also needs unusual help from his teammates; despite the tension that prevails in any no-hit game, they must not bobble even one ball.

There have been only seven nine-inning perfect games pitched in regular season competition since the turn of the century, which is mute testimony to how difficult a feat it is. Three of those perfect games—by Cy Young, Ernie Shore and Sandy Koufax—are described in other chapters, as is the Harvey Haddix effort which is in another category.

Form does not always tell with perfect games, any more than it does with no-hitters: Charley Robertson, with a lifetime record of 49–80, and Shore, who won only 63 games in his career, both pitched perfect games.

But generally speaking, the pitchers who have pitched perfect games have been outstanding. Young and Koufax are both in the Hall of Fame; Jim Bunning won more than 200 games in his career, and Catfish Hunter will certainly reach 200—and may even win 300—before he ends his career.

Fittingly enough, the first perfect game of modern times was pitched by Young in 1904. The next came four years later, when Addie Joss pitched one for Cleveland against Chicago.

The year 1908 was a vintage one for no-hitters. Six regulation ones were pitched, as well as a six-inning no-hitter by John Lush that was stopped by rain. Joss's perfect game was the last and best of the no-hitters that year, and it came in the last week of the season, on October 2. His game and Sandy Koufax's perfect in 1965 were the only ones thrown in the last month of the season, when the pennant race pressure was chokingly tight; all the others have been thrown in early season.

Joss's perfect game was no fluke. Addie Joss was an excellent pitcher. Had he not died just two days past his thirty-first birthday, he might have gone on to become one of the all-time best. Four times in his nine-year career he won 20 games or more and he finished with a total of 160–97, with a remarkable 1.88 earned run average.

The year before, 1907, had been his best winning year, as he led the league with 27 wins against 10 losses and had an ERA of 1.83. He also pitched three one-hitters, still an American League record. In 1908, he had a league-leading 1.16 ERA and won 24 games, but none of his other wins came close to matching the drama of his perfect game.

This one would have been dramatic even if it hadn't been perfect. The American League had an unusually tight pennant race that season, with Cleveland, Chicago and Detroit going down to the wire virtually tied. Detroit finally won it on the last day; it was the first American League pennant to be decided on the last day of the season and that did not happen again until 1944.

It was with this background that Cleveland and Chicago met on October 2. Each had its ace ready; Joss, of course, for Cleveland; big Ed Walsh for Chicago. Walsh was having an incredible year. Starting and relieving, he appeared in 66 games and 464 innings that year. He won 40 games, leading the league in wins, games, games started, complete games, innings pitched and strikeouts.

He was working with only two days' rest against Cleveland that day and he pitched an excellent game, allowing only four hits and one walk and striking out 15. But it wasn't enough because Joss didn't allow anything.

The one run that Cleveland scored to win the game came in the third, and it was tainted. Joe Birmingham opened the inning with a short fly to center which fell for a hit when Eddie Hahn couldn't quite reach it. That was the first hit of the game.

Walsh tried to pick Birmingham off first and probably would have done it, but Birmingham dashed toward second instead of trying to get back to first. First-baseman Frank Isbell's throw hit Birmingham on the head and caromed into the outfield, and Birmingham went to third.

Walsh got George Perring to hit an infield grounder on which Birmingham was forced to hold third, then struck out Joss. With two strikes on Wilbur Goode, the next pitch got away from Ossee Schreckengost for a passed ball and Birmingham scored.

Then Walsh struck out Goode, who was to strike out four times in the afternoon, but that one tainted run was all Cleveland needed.

Schreckengost was the goat of the game, of course, but it wasn't all his fault. For one thing, Walsh's big pitch was a spitter, a ball which breaks with extraordinary quickness and is often hard to catch. For another, he wasn't Walsh's regular catcher. Billy Sullivan was, but Sullivan was out of the lineup that day.

The next perfect game was a disputed one thrown by Shore in 1917 (discussed in a later chapter), but on April 22, 1930, Charlie Robertson threw a 2–0 perfect game against the Tigers about which there could be no dispute.

That Robertson would throw a perfect game at this particular time is one of the twists of fate that make baseball so interesting. Before the game, the most reasonable prediction for Robertson that day would have been an early shower.

Robertson was facing an awesome lineup. The Tigers finished third in the American League race that year, almost entirely on their hitting. They had no 20-game winners, but they hit .305 as a team.

The leading hitter, of course, was Ty Cobb, who hit .401 that year, but Cobb had plenty of help. In the lineup that raced Robertson that day were Cobb and four others who went on to hit at least .300 for the season. Harry Heilman hit .356, Bobby Veach .327, Lu Blue and Topper Rigney an even .300.

Before and after his great feat, Robertson was a mediocre pitcher, never winning as many as he lost on any of his eight major league seasons. He had come up briefly to the White Sox in the 1919 season, pitching two innings in one game, then returning to the minors for two more years. Thus, 1922 was regarded as his rookie season. To stack the odds even higher against him, he was pitching in the Tiger's home stadium in Detroit.

None of that mattered on this day, however, as Robertson pitched his way past the dangerous Tigers with ease, 27 men up and 27 down.

The Tigers protested early in the game that he was throwing an illegal pitch (spitballs and other trick pitches had been banned after the 1920 season, when Cleveland's Ray Chapman had died after being hit on the head by a Carl Mays' pitch), but the umpires could detect no illegalities. The protests did not seem to bother Robertson, who was in perfect control.

Perfect control is indeed the proper phrase. Only once all day was Robertson behind a hitter. He was able to put the ball just where he wanted it almost all the time: Thus, the Tigers had to hit the pitch he wanted them to hit, not the one they wanted. There is a substantial difference.

Robertson struck out six men in the game. Seven men grounded out and fourteen flied out, to either the outfielders or infielders. Of those seven groundouts, three were handled by Hall of Fame second baseman Eddie Collins, who also caught four flies. It was a busy day for Collins.

Only six balls were hit deep enough to cause Robertson any concern: Right fielder Harry Hooper and left fielder Johnny Mostil gathered them all in, without extraordinary effort. Only in the second did Robertson appear shaky at all as the Tigers hit three long drives, Veach's being caught by Mostil, Heilmann's and Bob Jones's being caught by Hooper.

In the ninth, Cobb, who was also the Detroit manager that year, sent up two pinchhitters in an attempt to break Robertson's spell. The first was Dan Clark, a .292 hitter during the 1922 season; he was soon Robertson's sixth strikeout victim. Catcher Clyde Manion batted for himself and popped out to Collins.

Finally, Cobb sent up Johnny Bassler, usually the Tigers' starting catcher but resting on this day. Bassler was an excellent hitter—he average .323 in the 1922 season—but he was no threat that day. Pinchhitting for pitcher Herman Pillette, he hit a foul fly down the left field line that Mostil came in and grabbed.

The Detroit fans, as partisan as any, had howled at Robertson in the early innings when the Tigers were complaining of illegal pitches. But by the late innings, they were aware of what they were seeing and were rooting for the lean Texan. At the end of the game, some of the estimated 25,000 who watched the game broke out onto the field and carried Robertson off on their shoulders.

As often seems to happen in no-hit games, Robertson's pitching opponent, Pillette, had also pitched an excellent game, allowing only seven hits. He gave up both the Chicago runs in the second inning but was in command from that point. Those two runs, though, were too much: that game was to keep Pillette from a 20-win season; he finished at 19–12.

Robertson's feat got more attention in subsequent years than the earlier perfect games because it seemed for a long time that it might be the last such game pitched. In stories on no-hit games, it was routine to include the phrase, "There hasn't been a perfect game pitched since Charlie Robertson did it on April 30, 1922 . . ." There wasn't another perfect game thrown in championship competition until Don Larsen did it in the World Series

in 1956, and it was another eight years before one was thrown in
the regular season.

When Jim Bunning broke through on June 21, 1964, with the
first perfect game in the regular season in 42 years, it seemed to
break a psychological barrier. The next season, Sandy Koufax
threw his fourth no-hitter and first perfect game; in 1968, Catfish
Hunter threw a perfect game. Forty-two years without a perfect
game, then three of them within a four-year span!

That Bunning would throw a no-hitter was no surprise, because
he had done it once before, on July 20, 1958, against the Boston
Red Sox in Fenway Park. He was an outstanding pitcher, winning
224 games in his career and finishing with 2,855 career strikeouts,
trailing only Walter Johnson and Bob Gibson.

He was the kind of pitcher managers like to have throwing in
Fenway Park—with its cozy left field wall that could be so easily
reached by righthanded hitters—because he had a fastball that
seemed to explode and he liked to come sidearm to righthanded
hitters, his right arm seeming to whip in from somewhere around
third base. Righthanded hitters who stayed close to the plate
against that pitch were advised to have their life insurance pre-
miums paid.

His first no-hitter came for the Detroit Tigers and he was only
the third Tiger pitcher to throw a no-hitter. Virgil (Fire) Trucks
had thrown two of them in 1952; George Mullin had done it once
back in 1912.

His most anxious moments came early. The leadoff hitter,
Gene Stephens, hit a drive deep into right field. Al Kaline backed
up onto the warning track and hauled in the ball just a few steps
from the wall.

The next batter was Pete Runnels, leading the American
League in hitting at the time. Runnels hit a ball sharply down the
third base line. Ossie Virgil made the stop deep behind the bag
and his throw just got Runnels at first. Runnels was limping because of a pulled leg muscle and left the game shortly after that.
Had he been healthy, he probably would have beaten out the
grounder. That's what pitchers mean when they say they need
luck to pitch a no-hitter.

After that, Bunning had little trouble. He struck out 12,
walked Stephens twice (not taking any chances after that first
drive) and hit Jackie Jensen in the arm; Stephens and Jensen were
the only Red Sox baserunners. Only seven times did the hard-
hitting Red Sox even get the ball out of the infield.

Bunning made his teammates uneasy because he defied the
old tradition of the dugout by talking freely about his no-hitter. "I

was going after it from the sixth inning," he said. "In fact, I told some of the fellows to keep digging those balls because I was going to make it."

By the ninth inning, Bunning was throwing almost exclusively fastballs, challenging the Red Sox hitters, not wanting to lose the no-hitter on an off-speed pitch. With the 29,529 Boston fans now behind him, he struck out the pesky Stephens and also Ted Lepcio to come within one out of a no-hitter.

The last hitter was Ted Williams, who was certainly the best hitter of his time. Williams had been the last to hit .400, with a .406 mark in 1941; he had hit .388 just the year before and he was to lead the American League with a .328 average in 1958. Bunning brushed Williams back from the plate with his first pitch, then Williams lined the next pitch to right field. Kaline took a few steps to his right and caught the ball to end the game, giving Bunning a 3–0 win and his first no-hitter.

By 1963, Bunning seemed to be tailing off, winning only 12 and losing 13 that year, and the Tigers traded him in the off-season to the Philadelphia Phillies, little knowing they were setting the stage for baseball history in so doing.

Though fans marvel at the ability of a major league pitcher, it is really his emotions that are more important. At that level everybody has ability; although some have more than others, what separates the best from the mediocre is usually mental attitude, the desire to be the best. Certainly, that was true in the case of Bunning, who was always what is known as a "competitor" in the baseball world. After his trade, he was determined to prove that the Tigers were wrong, and he carried a 6–2 record to the mound to face the New York Mets in the first game of a doubleheader in New York on June 21, 1964.

Bunning also had a good sense of the dramatic. He pitched with such exertion that his motion carried him far off to the left side of the mound; occasionally, he even fell.

And now, he picked Father's Day to throw his perfect game. It was surely appropriate, for he was the father of seven. His wife, Mary, and oldest daughter, Barbara, were in the stands watching the game that day.

As with his first no-hitter, Bunning had his only real trouble early in the game. In the fifth, Jesse Gonder drove a hard ground ball between first and second. Tony Taylor made a spectacular diving grab of the ball, bobbled it momentarily, then threw to first baseman John Herrnstein for the out, getting Gonder by a stride. Again, the pitcher's no-hit luck: Gonder was a slow runner; a faster runner might have beaten the throw.

Aside from that play, the Mets gave Bunning no trouble. Of course, the Mets gave nobody any trouble that year, winning only 53 games, but this was exceptional even for them. Only four balls were even hit to the outfield and the hardest hit ball by the Mets all day was a foul drive to right by Ron Hunt in the fourth.

Bunning struck out ten and went to a three-ball count on only two batters in the game. The last time came with two outs in the eighth when Bob Taylor went to a 3–2 count, but Bunning slipped a third strike past him to end the inning.

There was little suspense about the outcome of the game because the Phillies got single runs in the first and second, then four more in the sixth for the final score of 6–0.

A walk to Johnny Briggs, Herrnstein's sacrifice and a single by Dick Allen scored the first run. A walk to Taylor, Cookie Rojas' sacrifice and a double to left by catcher Gus Triandos made it 2–0. Triandos had been part of the Bunning deal, coming over with Jim in exchange for pitcher Jack Hamilton and outfielder Don Demeter.

In the sixth, John Callison opened with a home run over the right-field fence. A walk to Wes Covington and singles by Taylor and Triandos brought in another run, then Bunning doubled in the final two runs himself.

After that, Bunning's chief threat was the 90-degree temperature in humid Shea Stadium. To take his mind off that, he talked about the no-hitter—even when he was on the mound. "He was chattering like a magpie out there," Triandos told Dick Young of the *New York Daily News* later.

Heat or no, however, he got better as he went down the stretch; it was the Mets who wilted, not Bunning. He struck out six men in the last three innings and threw only 25 pitches in that span; for the game, he had 90 pitches, 69 of them strikes.

Most of the 32,026 fans were standing by the ninth inning, unable to bear the tension any other way. Bunning went to a 2–2 count on the first batter, Charlie Smith, and then threw a slider in on Smith's fists to get him to lift a high foul behind third, taken by shortstop Bobby Wine.

Next up was George Altman, pinchhitting for Amado Samuel. Altman fouled off the first two pitches, then swung at a low outside pitch and struck out.

Bunning sighed, took off his cap and wiped his brow and called Triandos out to the mound. He wanted the catcher to tell him a joke to relax him. Triandos was astounded and could think of nothing to say; he was probably more tense than Bunning at that point. Finally, Triandos told Bunning just to throw the ball and get it over, and he went back behind the plate.

The third hitter of the inning and the only man between Bunning and a perfect game was Johnny Stephenson, pinchhitting for the third Met pitcher, Tom Sturdivant. Like Altman, Stephenson was a lefthanded hitter. Casey Stengel, the Mets' manager, was always a believer in the lefty-against-righty percentage, and never more than now.

By this time, though, it didn't matter to Bunning which way the Mets were swinging. He threw a low-breaking ball, which Stephenson missed, then a fastball which Stephenson took for a strike. Ahead at 0–2, Bunning then tried to get Stephenson to chase a bad pitch, but the Met hitter let two balls go, one low and outside, the other high and outside.

Then Bunning came back with a curve at the knees on the outside—a perfect pitch—and Stephenson could do nothing but swing and miss. The Phillies poured out of the dugout to escort Bunning in to face the inevitable interviews.

"It's a wonderful feeling," said Bunning. "I still can't believe it. I had everything going for me. My fastball was working good, but the slider was my best pitch."

He was less excited than his wife. "I was so excited, I lost my sunglasses twice," said Mary Bunning.

As Bunning was being interviewed, Callison shouted across the room, "It's easy in the National League, isn't it?" Callison, too, had started his career in the American League, with the Chicago White Sox, before being traded to Philadelphia.

Bunning had indeed showed the Tigers how wrong they had been in trading him. He went on to win 106 games—almost half his major league total—for the Phillies, including three straight seasons of 19 wins. His perfect game made him only the second pitcher in modern times to pitch no-hitters in both leagues, Tom Hughes having done it for the New York Highlanders in 1910 (a game covered in an earlier chapter) and the Boston Braves in 1916.

Jim had made his point.

The three perfect games of the '60s were no flukes. All were thrown by excellent pitchers: Bunning, Koufax and Hunter. But there is a difference. Bunning and Koufax were established pitchers when they threw their perfect games; Hunter's game was the first indication that he was going to be an outstanding pitcher.

Hunter was signed to a $75,000 bonus contract by Charlie Finley in 1963, after he had won 23 games and lost only 2 in his last two high-school seasons. He already had some no-hit experience. He remembers that he threw five no-hitters in high school, one of them a perfect game, though only seven innings.

He spent the 1964 season on the disabled list because of a

hunting accident; part of his foot was removed. He was put on the major league roster in 1965 and never pitched an inning in the minor leagues. His ability was obvious even then and the A's had nothing to lose by pitching him, since they were to finish tenth in two of his first three seasons.

He was 8–8 in 1965, 9–11 in 1966 and 13–17 in 1967, bringing his earned run average down to 2.81 that year. He was 2–2 when he went out on a cool Oakland night, May 8, 1968, to face the Minnesota Twins.

The A's had moved from Kansas City to Oakland just that season, culminating several years of effort by Finley to get out of Kansas City. The move had changed Hunter's pitching habits. In Kansas he had been pitching in a large park where control didn't seem so important. The first night in Oakland, four home runs sailed out of the Coliseum and Hunter and the other A's pitchers immediately assumed the Coliseum would be a hitter's park. It didn't turn out that way, but it still made Hunter work more on his control, because he feared that any mistakes he made in that park would immediately be sent crashing into the seats.

That work on his control made a big difference the night of May 8. By his own later admission, Catfish threw only one bad pitch that night, a hanging curve that Harmon Killebrew took dead aim at—and missed. It was the only curve Hunter threw all night. Catcher Jim Pagliaroni stood up and started to come to the mound, but then stopped. Hunter got the message: Don't do that again. He didn't.

Hunter's perfect game was achieved with remarkable ease. There were only four hard-hit balls against him. In the fourth, Cesar Tovar lined out to rookie Joe Rudi, making his first start in left field after reporting from Vancouver of the Pacific Coast League that day.

In the fifth, Ted Uhlaender flied deep to right fielder Reggie Jackson. The next batter, Bob Allison, hit a one-hopper to third baseman Sal Bando that took a bad hop, but Bando grabbed it anyway and threw out Allison at first.

In the seventh, Rod Carew lined to Rudi. That was the only one that really scared Hunter. It scared Rudi, too. "I thought that one was over my head," said Rudi, later to become the best left fielder in the league. "I was hoping the ball wouldn't be hit to me, I was so nervous."

Hunter went to a three-ball count on Minnesota hitters three times, the worst being a 3–0 count to Tony Oliva in the second. Oliva was a dangerous hitter—he had hit over .300 in three of his first four major league seasons—but Hunter put over three straight strikes to get him out.

In retrospect, it was not at all typical of Hunter's later efforts when he became a big winner. His style now is to make the hitter hit his pitch. He is not a big strikeout pitcher because he does not like to throw all the pitches you need to get strikeouts, and his games are usually over very quickly when he is pitching well; one season, I covered successive games by Hunter that went only 1:54 and 1:56.

In contrast, in his effort against Minnesota, he struck out 11, threw 107 pitches—only 38 of them balls—and took 2:28 to finish the 4-0 game.

Both Hunter and the Minnesota starter, Dick Boswell, were helped by the unusual 6 o'clock start for the game, because the batters had trouble picking up the ball in the twilight. Thus, for the first six innings, neither team scored.

In the seventh, Rick Monday led off for the A's with a double and went to third on a wild pitch while Rudi was striking out. That brought Hunter to the plate. There was some mild joking in the press box about a pinchhitter for Catfish, but Hunter took care of everything by laying down a bunt that was so good he beat it out for a hit as Monday was scoring.

As if that weren't enough, Hunter also knocked in the last two runs in the eighth. The inning started with successive singles by Sal Bando and Ramon Webster. Sacrifice bunts by John Donaldson and Pagliaroni both failed, the runners being forced, but then Monday walked to load the bases.

Floyd Robinson came in as a pinchhitter for Rudi and went to a 2-0 count on Boswell. At that point, Minnesota manager Cal Ermer—not aware that the Twins had already lost the game—brought in Ron Perranoski from the bullpen. Oakland manager Bob Kennedy countered by sending up righthanded hitting Danny Cater against the lefthanded throwing Perranoski. Managers must have their fun.

Perranoski then completed the walk, which forced in Webster with the second run, and Hunter singled to right to score the third and fourth runs of the game. It was Hunter's third hit of the game, which is not as surprising as it sounds. He was good enough to hit .350 one year before the American League's designated hitter rule kept him in the dugout while his team was at bat.

He did his hitting this time, though, almost without benefit of batting practice. "Before the game," he said, "we were taking batting practice. Everyone was supposed to take six swings and a bunt. Well, Jim Nash was pitching and he threw ten pitches. Eight of them were balls. Heck, one of them almost hit me.

"Kennedy came around and told me to get out of the cage, because I had already been in there four minutes. He said I was fouling up the hitters. I just took my bat and when I got to the dugout, I threw it. I was mad."

He took out his anger on the Twins.

There were only 6298 fans in the park that night, but they were all aware of what was happening as the game reached its late innings.

"The ninth inning," wrote Dick Friendlich of the *San Francisco Chronicle*, "found everybody in the park, except Hunter apparently, tighter than a G-string on a violin.

"There was, as the Catfish's catcher, Jim Pagliaroni, remarked, an uneasy quiet in the A's dugout from the fifth inning on. But nobody said anything. Everybody, Hunter included, knew what was going on."

John Roseboro batted for shortstop Jack Hernandez to lead off the ninth and grounded out to Donaldson at second base. Catcher Bruce Look struck out for the third straight time, this time on a called strike, and then Rich Reese came up to swing for relief pitcher Perranoski.

Now, all the tension was focused on one batter and Reese, hitting only .154 at game time, made the most of it. Pinchhitting was Reese's speciality—he had hit .317 in pinchhitting roles the previous year—and the pressure didn't bother him. He fouled off a fastball and then took two balls inside and low that just missed the corner.

Then he fouled the next four pitches into the stands, the fans sucking in breath and then exhaling at each pitch. Next, Hunter fired a fastball just a little high and inside. Pagliaroni thought it was close enough to be called a strike and he started to the mound. Umpire Jerry Neudecker called him back; he had called the pitch ball three. It was a gutsy call by the umpire, who was rewarded only by boos from the fans.

Hunter, the weight of his great performance on his back, never hesitated. On the 3–2 count, he challenged Reese with a fastball on the inside corner and Reese swung and missed. Catfish had his perfect game and his teammates mobbed him on the mound.

"Nervous in the ninth; you'd better believe it," said Hunter after the game. He'd known full well he had a no-hitter going. "I'd been going with fastballs and sliders—I threw only three changeups and one curve all night—and just made up my mind to stick with those pitches. I felt strong all the way in this cool weather."

Hunter thought his control had been the best he'd ever had, and catcher Pagliaroni agreed. "He never lost his fastball," said

Pagliaroni, "and his slider was outstanding. But mainly his control was fantastic."

It was the second no-hitter Pagliaroni had caught—his first had been one with Bill Monbouquette for the Boston Red Sox in 1961—but he said this one was easier. "He only shook off two of my signs. I called for a couple of breaking balls and he wanted to stick with the fastball. It was his ball game and he was throwing with confidence."

All was well with the A's world after the game. Hunter sent his uniform to the Hall of Fame but kept the ball he threw for the last strike. Finley called him from his home in LaPorte, Indiana, where he had been listening to the game, and said he would give the Catfish a $5,000 bonus. Finley also gave Pagliaroni a $1,000 bonus and Hunter surprised his catcher with an engraved gold watch.

Hunter's relationship with Finley later turned sour, as often happens with Charlie O. The break came because of a $150,000 loan Finley made to Hunter in 1970 to buy a 500-acre farm near the pitcher's home in Hertford, North Carolina. Hunter told this story about the loan to Ron Bergman of the *Oakland Tribune*:

When he first lent me the money, we had a verbal agreement, never anything written down. He sent the money straight into my bank under my name. He didn't have any attachments to it.

The only agreement was that I was to pay him back at least $20,000 a year at the end of every baseball season with six per cent interest until it was paid off.

Then, after three or four months, he'd start calling me. And the days he would call me were the days I was going to pitch. He'd say, "Jim, you know you owe me $150,000, and I need the money to buy the hockey team and basketball team [the California Seals and the Memphis Tams]."

I would say, "Mr. Finley, how do you think I can make it playing ball? Let me go home in between starts and I'll make the arrangements to get the money."

Mr. Finley would say, "No, you've got to stay and pitch. You can't worry about that."

He phoned me in August and I didn't win a game in August. He never phoned me one time on a day I wasn't pitching. I think it affected me and it liked to have run my father crazy, too.

I tried to tell him that he deliberately called me on my pitching day, but he said he didn't know when I was going to pitch. But he knows more about this ballclub than anyone else, even the players.

As soon as the season was over, I went home and tried to get a loan to pay him back. I couldn't get a loan right away, so I said the hell with it and sold 400 of the 500 acres and paid him back, interest and everything. Later, he refunded the interest.

Four years later, Hunter had a contract with Finley for $100,000 which called for half of it to be paid to an insurance company. When Finley did not, Hunter brought the case to arbitration and was made a free agent, eventually signing with the New York Yankees for a multimillion dollar package which included a five-year, $150,000 a year salary, a bonus and a $1 million insurance policy on his life.

Among other things, that makes him the richest perfect game pitcher in history.

9

Some needed help

Babe Ruth started his professional career as a pitcher and he was a very good one, a fact which was obscured by his later success as a hitter. Until Whitey Ford surpassed it in the 1961 World Series, his 29²/₃ consecutive scoreless innings were a Series record. He pitched only three complete seasons, but in two of them he won more than 20 games and in the third, he won 18. He finished with a record of 94–46 and an excellent 2.28 earned run average.

His best season was 1917, when he won 10 of his first 11 and went on to post a 24–13 record. But 1917 was also the year Ruth first displayed signs of temperament, most of them aimed at the umpires. It started with the first game of the season, when the Babe pitched a 10–0 shutout for the Boston Red Sox over the New York Yankees. That winning margin would have seemed to have been enough to satisfy Ruth, but he disputed two calls by plate umpire Tom Connolly in the fourth; the first when a Yankee batter walked and the next when Connolly ruled that Ruth had hit a batter with a pitch. He also glared at the umpire when he was called out on strikes in the seventh inning.

Ruth's crankiness was probably just as much due to his off-field problems, most of which he brought on himself by his cavalier attitude toward marriage; Babe couldn't even find monogamy in the dictionary, let alone practice it.

At any rate, he became more and more ill-tempered toward umpires, so much so that he was scolded by a Boston sportswriter, Edward Martin of the *Morning Globe*. On May 25, 1917, Martin wrote: "Ruth has added something to his repertoire which he might just as well eliminate before it gets chronic. It is nagging the umpire behind the plate. Babe puts on a stubborn child sketch every time the arbiter calls one wrong. . . ."

His bad temper crested on June 23, when he was the starting pitcher against the Washington Senators in a game at Boston. The umpire behind the plate was Brick Owens, who had a temper himself.

Ruth threw only four pitches, to leadoff hitter Ray Morgan, and they were all called balls. He disagreed with each of the calls. After the third, he yelled, "Open your eyes! Open your eyes!"

"It's too early for you to kick," Owens yelled back. "Get in there and pitch!"

After Morgan had walked on the fourth pitch, Ruth ran in toward the plate screaming at Owens, who told him to get back out to the mound or he would throw Ruth out of the game. Ruth reacted by threatening to punch him in the nose and Owens stepped across the plate and waved his arm. "Get the hell out of here! You're through."

Boston catcher Chester Thomas got between pitcher and umpire, but Ruth threw a couple of punches anyway, over Thomas's shoulder. One of the pitches caught Owens on the back of the neck, and Ruth finally had to be led away from the field by a policeman.

Ruth later apologized through the newspapers and he was let off with a ten-day suspension and a $100 fine by American League President Ban Johnson. It was light punishment for what he had done, but Johnson said he felt it would be unfair to Boston to keep Ruth sidelined longer. No doubt, Ruth's punishment was also less than he deserved because one of the great games in baseball followed his expulsion, causing everybody to overlook the Ruth-Owens fracas that had preceded it.

Boston righthander Ernie Shore was rushed into the game and allowed only eight warmup pitches, as the rules then provided; in a similar situation today, a pitcher would have as many warmup pitches as he wanted.

On Shore's first pitch, Morgan broke for second in an attempt to steal, but Thomas threw him out. Shore got the next two men in the inning, Eddie Foster and Clyde Milan, then retired the Senators 1–2–3 in the next eight innings for a perfect game and a 4–0 win.

It was a remarkable effort by Shore, especially since he had been rushed into the game so quickly. He had the Senators hitting the ball on the ground all day and none of the plays made behind him were remarkable. Only six balls were hit to the outfield—two of them to left field and four to center; right fielder Harry Hooper could have stayed on the bench all day without being missed. And the game was over quickly, as games often were in those days, in 1:40.

Catcher Thomas, who got the only out that Shore didn't, was taken out early in the game and replaced by Sam Agnew. Agnew's offensive contribution was considerable—three hits and one run—but who can say whether he would have made the same kind of throw that Thomas did on Morgan's attempted steal?

The Washington starter, Yancy Wyatt (Doc) Ayers, pitched an excellent game himself for six innings, allowing only one Boston run. He weakened and gave up three more in the seventh, but Washington manager Clark Griffith left him in the game, possibly because he had no confidence in anybody else. After the great Walter Johnson, the Washington pitching wasn't much that year and Johnson was scheduled to pitch the second game of the doubleheader that day.

Griffith, in fact, seemed mesmerized by Shore's effort. Not until two were out in the ninth inning did he send up a pinch-hitter, Mike Menosky hitting for Ayers and going out to give Shore his perfect game.

There was considerable debate, at the time and later, as to whether Shore deserved credit for a perfect game. Those who argued against giving him credit said that he had only gotten 26 outs himself and that one batter had reached first, in which case it could not be a perfect game. Generally, however, Shore's game has gone into the record books as a perfect game, the third of the century to that point.

It was fitting that Shore was the one to do it after Ruth's ejection, because the two men had been linked together a great deal of the time; inevitably, Shore had been overshadowed.

Shore and Ruth pitched together in the minors at Baltimore and Shore was the better of the two. Yet, when they were sold to Boston, it was Ruth who got most of the attention in the deal. Shore moved right in as a starting pitcher, while Ruth was sent back to the minors for a brief period. Shore pitched two games in the 1915 World Series, winning one of them, before Ruth ever threw a ball in Series play. Yet Ruth always got more attention, which is the nature of things; some athletes get far more publicity than others and it is not always easy to explain why.

Shore and Ruth even roomed together, both in the minors and majors, and various stories have come out of that. One insisted that Ruth used Shore's toothbrush (or shaving brush), and Shore demanded that he be moved in with somebody else. Another was that Shore refused to room with a man who didn't flush the toilet after he used it. Yet, Shore told Robert Creamer years later, "Hell, I roomed with him in 1920 when we were both with the Yankees. I was the only one he would listen to. He was the best-hearted fellow who ever lived. He'd give you the shirt off his back."

Ruth had already eclipsed Shore as a pitcher by the time of the perfect game, but Shore seemed on his way to a reasonably long major league career. He was only 26 and he had won 18 and 15 games in his previous two seasons; though he won only 13 in 1917, it was with a 2.22 earned run average. But Shore went off to war in 1918 and he was not the same pitcher when he returned. He was 5–8 and 2–2 in two years with the Yankees, then retired to be a sheriff in North Carolina, his home state.

Shore's great effort could be looked on in another light, as a shared no-hitter, though Ruth's share of the game was entirely negative. There have been three other games in baseball history where two or more pitchers have had a share in a no-hitter.

The first was a May 26, 1956 game in Milwaukee, matching the visiting Reds against the Braves, who finished second by a game to Brooklyn that year, getting ready for their two straight pennants in 1957 and 1958. The Reds finished only one more game back of Milwaukee, in third place, and it was this game that ultimately meant the difference in their positions.

Any time these two teams met in the 1956 season, it figured to be a high-scoring game because they were both good-hitting teams playing in parks that favored the hitters.

The Braves that year were led by Hank Aaron, who hit 44 homers in the first of his eight 40-homer seasons. The Reds, though, had a more balanced attack with Ted Kluszewski (35 home runs, 102 RBIs, .302 average); Wally Post (36 homers, 83 RBIs); Gus Bell (29 homers, 84 RBIs, .292 average); Frank Robinson (38 home runs, 83 RBIs, .290 average); and Ed Bailey (28 home runs, 75 RBIs, .300 average). That was the year the Reds hit 221 home runs, which tied the major league record, since extended to 240 by the New York Yankees in 1961.

Had the Reds had any pitching that year, they would have run away with the pennant, but they did not have a 20-game winner, nor a starter with an ERA of under 3.70.

Over the course of a season, the law of averages evens things out, but in an individual game anything can happen. The Reds, a team with no outstanding pitching, got a no-hitter for 9²/₃ innings, with three different pitchers; they also lost the game 2–1 in the eleventh.

Johnny Klippstein started for the Reds and manager Birdie Tebbetts had no reason to expect great things from him; Klippstein was to be only 12–11 for the year, with a 4.09 earned run average. Nor did it seem Klippstein was going to surprise Tebbetts. He was in trouble almost all the time during the seven innings he pitched and only a great catch by Robinson saved him from a shower as early as the second inning.

In that inning, the first three Braves to face Klippstein reached base. He hit Aaron in the back and then walked Bobby Thomson and Bill Bruton, getting only one strike while throwing eight balls.

Frank Torre, getting a fastball, hit a drive to deep left center. But Robinson ran and ran and ran, and finally caught up with the ball. Aaron scored easily after the catch, because Robinson was not in a position to throw, but Klippstein then got the next two men out to end the inning.

In the seventh, the Braves threatened again in much the same manner. This time, Klippstein walked three men but, with two outs, got pinchhitter Wes Covington to go down swinging.

The Braves, though they had a run, still did not have a hit; that situation remained unchanged in the eighth inning as Cincinnati relief pitcher Hershell Freeman set them down in order. Still, it seemed the Braves might be able to win without a base hit because, in the first eight innings, Milwaukee's Ray Crone had limited the Reds to four hits and had kept them from getting beyond second base.

Then, with two outs in the ninth, the Reds tied the score. Kluszewski, trying to even it up with one swing, as he could, instead hit the ball weakly off his fists—but it dropped into short center for a single.

Post, hitless in two other official times at bat, was next up and he dribbled a 1–2 pitch down the third base line for what was first ruled a fair ball by third baseman Frank Dascoli, which would have given Post a hit. But plate umpire Frank Secory overruled Dascoli and called it a foul ball. Tebbetts protested the call, but all was forgiven moments later when Post doubled to score Jim Dyck, running for Kluszewski.

Joe Black set the Braves down 1–2–3 in the bottom of the inning and the game went into the tenth inning tied at 1–1, with the Braves still hitless. The Reds got a chance to win in the top of the inning when Roy McMillan reached first after Torre misplayed his bunt, but then Crone struck out Joe Frazier and got Rocky Bridges to ground out.

Black got the first two men to face him in the last of the tenth but then the no-hit string ended as Jack Dittmer doubled off the right field wall. Shortstop McMillan then grabbed Johnny Logan's liner to end the inning and send the game into the eleventh.

The Reds had another chance to win the game in the top of that inning as Dyck singled and Post walked. With two outs, Ray Jablonski was at bat. Though he was to tail off badly later, Jablonski was leading the Reds in RBIs at that time, but he did nothing to fatten his totals this time. He swung hard but ineffectively at a half-speed curve for the third strike and final out.

Aaron got the Braves off strongly in the bottom of the inning as he slashed a drive down the right-field line. The ball, bounding off the wall, eluded Post and Aaron went all the way to third base before the throw came in from the outfield.

Milwaukee manager Charley Grimm sent up the lefthanded swinging Chuck Tanner to hit for Thomson; Tebbetts ordered Tanner walked and Bruton, too, to set up a force play at home plate.

For a moment, it seemed Tebbetts might bring in Joe Nuxhall to pitch to Torre, but he decided to stick with Black. It was the wrong decision. On the first pitch, Torre slammed a hit into right to score Aaron with the winning run.

That game, weird as it was, was probably no stranger than another shared no-hitter, this one shared by Steve Barber and Stu Miller—and lost.

Barber had been Bo Belinsky's friend and nemesis in the minor leagues. They had both been in the Baltimore minor system, but the Orioles, looking for a solid lefthanded starter, had looked right past Belinsky because they figured Barber was the better prospect.

They were right. For a time, Barber was an excellent major league pitcher—in alternate seasons. He won 18 games his second season, 20 his fourth, 15 in his sixth. Even in his best seasons, however, he was very wild; by 1967, he was already on a downhill slide and the Orioles would trade him to the Yankees before the season was over.

Barber had won two games and lost none when he took the mound on April 30 for the first game of a doubleheader at Baltimore against Detroit. It was some game. The Tigers were so busy ducking pitches, they forgot to hit them. Barber did not give up a hit, but he walked ten batters, hit two, threw a wild pitch and even committed an error.

Detroit's Earl Wilson pitched a more routine game, allowing two hits but walking only four. He matched zeroes in the run column with Barber until the eighth inning, when he gave up three walks. Luis Aparicio then hit a sacrifice fly which gave Barber and Baltimore a 1–0 lead going into the ninth inning.

It wasn't enough. Barber, who had thrown almost enough pitches for two games, couldn't finish the inning and wound up losing the game.

Barber started the inning by doing what he had been doing for the whole game, as he walked pinchhitters Dick Tracewski and Jake Wood. That was a tipoff how tired he was because Tracewski and Wood certainly didn't scare him with their lifetime averages of .213 and .250, respectively.

Wilson was next and he moved both runners up with a sacrifice bunt. Pinchhitter Willie Horton fouled out, but Barber then wild-pitched Tracewski home with the tying run.

Baltimore manager Hank Bauer was in a quandary. He certainly didn't want to take Barber out while he was pitching a no-hitter, yet it seemed Steve might never get that last out. Bauer finally made up his mind when Mickey Stanley walked: Stu Miller was brought in.

Miller was in the next-to-last year of a 16-year major league career, but he was still effective in short stints. This seemed to be one of them as he got Don Wert to hit a ground ball behind second that Aparicio handled easily. Aparicio flipped it to rookie second baseman Mark Belanger for what should have been the third out, but Belanger dropped the ball for an error, allowing Wood to come home with the tie-breaking run. Miller then retired Al Kaline for the final out.

In the bottom of the ninth, the Orioles could do nothing against Detroit reliever Fred Gladding and the Tigers won the game 2–1. Barber took the loss philosophically. "I was so wild," he said, "I didn't deserve to win."

The game was the first in which two pitchers had been involved in a nine-inning defeat in which neither gave up a hit. Until the Barber-Miller feat, the only pitcher in modern times who had been defeated in a nine-inning no-hitter was Ken Johnson of the Houston Astros: He had lost to the Cincinnati Reds, 1–0, on April 23, 1964.

Johnson's game deserves a mention somewhere and it might as well be here, since it cannot be easily categorized. It was probably inevitable that it would be Johnson who lost this kind of game because he was always a hard-luck pitcher; moreover, he had already lost two previous 1–0 games to the Reds.

He contributed to his own downfall in this one. With one out, Pete Rose bunted toward the third-base side of the mound. Johnson picked up the ball but his throw to first baseman Pete

Runnels was wide. The ball rolled to the seats and Rose raced to second.

There was little doubt that the play was an error, especially in Johnson's mind. "When I came up throwing," he said, "I knew I had him. I just didn't get a good grip on the ball. I can truthfully say a good throw would have got him."

The next batter, Chico Ruiz, came the closest of any Cincinnati player to getting a hit as he lined a shot off Johnson's shin. But the ball caromed directly to third baseman Bob Aspromonte, who threw Ruiz out, with Rose going to third on the play.

Johnson was only one out away from sending the game into extra innings when he got Vada Pinson to hit a grounder to second baseman Nellie Fox. But the usually reliable Fox fumbled the ball and Rose raced home with the winning run.

Johnson had walked only two and struck out nine. He had a right to be bitter about the loss, but he wasn't. "I'm not happy about losing the game," he said, "but I know that if we'd won, people would have forgotten by next year that I'd pitched a no-hitter. This way, they'll talk about it for maybe the next 20 or 30 years. It's a heady feeling to know you have a niche in history."

Vida Blue wasn't looking for a niche in history when he started for the Oakland A's in the final game of the 1975 season, but that's what he got—along with pitching teammates Glenn Abbott, Paul Lindblad and Rollie Fingers.

The A's had clinched their fifth straight American League West divisional championship earlier in the week, and manager Alvin Dark just wanted Blue to stay sharp in preparation for the upcoming playoff with the Boston Red Sox, winners of the American League East. So, Dark told Blue he would pitch five innings—the minimum for a starting pitcher to get a win—as the A's closed out the season at home against the California Angels.

Blue wasn't as overpowering as he can sometimes be, striking out only two in his five innings, but he was very effective, not yielding a hit. There were only three California baserunners off Blue. With one out in the first, Dave Chalk walked but was erased on a double play. Lee Stanton was safe in the fourth when shortstop Campy Campaneris bobbled his two-out grounder and Bob Allietta walked with two outs in the fifth.

Blue left with no complaints after the fifth. He had already pitched a no-hitter earlier in his career. His twenty-second victory seemed safe, because the A's had a 3–0 lead over the punchless Angels.

An apprehensive Abbott followed in the sixth. Some of the Oakland fans booed, thinking that Dark should have left Blue in. "I hated coming in in that situation," said Abbott, "because I thought they might leave Vida in. I was conscious of what was going on. I was glad they didn't get a hit off me. I could have really been the goat."

Third baseman Sal Bando cut in front of Campaneris to throw out Jerry Remy for the second out of the sixth in the toughest fielding play of the day, and Abbott got the Angels out 1–2–3 in the sixth. Lindblad followed in the seventh and did the same. There was no pressure for Lindblad. He hadn't been paying much attention to the game while he was warming up and didn't realize there was a no-hitter in progress. "I didn't know there hadn't been a hit until I got into the clubhouse," said Lindblad.

Fingers followed, because Dark wanted him to pitch the 1^2/$_3$ innings of scoreless ball that Rollie needed to bring his ERA below 3.00. "The way Rollie was pitching, he must have thought it was the World Series," said plate umpire Bill Kunkel. "He was throwing sliders that broke three feet in front of the plate and then just exploded for strikes."

Fingers retired six straight men, though California manager Dick Williams sent up four left-handed pinchhitters against him. Mickey Rivers grounded out to shortstop to end the game, and the A's were in the record book with the first no-hitter shared by four pitchers. Quite likely, it will be the last.

10

Bob Feller . . . fast

Baseball is a great game for trivia questions and one of the favorites is this: Which team played a game in which every player ended the game with the same batting average with which he started it?

The answer is the Chicago White Sox, on April 16, 1940. The White Sox players all started the game batting .000, because it was Opening Day; they all ended the game batting .000, because Cleveland's Bob Feller threw a no-hitter, the first on Opening Day in baseball history.

It was the kind of raw, gusty day that Chicago often gets in the early spring when Feller took the mound. He did not have what he regarded as his best stuff, but even when he wasn't in top form, Feller was overpowering in those days. He had just turned 21 a month after the end of the 1939 season, but he had won 24 games that year, with 246 strikeouts; he was to go on to win 27 in 1940, with 261 strikeouts.

Feller, often bothered by wildness in his early days, had trouble getting loose in the early innings. He walked four men in the first two innings, but he did not allow a hit and the White Sox could not get a run.

In the top of the third, the Indians bunched two of the only six hits they got off Chicago starter Edgar Smith for their only run, with Jeff Heath singling and catcher Rollie Hemsley doubling.

That seemed to inspire Feller: He got tougher and tougher from that point, retiring 20 White Sox batters in a row from the third inning into the ninth. He had excellent support behind him, as he pointed out after the game, with right fielder Ben

Champman making a couple of nice catches on long fly balls, and third baseman Ken Keltner and second baseman Ray Mack making good plays on ground balls.

Mack made a tough play in the eighth on pinchhitter Larry Rosenthal, batting for Smith. Mack had to come in quickly for Rosenthal's slow roller and throw off balance, but his throw just nipped Rosenthal at first.

In the Cleveland dugout, Feller's teammates were feeling the pressure more than he was. By the seventh inning, the dugout was quiet as a tomb. Feller mopped his sweating face with a towel, looked straight ahead and said nothing. The other members of the team fidgeted uneasily and said nothing.

Finally, Heath could stand it no longer. He cleared his throat and began to speak. "Well, Robert," he started. He got no further.

"Another word," said Harry Eisenstat, "and I'll stick my hand down your throat to the elbow." Heath subsided, realizing what Eisenstat meant: He shouldn't jinx the no-hitter.

Shortly after that, a newspaper photographer came up to the dugout steps and started to take a picture of Feller. Before he could, Lefty Weisman leaped to his feet and stood between them. "Amscray," he told the startled photographer, who then did as he had been told.

Feller went out for the ninth inning with only that 1–0 lead, fully aware of what he was doing. "I knew I had a chance for a no-hitter," he said after the game, "but I tried to put the thought out of my mind by reminding myself you never have a no-hitter until the last man is out. I got to thinking I'd just pitch my own ball game. A pitcher can't be any better than he is."

Feller got the first two batters, then Luke Appling came to the plate. Appling was probably the last hitter Feller would have chosen to face in that situation. The White Sox shortstop was an excellent hitter who had hit over .300 for six straight seasons, including a .388 season in 1936, and who seldom struck out; in a 20-year career, Appling struck out only 528 times.

Working as carefully as he could, Feller went to a 3–2 count on Appling, then Luke fouled four straight pitches down the right field line. In the dugout, Cleveland manager Oscar Vitt and coach Luke Sewell sat side by side. Vitt said to Sewell, "Oh, God, just let him get by Appling."

He couldn't get Appling, walking him on the tenth pitch. Feller then faced the lefthanded hitting Taft Wright, who lashed a hard grounder that looked for a moment as if it would get through to right field. Instead, Mack knocked it down, retrieved it and then threw out Wright. Feller had his no-hitter.

Neither Feller nor his catcher, Hemsley, thought the game

was Feller's best. Feller had already thrown three one-hit games, two of them in 1939, and Hemsley thought all three of those had been better games. But they didn't look as good in the box score.

Fewer than 15,000 people had come out on the chilly day, but three of them were very important to Feller—his parents, Mr. and Mrs. William Feller, and his sister, Marguerite. None of them said anything about the no-hitter, but they were all aware of it. "It would be an understatement to say we were holding our breath in that ninth inning," said William Feller.

It was altogether fitting that Feller's father was there to see him pitch his first no-hitter, because it was the senior Feller who had gotten Bob off to his start in baseball.

William Feller had been a semipro baseball player in his youth and he dreamed of having a son who would do better than he had. As soon as Bob was old enough, he and his father were playing catch behind the barn on the family farm at Van Meter, Iowa.

The famed Feller fastball showed up early—there is an apocryphal story that he broke three of his father's ribs with a pitch when he was only 11—and he became the star pitcher of every team he played for on the steps of the baseball ladder. As a sophomore on the high school team, he pitched five no-hitters.

Eventually, when Feller was still only 16, he got into a semipro league in Des Moines, where he was competing against adults, and caught the eye of Cleveland executive Cy Slapnicka, who signed him to a Cleveland contract, though his high school class had not yet graduated. The signing was contrary to baseball law of the time; though it was a common practice, major-league teams were not supposed to deal directly with semipro players.

The original plan had been to send Feller to the Indians' farm team of Fargo-Moorehead, North Dakota, in the Northern League, but Feller developed a sore arm, so Slapnicka had him report directly to Cleveland. With rest and treatment, Feller's arm returned to normal and Slapnicka had him pitching for the Cleveland Rosenblooms, a semipro team. Then, in July of 1936, the Indians had an exhibition game scheduled with the St. Louis Cardinals: Slapnicka decided to give Feller his chance against major league opposition.

Few pitchers have broken in as spectacularly as Feller did that day. Even on the sidelines, warming up, he was impressive. St. Louis manager and second baseman Frank Frisch was talking to Harry Grayson, then the sports editor of Newspaper Enterprise Association. Frisch said, "Who in the hell is that fireballer?" Grayson told him Feller was a kid Slapnicka had just signed. "That kid's the fastest pitcher I ever saw," said Frisch. He turned to reserve infielder Stu Martin and said, "Stu, how'd you like to play second base tonight?" and then he turned back to Grayson and winked. "They're not gonna get the old Flash out there against that kid," he said.

Frisch may have been the first of the Cardinals to recognize Feller's speed, but he certainly wasn't the last. The first hitter to face Feller, Bruce Ogrodowski was out trying to bunt his way on, then Feller got the next eight outs of his three-inning stint by strikeout, getting Pepper Martin, Charley Gelbert, Rip Collins and Art Garibaldi once each, and Leo Durocher and pitcher Les Munns twice each.

Feller went on from that exhibition game to strike out 15 men in a regular season game against the St. Louis Browns in August, then topped that with a 17-strikeout game against the Philadelphia Athletics just three weeks later. He was not yet 18 and he had tied the major league strikeout record set by Dizzy Dean of the Cardinals only three years earlier.

He was hardly a polished pitcher. All he really had was a fastball. His curve wasn't much and he tipped it off when he was going to throw it. He had no idea what a change of pace was and he knew nothing about holding runners on base; players stole bases while he was holding the ball on the mound.

And his control was very shaky, though there is a question whether this hurt or helped him. Certainly, batters didn't dare take much of a foothold at the plate when his fastball was zipping in and around them, because nobody—even Feller—really knew where the pitch would go. The first time the Boston Red Sox faced Feller, Billy Werber led off and the first pitch went behind Werber!

"When this ball whizzed behind him," recalled Al Schacht, a Boston coach at the time, "Werber went sprawling across the plate. He was white and shaken when he got to his feet. He knew this was just wildness, no deliberate attempt to dust him off. I looked in at our bench and saw the players look from one to another in silent amazement. I said to myself, 'No wonder this kid gets so many strikeouts. I wouldn't be surprised if he got all 27 of us today!' As a matter of fact, he did wind up with 16."

Feller won five and lost three for the Indians in his first season, striking out 76 in 62 innings; it was obvious that despite his lack of polish he was going to be a great pitcher. But perhaps not for the Indians, because Lee Keyser, who owned the Des Moines franchise in the Western League, had filed a complaint with commissioner Kenesaw Mountain Landis that the Indians had illegally signed Feller.

The facts of the case were unarguable, but Landis realized

two things: 1) the Indians were not the only club to break that rule; and 2) after Feller's sensational debut, if he were made a free agent, there would be furious bidding for him. The commissioner ruled that Feller would remain Cleveland property, ordered Cleveland to pay Des Moines $7500 as damages and rescinded the oft-broken rule against major league clubs dealing for sandlot players.

Feller went on to win 9 games his second season, 17 his third and then had seasons with 24, 27 and 25 wins, striking out 1007 batters in seasons three through six. Then, World War II became a reality for the United States and Feller went off to war. He lost three full seasons and most of a fourth in his pitching prime: That cost him a chance to get into the all-time top ten, and possibly top five, in career wins. He finished his career with 266 wins. Considering that he won 102 games in the three seasons preceding military service and the one full season after it, his service time may have cost him as many as 100 wins. Another 100 wins would have put him in fifth place in the all-time standings, just ahead of Warren Spahn's 363.

The war also cost Feller a chance to become the all-time career strikeout leader. He finished in sixth place with 2581, far behind Walter Johnson's leading total of 3508, but in the previously mentioned four seasons which surrounded his military service, he struck out 1115. Assuming good health, he would obviously have had around 1000 strikeouts in the nearly four seasons he lost, which would have been enough to vault him past Johnson.

Feller returned late in the 1945 season, just long enough to win five games and lose three, after serving 44 months in the Navy and earning eight battle stars. After the season, he went on a barnstorming tour to get himself back into pitching shape for 1946, when all the players would be back from the war.

He started the '46 season with an Opening Day 1–0 win against the same Chicago team which he had no-hit in 1940, but then he lost his next two decisions. Reports started that Feller had left his fearsome fastball in the service, though—halfway between the ages of 27 and 28—he should be in his prime.

It was with this in mind that he went out to face the New York Yankees on April 30 at Yankee Stadium. A weekday crowd of 37,144 had come to the Stadium that day, mindful of the stories that the Feller fastball was gone and anticipating that the Yankees would win the game.

The Yankees had been a hard team for Feller to beat, as they had been for every pitcher; in his first six seasons in the league, they had won five pennants. In his first start in New York, in 1936, he had given up five runs in just one inning. The next year, coming back after a sore arm, he had battled to a 1–1 tie until Joe DiMaggio had hit a grand slam homer.

DiMaggio, in fact, was Feller's particular nemesis; Joe had knocked in seven runs against Feller in one game in 1938. And DiMaggio was hitting cleanup in 1946 in a lineup which also included Tommy Henrich, Joe Gordon, Charlie Keller, Bill Dickey and Phil Rizzuto.

As it had in the Opening Day no-hitter, Feller's wildness got him into minor trouble early. He walked Henrich with two outs in the first, but then got DiMaggio to ground into a force out. Keller led off the second with a walk, but then was thrown out trying to steal as Nick Etten and Gordon struck out.

Dickey walked to open the third, but Feller then struck out the side, pitcher Bill Bevens, Rizzuto and George Stirnweiss. Again in the fourth, he walked the first man, Henrich, but got DiMaggio to pop out and struck out Keller and Etten.

With two outs in the eighth, Rizzuto popped a foul to third baseman Keltner but Keltner, feeling the pressure of the situation, dropped the ball. No-hitters are often lost on just such plays, and Rizzuto then slammed a shot deep to short. But Lou Boudreau, the master of position, was there to grab it and make the long throw to beat Rizzuto by a step.

Bevens, meanwhile, was pitching an excellent game himself, yielding only six hits through the first eight innings. Then, in the top of the ninth, Cleveland catcher Frankie Hayes hit a home run for the first score of the ball game.

Feller had known for some time that he was pitching a no-hitter and said later he had tried harder from the sixth inning on. As he went out for the ninth inning, he knew it wouldn't be easy because the heart of the Yankee batting order was up that inning.

Stirnweiss, leading off, hit a ground ball to first baseman Les Fleming who had plenty of time to make the play but bobbled the ball, giving Stirnweiss—and the Yankees—life. Henrich was next and the Yankees' "Old Reliable" was a tough out. He often boasted that he never had trouble hitting Feller and he had walked twice in this game. But manager Joe McCarthy was playing the percentages—play for the tie at home, for the win on the road—and he ordered Henrich to sacrifice Stirnweiss to second, which Tommy did.

The next hitter was DiMaggio and he hit a hard grounder to Boudreau, who threw him out at first as Stirnweiss raced to third. Then, Keller hit a ground ball to Mack at second base, an easy chance. Mack stumbled fielding the ball, but he recovered in time to throw out Keller: Feller had his no-hitter, his second and the first against the Yankees since September 10, 1919. It was, of course, the first ever against them in Yankee Stadium, which had opened in 1923.

Feller had answered his critics; he had used his fastball most of the time and had struck out 11 Yankees. He got every Yankee but Henrich and DiMaggio at least once, and he struck out Etten three times.

Feller always considered this no-hitter his masterpiece, with good reason. The only really tough play behind him had been made on the second Yankee hitter of the game, Stirnweiss, who had hit a chopper behind the mound. Boudreau had raced in from shortstop and just got Stirnweiss at first; a picture showed Stirnweiss's foot just about to come down on the base as Fleming grabbed the throw.

And yet, his third no-hitter, on July 1, 1951, was in one way his most remarkable, because his days as an overpowering pitcher were behind him by then. The fastball that had frightened Frank Frisch out of the lineup 15 years earlier was no longer his out pitch. The statistics tell the story. In 1946, Feller set what was then an American League strikeout record of 348. In the years 1949–51 combined, he struck out only 338 batters.

But Feller was more than a man with a live fastball. Early in his career, he had taught himself to throw a curve, which came in nearly as rapidly as his fastball and broke sharply; that curve was responsible for many of his strikeouts. And when his fastball receded, he taught himself to throw a slider with excellent results.

With the slider his big pitch, Feller came back in 1951, after three straight years with less than 20 wins, to win 22 games—and pitch a no-hitter, making him the first pitcher to get three no-hitters since the lively ball had come into use.

His third no-hitter, thrown against the Detroit Tigers, was the only one he pitched at home in Cleveland's Municipal Stadium. It was also the only one of the three in which he yielded a run.

Feller lost his shutout in the fourth inning. Leadoff batter Johnny Lipon was safe at first when shortstop Ray Boone threw wildly after fielding Lipon's grounder. Lipon then stole second, went to third when Feller's attempted pickoff throw sailed into center field, then scored on George Kell's outfield fly.

The Indians had scored one run in the bottom of the first and they finally got another in the bottom of the ninth to win the game 2–1. Feller faced 31 Detroit batters, Lipon getting on through Boone's error and three Tigers walking.

Despite Feller's 266 career wins, his league strikeout record and his selection to the Hall of Fame in 1962, his career was a series of what-might-have-beens. I have already mentioned how many wins and strikeouts he lost because of the war.

Although Cleveland appeared in two World Series, Feller never got a Series win. In 1948, their first Series appearance since he had been with them, he pitched the opening game and gave up only two hits, yet lost to Johnny Sain, 1–0.

A controversial umpire's decision cost Feller the game. In the eighth, Bill Salkeld opened the inning by walking. Phil Masi went in to run for Salkeld and was sacrificed to second by Mike McCormick. Playing manager Lou Boudreau ordered an intentional pass for Eddie Stanky, to set up the double play.

With Sain at bat, Boudreau called for the pickoff play which had worked so effectively for Cleveland that year. Feller whirled and threw to Boudreau covering second, and Boudreau tagged Masi diving back to the bag. From the stands it seemed that Masi was out and later pictures seemed to verify that, but umpire Bill Stewart called him safe. The Indians protested, with the usual results.

Feller then got Sain to fly out, but Tommy Holmes followed with the Braves' second hit to knock in Masi with the game's only run.

Cleveland won the next three games and Feller was given a chance to win the Series with a second start before the largest Series crowd to that time: 86,288 in cavernous Municipal Stadium. Feller didn't have much that day, but neither did Boston pitcher Nelson Potter, so Boudreau stayed with him longer than he would have another pitcher, in the hope that Feller would be able to get his first World Series win.

Bob Elliott hit a three-run homer off Feller in the first inning and a solo homer in the third, but Jim Hegan hit a three-run homer for Cleveland in the fifth to give Feller a 5–4 lead. He couldn't hold it and he was finally taken out in the seventh as the Braves went on to an 11–5 win which sent the Series into the sixth game.

As the writers boarded the train for Boston for the sixth game, Francis Stann of the Washington Star remarked, "This trip well might be entitled 'A Sentimental Journey.'" Like the other writers, Stann felt the Indians would have won if Boudreau had not stuck so long with Feller.

The second time the Indians got into the Series during Feller's career was 1954. By this time, he was nearing the end of the line, but he had managed to win 13 and lose only 3 as the Indians had won a league record 111 games in the 154-game season.

The World Series, though, was a different story, as the New

York Giants swept the Indians in four games. Feller never pitched, even in relief. When the Giants took a 3–0 lead in games and it was obvious they would win the Series, some thought Cleveland manager Al Lopez might give Feller a shot at a win, but Lopez stuck resolutely with the pitching rotation that had been so successful in the regular season and started Bob Lemon, who was knocked out in the fifth inning.

Feller might have gotten a chance at a World Series win eight years earlier, when he was in his prime, but for a most unexpected turn of events. In 1940, the year he set a personal record with 27 wins, Cleveland and Detroit were tied on the last day of the season. Detroit had only Floyd Giebell, who had won just one game that season, available; Cleveland had Feller, which made the Indians overwhelming favorites. But Giebell and Detroit won the game 2–0 and went into the World Series.

Even in the category of no-hitters, where Feller stood alone among pitchers in the lively ball era until Sandy Koufax, and then Jim Maloney, arrived, Feller's career was a case of what might have been.

With just a normal amount of luck, Feller could have had even more no-hitters because he pitched a record 11 one-hitters. That means that 14 times he had a reasonable chance at a no-hitter but he only got one three times.

He stands alone in that department. Koufax, for instance, had four no-hitters and only two one-hitters. In modern times, the closest to Feller in one-hitters are Mordecai Brown, Grover Cleveland Alexander and Maloney, all with five.

Feller even pitched a game one time where both he and the opposing pitcher, Bob Cain of St. Louis, had one-hitters. Feller lost the game 1–0, which was indicative of the kind of luck he had.

When baseball people talk of fastball pitchers over the years, there are always a few names which come immediately to mind and Feller is one of them. In his day, the constant argument raged over whether he was faster than Johnson, the all-time strikeout leader.

Feller, though, was the first pitcher whose fastball was timed electronically. A machine was devised to test his fastball and it registered at 98.6 miles per hour, which will give you an idea why batters stayed loose when Feller was pitching.

From time to time, other pitchers were timed, but nobody exceeded Feller's mark until 1973. Read on.

11

Nolan Ryan . . . faster

Everybody has his own favorite as the fastest pitcher of all time, but only one pitcher has been officially tested as faster than Bob Feller. In 1974, Nolan Ryan of the California Angels was tested twice: Each time his fastball was timed at faster than 100 miles an hour.

The first time Ryan was tested came on August 20, before and during a game with the Detroit Tigers. Ryan was first tested during five warmup pitches before the game and his fastest was "only" 88.5 mph. The scientists continued testing his pitches during the game; Dick Brandewie of Rockwell International later announced that Ryan had thrown two pitches that were clocked at an astounding 100.9 mph. The Tigers could believe that; Ryan struck out 19 of them in 11 innings that night.

The results of that test were not announced immediately—the scientists said they were only testing their equipment, rather than Ryan's speed—and on September 8, the Angels conducted an official testing during a game against the Chicago White Sox. Ryan virtually matched his previous performance, with a fastball timed at 100.8 mph during a 3–1 win over the White Sox.

Lee Richard was at bat for the White Sox when Ryan threw his fastest pitch. "I've watched Ryan and I knew he was the fastest I had ever seen," said Richard. "The one tonight that was really fast came with the count 3-and-1, I thought. It was a zinger."

The news that Ryan was officially the fastest ever was hardly a surprise to any of the American League batters who had been forced to hit against him. By the time of the tests, he had already thrown two no-hitters; his third and fourth came later. Hitters were thinking less of getting a hit than of preserving their lives. "He's baseball's exorcist," said Detroit's Dick Sharon. "He scares the devil out of me!"

Sandy Koufax, to whom Ryan is often compared in terms of speed, said, "Pitching is the art of instilling fear, making a man flinch by making him look for the wrong pitch. You're trying to control his instincts. But if your control is suspect, like Ryan's is, and the thought of being hit is in the batter's mind, you'll go a long way."

Ryan hit Boston's Doug Griffin in the head early in the 1974 season and the Red Sox have been exceptionally wary of him since. "The intimidation factor works on your psyche," said Boston catcher Carlton Fisk.

"Ryan is the only guy who puts fear in me," said Oakland slugger Reggie Jackson. "Not because he can get you out, but because he can kill you. There are just no words to describe what it is like standing up there and seeing that ball come at you. I simply couldn't do him justice. It's like trying to drink coffee with a fork."

Ryan had overwhelming speed from the start, but he also had the curse of all extremely fast pitchers—wildness. The Mets had him for four seasons, during which he struck out 493 batters in 510 innings, but they gave up on him because it seemed he would never control his wildness enough to be a consistent pitcher; he also walked 369 batters during that stretch. He was only 29–38 during his four years with the Mets. In his last year, he was 10–14 with a 3.97 earned run average. Knowing his potential, the Mets still traded him to California, along with three other players, for Jim Fregosi.

California manager Del Rice wasn't so sure he liked what he saw of Ryan in spring training. "He was very wild and inconsistent," said Rice. "I was pessimistic about the trade. But this was the type of fellow you have to stick with because of his great potential."

The Angels worked with him and Ryan got more confidence in what he was doing. He was maturing as a man as well as a pitcher and the comparisons to Koufax no longer bothered him.

"That put added pressure on me when I was younger," he said, "because I felt I had to live up to it. But I don't pay any attention to those things any more. I realize I have to pitch my type of game and throw as I'm capable of throwing. You can't try to throw like somebody else."

After an initial disappointment at being traded, Ryan found he liked the idea. "I felt like it was a new start for me. I came to the club with the attitude that I was going to be a starting pitcher and I was just going to do my best."

His best was very good. In his first year with the Angels, he won 19 and lost 16 and struck out 329 batters. His next year, he won 21 and struck out a major-league record 383 batters—and he also pitched two no-hitters. That surprised nobody, except perhaps himself.

"I never honestly felt I was the type of pitcher to pitch a no-hitter," Ryan said after his first one. "My curveball isn't overpowering and, after you've gone through the lineup once or twice, the hitters can get on the fastball better. A lot of that is timing. I don't have the type of fastball that really moves. A lot of guys have that explosive type of fastball that really moves. Also, I jam the hitters a lot, so the really strong guys can just bloop the ball over the infield for singles."

When Ryan was scheduled to pitch against the Kansas City Royals in Kansas City on May 15, 1973, neither he nor anybody else was looking for a no-hitter. For one thing, Kansas City was a good team, destined to finish second in its division that year, and a good—though not spectacular—hitting team. For another, the Royals have an artificial turf field which presents yet another hazard to a potential no-hit pitcher, because ground balls skip very quickly through the infield.

Ryan was hardly at his most effective, either. In his last start before the no-hitter, Ryan lasted one out and 17 pitches against the White Sox. In the game before that, he walked seven Orioles in a 5–0 loss.

Ryan and California shortstop Bobby Valentine walked down the visitors' tunnel to the field that night, neither of them saying a word. Valentine had not gotten a hit in his last 26 at-bats. Finally, Ryan said, "Why don't we break out of our slumps tonight?"

Valentine broke his slump with an infield single, but Ryan wasn't so confident he would. When he was warming up, he didn't feel he had particularly good stuff, so he thought he would have to keep the ball down on the hitters.

Then, Kansas City manager Jack McKeon protested the game early because he claimed Ryan was taking his foot off the pitching rubber early in his motion. McKeon claimed first base umpire John Rice had said Ryan was lifting his foot off the rubber. Rice remembered it differently. "I said he was lifting his foot up in the act of his pivot and that's legal," he said. "Every pitcher in baseball does it."

"His foot pivoted," agreed Evans, "but he didn't take it off the rubber. What he was doing was legal. I went out and warned him not to exaggerate."

The warning helped Ryan. "When I bring my foot off the rubber," he said, "it usually means that I'm rocking back too far and I get wild, high. McKeon didn't shake me up, he settled me down. I cut my back stride and everything turned out just fine."

Despite Ryan's worries about not having his best stuff, it was obvious early that he had brought his fastball with him. He struck out the side in the first inning and had six in the first three innings, en route to a 12-strikeout performance. "He was throwing the ball harder than any man I ever saw in my life," said Kansas City first baseman John Mayberry, the American League's RBI leader at the time. "If they had a higher league," said outfielder Hal McRae, "he could be in it. As a matter of fact, he could be it."

The left side of the California defense could almost have taken the game off. Third baseman Alan Gallagher and left fielder Vada Pinson didn't handle a chance all night. Shortstop Rudy Meoli had only two chances, one a routine grounder.

Meoli's second chance, in the eighth inning, came on the closest thing the Royals had to a hit all night. Pinchhitter Gail Hopkins, who had broken up a no-hitter with an eighth inning single against Ryan in a game the year before, hit the kind of off-the-fist bloop fly that Ryan had feared, but Meoli raced back and made an over-the-shoulder catch to prevent a base hit.

Amos Otis scared Ryan a bit when, with two outs in the ninth, he laced a drive that sent California right fielder Ken Berry back to the wall to catch it for the final out. Otherwise, there were no tough chances in the 3–0 California win.

"Nolan really had great stuff," said catcher Jeff Torborg. "He has thrown this hard before, but you get to the point where it's humanly impossible to throw any harder. He was very fast, really great, and his curve was excellent, too."

Ryan's no-hitter was the first by a righthanded pitcher in the Angels' brief history. Lefthanders Bo Belinsky and Clyde Wright had earlier thrown no-hitters.

McKeon's protest early in the game about Ryan's illegal delivery seemed to be supported by filmed replays by Los Angeles station KTLA—a station which was owned by Gene Autry, chairman of the board of the Angels. But McKeon withdrew his protest. He knew he had no chance of having a no-hit game thrown out because of a protest.

Only three times before in baseball history had a pitcher

thrown two no-hitters in the same season; when Ryan did it exactly two months later, he almost set a strikeout record as well.

The Angels had lost four straight and five of their last six going into the game, and Ryan was below .500, at 10–11. Ryan knew he would have to do something special for this game, against the Detroit Tigers in venerable Tiger Stadium. "When I woke up in the morning, I was 'up' for the game," he said later. "I decided to shut them out. I needed it, and the team needed it, the way we were going."

Ryan was at his overpowering best in this game. Twelve of his first fourteen outs came on strikeouts and he wound up with seventeen for the game. "It wasn't fabulous, it was fantastic," said Detroit catcher Duke Sims, who struck out three times. "I've had no-hitters thrown against me before but never as overpowering as this one."

Veteran Frank Robinson agreed. "I've never seen anyone throw harder," said Robinson, "and that includes Sandy Koufax. I've seen six no-hitters and that one was the best. He was in complete command, just overpowering."

Ryan was throwing so hard that catcher Art Kusnyer got a bone bruise on the first finger of his left hand. "I've never had anything like it before," said Kusnyer, "but Nollie was throwing so hard . . ."

The Tigers were so overmatched that Norm Cash even carried a paddle to the plate in the fifth inning, as a gag. Plate umpire Ron Luciano, though probably sympathizing with Cash's plight, threw the paddle out of the game.

As in his first no-hitter, Ryan didn't require any extraordinary help from his defense. Ken Berry went deep into left center to catch a line drive by Jim Northrup in the eighth inning, but he had a line on it all the way. Shortstop Meoli again made a key play, this time by stabbing a Gates Brown line drive, about a foot over his head, in the ninth inning.

The Angels got one run in the third inning and that was obviously going to be enough as Ryan moved easily through the Detroit lineup. By the end of seven innings, he had 16 strikeouts, two short of Feller's American League record and three short of the major league record shared by Tom Seaver and Steve Carlton. He seemed on his away to 20 strikeouts, as well as a no-hitter.

In the top of the eighth, the Angels got five runs, with the key hits being two-run singles by Gallagher and pinchhitter Winston Llenas. That was a mixed blessing. It took the pressure off Ryan as far as winning the game, but it also gave his arm a chance to cool off. He got only one strikeout the last two innings.

"I could feel the difference," he said. "I know I didn't have as good stuff, because of the wait. That was my concern at the time. I really wanted the strikeout record. I honestly believe it will be easier for me to strike out 20 than pitch another no-hitter."

Ryan is a better pitcher than prophet. He got his third no-hitter, without getting a game strikeout record before. In fact, he almost got his third no-hitter in his next start. Going for a second straight no-hitter, which would have tied him with Johnny Vander Meer, Ryan held the Baltimore Orioles hitless for the first seven innings. Then Baltimore shortstop Mark Belanger lined a clean single to left to lead off the eighth and end Ryan's consecutive hitless streak at 16 innings.

Ryan had yielded a run in the first inning of that game when he walked Rich Coggins, who then stole second; Ryan wild-pitched Coggins to third and then gave up a groundout to Tommy Davis that scored Coggins. The Angels could score only one run themselves in the regulation nine innings and Ryan eventually lost the game in the eleventh, 3–1.

Ryan had nearly become the first man in history to pitch three no-hitters in a single season, but he failed to overwhelm his mother. "I think it's wonderful what he's done," she said, "but I have six children and I've lived through so many things with these kids, I don't get too excited about the things they do any more. What I'm waiting for Nolan to do is pitch a perfect game."

That may come, too.

Ryan got his third no-hitter at the end of the 1974 season, September 28 against Minnesota at Anaheim.

Again, he had his fastball working as he got 15 strikeouts, but unlike his earlier efforts, he had to labor because of control problems, which caused him to walk eight batters in the 4–0 California win.

"I think I was throwing as hard right from the start as I have in any game this year," said Ryan, "but it was a struggle. When you throw as many pitches as I did, you have to be lucky. The only time I had a little lag was in the seventh inning, when I made a mistake against Glenn Borgmann."

Ryan tried to get a breaking pitch past Borgmann, who slammed it to deep left. Rookie John Balaz made an excellent running catch to preserve the no-hitter.

Harmon Killebrew came up as a pinchhitter with one out in the ninth and walked. "I wasn't working around Killebrew," said Ryan, "but I knew he was looking for something to pull and I had to keep the ball away from him."

Ryan finished the game with a flourish, striking out Eric Soderholm for the final out.

Then, on the first day of June, 1975, Ryan tied Koufax's record by pitching his fourth no-hitter, a 1–0 win over the Baltimore Orioles at Anaheim. He struck out nine and walked four in winning his 100th major league game.

Ryan was at his overpowering best, and the Orioles seldom hit a ball solidly. The best effort by a Baltimore batter was Lee May's drive in the fifth which went right to Angel left fielder Winston Llenas.

A fine defensive play by second baseman Jerry Remy saved Ryan in the seventh. Pinch-hitter Tommy Davis led off with a high bouncer over the mound. Remy raced to his right to grab the ball and throw out the slow Davis.

The seventh inning was Ryan's most difficult. After Remy's fine play, Nolan walked Bobby Grich and May was safe on an error. Both runners advanced on Brooks Robinson's infield out, and a hit at that point would not only have broken up the no-hitter but would probably have won the game. The Orioles couldn't get it. Ryan induced Ellie Hendricks to pop out to Dave Chalk behind third base to end the inning.

The crowd of 18,492 gave Ryan a standing ovation at the end of the eighth inning and again at the start of the ninth. After his trouble in the seventh, Ryan got the Orioles 1–2–3 in each of the last two innings.

Fittingly, Ryan struck out Grich on a called third strike for the final out. Chalk rushed to the mound from his spot at third base and shook Ryan's hand, almost casually, and Ryan hugged his catcher, Ellie Rodriguez. He then strolled to the dugout. No-hitters were becoming commonplace.

Koufax, at his home in Paso Robles, California, commented somewhat wistfully that, "He may pitch ten no-hitters before he's through."

Indeed he may. He almost pitched another one his next time out, against Milwaukee. Hank Aaron broke that one up with a sixth-inning single, and Ryan eventually settled for a two-hit win.

Despite Ryan's early disclaimers about never expecting to pitch a no-hitter, his no-hit efforts are no flukes. Like Koufax, Maloney and Feller before him, he has such overpowering speed that he has a chance to pitch a no-hitter any time he works. That's what it's like when you're officially the fastest pitcher of all time.

12

Back-to-back

Baseball officials like to maintain that the baseball used in major league games remains the same year after year. The winding is supposedly no tighter or looser one year than the next, and that talk of injections of rabbit is just so much idle chatter. It is thus incumbent upon you, should you happen to find yourself talking to one of these men at a party, not to mention the years 1930 and 1968, unless you like to see grown men cry.

For the hitter, 1930 was Christmas come early. It was an incredible year and nowhere more so than in the city of Philadelphia, where the Phillies averaged .315 as a team. Five starters averaged over .300; Lefty O'Doul hit .383; and Chuck Klein hit .386 with 40 home runs and 170 RBIs. That offensive display earned the Phillies last place, because their pitchers were surrendering runs faster than the Phillies could score them; the Philadelphia staff had an astounding 6.76 earned run average that year.

In the years since 1930, it has been a rarity when a team finishes with a .300 batting average, but 9 of only 16 clubs did it that year. The batting average of the entire National League was .303! The New York Giants averaged .319 and Bill Terry hit .401.

Other clubs did almost as well as the Giants in the hitting department. The St. Louis Cardinals had all eight starters, excluding the pitcher, above .300.

Individually, Hack Wilson of the Cubs set a National League record with 56 home runs and a major league record with 190 RBIs.

It was a year of torment for pitchers. Only one staff in the majors, Washington, had an earned run average of under four runs a game. The great Lefty Grove won 28 games and had an ERA of 2.54 for the Philadelphia A's, who went on to win the World Series in six games. But even with Grove, the A's staff had a 4.28 ERA; George Earnshaw won 22 games with an ERA of 4.44!

It took 38 years, but the pitchers finally got their revenge in 1968, undeniably the Year of the Pitcher, just as 1930 had been the Year of the Hitter. In 1968, the ball was either given the consistency of a canteloupe (hitters' version) or all the hitters in both leagues went into a massive, simultaneous slump (official baseball version).

On any level, hitters suffered in 1968. The four greatest hitters of the time—Hank Aaron (.287), Willie Mays (.289), Frank Robinson (.268) and Roberto Clemente (.291) all hit below .300. Clemente's average, it should be noted, was sandwiched between years in which he hit .357 and .345. Almost from the time they started playing, it was obvious that Aaron, Mays, Robinson and Clemente would eventually make the Hall of Fame, but they couldn't help their causes that year.

Only a fast finish enabled Carl Yastrzemski of the Boston Red Sox to hit .301 and save the American League the embarrassment of not having a .300 hitter. The National League hitters fared better, but not much; only five exceeded .300 for the year.

The pitchers were having a great time. Nearly a fifth of the games ended in shutouts—335 in all. Great individual pitching performances were common. Don Drysdale broke a record set by Walter Johnson in 1913 when he pitched 58⅔ consecutive scoreless innings, a streak which included six shutouts. Denny McLain became the first pitcher in 34 years to win 30 games when he finished with a 31–6 mark. Bob Gibson won both the Cy Young Award for pitching and the Most Valuable Player award in the National League as he won 21 games, 13 of them shutouts, and posted an ERA of 1.12, lowest since the lively ball was introduced in 1920.

And 1968 was also the first year in modern baseball history when no-hitters were pitched in consecutive games, the great feat coming at windy Candlestick Park in San Francisco in a night game on September 17 and an afternoon game on September 18.

The first was pitched by Gaylord Perry and nobody knew better than Perry that the Year of the Pitcher was a mixed blessing even for the pitchers; he had pitched very well all season (2.45 ERA for the year) but he was only 14–14 coming into the game because the Giants hadn't been getting runs for him any faster than he had been yielding them.

Gaylord and his brother, Jim, were the winningest brother combination in baseball history and he didn't need the extra help pitchers got in 1968. With the help of a spitball which he claimed later to have abandoned, Perry had won 36 games in the two seasons prior to 1968; he later went on to win a career high of 24 games with Cleveland in 1972.

In 1968, Perry seemed to be continually flirting with a no-hit game, a feat that had escaped him in previous years. He had two two-hitters and two three-hitters in the first two thirds of the season, then came within one hop of throwing a perfect game on August 26 against the Chicago Cubs.

For five innings that day, Perry retired the Cubs in order with only one difficult chance, a grounder into the hole by opposing pitcher Bill Hands in the third, on which shortstop Hal Lanier made an excellent play and throw.

With one out in the sixth, Perry was thinking no-hitter with Chicago catcher Randy Hundley, an ex-Giant, at the plate. Hundley slammed a line drive into the left field corner and Giant left fielder Ty Cline timed the drive perfectly, making a leaping catch as he crashed into the fence. Perry called catcher Dick Dietz out to the mound. "Please, please, don't let me throw that pitch again," he said.

Then, with one out in the top of the seventh, Glenn Beckert hit a grounder right through the middle of the pitching mound. Lanier and second baseman Ron Hunt converged on it but neither could grab it as the ball went through for a hit.

Had the ball bounced slightly higher on its way past the pitching mound, Perry might have got it himself—and thus got his no-hitter, because that was the only hit the Cubs got. As it was, Perry pitched almost as good a game as was humanly possible. He threw only 75 pitches, just 22 of them balls. He not only did not walk a man, he never got to a three-ball count. Only Cline and Lainer had tough chances in the field, and only 7 of the 27 outs were hit out of the infield.

Three weeks later, Perry got another chance for a no-hitter and this time he made the most of it. He knew when he took the mound that he almost had to pitch a no-hitter to win—his pitching opponent was the overpowering Gibson of the Cardinals—and he was right; he won the game 1–0 when Hunt hit a home run in the first inning off Gibson. "Larry Jansen [Giants pitching coach] told me before the game that if I shut out the Cardinals, I might get a draw," said Perry after the game.

Perry's control was not quite as sharp in this game as it had been in his one-hitter against the Cubs. He walked two men, Mike

Shannon with two outs in the second inning and Phil Gagliano with two outs in the eighth. Despite those walks, however, Perry was in command; in his story in *The San Francisco Chronicle,* Bob Stevens noted that Perry had thrown a strike on the first pitch to 23 batters.

Perry threw 101 pitches, 69 of them strikes (according to the statistics-mad Stevens) and struck out nine batters. Only twice did he need good fielding plays and he supplied one of them himself: Both came in the sixth inning. Dal Maxvill hit a strangely bouncing grounder to Perry's right, but Gaylord came quickly off the mound to grab it and throw out Maxvill. Then, Bobby Tolan hit a grounder between first and second that Willie McCovey strained for and reached, McCovey then throwing to Perry for the out.

Perry could feel the tension as the game went on with the Cardinals hitless. "Hearing the stands yell on every pitch in those last innings was a tremendous thrill," said Gaylord, who told Dick Friendlich of *The Chronicle* that he was thinking about the no-hitter from the fifth inning on.

"I knew I hadn't given any hits, and nobody said anything about it, but Lanier and Hunt were saying, 'Come on, you gotta go hard.' I knew what they were talking about."

In the ninth inning, the Cardinals sent up Lou Brock as a pinchhitter for Gibson. Brock was taking a rare rest that night, but his presence at that point worried Perry. "I was worried about his great speed," said Perry. "I thought he might drag one and beat it out."

Instead, Brock hit a grounder to shortstop, which Lanier handled, throwing to first for the first out of the inning. Tolan, another fleet runner, was the next hitter and he grounded to Hunt for the second out.

Only Curt Flood stood between Perry and his no-hitter and Flood worried him. "I figured Flood would be up there swinging," said Perry. It didn't work that way. Perry threw a called strike, then another. The next pitch was a ball and the fourth one a foul, leaving the count at 1–2.

Then, Perry threw a fastball on the outside corner. Flood let it go and plate umpire Harry Wendlestedt shot his right arm up to signal the third strike that ended the game, giving Perry his no-hitter.

It was the first no-hitter Perry had thrown since his high school days, but despite the fact that it had come in 1968, it was no fluke. Catcher Dick Dietz said Perry had made only three bad pitches all night, all of them high sliders, to Gagliano in the second, to Gibson in the sixth and to Cepeda in the seventh. Only two balls were hit to the outfield, an indication that Perry's spitter, or "hard slider," was working very well.

The no-hitter was only the second thrown in 49 years against the Cardinals and it was the first at Candlestick Park since June 15, 1963, when Juan Marichal had thrown one against the Houston Astros. It would have been nice if Perry could have savored it for a while, but his moment of glory lasted less than 24 hours, until Ray Washburn pitched a no-hitter against the Giants the next afternoon.

All no-hitters are satisfying to the pitchers who throw them, but Washburn provided a special satisfaction because he had been laboring. He had started out well with the Cardinals, winning 12 games and being named Rookie of the Year in 1962, but a shoulder injury in 1963 had reduced the effectiveness of his fastball and made him a part-time pitcher who had won only 38 games in five years.

While he was struggling, Washburn came up with another pitch, a slow curve, to reduce his dependence on the fastball. It was this curve that was the chief ingredient in his no-hitter, a 2–0 win. "I never saw a guy throw a curve much better," said Willie Mays. "It floated, but you couldn't hit it."

The precise breakdown in Washburn's mix was 42 curves, 89 fastballs and 7 sliders—138 pitches in all, far more than Perry had thrown the night before and more than a no-hit pitcher normally throws. Washburn also walked five batters, but catcher John Edwards said this was less wildness than a determination to make the Giants hit his pitch.

"If he was wild with his fastball," Edwards told Charles Einstein of *The Chronicle*, "he didn't mind coming in with his breaking pitch when he was behind in the count."

Two or three times, Edwards thought (and the Giants agreed), Giant players helped by swinging at what would have been ball four.

Washburn, who duplicated Perry's feat by allowing only two balls to be hit to the outfield all day, had minor trouble early. In the first inning, he walked Mays with two outs but got McCovey on a grounder. In the second, Dietz walked but was erased on an inning-ending double play.

Washburn then retired 12 straight Giants before getting into his most serious trouble. Hunt walked to open the Giants' seventh. Mays struck out, bringing McCovey to the plate. McCovey got the sparse crowd of 4703 excited for a moment as he hit a long foul into the right field seats, but the ball didn't especially worry Washburn. "That was a low inside slider," said catcher Edwards later, "and it was a real good pitch. If he does hit it, it has to go foul."

McCovey then walked; both he and Hunt advanced on Jim Hart's ground ball, giving the Giants a runner on third for the first time in the game. But then, with his curve especially sharp, Washburn struck out Dietz to end the inning.

It was at that point that Washburn allowed himself to think seriously of a no-hitter. Once before, against the Dodgers in 1963, he had come close, not giving up a hit until two were out in the eighth inning. "I told myself to make them hit my pitch," he said later.

In the eighth, Washburn walked Dave Marshall, pinchhitting for losing pitcher Bob Bolin, with two outs but got Bobby Bonds to foul out. His no-hitter was still intact.

The Cardinals made it easier for Washburn than the Giants had for Perry by getting him two runs. The first run came in the seventh when Orlando Cepeda singled and Mike Shannon hit a two-out double. In the eighth, Dick Schofield doubled, Washburn sacrificed and Curt Flood singled—again with two outs—to get the second run home.

As he came out for the ninth inning, acutely aware that he was throwing a no-hitter in a park he had cursed in the past, saying he never wanted to pitch there again, Washburn had the toughest part of the Giants' order facing him: Hunt, Mays and McCovey.

He threw what his catcher called his worst pitch of the game, a slider that was supposed to be low but came high instead, to Hunt, but he then got the kind of luck every no-hit pitcher needs. Hunt hit the ball on the ground directly to Gagliano at second base and Gagliano threw him out.

Washburn's first pitch to Mays was a ball that got past Edwards, but then Mays bounced out to Shannon at third. The Cardinal pitcher went ahead 0–2 on McCovey, wasted a pitch and then got him on a soft liner to Flood in center, and he had his first no-hitter of his professional career.

As Washburn came into the clubhouse, he saw Perry. "I was watching you last night," he said.

"So I noticed," said Perry.

The most bemused man in the place had to be Detroit scout Rick Ferrell, who had just come to San Francisco to scout the Cardinals—later Detroit's opponent in the World Series—and had to send back a report on a no-hitter for the second straight day, fully aware that the Detroit front office might send him a message to sober up.

There were other oddities to the double no-hitters. One was

that neither Cardinal manager Red Schoendienst nor outfielder Roger Maris had seen a no-hitter before that week; then, they saw two in succession.

On the other hand, no-hitters were commonplace to Mays, who had played in six. Two of them, by Perry and Marichal, had come for the Giants; four of them, by Sandy Koufax, Warren Spahn, Carl Erskine (in the Brooklyn-New York days) and Washburn, had been thrown against the Giants.

The players on both teams were caught up in the excitement of the moment, knowing they had seen something that had never happened before and might never happen again. Little did they know; less than a year later, it happened again.

The second time was even more noteworthy than the first because it involved two pitchers, Jim Maloney and Don Wilson, who had already thrown no-hitters.

Maloney was the first to throw his no-hitter, a 10–0 win for Cincinnati against Houston in a game covered in an earlier chapter. The next night, Don Wilson of the Astros came back to pitch a 4–0 no-hitter against the Reds, who didn't like it at all.

Wilson had thrown his first no-hitter as a rookie—the first since the famed Bo Belinsky five years earlier—on June 18, 1967, against Atlanta. It was the first no-hitter in the Astrodome and, at this writing, still the only one, though the Astrodome with its constant temperature and "dead air" is very definitely a favorite of pitchers.

As often happens, there was no prior warning that Wilson would throw a no-hitter; indeed, it seemed unlikely he would last the full nine innings. In his previous start, he had struck out 13 Giants in a 7–4 win in which he had thrown 155 pitches, and he was working with three days rest, instead of his usual four.

The lack of rest didn't bother Wilson. He retired the first 14 batters he faced before yielding a walk to Denis Menke in the fifth. He also walked Hank Aaron in the seventh and Menke again in the eighth—but he also struck out 15 Braves.

The closest the Braves came to a hit against Wilson was in the sixth inning when Felipe Alou drilled a grounder into the hole between third and short. Third baseman Bob Aspromonte made a diving stab of the ball and threw out Alou while on his knees.

The Astros got two runs in the fourth and that was the margin as Wilson went into the ninth against the top of the Atlanta batting order, Alou, Tito Francona and Aaron. Knowing he would have to face Aaron, he was—he later said—"petrified," but it didn't show.

Wilson, who had struck out the side in the eighth, got Alou on a foul pop to Aspromonte on a one-and-one pitch. Francona fouled off the first Wilson pitch and then went down swinging on his next two pitches.

That left only Aaron, who was on his way to another of his typical seasons: 39 home runs, 109 RBIs, .307 batting average. Hank worked the count to two-and-two and then smashed a long foul into the left field stands. Wilson took a deep breath on the mound and then whistled his best fastball past Aaron for his fifteenth strikeout and the no-hitter.

"That last pitch to Aaron was as hard as any pitch he threw all day," said an amazed Houston manager Grady Hatton.

Aaron, who had struck out three times, said, "It's young guys like this who make me want to retire." Aaron was joking, of course; he had some history yet to make.

Throughout his career, Wilson was an in-and-out pitcher, brilliant in one outing, poor in the next, depending on whether he could get his good fastball consistently over the plate. The Reds probably should have been thinking of that on May 1, 1969, the night after Maloney had no-hit the Astros, because Wilson was due; in his last outing against Cincinnati, the Reds had won 14–0.

Wilson was also angry as he went to the mound in Cincinnati. He felt the Reds had tried to make the Astros look bad in front of the Houston fans—particularly in the 14–0 victory—and he was also upset because he had been hit by a Jim Merritt pitch in that lopsided loss.

He channeled his anger into his fastball, striking out 13 Reds. At times, he seemed to be trying too hard, as he walked six men. And, while the Reds could not hit him, he hit them, literally. He hit Merritt, in what only the most naive could regard as a coincidence, and Johnny Bench.

The strain seemed to be telling on him in the eighth inning when he went to a 3-and-2 count on the first three batters. Pete Rose got a lift when catcher Don Bryant dropped his foul pop, but Wilson worked out of trouble. In the ninth, he walked the leadoff hitter but then retired the side on three straight shallow fly balls for his second no-hitter.

The Cardinals and Giants, perhaps because the games had come late in the season when the race was all but decided (the Cards winning by nine games over the Giants), had a mutual feeling of good will after their back-to-back no-hitters. The same could not be said for the Astros and Reds. A picture taken immediately after the game showed Wilson's anger had not abated and the Reds had very sparing praise for Wilson. History be damned.

"I'm not going to say anything good about him," said Cincinnati outfielder Rose. "He's always got good fast stuff, and he usually throws hard. But he usually goes only about five or six innings. All I've got to say is he should be a much better pitcher than he is."

Maloney, asked about the game, was brief and ungracious. "What am I supposed to say? The guy pitched a good game. You don't have much feeling when you get beat. I don't want to say anything more about it."

Rose, one of the few Reds willing to talk, said Wilson's pitches were coming in high, around the letters, and the Reds were hoping he would get it down.

"He's one of those guys, when he gets that fastball up, it takes off," said Rose. "I thought I was going to get a hit in the eighth. He was extending himself. He could taste that no-hitter and he was trying too hard. Heck, we all thought we were gonna get a hit."

But none of them did.

Wilson's career continued to be up and down for the next five seasons. Then, on January 5, 1975, he died of carbon monoxide poisoning after he apparently fell asleep in his car. He would have been 30 the following month.

Technically, something very similar to the Perry-Washburn and Maloney-Wilson games occurred on May 5 and 6, 1917, when Ernie Koob and Bob Groom of the St. Louis Browns threw no-hitters on successive days. The feat wasn't the same, however, because the games did not come consecutively (Groom's was in the second game of a doubleheader) and one was tainted.

The tainted one was Koob's. He gave up an infield single in the first inning in a 1–0 win over the Chicago White Sox. When the game ended with that the only hit by the White Sox, the official scorer called a meeting of the writers covering the game and it was agreed to change that hit to an error on third baseman Jimmy Austin.

In no-hit games since, there have been questionable calls which were changed from hit to error when the scorer talked to the fielder involved and learned that the play should have been an error. But in Koob's game, a clean hit was simply erased.

There was no taint to Groom's effort the next day. Not only did he pitch a legitimate no-hitter, but he held the White Sox without a hit for 11 innings.

Groom's streak started in the first game of the doubleheader on May 6. With St. Louis ahead 5–4 going into the eighth inning, Groom went in for Eddie Plank, the Hall of Fame pitcher who was in his final season, after Plank had come out for a pinchhitter in the previous inning. Groom walked three batters in the final two innings but did not allow either a hit or a run, and St. Louis won the game 8–4.

Pitchers were not pampered in those pre-lively ball days and so, after the rest between games, Groom was handed the ball again by St. Louis manager Fielder Jones and sent out to pitch.

Groom's control was still not sharp—he walked three more batters in the second game and hit another—but he continued to baffle the White Sox, who could not get a hit off him. He struck out four.

The suspension of the law of averages that is present in every no-hit game was never more obvious than on these two days, when the Browns beat the White Sox three times. The White Sox were the best team in baseball that year, winning the American League pennant by nine games and then beating John McGraw's Giants in the World Series in six games; the Browns, conversely, finished only a game and a half out of last place, trailing the White Sox by a whopping 43 games.

Nor were Koob and Groom especially good. Koob's win was one of only 6 he got all year, against 14 defeats. Groom led the league three times in losses during his career, and this was one of those years, as he finished with an 8–19 record.

But even though Koob required help from the official scorer, for those two days in May, 1917, they were participants in a feat which would not be surpassed until Perry and Washburn came along more than 50 years later.

13

Two in a year

Until Johnny Vander Meer threw no-hitters back to back in the 1938 season, no pitcher had ever thrown two no-hitters in the same season in modern times. No pitcher did again until 1951 and then, curiously, two no-hitters by the same pitcher in a season suddenly became a much more common event. In 1951, Allie Reynolds of the New York Yankees did it and the very next year, Virgil Trucks of the Detroit Tigers threw two; in 1965 and 1973, Jim Maloney of Cincinnati and Nolan Ryan of California threw two no-hitters each, in games discussed in earlier chapters. By stretching a point, Dean Chance of the California Angels can also be included; Chance threw one 9-inning no-hitter in 1967 and had another one halted by rain after 4½ innings.

These five pitchers were all righthanders who depended on their fastballs as their out pitch. Interestingly, the three being discussed in this chapter—Reynolds, Trucks and Chance—had a lot in common, besides their right arms and their fastballs. In each case, they had years when they were overpowering, and in the case of Reynolds and Chance particularly, seemed as if they would eventually take their place among the best pitchers in the game's history; yet, their career marks fell far short of any criteria for greatness.

Reynolds' problem was that he learned how to pitch at a time when his skills were fading. Early in his career, he had a great fastball but didn't know what to do about it. Late in his career, he became a smart pitcher, but by then it was almost too late; he didn't win 20 games until he was 37 and he had only two seasons left after that.

Reynolds made a brief appearance in the majors in 1942, pitching five scoreless innings in two games for the Cleveland Indians, but he was not a full-fledged major leaguer until the following season, when he was already 28.

He gave little indication of the pitcher he would be later with the Yankees as they won five straight pennants in the 1949–53 period. His fastball was impressive, but often misguided; he led the American League with 151 strikeouts in 1943, but then led the league in walks two years later with 130. He won 11 games in each of his first two seasons and was 18–12 in his third, but that was in the last war year, 1945, when so many quality players were in the service and the competition was not precisely fierce. Many who looked good in the war years found their careers taking a nosedive when players like Bob Feller, Ted Williams and Joe DiMaggio came back from the war; Reynolds seemed to be one of them as he slipped to an 11–15 record in 1946.

It was a big surprise, then, when the Yankees traded for him before the 1947 season, particularly when they gave up star second baseman Joe Gordon. It was not a trade that made Yankee fans happy, but it grew on them.

Cleveland was looking for a second baseman to team with playing manager Lou Boudreau at shortstop. The Indians offered the Yankees either Steve Gromek or Reynolds. It wasn't really much of a choice, because Gromek had been only 5–15 the previous year, and the deal was made for Reynolds when DiMaggio told the Yankee front office, "He can buzz the high, hard one by me any time he feels like it."

Gordon had been an excellent second baseman for the Yankees until he went into the service after the 1943 season, but the war seemed to have rusted his skills. He batted only .210 in 112 games in 1946 and he had obviously lost some fielding range. The Yankees were willing, perhaps even eager, to get rid of him.

Baseball people often talk about the best trade being one that helps both teams and this was one of those trades. Gordon was far from through. He learned to compensate for his decreasing range in the field—just as shortstop Boudreau did—and he and Boudreau became one of the great double-play combinations of all time.

Gordon's bat, too, came back to life in Cleveland. In 1947, he hit 29 home runs; the next year, he hit 32 with a .280 batting average. Boudreau had the spectacular year in 1948, hitting .355 as the Indians won their first pennant in 28 years, but the Indians could not have done it without Gordon. He played two more seasons with the Indians, tailing off to 20 and 19 homers and batting averages of .251 and .236 before retiring.

Meanwhile, Reynolds was even more help to the Yankees, winning 19 games in 1947, as the Yankees won the American League pennant and World Series. He followed with years in which he won 16 twice, 17 twice, and 20. He pitched eight years for the Yankees and was an effective pitcher to the end; though reduced to a part-time pitcher in his final two seasons, he won 26 and lost only 11 in those two years.

Yet, it took Reynolds a long time to gain the recognition he deserved. Early in his Yankee career, he gained the reputation of a pitcher who couldn't pitch his way out of trouble. That reputation seemed deserved in 1949 when, though he won 17 and lost only 6, he finished only 4 games. He owed most of his success, said his critics, to star Yankee reliever Joe Page; some insisted that the best Yankee pitcher was named Reynolds-Page.

Reynolds' reputation for being unable to finish what he started, though, was due less to his own pitching than to the quick thumb of manager Casey Stengel. In fact, Allie was an excellent clutch pitcher, as he proved in World Series competition, where he won seven and lost only two.

He started to turn his reputation around with a two-hit 1–0 win over the Brooklyn Dodgers in the opening game of the 1949 World Series; by 1951, he was the ace of the Yankee staff and nobody appreciated that more than his old club, Cleveland. When Reynolds took the mound on July 12, he had already beaten the Indians three times, twice on shutouts. They had scored only two runs off him in 27 innings.

Allie was a better pitcher in 1951 than he had ever been, for a strange reason: He had bone chips rattling around in his right elbow, which necessitated an operation after the World Series that fall. "I couldn't bend the arm too good," Reynolds said after that season, "and as a result, I seemed to get better control than I had in other years."

Still, a no-hitter was the furthest thing from his mind that day. "After you've been in the majors nine years," he said, "you don't go around thinking about whether you're going to pitch a no-hitter. You just keep wondering how much longer you're going to stay up."

And, despite his success against the Indians, he knew it wouldn't be easy to win the game. The Cleveland pitcher that day was Bob Feller, who was on his way to a 22-win season; Feller had pitched a no-hitter, the third of his career, just 11 days before.

In this game, Feller was almost as good, yielding only four hits, two of them scratch singles. But one of the four hits was a solo home run by Gene Woodling in the top of the seventh; that was the only run of the game.

Reynolds walked three and struck out four, but he was faster than the strikeout figure revealed. An indication of the effectiveness of his fastball was the fact that left fielder Hank Bauer handled seven fly balls: Five of them were by lefthanded Cleveland hitters, showing that the hitters were not getting around on Reynolds' fastball.

Reynolds, who relied on curves and sliders early in the game but then switched mainly to fastballs in the later innings, had some anxious moments early. The worst was the second, when the Indians got a runner—Luke Easter—to third base for the only time in the game. With two outs and Harry Simpson on first in addition to Easter on third, Jim Hegan hit a grounder through the box. Shortstop Phil Rizzuto had committed what turned out to be the only error in the game when he misplayed Bobby Avila's slow roller in the first inning, but he atoned for it by grabbing Hegan's grounder behind second and throwing to Jerry Coleman to force Simpson.

Rookie third baseman Gil McDougald made two good plays on slow rollers, against Avila in the third and Hegan in the fifth, coming in fast to grab the grounders and fire to first for the outs.

Reynolds knew all the time that he had a no-hitter going—"I can see the scoreboard as well as anyone else in the park," he said after the game—and it didn't bother him to talk about it. On the bench in the seventh inning, right after Woodling hit the home run that put a run on the board, Reynolds turned to fellow pitcher Eddie Lopat and asked, "Think I can pitch a no-hitter, Eddie?" Lopat just looked at him and gulped.

Allie's flaunting of the no-hit jinx seemed about to catch up with him in the eighth inning. Sam Chapman, who had come in for the injured Larry Doby, hit a bad pitch deep to left. Bauer backed up as far as he could against the fence in Cleveland's Municipal Stadium and at the last moment, the stiff wind slowed the ball just enough to enable him to make the catch.

In the early innings, Reynolds had been missing the corners with both fastball and curve, and he had feared he would have a long night—or a quick shower. After his shaky second inning, however, his control came back and he retired 17 straight Indians at one point. In the eighth, he told catcher Yogi Berra that he wanted to stick with fastballs because he didn't want to take a chance on losing his no-hitter. Throwing fastballs, he again set the Indians down without a hit.

In the ninth, Cleveland manager Al Lopez sent up Bob Lemon as a pinchhitter for Feller. Lemon, who had won 20 games in each of the previous three seasons, had started his major league career as a third baseman and outfielder before being switched to the mound; he was a good enough hitter to have averaged .272 in 1950. He was no threat to Reynolds at this point, however. Allie was wide with his first pitch but then threw three straight fastballs by Lemon.

The next batter was Dale Mitchell. With a count of one ball, two strikes, Mitchell tapped weakly to Coleman at second. Only one out between Reynolds and his no-hitter.

The final batter was Avila, a good hitter who was on his way to the first of three .300 seasons. In May of 1951, Avila had broken up a no-hit bid by Joe Dobson of the Chicago White Sox.

The first pitch was low, then Reynolds threw a strike. The third pitch was fouled back by Avila and Reynolds fell as he made the pitch. He'd had trouble all night because Feller took a longer stride and he kept stepping in the hole that Feller's foot had made. This was the only time he had fallen, however, and Berra rushed out to the mound to make sure Reynolds had not hurt himself. Allie brushed himself off and sent Berra back behind the plate.

The next ball was just low. Reynolds wondered how Avila could take that close a pitch with two strikes, but the Cleveland second baseman did—and he also took the next pitch, which was similarly just off the plate. With the count 3–2, Avila fouled a ball to the screen and then another into the stands.

Reynolds got a new ball and rubbed it vigorously. He stood on the mound for a moment, took the fastball sign from Berra and then fired. Avila swung and missed and Reynolds had his no-hitter.

Jim Turner, the Yankees' pitching coach, said Reynolds' ninth inning effort was the strongest he had ever seen. "That guy never worries, isn't superstitious and is in good condition, but that ninth inning was something, and I've seen plenty of them."

The fact that Reynolds had talked about the no-hit game while it was in progress, in violation of baseball tradition, had bothered many fans, who wrote to Allie about it. So the next time he had a shot at a no-hitter, he was all business.

The next time came on September 28 against Boston, with only two days of the season remaining: It was a much different game than the first. This time the Yankees scored early and often, getting two runs in the first inning and then coasting to an 8–0 win.

The eight runs made it easy for Reynolds to win the game, but they didn't make it any easier for him to pitch his no-hitter, and the Red Sox were tough to stop. They were a strong hitting team: Ted Williams, Bobby Doerr, Walt Dropo, Johnny Pesky and Vern Stephens were in the lineup; Billy Goodman, a .297 hitter, could not even win a starting position.

Reynolds' game was the first of a doubleheader and was being played on American Indian day, fittingly enough for Allie, who was known as Super Chief because of his Creek Indian heritage. It was also the game in which the Yankees clinched their third straight AL title.

In contrast to the first game, Reynolds had his fastball with him all the way in this game, striking out nine Red Sox. He also walked four and threw 119 pitches, which bothered him a little. Not much. "I should have done better with my control," he said.

Until the eighth, no Red Sox hit the ball hard off Reynolds. Then, Aaron Robinson hit one deep to right field. Allie didn't turn around because he was sure the ball was going into the stands, but Bauer caught it against the fence.

In the ninth, Reynolds got the first two batters and then faced Williams, the best hitter of his time. With a count of 1–1, Williams hit a high foul behind the plate. Berra went over and watched it come down, but the shadows at Yankee Stadium are very tricky in September and Yogi dropped it.

Reynolds told Berra, "Don't let it bother you. Let's get that guy now." Williams was even more determined than before. "I wanted Berra to catch the foul he dropped, but then I became more eager than ever to break up that no-hitter," he said later.

Reynolds threw the ball as fast as he could and Williams lifted another pop foul. Again, Berra got under it. This time, though, he caught it.

As Reynolds came off the mound, he passed manager Stengel. "You can have the rest of the season off," said Casey.

Virgil Oliver (Fire) Trucks received his nickname early in his career because it seemed such a natural, considering his last name and the speed with which his pitches arrived at the plate.

Like many fastballers, Trucks was often bothered by a lack of control, probably the main reason he never became the great pitcher he seemed capable of becoming when he first came to the majors. His was an erratic career, going from good seasons to bad and back again. Though he won 19 games twice and was in double figures in wins in 10 of his 17 seasons, Trucks only once won 20 games. Fittingly enough, that was in the 1953 season, when he pitched for two teams: St. Louis, for whom he won five games; Chicago, for whom he won 15.

The most erratic season of his erratic career came in 1952. He lost 19 games that year and won only 5—but 2 of his 5 wins were no-hitters.

It was not the first time Trucks had pitched two no-hitters in a season. In 1938, when he was only 19, he had pitched two for Andalusia in the Class D Alabama-Florida League.

Those no-hitters, though, came when Trucks had youth and a live fastball going for him. In 1952, he had obviously lost the first and seemed to have lost the second: The Tigers were to trade him at the end of the season, certain that he was on his way out.

For two days of the 1952 season, however, Trucks was never better. The first no-hitter came on May 15 against the Washington Senators in Detroit. He had lost his first two decisions that year, but the Senators were an ideal club to face in his attempt for his first win; they did not have a .300 hitter in the lineup.

Trucks walked only one batter in the game (curiously, he hit two) and struck out seven. The Senators gave him no trouble. The Tigers were not giving Washington pitcher Bob Porterfield much trouble, either, getting only three hits and no runs going into the bottom of the ninth inning. It seemed Trucks might be another of those unfortunate pitchers who threw extra-inning no-hitters but couldn't win.

Then, with two outs in the ninth, Vic Wertz smashed a Porterfield fastball into the right field seats. Trucks had a 1–0 win and, more importantly, a no-hitter, in a game that took only one hour and 32 minutes to play.

Trucks almost duplicated Vander Meer's feat by throwing a no-hitter his next time out. He held Philadelphia without a hit until Billy Hitchcock singled with one out in the seventh; he wound up with a two-hit, 5–1 victory.

Then, on August 25, Trucks pitched his second no-hitter. His first one had come at home against a weak opponent, but he didn't pick a soft spot for his second one: This one came against the New York Yankees, on the way to their fourth straight American League pennant, at Yankee Stadium.

This one was a story within a story. In the third inning, Yankee Phil Rizzuto slapped a ground ball at Detroit shortstop Johnny Pesky, who seemed to have trouble getting the ball out of his glove. When he finally got it, his throw to first was too late to catch Rizzuto.

John Drebinger of the *New York Times*, scoring the game, immediately called it an error, but other writers in the press box disputed the call. Their position was that the ball had stuck in the webbing of Pesky's glove, which technically made it a base hit and not an error. Finally, Drebinger changed his ruling to hit.

As the innings went on, Trucks had not yielded another hit and Drebinger was increasingly worried about his call on Rizzuto's ball. Finally, he called down to the Detroit dugout and talked to Pesky, who said it should have been an error. Pesky said the ball had not stuck in his glove but that it had spun out and, as a result, he'd had trouble closing his right hand on it in time to make a good throw. "I just messed it up," said Pesky.

So, Drebinger changed his ruling back to error and Trucks had his no-hitter again. The ruling was announced just as the Tigers finished batting in the top of the seventh and the crowd of 13,442 roared its approval.

The Tigers had taken a 1–0 lead in the seventh when Walt Dropo doubled down the left-field line, only the second Detroit hit off Yankee starter Bill Miller, and Steve Souchak singled.

Now, the pressure was on Trucks to maintain the no-hitter and to win. He had been magnificent since the third; after allowing three Yankees to reach first in the first three innings, on a walk and two errors, Trucks had set down the New Yorkers in order since. The closest thing to a hit had been a vicious line drive off Rizzuto's bat in the fifth inning that was grabbed by Trucks himself.

Trucks mowed the Yankees down 1–2–3 in the seventh and eighth, then he faced Mickey Mantle, Joe Collins and Hank Bauer in the ninth. All were solid hitters, with Mantle the best. Mickey hit .311 that year; he also struck out 111 times and this was one of those occasions. He went down swinging for the second time, bringing Trucks's game total to eight.

Collins then hit a long drive that seemed for a moment as if it would go for extra bases in left center, but center fielder Johnny Groth caught it after a long run. Only Bauer was left.

Hank hit a sizzling one-hopper to Detroit second baseman Al Federoff that almost knocked Federoff down, but the second baseman grabbed it and tossed to Dropo for the final out.

Trucks had become the third pitcher in modern history to throw two no-hitters in a season, the first to throw two in afternoon games. Vander Meer's second no-hitter and Reynolds' first had come in night games.

Despite what the Tigers thought, Trucks was hardly through. Traded in the off-season, he went on to win 20 games for Chicago and St. Louis the next season. He lasted six more years, finishing with 177 career wins. Included in those wins were two one-hitters in 1954, against Boston and his former teammates at Detroit. But nothing before or after gave him the thrill he got from pitching two no-hitters in one season.

A footnote. must be added to this chapter on Dean Chance, who might have been the fifth to pitch two no-hitters in a single season had it not been for untimely rain.

For a while, it seemed Chance would be known only as Bo Belinsky's buddy. The two were inseparable in their rookie year of 1962 with the Angels. Chance had been up briefly late in the 1961 season, long enough to pitch in five games and 18⅓ innings, but not long enough to lose his rookie designation.

When Belinsky was involved in an early morning fracas in which a woman claimed he had hit her, Chance was there. When Belinsky was involved in his famous fight with sportswriter Braven Dyer, Chance was in the vicinity, though versions of exactly where he was differed. Only 21 and from rural Ohio, Chance seemed a naive young farm boy, along for the ride.

Farm boy, yes; naive, no—as the California front office learned when he started negotiating midseason raises in his contract. Belinsky had talked about getting his contract raised before reporting to camp in 1962 and got a lot of publicity about it, but he didn't get the raise. Chance didn't talk about getting a raise, he just got it. In retrospect, there is considerable doubt about who was the leader and who was the follower in the Belinsky-Chance pairing.

Chance also turned out to be a better pitcher than Belinsky, even in Bo's best year, 1962. Belinsky got all the publicity, before and after his no-hitter, but it was Chance who had the better record, 14–10 with an excellent 2.96 earned run average.

Two years later, he was the best pitcher in his league, winning 20 games and losing only 9 for a California team which had a team batting average of only .242. He had a sparkling ERA of 1.65, threw 11 shutouts (often the only way he could win with the Angels) and led the American League in wins, ERA, complete games, innings pitched and shutouts. He won the Cy Young Award as baseball's best pitcher.

When he slipped to a 12–17 record in 1966, the Angels traded him to Minnesota. He almost led the Twins to the pennant in 1967 with his second 20-win season. And in 1967, he almost threw two no-hitters.

Chance was no stranger to no-hitters: In high school in Wooster, Ohio, he had thrown 18 of them. He was a natural, as his high school coach, Dan Baker, realized. Dean had tried to work on a breaking pitch and couldn't throw one—but when he threw his fastball, said Baker, "It broke so sharply, it was as crooked as a dog's hind leg."

In 1962, pitching against the Minnesota team for whom he was now playing, Chance had come within two outs of a no-hitter; with one out in the ninth, Zoilo Versalles had singled for the only Minnesota hit of the game.

Then, on August 6, 1967, Chance was even sharper than he had been in the one-hitter as he pitched five perfect innings against the Red Sox, striking out four in that time. The Red Sox hit only four balls to the outfield, with the longest being Jim Lonborg's drive that backed Bob Allison against the left-field fence in the third inning and Elston Howard's liner to center in the third.

The only difficult play for the Minnesota defense came in the fourth, when Dalton Jones grounded sharply to Harmon Killebrew at first. He blocked the ball in front of him, recovered quickly and tossed to Chance at first for the out.

But Chance's perfection all came to naught when a deluge of rain hit Metropolitan Stadium in Bloomington, after the Red Sox had gone down 1–2–3 in the top of the fifth inning, rendering the field unplayable.

Since the Twins had scored two runs in the bottom of the fourth, Chance got credit for a win and a complete game, but he did not get credit for a perfect game because it had not gone nine innings.

Chance got another opportunity for a no-hitter less than three weeks later, this time against the Indians in Cleveland. The game was played only 50 miles from his home town; his parents and high school coach, Baker, were in attendance. That didn't bother Chance. He was no stranger to pressure, having won thirteen 1–0 games in his major league career.

Dean was wild in this game, as he had not been in his aborted perfect game attempt, walking five batters; he struck out nine. His wildness cost him a run in the first inning, as the Indians scored on two walks, an error and a wild pitch.

The Twins came back to tie the score with a run in the top of the second and then went ahead in the sixth with another single run. By that time, Chance had settled into a groove and was retiring the Indians without a hit inning after inning. Unfortunately, he was doing it in virtual privacy. Chance's game was the second of a twi-night doubleheader and only about 4000 of the 10,519 that had been there for the start of the first game were still around.

Perhaps because of the lack of people, Chance was calm about the no-hitter. "I saw Bob Feller, Bob Lemon and Sonny Siebert pitch no-hitters for Cleveland," said pitching coach Early Wynn, "and they all were calm. So was Chance. Sometimes we talked over the hitters coming up the next inning. There was no tension in his eyes or face. He was all business."

Crowd or no crowd, though, Chance probably wouldn't have been bothered. He had always been a pitcher who had done his best under pressure.

"I don't want to say I've got ice water in my veins," said Chance after the game, "but, in four years, I've lost only two games in which I had a lead by the eighth inning.

"I've had to pitch in tight games all through my career. I hate to lose close ones when I get a lead. I think having to pitch in so many games like that was good preparation for pitching a no-hitter. I don't think I ever was tense. And I knew it was a no-hitter."

Chance's father, who never played baseball, asked Baker in the ninth inning if he thought Dean could make it. Both feared something would happen, but it didn't. Chance retired the Indians without a hit in the ninth and had his first official no-hitter.

After the game, he got a telephone call from the Twins' No. 1 fan, then Vice-President Hubert Humphrey. A longtime baseball aficionado, Humphrey watched minor league games from the roof at old Nicollet Park when he was mayor of Minneapolis. He had visited the Twins' dressing room many times, first as U.S. Senator, then as Vice President.

Chance spoke without visible emotion to the Vice President and then casually told writers, "That was Humphrey. He's a real fan, a great baseball man. Just wanted to say nice going to me and all the guys. He calls all the time and talks to the guys."

At the time of his no-hitter, Chance was still only 26 and seemingly on his way to a great and lengthy career. It didn't happen that way. He pitched only four more years, winning just 34 games, then retired to manage horses and boxers, with the memory of one no-hitter and an aborted perfect game.

14

Hall of Famers who did . . .

Through 1974, there were 31 pitchers elected to the Hall of Fame who had pitched at least part of their careers in the twentieth century. You would expect these men to be proficient at pitching no-hitters and in some cases they were. Sandy Koufax, for instance, pitched four, and Cy Young and Bob Feller had three apiece; all were discussed in previous chapters. Christy Mathewson and Warren Spahn each pitched two, Walter Johnson and Ed Walsh each had nine-inning no-hitters and an additional no-hitter for less than nine innings.

And yet, it will give you some idea of the special ingredients that go into a no-hitter to know that only six other Hall-of-Famers pitched no-hit games: Carl Hubbell, Chief Bender, Ted Lyons, Dazzy Vance, Jesse Haines and Rube Marquard. The remaining 18 pitchers never had a no-hit game.

In any discussion of great pitchers, Christy Mathewson's name always comes up. Mathewson won 373 games in his career, tying him with Grover Cleveland Alexander for most wins by a National League pitcher, and he was a dominant pitcher from the start. In his first full season, 1902, Mathewson won 20 games and pitched a no-hitter.

Mathewson's first no-hitter came on July 15, 1901, against the Cardinals at St. Louis. It was not quite the masterful type of game for which Mathewson would become famous. He walked four, a remarkably high number for a pitcher who specialized in control—but it was still an impressive feat for a rookie.

The management of the Giants, however, was not impressed.

Horace Fogel, manager at the time, decided that Mathewson should be a first baseman! The thinking of baseball managers is often mysterious, but never more so. Later, Fogel was replaced as manager by George Smith, but he remained as an advisor and suggested that Mathewson be tried at shortstop, too.

Fortunately for Mathewson and the Giants, John McGraw jumped from Baltimore in the American League to the Giants in July that year. McGraw had a better appreciation of what Mathewson could do. He told owner Andrew Freedman to get rid of Fogel. "Anybody who doesn't know any more about baseball than he does has no right in a ball park," said McGraw. "Trying to make a first baseman out of Mathewson! There's a kid with as fine a pitching motion as I ever saw, and as much stuff as any young fellow to come up in years."

McGraw was right, of course. Mathewson, a big man by the standards of his day at six feet, one and a half inches and 195 pounds, was a natural pitcher. He was a great control pitcher who, it was said, could consistently put the ball in an area which could be covered by a grapefruit. That is no doubt an exaggeration, but Mathewson had one year, 1913, when he walked only 21 batters in 306 innings, an average of one in almost 15 innings.

In that same year, Mathewson set a major league record by going 68 consecutive innings without walking a man. He had other impressive statistics. Starting in 1930, he won 30 or more games for the next three seasons, and he went on to win 20 or more games for 12 consecutive years, a league record. In the 1905 World Series, he pitched three shutouts.

Mathewson had such a smooth motion that his fastball was often in on hitters before they realized it. He also had a good curve and the pitch that made him famous, the "fadeaway," known in modern times as the screwball. By whatever name, it is a curve that breaks the opposite way—in Matty's case, away from lefthanded hitters. The pitch is usually hard on a pitcher's arm, because the motion twists the arm out, but that did not bother Mathewson or Hubbell, another who specialized in that pitch.

It is a measure of Mathewson's talent that he did things he wasn't even trying to do. He seldom tried for strikeouts, for instance; yet, his assortment of fastball and curves was so bewildering that he five times led the National League in strikeouts, setting a league record of 267 in 1903.

He never tried for a no-hitter, either. Mathewson's idea of pitching was simple. He believed in letting the batter hit the ball; with his remarkable control, he could usually make the batter hit a pitch on the corner of the plate and, in that pre-lively ball era, he didn't have to worry about a mistake being hit out of the park.

Fred Lieb, author of several books and articles on baseball, once told of a game he had seen Matty pitch against Cincinnati. Mathewson had allowed 14 hits and still pitched a shutout. In each of the first seven innings, he had retired the first two batters and then given up two singles. In the eighth and ninth, he retired the Reds 1–2–3. He did not, of course, give up a walk.

Even without trying, Mathewson pitched two no-hitters. His second was easily the better of the two, one of the finest games ever pitched. With better support, the 1–0 win over the Chicago Cubs could have been a perfect game; he did not walk a man and the only Cubs to reach base got there because of errors. Mathewson faced only 28 men, with one of the baserunners erased as right fielder George Browne made an excellent running catch of a fly ball and turned it into a double play.

The newspaper account of the day said the game ranked next to the "wonderful game" by Young (his perfect game) pitched the previous year. "Inning after inning," read the account, "the locals [Cubs] came up and retired with a dazed look on their faces. The chances they hit were mostly of the easiest kind and gave the New York fielders little worry."

Mathewson had to pitch this kind of game to win—which is probably exactly why he did pitch it—because his opponent, Mordecai (Three Finger) Brown was shutting out the Giants until the ninth, although the anonymous writer of the day said, ". . . the vicious way the visitors kept driving the long flies across the gardens presaged final disaster." I told you they don't write like that any more.

Brown, one of the Hall of Fame pitchers who could never pitch a no-hitter, had a one-hitter going until the ninth—despite the "vicious way" the Giants were hitting the ball. But in the top of the ninth, he allowed four hits and the only run of the day. Mathewson set the Cubs down 1–2–3 in the ninth, and he had his second no-hitter.

That game came on June 13, 1905, and there was more than a little irony to that in retrospect: Brown soon gained respect as the one pitcher who could beat Mathewson consistently. One day less than a month later, he started a string of nine consecutive wins over Mathewson that stretched through the 1908 season. But nobody could have beaten Mathewson on that day in 1905.

A contemporary of Mathewson's, Big Ed Walsh, almost duplicated his feat of two no-hitters, but the weather would not cooperate.

The period when Walsh and Mathewson were pitching was one when pitchers used a number of trick pitches; Mathewson was an exception because he did not. Pitchers used emery board to rough up the ball or cut nicks in it with a razor blade; in each case, it was to make the ball curve more sharply.

One of the most effective of the trick pitches, for the few who could master it, was the spitball. In the early days of the century, the spitter was known as a pitch that was hard on the arm—because Jack Chesbro and Elmer Stricklett, who used the pitch effectively, spread the myth so they could keep a monopoly on the pitch. In fact, it was easy on the arm because it did not require an unnatural motion.

Spit is applied to the tips of the first two fingers of the throwing hand and these fingers are placed on the top side of the ball, with the thumb underneath. The ball is held firmly, but not tightly, and is delivered with a wrist snap that makes it come off the thumb and slip from under the moistened fingertips. The ball rotates with a forward spin and sinks as it nears the plate.

Or, at least, that's the way the pitch used to be thrown. It has been illegal since 1920 and, of course, nobody throws it now. If you don't believe me, ask Gaylord Perry.

When Walsh came to the Chicago White Sox in 1904, he was advised by manager Fielder Jones to learn how to throw the spitter. Walsh had a live fastball, but he was often wild with it; his curve was no better than average. It took him a couple of seasons to learn how to control the spitter but once he did, he was very effective; he had one five-year stretch in which his highest earned run average was 1.88!

Walsh's first pass at a no-hitter came on May 26, 1907, in a game with the New York Highlanders at Chicago. His control was not sharp at the start and it cost him a run in the first inning. Kid Elberfeld of the Highlanders walked, stole second, went to third on a passed ball and scored on a wild pitch.

The White Sox responded in uncharacteristic fashion. Known as the "Hitless Wonders" for entirely logical reasons—they had averaged only .230 in winning the American League pennant and the World Series the previous year—the White Sox managed to score eight runs in five innings in this game.

Meanwhile, Walsh was holding the Highlanders hitless, though yielding one more walk. But rain delayed the game once and finally stopped it with one out in the bottom of the fifth, the White Sox batting. Walsh got a win, but he did not get official credit for a no-hitter. He was lucky even to get the win. The White Sox were ahead 4–1 at the time of the first shower, after the third inning, and New York manager Clark Griffith knew the game was as good as lost. When the teams took the field again, Griffith went to the mound in place of starter Al Orth and tried to stall, until the umpire told him to stop it.

Walsh won 25 games in 1907, but 1908 was his finest year. That year he won 40 games, pitched in 66 games and 464 innings. In the last eight games of the season, he pitched in six, including a doubleheader against Boston when he allowed just three hits in the first game and four in the second. Yet, his first official no-hitter did not come that year but three years later, on August 27, 1911, in Chicago against the Boston Red Sox.

This one was very nearly a perfect game. The only Red Sox baserunner got there on a walk; Walsh struck out eight. It was a good hitting (.274 team average) Red Sox team that Walsh faced, with all-time great Tris Speaker leading the attack, but they could do nothing with his pitches on this day.

As in the no-hitter that didn't count, the White Sox made it easy for Walsh to win, scoring five runs. They were not customarily that generous.

Walter Johnson, another who missed the accomplishment of two no-hitters because of rain at an inopportune moment, is still considered by those who saw him as the fastest pitcher of all time. Unlike fastball pitchers such as Feller and Lefty Grove, who had to switch to other pitches late in their careers when their fastballs faded, Johnson's fastball remained his best pitch right to the end of his career.

Indeed, it was probably his only effective pitch. He had a mediocre curve, which he often insisted on throwing when he had two strikes on a hitter. Eddie Collins said that he would take two strikes from Johnson so he could have a chance to hit the curve instead of the fastball. Johnson has the career record for strikeouts——3503—but old-timers insist he would have had far more if he had thrown the fastball more often with a two-strike count.

Johnson also had unusual control for a fastballer. He averaged about two walks for a nine-inning game during his career and in 1913 he walked only 38 men in 346 innings, an average of one every nine innings.

Though pitching for a team which was almost always in the second division, Johnson compiled some impressive statistics. He won either 413, 414 or 416 games (statistics in the first 20 years of the century were often incomplete or lent themselves to interpretations); whatever figure you accept, and the third figure is generally accepted now, only Cy Young ever won more games.

His strikeout total was the best in history and nobody has ever equaled his career shutout record of 113. Many of those shutouts were pitched out of necessity, the Senators' hitting being what it was—or wasn't; 20 times during his career, Johnson lost games by 1–0.

It was not until 1920, however, when Johnson was in his fourteenth big league season, that he finally pitched a no-hitter. Ironically, it was not a good season for him, either; he was only 8–10 and pitched only 143 innings as he suffered with the only sore arm of his career.

He didn't have a sore arm on July 1, however, as he stopped the Red Sox without a hit in Boston, striking out ten in the process. He could have had a perfect game except for an error by second baseman Bucky Harris in the seventh. Johnson was noted for his easy temperament, but even if he had been more volatile, he couldn't have gotten mad at Harris: Bucky also singled in the Senators' only run, also in the seventh inning.

Boston manager Ed Barrow—the same man who turned Babe Ruth into an outfielder and later bacame the general manager who started the Yankees on their road to success—didn't concede anything to Johnson, sending up pinch hitters Ben Karr and Hack Eibel in the ninth inning. It made no difference to Johnson, who sailed through the Red Sox as easily in the ninth inning as he had the rest of the game.

There was a footnote to that game. Washington, which finished in sixth place that year, was drawing small crowds, but Clark Griffith, by now owner and manager of the Senators, saw a chance to make some money. The Yankees, with Ruth having the first of his great home run years, were in town for a July 4 doubleheader and Griffith advertised that Johnson would pitch against them.

More than 25,000 came out for the doubleheader—but one of them wasn't Johnson. The seldom-sick, seldom-injured Walter was home in bed and somebody had to take his place. Al Schacht volunteered to do it.

When Schacht was announced as the pitcher, the crowd threw cushions, bottles, and score cards. They booed vigorously as Schacht walked New York's leadoff hitter, Whitey Witt, on four straight pitches. But ultimately, Schacht won the game 9–3 and the crowd somewhat mollified. Griffith was grateful and he promised Schacht a job for life, if he wished. He kept his word, hiring Schacht as a coach and encouraging the clowning which Schacht later developed into a profitable routine.

After his slump in his no-hit year, Johnson bounced back and had an excellent year in 1924, when the Senators won the pennant for the first time since he had been with them. He won 23, lost only 7 and —though nearly 37—led the league in strikeouts. He won a World Series game that fall and he almost pitched another official no-hitter. That he didn't was no fault of his.

Johnson wasn't as dominating in this game, played on August

25, 1924, at Washington against the St. Louis Browns, as he had been in his nine-inning no-hitter, but he was nearly as effective. He walked two batters but did not give up a hit in seven innings, as the Senators took a 2–0 lead. Then, rain washed out the rest of that game and the second game of the doubleheader scheduled for that day, and Johnson missed his chance to go into the record books with two official no-hitters.

Johnson was nearly 33 when he pitched his no-hitter, but that was nothing compared to Spahn; Warren was nearly 40 when he pitched a no-hitter. Once he got the hang of it, he came back a few months later to pitch a second no-hitter. This time, he *was* 40.

It was fitting that Spahn's no-hit accomplishments came late in his career, because he had been a late starter through no fault of his own. He didn't win a major league game until he was 25, but from that point, he won 363 of them. No lefthander has ever won as many.

Spahn came up to the Boston Braves in 1942, but he didn't last long. He was pitching against the Brooklyn Dodgers when Boston manager Casey Stengel advised him to throw his fastball, which was a good one, in the vicinity of Pee Wee Reese's cap. Spahn declined. Stengel sent him back to the minors.

During the ensuing three years, Spahn was in the Army in the European theater; he won only eight games his first season back with the Braves. The next season, though, he won 21 games and started an amazing streak; in a 17-season span, he won 20 or more games 13 times and he never had two consecutive seasons in which he did not win 20. In the Boston pennant year of 1948, the Braves' pitching rotation was described as "Spahn, Sain and two days of rain." At the age of 42, he won 23 games. In midcareer, his fastball lost several miles an hour, but he simply learned other pitches and became a clever pitcher, working the corners and never giving the hitter anything good to hit. He accomplished everything a pitcher ever would want, from World Series wins to an eventual place in the Hall of Fame.

But for years, one objective eluded him: a no-hit game. His frustration became even more pronounced when his best friend, Lew Burdette, threw one against the Philadelphia Phillies on August 25, 1960. Not to be outdone, Spahn came back and threw a no-hitter against the same club just 31 days later.

Spahn, who had thrown one-hitters twice before, missed a perfect game when he walked Ken Walters in the fourth and Cal Neeman in the fifth. No matter. It was a notable game even though it was not perfect. For one thing, it was his twentieth win of the season. For another, it was a throwback to the days of his youth, when his fastball could match almost anybody's; mixing fastballs and curves, he struck out 15 Phillies.

A drizzling rain that lasted throughout the game in Milwaukee kept the crowd down to 6117 fans, but it didn't bother Spahn. He was on target most of the time with 71 strikes among his 105 pitches, and there were no tough plays behind him until the ninth.

In the ninth, he almost lost it. With two outs, Bobby Malkmus hit a hard grounder toward the mound. Spahn, a good fielding pitcher, stuck up his glove, but the ball bounced away. The crowd groaned as it appeared Malkmus would beat out the ball for a hit.

But shortstop Johnny Logan cut behind the mound to grab the ball, and then fired to first. Joe Adcock stretched his six-foot, four-inch body as far as it would go to take the throw, a half-step before Malkmus reached the base.

"I had to be a copy cat," said Spahn after the game. "Burdette threw a no-hitter and I wanted one, too. I knew it was there and I wanted to win it. I knew it in the second inning. I usually give up a hit about that time."

Spahn shook his head. "It's just a crazy game. How many years—16?—I've been pitching, and now I get a no-hitter."

It was to get stranger. On his third start of the 1961 season, April 28 in Milwaukee, Spahn would pitch another no-hitter, this one against the Giants. This one surpassed the first in two respects: 1) Spahn had no working margin; the Braves won his first no-hitter 4–0, the second one only 1–0; and 2) the Giants were a far better team than the Phillies of the previous year; they had narrowly lost the pennant the previous year and were leading the league at the time they ran into Spahn.

The Braves got their only run in the first inning. With one out, Frank Bolling singled and went to second on a passed ball. Hank Aaron then lined a single into right and Bolling scored.

Meanwhile, Spahn was having little trouble with the Giants. He struck out six, and walked only two and he faced only the minimum of 27 batters. His walks went to Chuck Hiller and Willie McCovey, in the fourth and fifth, respectively; in each case, Spahn started a double play himself on the next batter, first Harvey Kuenn and then Orlando Cepeda.

"It was so easy it was pathetic," said Spahn after the game. "Everything went my way and they kept guessing wrong. But let's face it: I was just plain lucky. I walked a man to start an inning— a cardinal sin with a one-run lead—not once, but twice, and got away with it."

Only twice in the first eight innings was Spahn's no-hitter in doubt. In the sixth, shortstop Roy McMillan went far to his left and momentarily fumbled Jose Pagan's grounder before throwing him out. In the seventh, McMillan had a little trouble with Kuenn's grounder, but again he recovered in time to make the play.

All the excitement came in the ninth. Spahn got two strikes on Bailey, whose passed ball had let in the only run, then got Bailey to hit a foul pop. Catcher Charlie Lau dropped it. Bailey fouled off the next four pitches and Spahn was worried. "I was afraid he would straighten one of them out. He was swinging good." Finally, though, Spahn slipped a third strike past Bailey.

The next hitter was Matty Alou. Most players will not bunt in the ninth inning of a no-hitter, figuring that if they break up the no-hitter, it should be on a good hit. Alou did not believe that. He laid down a bunt that hugged the first base line. Spahn came quickly off the mound, scooped it up and underhanded it to Adcock, just ahead of the fleet Alou.

Now, Spahn was just one out away from his second no-hit game. Joey Amalfitano came in to hit for Sam Jones, who had pitched a magnificent game himself. Amalfitano hit a sharp grounder directly at shortstop McMillan. The ball popped out of McMillan's glove but he grabbed it in the air and then threw to Adcock for the final out.

The other no-hitters thrown by Hall of Fame pitchers deserve mention because of their relative rarity, if for no other reason. In chronological order, then:

Charles Albert (Chief) Bender was the pitcher Connie Mack once said was his best money pitcher, an impressive compliment from a man who handled such pitchers as Lefty Grove, Rube Waddell and Eddie Plank.

Bender, called Chief for the obvious reason—he was one of 13 children born to a Chippewa mother at Brainerd, Minnesota—won 212 games in his major league career. He was noted for his fastball. Eddie Collins, who hit against Walter Johnson and played behind Bender in his prime, said he doubted that Johnson was any faster than Bender at his best.

Bender was definitely at his best in 1910, when he won 23 games and lost only 5 for the Philadelphia Athletics, with an earned run average of 1.58. That was also the year he pitched his no-hitter, on May 12 against the Cleveland Indians, appropriately enough at Philadelphia.

The no-hitter came within an eyelash of being a perfect game. The only Cleveland baserunner was shortstop Terry Turner, who walked. Turner was out trying to steal second, so Bender faced only the minimum of 27 men.

Rube Marquard was no stranger to no-hit games. Pitching for Indianapolis of the American Association in 1908, he had won 28 games—and the last one was a no-hitter. After that game, he was auctioned off to major league clubs and the New York Giants bought him for $11,000, at that time the highest price ever paid for a baseball player.

When Marquard won only nine games for the Giants in his first two seasons, he became known as the "$11,000 Lemon." He quickly shook that tag, though, when he won 24, 26 and 23 in the seasons of 1911–13. In 1912, he set a record by winning 19 straight games. In *The Glory of Their Times*, Marquard claimed the figure should have been 20. In one game, he had relieved Jeff Tesreau when the Giants were trailing 3–2 in the eighth. The Giants scored twice to win the game 4–3 in the ninth, but the scoring rules of the day gave the win to Tesreau, not Marquard.

Marquard jumped to the Brooklyn team in the Federal League in the winter of 1915, but then jumped back again to the Giants before the season started. He celebrated his return to the Giants on April 15 by pitching a no-hit game in New York against the Brooklyn Dodgers.

Nap Rucker, who had pitched a no-hitter himself seven years earlier, opposed Marquard. It was a great pitchers' duel, finally ending 2–0 in the Giants' favor.

Only three men reached first for Brooklyn, two on walks and one on an error by shortstop Art Fletcher, and only three balls were hit to the outfield. Marquard helped to win his own game by knocking in the second run.

That year, though, was the end of Marquard's career with the Giants. McGraw was unhappy with his pitching most of the time and finally gave Rube permission to make his own deal. Marquard phoned up Wilbert Robinson, manager of the Brooklyn team he had no hit earlier in the year, and told him a deal could be made for $7500, which it soon was. Baseball was simpler in those days.

When Jess Haines pitched a 5–0 no-hitter against Boston in St. Louis on July 17, 1924, it was a game of firsts: the first no-hit game of Haines' career, the first of the season, the first by a National League pitcher in St. Louis in modern history and the first at Sportsmans Park since Bob Groom had done it in 1917.

Haines walked three men in the game, striking out five, and was seldom in trouble. There were three occasions when it seemed the Braves might get a hit, but they came to naught.

In the second inning, James (Cotton) Tierney hit a drive to the left of St. Louis second baseman Rogers Hornsby and it seemed the ball might go through. But Hornsby stabbed it after it had bounced once off the infield and threw to first for the out.

In the third, Hornsby made another fine play when he grabbed a line drive by Gus Felix; in the eighth, a short fly by Mickey O'Neil almost fell in before St. Louis center fielder Wattie Holm was playing a shallow center and he grabbed the fly.

Haines breezed through the ninth, usually the toughest inning for a no-hit pitcher, on just six pitches. He got Felix to fly out on the first pitch, went to 1–2 on Bill Cunningham before Cunningham popped to James Cooney at shortstop.

Only one out remained and the batter was the ubiquitous Casey Stengel, a World Series hero with the Giants the previous fall before being traded to the Braves. Haines whipped the first pitch into the strike zone and Stengel swung, sending an easy grounder to Hornsby for the final out of the game.

No Hall of Fame pitcher ever got a later start than Dazzy Vance, who was 29 when he pitched his first full season in the majors of Brooklyn. Vance once said it would be impossible to trade him to a minor league where he didn't know somebody and he was probably right. He bounced around for years from one league to another before a manager discovered the key to success for Vance: he needed four days of rest instead of the normal three. Given that extra day of rest, he was overpowering.

Once he got to the majors, Vance made up for lost time, winning 20 or more games in three seasons and finishing with 197 wins in a career which did not end until he was 44. He had an exaggerated windup in which he threw his left leg higher than his head; Garry Schumacher, who saw both men as first a writer and then a public relations man, said that Vance and Juan Marichal had very similar windups.

With that motion, Vance poured in an overhand fastball which was one of the best of all time. Indeed, he set a National League record by leading the league in strikeouts for seven consecutive seasons, from his rookie year of 1922 through 1928.

His best season was 1924 when he won 28 games, had an earned run average of 2.16, completed 30 games and struck out 262 batters—all personal highs—but his no-hit game came a year later, on September 13, 1925.

There was an interesting prologue to that game. Vance had pitched a one-hitter in his previous start, against Philadelphia, when Philadelphia first baseman Nelson (Chicken) Hawks had dropped a short fly into right center for a single in the second inning. Hawks was caught stealing and no other Philadelphia batter reached first. Thus, Vance pitched to only 27 men, winning the game 1–0.

Five days later, Vance was scheduled to pitch again against the Phillies. Again, Vance's game was the first game of a doubleheader, and again, the game was played at Ebbets Field in Brooklyn. As Vance went to the pitching mound in the first inning, Philadelphia manager Art Fletcher yelled at him from the coach's box at first. "Well, you lucky stiff, you'll get no one-hitter today."

"I wouldn't be too sure about that, Art," Vance responded. "With these humpty-dumpties you've got, anything can happen."

And anything did. Unlike the previous Vance game against Philadelphia, this one was no contest. The Dodgers scored early and often, ten runs in all. The Phillies also got an unearned run in the second inning. Jimmy Johnston, usually an infielder but playing in left field in this game, made a two-base error on a fly by Hawks, then compounded his error by throwing wildly to second, allowing Hawks to take third. Barney Friberg followed with a sacrifice fly that scored Hawks.

Vance didn't have quite the perfect control of his first game against the Phils, walking one while striking out nine, but no Philadelphia player came within hailing distance of a hit until there were two out in the ninth. Then, Fred Leach smashed a curving liner down the left field line that nearly dropped in until Johnston redeemed himself for his earlier errors by making a fine running catch.

Vance had his no-hitter and Fletcher's prediction had come true, though possibly not in the form he had envisioned.

Ted Lyons, who pitched a no-hitter the following year, was a pitcher with two distinct careers, both with the Chicago White Sox. In his first career, he was a steady, everyday pitcher with a fine fastball who three times won 20 games in his first seven full seasons, though pitching for a weak ball club.

Then, Lyons hurt his shoulder while throwing a curve in a 1931 exhibition game at night in Texas. He was only 30 and in his pitching prime, but his arm never fully recovered after that. From 22 wins in 1930, he fell to four in 1931.

Lyons then taught himself a knuckle ball and managed to hang on for 12 full seasons; in fact, he even came back briefly in 1946 at the age of 45, long enough to pitch 42 innings. His shoulder-arm problems reduced both his effectiveness and his durability—he only three times again pitched more than 200 innings in a season and never won more than 15 games—but he was able to win 260 games in his career and pitch his way into the Hall of Fame.

He was in his prime, a three-year stretch in which he won 61 games, when he threw his no-hitter on August 21 in Boston against the Red Sox. He had come very close to a no-hitter the previous season against Washington, losing it when Bobby Veach singled with two outs in the ninth inning.

The game didn't start out well for Lyons as he walked the Boston leadoff hitter, Jack Tobin, but after that it was easy going. He didn't walk another man and the only other Red Sox baserunner was William (Baby Doll) Jacobson, who reached base with one out in the seventh when Chicago shortstop Bill Hunnefield, a rookie, fumbled his easy grounder. That broke a string of 19 straight retired by Lyons, but he then got the final eight in order, facing only 29 men in all.

Lyons, said an account of the day, "had such perfect control and so much stuff that apparently he could make the batters hit the ball exactly as he wished them to hit, and where the fielders had placed themselves to receive it."

There were only two tough chances, both ground balls hit to first baseman Earl Sheeley, on which Lyons had to cover first for the throw for the out.

The game was the first no-hitter in Boston since Johnson's game against the Red Sox six years earlier.

Carl Hubbell was the mirror image of Christy Mathewson for the Giants. Both were control specialists whose big pitch was the screwball. Hubbell, of course, won far fewer games—253 to 373—but he was also pitching in the lively ball era, when there was more strain on a pitcher's arm because a mistake could be hit out of the park, as it virtually never was in Mathewson's day.

The lefthanded Hubbell almost quit before he got a real start in the major leagues, because the Detroit Tigers, who owned his contract, thought little of his chances. Finally, he was traded to the New York Giants and he was a winner for them from his first year, 1928.

Hubbell was cautioned against throwing the screwball early in his career because it would hurt his arm and he didn't use it in his early days with the Giants. He threw it for the first time against Chick Hafey of the Cardinals on a 3–1 count. When Hafey missed his first screwball, Hubbell threw another and struck out the dangerous righthanded hitter. From that time, he threw the screwball frequently.

Along with his screwball, Hubbell had what baseball people regarded as unnatural control for a lefthander. "Such control in a left-hander is incredible," wrote Heywood Broun after a game in which Hubbell had not walked a man in ten innings. "There must be a skeleton in Hubbell's closet somewhere, such as a right-handed maternal grandmother."

The screwball did indeed hurt Hubbell's arm. As early as 1934, his left elbow would swell up after a game bacause of bone chips. In the 1933–37 stretch, he had five straight seasons with more than 20 wins and an overall total of 115, but he fell to 13 wins in 1938. An operation after the 1938 season failed to help him; he pitched five more years but won only 48 games.

Probably Hubbell's most noted feat was his performance in the 1934 All-Star game, only the second played. He gave up a single to leadoff hitter Charley Gehringer of the American League and walked Heinie Manush, but then struck out Babe Ruth, Lou Gehrig, Jimmy Foxx, Al Simmons and Joe Cronin in order.

Hubbell also had two great streaks. In 1933, he pitched 46⅓ consecutive scoreless innings; in 1936, he won 16 straight games at the end of the season; the next year, he won his first eight, as well.

Strangely, Hubbell's no-hitter came not in his great years but in 1929, his second season. It was a good year, during which he won 18 and lost 11, but not comparable to what was to come later.

The game was an easy one for Hubbell to win because the Giants got 11 runs, but not an easy one to pitch because the New York defense was not equal to the offense that day. Three Pittsburgh runners reached base on errors in the May 8, 1929, game and Hubbell also walked a man. Hubbell was in control of the game, however, with only six balls hit out of the infield all day.

In the ninth, the Giant defense became very nervous, though Hubbell remained cool. First, left fielder Chick Fullis misjudged and then dropped a liner off the bat of Harry Riconda. Then shortstop Travis Jackson fumbled a grounder by Sparky Adams and Hubbell was in a hole. The next two batters were the Waner brothers, Lloyd and Paul, "Little Poison" and "Big Poison." They were fearsome hitters, Paul finishing with a lifetime average of .333 and Lloyd with a .316 average, good enough to get both of them into the Hall of Fame eventually.

That didn't bother Hubbell, who first got Lloyd to take a called strike; it was one of only 173 strikeouts in Lloyd's 18-year major league career.

And then, Hubbell got Paul Waner to hit back to the box. Carl grabbed the grounder, fired to Jackson at second for the first out, then Jackson fired to first for the game-ending double play.

Hubbell, now an executive in the Giant organization, has a visible souvenir of his pitching days: Throwing the screwball, with its unnatural motion, twisted his left arm so much that, at rest, his palm faces outward. But that is a small price to pay for 253 major league wins and a no-hitter.

15

. . . And some who didn't

To pitch a no-hitter, a man needs both skill and luck: Some think the more important of the two is luck. Certainly, without luck, ability is not enough; some of the best pitchers of all time have not been able to pitch no-hitters.

Grover Cleveland Alexander, for one. In any discussion of great pitchers, Alexander's name always comes up; he is tied with Christy Mathewson at 373 for most wins by a National League pitcher.

Alexander had the most economical style of any of the great pitchers. His windup was brief, his stride short and he threw no more pitches than was absolutely necessary. He believed in making the batter hit the ball, on the first pitch if possible, rather than trying to strike everybody out. He wasted no time between pitches and once pitched a game in 58 minutes! He was an artist and other pitchers admired him as much as fans.

Alexander, who came to be known as "Old Pete" late in his career, was a winner from the start, breaking in with 28 wins for the Philadelphia Phillies in 1911, a total unmatched by a rookie since. He had a stretch of three seasons, 1915–1917, when he won at least 30 games each year, and he won 21 games in 1927, when he was 40. Not until his final year, when he was 43, did he have a losing season.

He did all this despite the twin handicaps of epilepsy and alcoholism. Alexander's drinking problem was well known throughout baseball, but his epileptic seizures were kept secret by the clubs for which he pitched. He apparently started having sei-

zures after his overseas service during World War I, but they
didn't become public knowledge until years later, when he would
sometimes be found unconscious in the streets.

His alcoholism caused him to be traded more frequently than
you would expect with a great pitcher. He was traded by the
Phillies, in fact, after the third of his 30-win seasons. The Chicago
Cubs traded him during the 1926 season to the St. Louis Cardinals, then he came back to the Phillies just long enough to lose
three games and win none in his final season.

In the winter of 1925–26, he checked into a sanitarium to cure
himself, but the cure didn't last. During and after his career, many
stories about Alexander pitching when he was drunk or hungover
were circulated and some of them may even have been true.

He lived 20 years after his career ended, but they were not
happy years. For a time he pitched for the House of David, some
semipro teams and worked with Hubert's Museum on West 42nd
Street in New York, which had a collection of novelty acts. He
made his last public appearance at the 1950 World Series, the first
one in which the Phillies had participated since he had pitched
them to a pennant in 1915.

A month later, Alexander died in a rented room in a boarding
house in St. Paul, Nebraska.

Alexander's pitching style was best suited to the pre-lively
ball era and his greatest years came then. But he was more than
just a product of his times. In the first year of the lively ball era,
1920, he won 27 games with an earned run average of 1.91; he
three times won 20 or more games in the lively ball era, though he
was past his physical prime.

It was during one of those years, too, that his single most
famous pitching exploit occurred. It came in the 1926 World
Series, when the Cardinals faced the Yankees. Alexander had
been traded during the year from Chicago because new Cub manager Joe McCarthy didn't think he could establish the proper team
discipline with Alexander around, breaking the rules whenever he
chose.

Down the stretch that year, Alexander won nine important
games for the Cardinals, and he won the second and sixth games
of the Series, though he was nearing his fortieth birthday. In the
seventh game, with two outs, the bases loaded and the Cardinals
ahead by only one run, 3–2, manager Rogers Hornsby called in
Alexander to face young slugger Tony Lazzeri.

The popular version of events is that Alexander was hungover
from a celebration the previous night. Alexander himself always
said that he had stayed sober the night before, at Hornsby's re-

quest. Since he made no attempt to apologize or cover up for his drinking problem, there is no reason to doubt Alexander's word.

Whatever the circumstances, it was a dramatic moment. Lazzeri took a ball and a strike and then exploded a drive into the left field seats, but foul. Alexander then struck out Lazzeri to end the threat and got the Yankees in the next two innings to save the win and the Series for the Cardinals.

Alexander's best year was probably 1915, when he won 31 games with an ERA of 1.22. He led the league that year in wins, winning percentage, ERA, complete games, innings pitched, strikeouts and shutouts. It was in 1915 that Alexander came closest to a no-hitter, too, as he pitched four one-hitters. In his career, he had five, and no National League pitcher since 1901 has done better. But the no-hitter always eluded him.

Lefty Grove is another name that always comes up in discussions of great pitchers. Grove was the first pitcher to win 300 games entirely in the lively ball era, and only two pitchers have done it since Grove won number 300 in 1941, Warren Spahn and Early Wynn. Grove lost only 141 games and his winning percentage of .680 is better than any other pitcher who has won 300 games.

Grove was an entirely different pitcher than Alexander, relying as he did chiefly on his fastball in his early career; in any discussion of fastball pitchers, Grove is usually mentioned with Walter Johnson, Bob Feller, Sandy Koufax and Nolan Ryan as the fastest of all time.

Nor did Grove get off to the same kind of start in the majors that Alexander had. Lefty had been a big winner for Baltimore of the International League (108 wins, 36 defeats in four years) and was sold to the Philadelphia Athletics for a then-record price of $100,600. Grove quickly learned that there was a substantial difference between the leagues. In the International League, Grove had simply fired his fastball and not worried about control, because if he walked a couple of batters, he could always strike out the next couple. In the American League, batters laid off his bad pitches and his frequent walks got him in trouble. He led the league in walks as a rookie and had only a 10–12 record.

Grove also had to learn to control his temper, which was fearsome. He would get so mad when he threw a bad pitch that he would throw the next one without thinking. Finally, he learned to slow down and to hold back his best fastball for critical situations. By his third season, he was a 20-game winner.

He went on to win at least 20 games for seven straight seasons and he also led the league in strikeouts for seven straight years, though only the first 5 of the 20-win seasons and the last 5 of the strikeout years coincided.

In 1930–31, Grove had the most remarkable pair of years of any pitcher in the lively ball era. In 1930, despite the hitting rampage that existed in both leagues, he won 28 and lost only 5. The next year he improved on that with a 31–4 record, winning 16 straight at one point to tie the American League record. Going for his seventeenth, he was beaten on a ninth-inning error, 1–0.

After the 1933 season, the last in his string of 20-win years, Grove was traded to the Boston Red Sox, with whom he finished his career. He hurt his arm in spring training that season and was never again the overpowering pitcher he had been in his youth, but he worked more on his curveball and added a fork ball, and he was in double figures in wins five seasons of his last eight. At the age of 41, he won game 300 and retired.

For all his success, though, Grove was never able to pitch a no-hit game.

There have been some eccentric baseball players, particularly in the early part of the century when the game was more relaxed and less competitive than it is now, but few of them have been outstanding players. On the major league level, players must concentrate and use their ability to full potential to become outstanding.

There are, however, two Hall of Fame pitchers who qualify as genuine eccentrics, one lefthanded and one righthanded: George Edward (Rube) Waddell and Jay Hanna (Dizzy) Dean.

Waddell was a country boy with immense talent who could not get serious about playing a game. He could not understand why he should not go chasing after a fire engine or go fishing when he chose to, even if his pitching turn was that day.

Rube was a great drinker, too. When he was with the Philadelphia Athletics, owner-manager Connie Mack used to pay him in dollar bills, trying to get Rube's money to go a little further; Mack knew if he paid Waddell his salary in a lump sum, it would be gone immediately.

Thus, Waddell seldom had drinking money, but that never stopped him. Sometimes he would claim to have lost his watch charm, a memento of the 1905 World Series, and Mack would have to pay a reward to get it back; a bartender always had it. At other times, Waddell would offer a bartender a baseball in return for drinks, the baseball supposedly being the one Waddell had used in pitching a 20-inning win over Cy Young.

At that, Waddell was no worse than his batter mate, catcher Ossee Schreckengost, who once showed his anger at being served a tough steak by nailing it to the restaurant wall.

Waddell for a brief time even played football, as Mack coached a pro football team in 1902, after the baseball season had ended. One night, Waddell came back to the team hotel, having stopped into at least one bar en route. Mack persuaded him to go to bed immediately. As Rube came to the desk for his room key, he pulled his handkerchief from his pocket. When he did, a loaded revolver fell from his pocket and went off, the bullet going into the office wall and fortunately not hitting anyone. The shaken Mack could only say, "That man is unpredictable."

With all his eccentricities, Waddell was a brilliant pitcher in his prime. He held the major league strikeout record for 42 years and, in a sense, even longer. Early baseball records are very skimpy and Waddell was originally credited with 343 strikeouts in 1904, a mark surpassed by Bob Feller's 348 in 1946. Historians since have credited Waddell with 349 that year. Both marks have since been surpassed by Sandy Koufax and Nolan Ryan.

His best years were 1902–05 when he won in succession 25, 21, 25 and 24. The last year would have been his best except for an incident on a train leaving Boston after the game of September 1. Rube was having a fine time going through the train smashing straw hats, an example of baseball humor of the day. Pitcher Andy Coakley, having been warned, swung a canvas bag at Waddell and knocked him down.

Waddell bruised his shoulder and could pitch no more that season, not even in the World Series. He never again won 20 games in a season, leaving the majors after the 1910 season, just short of his thirty-fourth birthday. He died at 38 of tuberculosis.

Waddell twice came close to no-hit games. The first came in 1904. The first Boston batter, Patsy Dougherty, beat out a bunt for a hit, but Rube then retired the next 27 men.

The next chance came a year later and it was even more of a heartbreaker. For five innings, Rube did not allow a hit and struck out nine, but then rain stopped the game with Philadelphia ahead 2–0, so Waddell did not get credit for a no-hitter.

Dizzy Dean—the nickname came for the obvious reason —was an original, first as a player and then in the broadcast booth. There has always been considerable question about his name and birthplace because he never liked to tell the same story twice; he wanted each sportswriter to have an exclusive story. Sometimes he said his name was Jay Hanna Dean, other times it was Jerome Herman Dean. It didn't matter, because everybody called him Dizzy.

Even in the World Series, Dizzy found it hard to be serious about the game. Before the last game of the '34 Series, for instance, he watched Detroit pitcher Eldon Auker warm up for some time and then yelled at Detroit manager Mickey Cochrane, "Is he gonna pitch? Is he the best ya got?" He then walked to the Cardinal bench muttering, "Won't do. Won't do."

He turned out to be entirely correct, as the Cardinals—behind Dean—beat the Tigers 11–0.

Before that same Series, the Tigers were engaging in a workout. Just as they finished batting practice, Dean came out in civilian clothes, took a bat from the Detroit player at the plate and hit a pitch into the outfield. Then he walked away and told the Tigers, "That's the way to do it, fellas!"

Frisch didn't mind when Dean pulled stunts like that, but others bothered him more. There were, for instance, Dean's periodic threats to quit the game. There was the time Dean was thrown out of the game for fighting and called umpire George Barr and National League President Ford Frick "a couple of crooks," a statement which got him suspended.

Dean also would occasionally tell opposing teams exactly how he would pitch to each batter. On another occasion, Dizzy walked by the Boston Braves bench and announced, "I'm throwing nuthin' but curve balls today, fellas. No fast balls." He kept his word—and he won the game.

He could do this because he had great ability and a sense of what was happening on the baseball field that was almost instinctive. He won 30 games in 1934; no pitcher did that again until 1968, when Denny McLain won 31. His time as a top pitcher was brief, because he hurt his arm trying to pitch after his toe had been fractured by an Earl Averill line drive in the 1937 All-Star Game, but nobody was better when he was at the top of his form.

Dean's pitching style probably kept him from getting a no-hitter, because he bore down only when he had to. He claimed he passed up the chance at several no-hitters just for the fun of it. That is an example of the Dean hyperbole, but there was at least one occasion when it might have been true.

On September 21, 1934, the Cardinals played a doubleheader against the Brooklyn Dodgers at Ebbets Field. The Cards were going down to the wire with the New York Giants—they eventually won the pennant by two games—and they needed both of these games. Frisch had Dean and his younger brother, Paul, ready for the doubleheader.

In the first game, Dizzy was in control all the way. He had a 7–0 lead as early as the third and finally won by 13–0. For seven innings he had a no-hitter, but he relaxed with that big lead and gave up three hits in the last two innings.

It was Paul's turn in the second game. Two years younger

than Dizzy, Paul was also inferior in pitching ability, but he had won 19 games in 1933 and added another 19 in 1934. This gave the Dean brothers a total of 49 for the season, more than half the 95 St. Louis wins.

Paul was even better than his brother on this day, though. He got the first two batters, Buzz Boyle and Lonnie Frey, in the first inning, then walked Len Koenecke. That was the last time a Dodger reached base as Paul retired the next 25 men in order for a no-hitter.

After the game, Dizzy congratulated his brother and then said, "Shucks, Paul, if I'da knowed you wuz gonna pitch a no-hitter, I'da throwed one myself."

There have been other great pitchers who have not pitched no-hit games. Kid Nichols, the first to use the "no-windup" style, won 360 games, most of them before the turn of the century, for the Boston Braves. He won 20 or more games his first ten years, 30 or more in seven of those years, but not one of them was a no-hitter.

Jack Chesbro won 41 games in 1904, the modern record, but could not pitch a no-hitter; Eddie Plank won 325 games, the record for a lefthander until Warren Spahn came along, but could not get a no-hitter; Early Wynn won 300 games, only the third to do that in the lively ball era, but not one was a no-hitter; Stan Coveleskie won 217 games and won three games in the 1920 World Series, but he could not pitch a no-hitter.

Red Ruffing (273 wins), Burleigh Grimes (270), Eppa Rixey (266), Urban (Red) Faber (254), Herb Pennock (240), Three-Fingers Brown (239), Waite Hoyt (237), Whitey Ford (236) and Lefty Gomez (189) are all in the Hall of Fame, but none of them ever pitched a no-hitter. Clearly, ability alone is not enough.

16

Two of a kind

The year 1905 was one of some remarkable ptiching accomplishments. Christy Mathewson won 31 games —one of them his second no-hitter—and then followed with three shutouts in the World Series. Rube Waddell won 24 games, even though he missed the final month of the season entirely.

In the American League, pitchers were so effective that only two hitters averaged more than .300 for the season. The pitching staff of the Chicago White Sox had a starting cumulative earned run average of 1.99; yet, the White Sox could only finish second. So much for pitching being 90 per cent of the game.

It was not surprising that a White Sox pitcher threw a no-hitter that year, on September 6 in Detroit against the Tigers. The surprising thing was that the White Sox scored 15 runs, about four games worth for them under normal circumstances.

The White Sox had won the first game of a doubleheader that day, 2–0, when Frank Smith took the mound and set the Tigers down hitless. Smith walked three men and all three were left on base. There were no difficult chances for the Chicago defense.

Frank Smith was a solid, but seldom spectacular, pitcher throughout his career. He won 136 games and had two 20-win seasons, but this was in a period when 20 wins were easier to come by than they are now.

In 1905, Smith won 19 games and lost 13, with an earned run average of 2.13. By modern standards, that would be an excellent year. By the standards of his time, it was scarcely above average. In that dead ball era, teams could get by with fewer pitchers because the pitchers could pace themselves, knowing that even if they gave up a couple of hits, they could bear down to keep the other team from scoring. Home runs were a rarity; the entire Chicago team hit only 11 that year and the league-leading team total was Boston's 29. Thus, the White Sox staff numbered only six that year: Smith was third in wins in the staff and fifth in ERA.

Still, he did pitch a no-hitter, which no other Chicago pitcher did that year, and he pitched another in 1908, on September 20 against the Philadelphia Athletics at Chicago. Unlike his first no-hitter, when he had been eight runs ahead before he even took the mound in the first inning, Smith had to pitch his best to win this game.

His pitching opponent was Eddie Plank—one of the Hall of Fame pitchers who never got a no-hitter—and Plank and Smith matched scoreless innings until the bottom of the ninth. Then, Frank Isbell beat out an infield hit, went to second on a wild pitch, to third on a passed ball and scored on an infield grounder for the only run of the game.

Smith's second no-hitter was a better game than his first one because he walked only one man. One other Philadelphia batter had reached first in an error by first baseman Isbell.

Thus, Smith became one of only 18 pitchers to throw two or more no-hitters in the years 1901–74, and only two pitchers did it before him—Mathewson and Cy Young.

The others who have done it—most of them covered in other chapters—are Addie Joss, Tom Hughes, Dutch Leonard, Johnny Vander Meer, Bob Feller, Allie Reynolds, Virgil Trucks, Carl Erskine, Warren Spahn, Sandy Koufax, Jim Bunning, Jim Maloney, Don Wilson, Ken Holtzman and Nolan Ryan.

As we have seen, anybody good enough to make the major leagues can throw one no-hitter, but throwing two usually separates the good from the mediocre. Hughes is the only one on the list above to win less than 100 games in his major league career; there are five Hall of Fame pitchers on it.

The next one to turn the trick after Smith was Joss: His second no-hitter was almost an anticlimax after his great perfect game battle with Ed Walsh in 1908. On April 20, 1910, at Chicago, Joss pitched Cleveland to a 1–0 win over the White Sox and did not allow a hit. The Indians got seven hits and scored the only run they needed in the sixth.

Joss walked two in this game and another man reached base on an error. One Chicago baserunner was out stealing, so Joss faced only 29 batters. An oddity of the game was that Joss had ten assists; two of them came on strikeouts, so he had eight fielding chances. It was a busy day.

For Hughes, too, the second no-hitter was not as dramatic as the first, though for different reasons than Joss's. On August 30, 1910, Hughes had pitched a no-hitter for 9⅓ innings, for New York against Cleveland, only to lose the no-hitter in the tenth and the game in the eleventh, 5–0.

The second time around, Hughes was luckier. In 1915–16, Hughes enjoyed the only good years of an otherwise mediocre career, winning 20 games and then 16, and he capped that with a no-hitter on June 16, 1916, at Boston. By now, he was pitching for the Braves against the Pittsburgh Pirates.

Hughes got the one run he needed so badly in his first no-hitter in the first inning of this game; the Braves added another in the eighth to make the final score 2–0. Meanwhile, Hughes was in command, walking only two and striking out seven.

Hughes was the joker in the two no-hit game deck, winning only 58 games in his career; he didn't have much else going for him, but he did have the no-hit knack.

There have been two men known as Dutch Leonard in baseball pitching history. The second, Emil (Dutch) Leonard was the better pitcher, with 191 career wins in a career which stretched 20 years.

The first Dutch Leonard—who started life as Hubert Benjamin Leonard in Birmingham, Ohio—was the one who pitched the no-hitters, two of them in fact.

Leonard's best year, when he won 18 games, was 1916, and fittingly, that was when he pitched his first no-hitter, on August 30 at Boston against the St. Louis Browns.

Oddly, Leonard had been knocked out of the first game of a doubleheader against the Browns the previous day in the first inning. Apparently reasoning that Leonard's arm would still be fresh the next day, Boston manager Bill Carrigan came back with Leonard. Carrigan never had a better idea.

The Red Sox got two runs in the second inning and another two in the sixth to remove any doubt about the game's outcome. Meanwhile, Leonard was pitching a perfect game until the eighth inning, when he walked Hank Severeid. In the ninth, he walked pinchhitter Grover Hartley; Severeid and Hartley were the only St. Louis baserunners. Leonard struck out three. For the most part, Leonard got the Browns to pop up and there were only three hard chances for the Boston defense in the game.

Leonard's second no-hitter was even more impressive than his first. This one came on June 3, 1918, in Detroit against a Tigers team which included Ty Cobb, who hit .382 that season. This time Leonard gave up only one walk, to Bobby Veach, as he struck out four.

Double no-hitters, like other unusual feats, follow unusual patterns. From the time Leonard threw his second no-hitter, there wasn't another pitcher who threw two until Johnny Vander Meer's back-to-back no-hitters 20 years later, in 1938.

There was another eight-year hiatus, until Bob Feller threw his second no-hitter in 1946, then there was a rash of double no-hitters. Feller, in fact, got his third no-hitter in 1951 and Allie Reynolds pitched two that same year. The next year, Virgil Trucks got two and Carl Erskine got his first no-hitter, to be followed by a second in 1956.

For the Brooklyn Dodgers, 1952 was the year they had to win. In 1950, they had lost the National League pennant on the final day of the season to a Philadelphia team that should not have been close to the Dodgers by then. In 1951, they had had a lead which reached 13½ games between games of a doubleheader in early August, and yet they had lost the pennant in baseball's most dramatic playoff to the New York Giants. In 1952, they had something to prove, to themselves as well as to others, and they did, winning the pennant by 4½ games over the Giants.

In those days, when they played in cozy Ebbets Field, the Dodgers' strength was their hitting; they could send Jackie Robinson, Gil Hodges, Duke Snider, Roy Campanella, Carl Furillo and Pee Wee Reese to the plate: That scared a few pitchers.

But the fences that made it so easy for the Dodger hitters also put a great strain on the Dodger pitchers; nobody could tell you more about that than Carl Erskine. For 12 major league seasons, Erskine threw every pitch knowing it had to be his best if he didn't want to see it going over or off one of the fences.

He paid a stiff price. For most of his career, every time Erskine threw his overhand curve, he had a sharp pain in his elbow, but he kept throwing it because it was his best pitch. One time he went to a surgeon at Johns Hopkins and was told that he should pitch sidearm. "But the only way I could get velocity and a good break was to come straight over," Erskine told Roger Kahn many years later. "Saying pitch sidearm was really telling me don't pitch. I kept pitching overhand and it kept hurting, but I got a dozen years in the big leagues."

For six straight years, 1951–56, Erskine was the steady man in the Brooklyn pitching rotation, winning in double figures every year during that stretch. He won 20 games once and he set a World Series strikeout record of 14 in a 1953 Series game against the Yankees, but probably his most significant accomplishment was pitching two no-hitters in Ebbets Field.

The first one, on June 19, 1952, was also his best. He had

gone into the game with a 5–1 record, but he hadn't completed a game in more than a month, since May 11. Pitching against the Chicago Cubs on this day, however, he was in complete control.

The Dodgers got Erskine working room immediately with three runs in the first inning, as Campanella and Furillo hit home runs off Chicago starter Warren Hacker. Andy Pafko got another home run in the second inning to knock out Hacker and bring in knuckleball reliever Willard Ramsdell, who was to figure in the dramatics of the game.

Erskine got the first eight Chicago batters, then Ramsdell came to the plate. Ramsdell, who had ironically started his major league career with the Dodgers, was one of those pitchers who batted only because the rules called for it; in 1952, he had just one hit in 19 at-bats.

But Erskine's control, which was otherwise excellent, suddenly left him and he walked Ramsdell on four straight pitches. That spoiled his chance to pitch a perfect game, a thought which was probably not in his mind, anyway, at that early stage. He then retired leadoff hitter Eddie Miksis to end the inning.

After Bob Addis came to the plate as the first Cub batter in the fourth inning, a thunderstorm hit the field and stopped play. For a time, it seemed Erskine's no-hitter—and the Dodgers' win—would be swept away in the storm. But then it stopped as suddenly as it had started and the game was continued after a 40-minute delay.

Often, a pitcher loses his effectiveness after such a long delay, but that didn't happen to Erskine. He got the next 19 men in succession for his no-hitter and there were only a few times when there was any doubt. Third baseman Bobby Morgan made two excellent plays and Furillo twice caught fly balls against the right field fence, the first by Ransom Jackson in the fifth and the second by Hank Sauer in the seventh. Only five balls were hit to the outfield; Erskine had learned the hard way that the key to success in Ebbets Field was making batters hit the ball on the ground.

Erskine threw 103 pitches, most of them curves. For once, the pain didn't bother him.

By 1956, Erskine was fading as a front-line pitcher; he won 13 games that year, his last in double figures. When he took the mound against the Dodgers' most hated rivals, the Giants, he was only 1–2, and the losses had come in his last two starts. But from the start, there was a different feeling about this game. In the clubhouse, shortstop and team captain Pee Wee Reese told Erskine he had a premonition that Carl would win this game.

Erskine's chance at a perfect game evaporated as early as the third batter, when he walked the dangerous Willie Mays before getting Dusty Rhodes out to end the inning.

In the second inning, with one out, Bill White sent a long drive over the right field fence, but it was a foul. Erskine then got White and Foster Castleman to end the inning.

In the third, the Giants went down 1–2–3. The Dodgers finally broke through for their first run of the game, on a walk to Reese, a single by Snider and walks to Hodges and Robinson.

Then, the Giants threatened in the top of the fourth. Alvin Dark walked as the leadoff hitter, then Mays slashed a drive that seemed headed down the left field line until Robinson made a diving catch. At the time, the catch seemed important because it had stopped a rally, not because it had saved a no-hitter; it was still early to be thinking of that.

Brooklyn scored twice more in the seventh on a single by Reese, a double by Snider and a single by Campanella. Meanwhile, Erskine was setting the Giants down 1–2–3 with very little trouble; the only tough play behind him had come in the fifth when Furillo had raced to the scoreboard in right center to make a catch of a fly ball hit by Ray Katt.

Erskine went into the ninth with that 3–0 lead, having retired 15 batters in a row. The first batter was George Wilson, pinchhitting for Giant reliever Marv Grisson. Wilson fouled out. That brought up Whitey Lockman and Lockman scared Erskine by lining a pitch over the right field wall—but foul by inches. Erskine settled down to get Lockman and only one out remained.

The batter was Dark and Erskine was particularly wary of pitching to Dark. "He's a very hard man to pitch to because he's a slap-hitter and can hit different pitches," Carl said later. His first pitch to Dark was a little too good and Dark hit a sharp foul wide of first base. That was the last good pitch he saw, however, as Erskine got Dark for the final out and his second no-hitter.

That was almost the last moment of glory for Erskine. Though he pitched three more seasons after 1956, he won only nine games in that span. Two months short of his thirty-third birthday, when he should have been in his pitching prime, he walked into the office of general manager E. J. (Buzzie) Bavasi and said he was quitting. The pain was no longer worth it. He had pitched 12 major league seasons and had some rich memories—including that of two no-hitters.

Another spate of double no-hitters started in the '60s, as Warren Spahn threw his two in 1960 and 1961. Sandy Koufax threw no-hitters in successive years in 1962, '63, '64 and '65.

Jim Bunning got his second in 1964, a perfect game, after

pitching his first in 1958; Jim Maloney got two in 1965; Don Wilson got two in 1967 and 1969; and Ken Holtzman pitched no-hitters in 1969 and 1971.

Holtzman had signed for an estimated $70,000 bonus with the Chicago Cubs, enough to make it worthwhile to cut short his college career, but he showed only sporadic flashes of brilliance in his first four years with the club. One year, 1967, he had been undefeated in nine decisions in a year cut short by National Guard duty, but overall, he was only 31–30 going into the 1969 season.

Ken had had trouble because of his inability to get along with Cub manager Leo Durocher, which hardly made Holtzman unique. An intelligent man, Holtzman didn't feel that Durocher's policy of instilling fear in his players was the best way to manage.

In addition, Holtzman could not feel confident in his home park, Wrigley Field, where the wind often turned what should have been easy fly balls into home runs. His best pitch was his fastball, which he could cause to break in different directions, depending how he held it, but he was forced to use breaking pitches more than he liked in an attempt to cut down on home runs.

Twice in his early career, Holtzman had flirted with no-hitters. In 1966, he had a no-hitter through eight innings against the Dodgers and Koufax but then settled for a 2–1 win. On June 28, 1969, he had pitched seven perfect innings against St. Louis, but he eventually lost the no-hitter and the game 2–0.

As he warmed up for an August 19 game in Wrigley Field against the Atlanta Braves, Holtzman noticed two things, one good, one bad. The wind was blowing in, which meant he had a much better chance than usual of keeping the ball in the park; but he had no control of his curve and change-up and would have to stick almost entirely with his fastball.

His fastball was enough, though just barely in one case. In the seventh, Hank Aaron drove one deep to left field, but the wind held it up just long enough to enable left fielder Billy Williams to make a leaping catch just off the ivy on the wall.

Chicago third baseman Ron Santo accounted for all the scoring when he hit a three-run homer off Phil Niekro in the first inning, and Holtzman's infield helped him three times on defense. Twice, second baseman Glenn Beckert made fine plays on grounders by Felipe Alou; shortstop Don Kessinger made a good play on a Niekro grounder.

Probably the most unusual aspect of the no-hitter was that Holtzman did not strike out a batter, although at that time of his career, he was averaging about six strikeouts a game.

Holtzman came close to another no-hitter in a most unusual

game in 1970. Pitching against the San Francisco Giants, Ken had a 9–0 lead after two innings and eventually won 15–0. With that kind of lead, pitchers almost always relax, but Holtzman had a no-hitter going until, with no one out in the eighth, the weak-hitting Hal Lanier singled.

Holtzman's first no-hitter had come in the stretch of a pennant race. The Cubs were leading the National League East at the time, though they were later passed by the Mets.

The second no-hitter, pitched against the Reds at Cincinnati on June 3, 1971, was a different matter. The Cubs were going nowhere; they eventually finished tied for third in a six-team division. The Reds were going in the same direction; they eventually tied for fourth in their division. And Holtzman was going nowhere but out of town at the end of the season; he had a dismal 2–6 record and a 5.40 earned run average going into the game.

There was one good omen, though: Just as in his first no-hitter, Holtzman had no luck with his curve and thus was forced to rely on the fastball, always his best pitch. This time, he struck out six while walking four.

Holtzman also scored the only run of the game in the third. He reached base on Tony Perez's throwing error, moved to second on an infield out by Kessinger and scored on a single to right center by Beckert.

Only twice was Holtzman's no-hitter in danger. In the seventh, second baseman Becker threw out the slow Tony Perez on a grounder just to the right of second base. Also in the seventh, Johnny Bench surprised Holtzman with a bunt, and for a moment Holtzman thought it would be a hit.

"When I got over there, though," he said later, "I saw the ball was spinning and knew it would roll foul."

The Cincinnati fans behind the dugout told Holtzman from the fifth inning on that the Reds would break up his no-hitter, but by the ninth, they were all cheering for Holtzman.

The ninth was no more difficult for Holtzman than the previous eight innings. He got Hal McRae to fly out for the first out, and then struck out Tommy Helms and Lee May to end the game.

It would be nice to think that game turned Holtzman's season around, but that kind of thing happens only in juvenile novels. Fast tiring of the constant battle with manager Durocher, he won only 9 games and lost 15 that season, with a 4.48 ERA. He was traded to Oakland after the season for Rick Monday.

That was the break of his career. Taking a cue from his no-hit games, Holtzman relied more and more on his fastball as he won 19, 21 and 19 games in his first three seasons with the A's—and the A's won three straight World Series. Better the Cubs should have traded Durocher. After all, Leo couldn't throw a no-hitter.

Somewhere in here, there has to be a mention of Sad Sam Jones II, who was kept from a three no-hitter career—two of them in a single season—only because of weather, an incompetent shortstop and a stubborn scorekeeper. Sam didn't get his nickname from these circumstances, but he could have.

As in the case of the Leonards, there were two Sad Sam Joneses, the alliteration irresistible to two generations of baseball writers. The first Sad Sam had a lengthy and productive career, stretching from 1914 through 1935. In his 22-year career he won 229 games: One of them was a no-hitter, on September 4, 1923, for the New York Yankees against the Philadelphia Athletics.

It is, however, the second Sad Sam we are concerned with here. This Sad Sam, also known as Toothpick Sam because of his habit of pitching with a toothpick in his mouth, got a late start in the majors. He had overpowering stuff, a lively fastball and a fast curve that had righthanded batters continually backing away from the plate, but he also had control problems. Because of that, he was almost 30 when he had his first full season in the majors, with the Chicago Cubs in 1955—and he led the National League in both walks and strikeouts that season.

In 1955, Jones also pitched his only nine-inning no-hitter on May 12 against the Pittsburgh Pirates, the first at Wrigley Field since the double no-hitter between Fred Toney and Jim Vaughn on May 2, 1917.

The Pirates gave Jones little trouble at any time. The closest they came to a hit was in the seventh when Dick Groat hit a liner back to the box that was deflected by Jones. It went directly to Gene Baker at second, who made the play. The Pirates hit only five balls to the outfield and center fielder Eddie Miksis made excellent catches on two of them.

Jones's main tormentor was himself. As always, he was wild. In the early innings, he could not control his curve at all, but it came around late in the game and catcher Clyde McCullough later called it the best curve he had ever caught. Through the first eight innings, Jones walked four and had one wild pitch, but the Chicago defense helped to protect his no-hitter and his lead with two double plays.

Going into the top of the ninth, Jones had a 4–0 lead. There is always enough excitement for anybody in a no-hit game, but Jones compounded it by walking the first three men to face him, Ed Freese, pinchhitter Preston Ward and Tom Saffell. Manager Stan Hack and the Chicago infielders huddled around Jones after the third straight walk, trying to calm him down. Though he didn't tell Jones at the time, Hack later said he certainly would have yanked Sam if he had walked one more batter.

Fortunately for both men, Hack never had to make that decision. Facing the heart of the Pittsburgh batting order—Groat, Roberto Clemente and Frank Thomas—Jones simply poured his fastball through the center of the plate and struck out all three men with just ten pitches.

Jones had once pitched three no-hitters in semipro ball in one year, 1949, but this was his first professional no-hitter. Officially, he never pitched another, but he came maddeningly close twice in 1959.

The San Francisco Giants had traded first baseman Bill White to the St. Louis Cardinals for Jones before the 1959 season in one of those trades that benefit both teams. White went on to a long and productive career, but the Giants had been well supplied at first base with Orlando Cepeda and Willie McCovey available. They needed pitching to make a run for the pennant and they thought Jones could provide it. They were right. Sad Sam won 21 games and saved another 4 in relief in his best year; it was not his fault the Giants finished in third place, a last week collapse erasing a two-game lead with eight games remaining.

One of the reasons the Giants lost the pennant that year was owner Horace Stoneham's quixotic belief that a former cricket player named Andre Rodgers could be made into a major league shortstop. Rodgers had the size—6 feet, 3 inches, 200 pounds—and the reflexes to play the game, but his lack of experience was too much of a handicap for him to overcome. Though the Giants had a good fielding shortstop available, Ed Bressoud, Rodgers played 66 games at shortstop that year and made critical errors when he played.

Unfortunately for Jones, Rodgers was at shortstop when the Giants played the Dodgers in a June 30 game in Los Angeles. Sam held the Dodgers hitless for seven innings, then fanned Don Zimmer and Ron Fairly to start the eighth. Jim Gilliam tapped a grounder that bounced over Jones's head. Rodgers, moving to his left, fielded the ball but it slipped out of his hands and he could not make a throw.

The official scorer, Charlie Park, called it a hit, ruling that Gilliam would have beaten the throw even if the ball had been fielded cleanly. The fans booed and many writers disagreed with Park, but the decision stood—even after Rodgers said it should have been an error. Jones ended the game with a 2–0 one-hitter.

Less than three months later, on September 26, Jones was back in the no-hit groove against the Cardinals in St. Louis. This was his last start of the season, as the Giants tried vainly to catch the Dodgers and Braves, who were to finish in a tie that was resolved when the Dodgers won two straight playoff games.

Jones was magnificent as a storm raced toward Busch Stadium. He walked Joe Cunningham in the first and Alex Grammas in the sixth, but did not give up a hit for seven innings. Only one runner, Grammas, reached second.

Meanwhile, he was getting plenty of support as Willie Mays hit his thirty-fourth homer and McCovey his thirteenth, the Giants scoring four runs. Then, with the Giants batting and two outs in the top of the eighth, the storm hit the stadium. Wind-lashed rains swept through the stands and the field; plate umpire Frank Dascoli called time.

For an hour and 37 minutes, Jones waited in the Giants' dugout, looking up at the black sky. Every time there was a letup in the rain, he would mutter, "Let's play ball," to nobody in particular. Finally, it was obvious the game could not be continued and Dascoli called it. The Giants won the game, but Jones did not get his no-hitter.

Chewing on his toothpick after the game, Jones tried to shrug off his disappointment, saying, "I'm not choosey. It was a big one and kept us going." He admitted the obvious, though: He had wanted to finish the game.

With a little bit of luck, Sad Sam Jones could have been the second pitcher to throw three no-hitters in a career and the fourth to throw two no-hitters in the same season. Instead, he didn't get credit for even one no-hitter in 1959. The breaks even out? You'd never have convinced Sad Sam Jones of that.

17

The might-have-beens:
Barney and Blackwell

There have been several no-hit pitchers who have not lived up to their early promise, but probably no two were more disappointing than Rex Barney and Ewell Blackwell. Barney and Blackwell both came up in the mid-1940s; both were right-handers with extraordinary speed; both seemed for a time on the way to excellent careers. It didn't happen. Blackwell had one great season and two good ones, Barney had only one good season; then, for different reasons, they faded out of the majors. The saddest words in sports: what might have been.

Barney came to the Brooklyn Dodgers in the war year of 1943 when he was only 18 and he impressed everybody with his speed and wildness. Later, New York sportswriter Dick Young was to say of Barney, "He'd be a great pitcher if the plate were high and outside."

The Dodgers were patient with Barney because they knew it was unreasonable to expect good control from a pitcher so fast and so young. Barney was probably only a shade wilder than Bob Feller had been at that age. So, the Dodgers brought Barney along slowly in '43, '46 and '47, and he seemed to be gradually gaining control of his awesome fastball.

By 1948, Barney's development had accelerated and he had a good season that seemed to promise a bright future. He won 15 games for the Dodgers, with an earned run average of 3.10. He gave up only 193 hits in 246²/₃ innings and, most important, walked 122. For another pitcher, that would have been a lot, but it was a considerable improvement over Barney's ratio of nearly one walk per inning during his first three seasons in Brooklyn.

As if to confirm that he had come of age, Barney narrowly missed a no-hitter on August 18 in Philadelphia, when Ralph Caballero's fifth-inning single was the only hit by the Phillies.

Less than a month later, Barney got another opportunity, this one on September 9 against the Giants in the Polo Grounds, and he won a 2–0 no-hitter.

The day did not start out well for Barney. Rain delayed the start of the game for 56 minutes, then the big righthander almost pitched himself out of the game in the first inning: He loaded the bases with one out on two walks and his own error. Willard Marshall then hit into a double play to end the inning and Barney was on his way.

In the third inning, Giant pitcher Monte Kennedy hit a roller to second that Jackie Robinson fumbled. But then Barney grabbed a ball hit by Jack Lohrke to the mound and turned it into a double play, to shortstop Pee Wee Reese and then to first baseman Gil Hodges.

The next batter, Whitey Lockman, grounded out to Hodges to end the inning and the Giants never got another baserunner. For the next six innings, Barney alternated his fastball, curve and change and got the Giants 1–2–3 each inning. He eventually faced only 29 batters, 4 of whom he struck out. He threw 116 pitches, a low nine-inning total for him.

The rain returned sporadically during the sixth, eighth and ninth innings, but it was not enough to stop either the game or Barney. In the eighth, Barney saved his no-hitter with a good fielding play. Pinchhitter Lonnie Frey hit a two-out chopper between first and home and Barney bounded off the mound to make the play just in time.

In the ninth, Joey Lafata pinchhit for Kennedy and struck out. Lohrke then popped to Hodges, and only one out remained. It was an easy one. Barney got Lockman to foul a ball back toward the screen and catcher Bruce Edwards raced back to catch it and end the game.

Mysteriously, that was virtually the last moment of glory for Barney. The idea that he was acquiring control turned out to be an illusion. The next year, he slipped to a 9–8 record as he gave up 89 walks in $140^2/_3$ innings; in 1950, he walked 48 batters in just $33^2/_3$ innings. That season was his last in the majors: Not yet 26, he was washed up after only 35 wins—and one no-hitter.

Blackwell's case was even sadder because only ill health kept him from a great career. In his brief prime, from 1947 through

1951, he was generally regarded by the hitters who had to face him as the best pitcher in the league, though his statistics don't support that claim.

Known as "The Whip" because of his sidearm delivery, Blackwell was a terrifying sight to righthanded hitters, particularly in his prime. At 6 feet, 6 inches and perhaps 185 pounds, he seemed to be all arms and legs as he released his fastball from somewhere in the region of third base. Dodger shortstop Pee Wee Reese once described Blackwell's pitching style succinctly: "He pitches like a guy falling out of a tree."

Blackwell was signed by Cincinnati in 1942 and, after spending some time in early season with the Reds, went to Syracuse of the International League. He won 16 games for Syracuse during the season, then pitched three shutouts in the playoffs and added another three scoreless innings in relief.

He didn't get a chance to pitch in the majors again until 1946, because he went off to war. He saw enough action to pick up two battle stars and then, after VE Day, pitched his outfit, the 71st Division, into the European Theater championship. He won 16 games, including 4 no-hitters.

The Reds thus expected great things of Blackwell when he arrived, but his first year, 1946, was disappointing. He was only 9–13, though six of his wins were shutouts, a league-leading figure.

In 1947, Blackwell had the kind of year everybody had expected of him: He won 22 and lost only 8 for a team which finished fifth in an eight-team league. No other Cincinnati pitcher won more than ten games that year.

Blackwell started slowly and by May 10, he was only 2–2. He then won 16 straight games with some incredible pitching. In all, he pitched 18 games between May 10 and July 30. Seventeen of those games were complete; he was relieved once, by Harry Gumbert, and though the Reds won the game, he did not get credit for the win. In the game which finally snapped the string, he was ahead 4–3 in the ninth, when Willard Marshall hit a home run to tie the score. The Giants went on to win the game in the tenth.

In that stretch, Blackwell had only one sloppy game, a 10–6 win over Philadelphia; that was also the only game in that stretch in which the Reds scored in double figures. He had an earned run average of 1.88 in those 18 games and 5 of his 16 wins were shutouts.

And one of the shutouts was a 6–0 no-hitter, on June 18 in Cincinnati against the Boston Braves.

The no-hitter was Blackwell's eighth consecutive win and the first game he had pitched at night during the season. He had said he thought he would be more effective at night than in the day-time, and he proved his point.

The Braves were the hardest-hitting team in the league going into the game, with 52 hits and 42 runs in their previous four games, but Blackwell quickly taught them humility. He walked four batters, but only three balls were hit hard during the nine innings.

Babe Young, a newly acquired first baseman, made it easy for Blackwell by hitting a three-run homer in the first and then duplicating that feat in the eighth.

In the ninth inning, everyone in Crosley Field was aware that Blackwell had a no-hitter going—except third baseman Grady Hatton, who shared an apartment with Blackwell in Cincinnati. Hatton had been on base every time he had been up that night and he simply did not realize what his friend was doing.

With two outs in the ninth, 'Bama Rowell was at bat for Boston. Hatton strolled to the mound and told Blackwell to throw one down the middle. "He'll either hit it out of the park or one of us will catch it," Hatton told Blackwell, who looked at him strangely. Blackwell then struck out Rowell to end the game and the roar from the crowd of 18,137 finally told Hatton what had happened.

The next time out, Blackwell faced the Brooklyn Dodgers. A comparison with Johnny Vander Meer's double no-hitter in 1938 was inevitable: Both Blackwell and Vander Meer pitched for Cincinnati; Vander Meer had thrown his first no-hitter against Boston and his second against Brooklyn, now Blackwell had the chance to do the same; and Vander Meer was still on the Cincinnati team as Blackwell took the mound against the Dodgers at Cincinnati.

The tension mounted as Blackwell turned the Dodgers back without a hit, inning after inning. As Blackwell took the mound in the ninth with only a 1–0 lead, Vander Meer was at the top of the dugout steps, wanting to be the first to congratulate Blackwell if he turned the double no-hitter.

As the 31,204 Cincinnati fans shrieked, Blackwell retired the first Brooklyn batter in the top of the ninth. Then, Eddie Stanky grounded a ball through the box. Blackwell went down to one knee to try to block the ball, but it got through and neither short-stop Eddie Miller nor second baseman Benny Zientara could get it. The fans then booed Stanky for breaking up the no-hitter, though it is not likely that bothered the combative Stanky.

Al Gionfriddo then flied out for the second out and Jackie Robinson added another single, so Blackwell ended with a two-hitter when he got the next batter. But if he had fielded Stanky's grounder, Gionfriddo would have been the third out and Robinson would never have batted.

Blackwell never pitched another no-hitter, but he came close twice in 1950, when he pitched one-hitters. The first game, on September 2, was the best. Blackwell held the Cubs hitless until the ninth and only four Cubs had hit the ball to the outfield. But Phil Cavaretta opened the inning with a single to end the no-hitter.

Ten days later, Blackwell nearly pitched another no-hitter. This one, however, was broken up early, when Gene Hermanski hit a looping fly that just eluded right fielder Johnny Wyrostek. To make it worse, Blackwell wound up losing the game 3–1, because of a combination of walks, wild pitches and his own error.

In 1951, Blackwell pitched another one-hitter, this time winning 1–0 against Boston, but this one was also broken up early with a fifth-inning double by Bob Elliott.

After his great 1947 season, Blackwell surprisingly tailed off to a 7–9 record in 1948 and could complete only four games, compared to a league-leading 23 the previous season. His trouble was finally diagnosed as a dormant right kidney and it was removed in January of 1949. The operation limited him to a 5–5 record in 1949 (he had left the hospital weighing only 150 pounds) but he recovered enough to win 17 and 16 games for the Reds in the next two seasons.

He might have won 20 games again in 1950, but he was struck by appendicitis after winning his seventeenth game and had to go to the hospital for more surgery.

Medical problems and a sore arm virtually ended Blackwell's career after 1951, though he should have been in his prime: he was only 29 the month after the end of the '51 season. He took the mound for portions of three more seasons but could win only six games, ending with a career total of 82, low indeed for someone with his promise. Health permitting, he would have won many more games—and might have pitched another no-hitter or two.

18

The ultimate frustration

If pitching a no-hitter is ecstasy, pitching a one-hitter is the ultimate frustration. The pitcher is left to consider what might have been. If only he had thrown a curve instead of a fastball, if only the pitch had been low instead of high, if only a fielder had been in a slightly different position, if only the wind had been blowing in instead of out, if only . . .

There have been some great accomplishments in one-hit games. Bob Feller threw 11 of them in his lifetime, along with 3 no-hitters. Grover Cleveland Alexander threw 4 in one season. There have been games in which each pitcher has thrown a one-hitter and, naturally, Feller figured in one of them.

Four pitchers have pitched one-hitters in their first major league games: Addie Joss, Cleveland, April 26, 1902; Mike Fornieles, Washington, September 2, 1952; Bill Rohr, Boston, April 14, 1967; and Juan Marichal, San Francisco, July 19, 1960. Marichal later got a no-hitter, and Joss got two, including a perfect game, but Fornieles and Rohr never came that close again.

Seven times, pitchers have thrown one-hitters in consecutive games. Put another way, that means they were just two pitches away from the successive no-hitter feat that only Johnny Vander Meer has accomplished.

Three of the consecutive one-hitters came before 1901; Hugh I. Dailey, Chicago of the Union Association, July 7 and 10, 1884; Thomas A. Ramsey, Louisville of the American Association, July 29 and 31, 1886; and Charles G. Buffinton, Philadelphia of the National League, August 6 and 9, 1887. Dailey had pitched a no-

hitter the year before in the National League, but Ramsey and Buffinton never got no-hitters.

Lon Warneke, known as the "Arkansas Hummingbird," was
the first to pitch consecutive one-hitters in modern times, in 1934.
At 25, Warneke was in his pitching prime, in the middle of a four-
year stretch in which he won 82 games, when he pitched the Chicago Cubs to a 6–0 win over the Reds at Cincinnati on Opening
Day of the 1934 season, April 17. He struck out 13 and walked
only 2 with a lively fastball and a sharp-breaking curve.

For 8⅓ innings, Warneke also held the Reds without a hit, but
then Cincinnati left fielder Adam Comorosky singled to center.
Warneke thus just missed being the first to pitch a no-hitter on
Opening Day, a feat later accomplished by Feller.

In his next start, Warneke pitched aginst Dizzy Dean of the St.
Louis Cardinals in what should have been a pitching duel but
wasn't; Dean was knocked out after three innings before the surprised St. Louis fans.

Warneke was not as sharp as he had been in his first game,
striking out only five and walking six, but he was just as stingy in
giving out hits. The only Cardinal hit was a double by Jim (Rip)
Collins in the fifth.

The Cardinals scored twice in the fifth, too. Virgil Davis had
walked ahead of Collins' hit and scored on a passed ball, with
Collins moving to third and scoring on Gene Moore's sacrifice fly.
Those runs mattered only to Warneke's earned run average, however, because the Cubs won the game 15–2.

Before the 1937 season, Warneke was traded to St. Louis and
he went on to have five good seasons with the Cardinals, en route
to a career total of 193 wins.

His last winning season was 1941, when he won 17 and lost 9,
and on August 30 of that year he pitched a 2–0 no-hitter against
the Reds in Cincinnati. He walked only one batter and was not
bothered by an occasionally shaky Cardinal defense, which erred
twice behind him.

No doubt that no-hitter was solace for Warneke for the ones
he had missed in the 1934 season, but the others on the consecutive one-hitter list had no such satisfaction; none of the three ever
got that elusive no-hitter.

The next pitcher to get consecutive one-hitters was Mort Cooper, the older of the Cardinals' unusual brother combination;
Walker Cooper was a catcher.

Mort Cooper was a big factor in the Cardinals' three successive pennants in the war years, 1942–44, though he faded quickly
after that. In 1942, he swept National League pitching honors,

leading in wins (22), earned run average (1.78) and shutouts (10) as he was named the league's Most Valuable Player.

In 1943, he was nearly as effective, winning 21 and losing only 8, and he was at his best when he blanked Brooklyn 7–0 on May 31. The only hit in the game was a twisting fly by Billy Herman in the fifth that fell just inside the right field line.

Four days later, in St. Louis, Cooper was even more effective as he shut out Philadelphia 5–0. For seven innings he held the Phils hitless, but in the eighth Jimmy Wasdell singled to break up Cooper's no-hitter. Mort did not walk a man and the only other Philadelphia baserunner came as a result of his own error. The Cardinals turned a double play behind him, so Cooper faced only 28 men. So close, and yet . . .

From the time he started pitching, Whitey Ford was a natural. In his first season, he was 13–4 at Butler of the Middle Atlantic League; manager Lefty Gomez, a Hall of Fame pitcher, commented: "I've never seen a kid like this. He throws his curves so easy, so natural."

When Ford came to the Yankees, pitching coach Jim Turner nearly echoed Gomez's words. "I can't teach him a thing," said Turner. "He sits there and watches and learns for himself. He's taught himself how to make his fastball alive. And his curve! For a kid his age, with his experience, it's a miracle!"

Ford started out a winner for the Yankees, 9–1 in his rookie season of 1950, and he remained one until the final two years of his career. He won 236 games with a .690 percentage, highest of all time for those with 200 or more wins. He was elected to the Hall of Fame and feels he should likewise be in the beer-drinkers' Hall of Fame with friend Mickey Mantle. He pitched in a record 11 World Series and a record 22 games and won a record 10 Series games. He did everything, in fact, but pitch a no-hitter.

He came maddeningly close in 1955. Twice, he pitched two-hitters that year, as he won an American League high 18 games, and he pitched one-hitters in succession, on September 2 and 7.

Oddly, neither of the games was a shutout, as Ford beat Washington 4–2, and Kansas City 2–1. In each case, the no-hitter was broken up in the seventh inning. Carlos Paula singled in the first game and Jim Finigan doubled in the second.

Eleven years later, Sam McDowell duplicated Ford's feat. Though both threw with their left arms, you could hardly find more different pitchers than Ford and McDowell. Ford was a clever pitcher who threw a variety of pitches and knew where each one was going; McDowell was terrifyingly fast, but with constant control problems.

In his prime, McDowell may have been as fast as anybody who ever threw a baseball. His strikeout statistics reflect that. For a seven-year period, 1964–70, McDowell averaged more than one strikeout an inning; only Sandy Koufax and Nolan Ryan have comparable records. Some pitchers celebrated for their fastballs—notably Walter Johnson, Lefty Grove, Rube Waddell and Bob Feller—did not have even one season in which they had more strikeouts than innings pitched.

Even when he was in his prime, however, McDowell was not a smooth worker. He labored, because his control was always uncertain. He threw hard and he worked hard. A huge man, at 6 feet, 5 inches and a weight which probably went as high as 250 on occasion, he would grunt as he let the ball go and it would pop loudly as it hit the catcher's glove, as loudly in the last inning as the first.

Typically, his one-hitters were sloppy but overpowering performances. Both games, April 25 and May 1, 1966, came in Cleveland's Municipal Stadium. The first came against the Philadelphia Athletics. McDowell walked six while striking out eight and the only hit was Jose Tartabull's lopping single to center in the sixth inning.

The next game was even more frustrating to McDowell. With two outs in the third inning against the Chicago White Sox, he walked Tommie Agee, one of five walks (against ten strikeouts) he had in the game. McDowell's first pitch to the next batter, Don Buford, was a fastball in on the fists. Buford hit it to almost the exact spot where Cleveland first baseman Fred Whitfield would normally have been playing, but Whitfield had been holding Agee on first and was not there. The ball squirted through for a double and McDowell held the White Sox hitless the rest of the way in a 1–0 win.

To make it worse for McDowell, there was a no-hitter by a Cleveland pitcher that year—Sonny Siebert, who pitched the only one of the year in the majors on June 10, a 2–0 win over Washington at Cleveland.

Pitching a one-hitter, or even successive one-hitters, in regular season play is frustrating, but even that cannot compare with the disappointment of just missing a no-hitter in the World Series, when there is so much more at stake.

Until Don Larsen pitched his perfect game in the 1956 World Series, there had never been a no-hitter pitched in the Series. This is not as surprising as it seems; the law of averages works against it. Consider this: In regular season play now, there are almost 2000 games played and there might be an average of four no-hitters thrown, or roughly one for every 500 games played. In all the World Series played from 1901 to 1956, there were not 500 games.

Four times, pitchers have come within one hit of that prized no-hit game in the Series. The first time came in the second game of the 1906 Series. The Chicago Cubs' Ed Reulbach, who had won 20 and lost only 4 during the regular season, was pitching against the Chicago White Sox, who seemed determined to live up to their nickname of "The Hitless Wonders."

For six innings Reulbach held the White Sox hitless, then Jiggs Donahue broke up the no-hitter in the seventh. Oddly, the White Sox had scored a run an inning earlier on a wild pitch and an error. Reulbach and the Cubs went on to win the game easily, 7–1, though the White Sox eventually won the Series in six games.

Not for nearly 40 years did another pitcher come that close to a Series no-hitter; again, it was a Chicago Cub righthander, this time Claude Passeau against the Detroit Tigers in the 1945 World Series.

Passeau had been an excellent pitcher for the Cubs for several years, winning 20 games in 1940 and following with seasons in which he won 14, 19 and 15 twice. Before the 1945 season, however, the calcium chips that accumulate in a veteran pitcher's elbow threatened to end his career.

As the season moved along, the pain in his elbow subsided and Passeau was as effective as ever, though his fastball had lost a little. Relying more and more on his curve, he won 17 games with an excellent 2.46 ERA.

As he took the mound for the third game of the Series on October 5 in Detroit, the Series was tied at a game apiece. Passeau then pitched what was considered the finest game yet in the World Series, shutting out the Tigers 4–0 on one hit.

The no-hit suspense never really got a chance to build as Rudy York lined a single to left field with two outs in the second inning. Only one other Tiger reached base, Bob Swift on a walk in the sixth, and the Cubs turned a double play immediately after that, so Passeau faced only 28 men.

There was plenty of no-hit suspense in the fourth one-hitter thrown in the World Series, this one by Jim Lonborg in a 5–0 win by the Boston Red Sox over the St. Louis Cardinals in the second game of the 1967 Series.

That was the year of the Impossible Dream, as the Red Sox came from half a game out of last place in a ten-team league in 1966 to a pennant in 1967, winning in a four-team race on the last day of the season.

Two men carried the Red Sox all season. Carl Yastrzemski had an incredible year, winning the Triple Crown (batting average, home runs and RBIs) and time after time coming up with the key hit or fielding play to win games.

Lonborg was almost as important. Jim led the league in wins (22) and strikeouts (246). He had won the game against Minnesota on the last day of the season that had won the pennant for the Red Sox. Because he had pitched in the season-closer, Lonborg could not start in the Series opener, won by the Cardinals, but he came back with a magnificent game in the second game.

Lonborg retired the first 19 men in succession, helped by some excellent defense. Twice, Boston second baseman Jerry Adair made excellent plays on balls hit by Lou Brock and short-stop Rico Petrocelli took a hit away from Dal Maxvill in the sixth with a great play.

The 6–5 Boston righthander had dreams of becoming the second to pitch a perfect game in the Series when Curt Flood walked on a close 3–2 pitch with one out in the seventh. It was the fourth time Lonborg had gone to a 3–2 count on a batter; this time it cost him, but it didn't bother him because the no-hitter was still intact.

Lonborg got Roger Maris to fly to Yastrzemski in left field, then Petrocelli made a nice play on a smash by Orlando Cepeda over second base, turning the smash into a force play.

The skies had turned dark in the seventh inning and light rain started to fall, and the lights were turned on. The rain stopped at the start of the eighth and Lonborg seemed as strong as ever, getting Tim McCarver and Mike Shannon on routine ground balls.

And then, Lonborg did what all pitchers dread: He hung a curveball. The curve was supposed to be low, but it came in high and Julian Javier lined a double down the left field line for the first hit.

Lonborg then retired the last four Cardinals to face him and won the game—Yastrzemski, of course, had provided the offense with two home runs—but he had lost the no-hitter that seemed within his grasp.

Lonborg's frustration, though, was nothing compared to that felt by Bill Bevens of the New York Yankees after one of the strangest games in World Series history in 1947.

Bevens was a tall righthander of no particular distinction; he was perhaps best known because he had been the losing pitcher in the second no-hitter thrown by Bob Feller, in 1946. Bevens had pitched well in 1945 and '46, winning 13 and 16 games, but he had slipped to a 7–13 record in 1947, though pitching for a team which won the pennant.

When he took the mound for the fourth game at Ebbets Field, the Yankees led the Series 2–1; it looked as if they were on their way to wrapping it up when they scored in the top of the first.

George Stirnweiss led off with a first pitch single off Brooklyn starter Harry Taylor, and Tommy Henrich duplicated that on the next pitch. Yogi Berra grounded to Jackie Robinson at second, but shortstop Pee Wee Reese dropped the throw and the bases were loaded. After Joe DiMaggio walked to force in a run, Brooklyn manager Burt Shotton brought in Hal Gregg to relieve Taylor, and Gregg got George McQuinn to pop out and Billy Johnson to hit into a double play.

Bevens started the first inning as he did four of the nine, by walking a man, this time Eddie Stanky. With two outs, he also walked Dixie Walker, but then got Gene Hermanski to foul out to end the inning.

It went that way inning after inning for Bevens, as he continually got into trouble because of his wildness. He walked ten batters, breaking a Series record of nine that had been set by Jack Coombs in 1910, and did not have a 1–2–3 inning until the eighth. But it was only his wildness that caused him trouble, because the Dodgers could not get a hit off him.

In the fourth, the Yankees got another run when Johnson led off the inning with a triple and Johnny Lindell followed with a double off Gregg.

In the fifth, the Dodgers scored but still could not get a hit off Bevens. Spider Jorgensen and Gregg walked to open the inning, and Stanky sacrificed to advance them. Reese then grounded to Rizzuto, who got Gregg sliding into third as Jorgensen was scoring.

After seven innings, the score was 2–1 and there had been nine Dodger baserunners, but Bevens still had not allowed a hit. He had now gone longer without giving up a hit than anybody else in World Series play, and there had been only two tough plays behind him. Left fielder Lindell made a diving catch of a foul fly by Robinson in the third (which would not have been a hit, anyway) and DiMaggio went to the center field fence to catch a drive by Hermanski in the fourth.

Hermanski almost got Bevens in trouble again in the eighth. After Bevens had retired the first two batters, Robinson and Walker, on grounders, Hermanski slammed a drive to right center. Right fielder Henrich raced to the fence in right center and, timing his leap perfectly, grabbed the ball just before it would have hit.

In the bottom half of the ninth, the Yankees clinging precariously to their 2–1 lead and Bevens struggling to pitch the first no-hitter in Series history, Bruce Edwards opened up by sending a long fly to left field, on which Lindell made a leaping catch.

Bevens then walked Carl Furillo and the still-hitless Dodgers had the tying run on base. Shotton sent in Al Gionfriddo to run for Furillo and Pete Reiser to pinchhit for relief pitcher Hugh Casey.

Bevens threw two balls and a strike to Reiser, who was limping because of an ankle he had hurt the previous day. On the next pitch, another ball, Gionfriddo raced to second and beat Berra's throw by a split second.

New York manager Bucky Harris then ordered a fourth ball to be thrown intentionally to Reiser, walking him and violating one of the basic baseball rules by putting the potential winning run on base.

Shotton sent Eddie Miksis in to run for Reiser and then called on Harry (Cookie) Lavagetto to pinchhit for Stanky. Lavagetto, who had been in the majors since 1934, had been used primarily as a pinchhitter for Brooklyn that year.

Lavagetto swung hard at the first pitch and missed, but on the second pitch, he connected and hit a drive toward right center, similar to the one hit by Hermanski the inning before on which Henrich had made an excellent catch. Tommy had no chance to get this one, however, as it struck the wall over his head. He tried to grab the ball as it caromed off the boards, but the fence in Ebbets Field sloped, producing erratic caroms, and it was some time before Henrich could catch up to the ball.

When he did, he fired it to the infield. First baseman Mc-Quinn caught it and relayed it to the plate, but it was too late. Gionfriddo and Miksis had scored on Lavagetto's double and Bevens had lost his no-hitter and the ball game with one swing of the bat. His only consolation was that he had gone further with a no-hitter than any other World Series pitcher, but it's doubtful that thought provided him many happy moments, then or later.

Bevens pitched briefly in relief later in the Series, but he never again pitched in the major leagues after that year, as a sore arm forced him out at the age of 31. It remained for another Yankee pitcher, Don Larsen, to finally pitch a World Series no-hitter as Bevens was left to reflect on what might have been.

Appendix

Major League No-Hitters Since 1901

Bold number denotes all pitchers who have hurled more than one no-hitter
Bold name denotes all pitchers who have hurled a perfect game

Year	Date	H/A	Pitcher/Teams	Score
1909	Apr. 15 H		2 Red Ames for NY vs Bkn (NL) no hitter for 9.1 innings, lost in 13th on 7 hits.	0–3
1910	Apr. 20 A		2 Addie Joss for Cle vs. Chi (AL)	1–0
	May 12 H		Chief Bender for Phi vs. Cle (AL)	4–0
	Aug. 30 H (2nd game)		Tom Hughes for NY vs. Cle (AL) no-hitter for 9.1 innings, lost in 11th on 7 hits.	0–5
1911	July 29 H (1st game)		Smokey Joe Wood for Bos vs. St. L (AL)	5–0
	Aug. 27 H		2 Ed Walsh for Chi vs. Bos (AL)	5–0
1912	July 4 H (P.M. game)		George Mullin for Det vs. St. L (AL)	7–0
	Aug. 30 A		Earl Hamilton for St. L vs. Det (AL)	5–1
1912	Sept. 6 A (1st game)		Jeff Tesreau for NY vs. Phi (NL)	3–0
1914	May 14 A		Jim Scott for Chi vs. Cle (AL) no-hitter for 9 innings, lost in 10th on 2 hits.	0–1
	May 31 H		Joe Benz for Chi vs. Cle (AL)	6–1
	Sept. 9 H (2nd game)		George Davis for Bos vs. Phi (NL)	7–0
1915	Apr. 15 H		Rube Marquard for NY vs. Bkn (NL)	2–0
	Aug. 31 A (1st game)		Jimmy Lavender for Chi vs. NY (NL)	2–0
1916	Jun. 16 H		2 Tom Hughes for Bos vs. Pit (NL)	2–0
	Jun. 21 H		Rube Foster for Bos vs. NY (AL)	2–0
	Aug. 26 H		Bullet Joe Bush for Phi vs. Cle (AL)	5–0
	Aug. 30 H		Dutch Leonard for Bos vs. St. L (AL)	4–0
1917	Apr. 14 A		Ed Cicotte for Chi vs. St. L (AL)	11–0
	Apr. 24 A		George Mogridge for NY vs. Bos (AL)	2–1
	May 2 A		Fred Toney for Cin vs. Chi (NL) 10 innings	1–0
	May 2 A		Hippo Vaughn for Chi vs. Cin (NL) no-hitter for 9.1 innings, lost in 10th on 2 hits.	0–1
	May 5 H		Ernie Koob for St. L vs. Chi (AL)	1–0
	May 6 H (2nd game)		Bob Groom for St. L vs. Chi (AL)	3–0
	June 23 H (1st game)		Ernie Shore for Bos vs. Was (AL), did not start game. Ruth walked the first batter and was ejected from the game. Shore relieved, the base runner was out stealing. Shore given credit for a perfect game facing only 26 batters.	4–0
1918	June 23 A		2 Dutch Leonard for Bos vs. Det (AL)	5–0
1919	May 11 H		Hod Eller for Cin vs. St. L (NL)	6–0
	Sept. 10 A (1st game)		Ray Caldwell for Cle vs. NY (AL)	3–0
1920	July 1 A		Walter Johnson for Was vs. Bos (AL)	1–0

Year	Date	H/A	Pitcher/Teams	Score
1922	Apr. 30	A	Charlie Robertson for Chi vs. Det (AL)	2–0
	May 7	H	Jesse Barnes for NY vs. Phi (NL)	6–0
1923	Sept. 4	A	Sad Sam Jones for NY vs. Phi (AL)	2–0
	Sept. 7	A	Howard Ehmke for Bos vs. Phi (AL)	4–0
1924	July 17	H	Jesse Haines for St. L vs. Bos (NL)	5–0
1925	Sept. 13	H (1st game)	Dazzy Vance for Bkn vs. Phi (NL)	10–1
1926	Aug. 21	A	Ted Lyons for Chi vs. Bos (AL)	6–0
1929	May 8	H	Carl Hubbell for NY vs. Pit (NL)	11–0
1931	Apr. 29	H	Wes Ferrell for Cle vs. St. L (AL)	9–0
	Aug. 8	H	Bob Burke for Was vs. Bos (AL)	5–0
1934	Sept. 18	H	Bobo Newsom for St. L vs. Bos (AL) no-hitter for 9.2 innings, lost in 10th on 1 hit.	1–2
	Sept. 21	A (2nd game)	Paul Dean for St. L vs. Bkn (NL)	3–0
1935	Aug. 31	H	Vern Kennedy for Chi vs. Cle (AL)	5–0
1937	June 1	H	Bill Kietrich for Chi vs. St. L (AL)	8–0
	Aug. 27	H	Fred Frankhouse for Bkn vs. Cin (NL) 7.2 innings	5–0
1938	June 11	H	Johnny Vander Meer for Cin vs. Bos (NL)	3–0
	June 15	H	2 Johnny Vander Meer for Cin vs. Bkn (NL)	6–0
	Aug. 27	H (2nd game)	Monte Pearson for NY vs. Cle (AL)	13–0
1940	Apr. 16	A	Bob Feller for Cle vs. Chi (AL)	1–0
	Apr. 30	A	Tex Carleton for Bkn vs. Cin (NL)	3–0
1941	Aug. 30	A	Lon Warneke for St. L vs. Cin (NL)	2–0
1944	Apr. 27	H	Jim Tobin for Bos vs. Bkn (NL)	2–0
	May 15	H	Clyde Shoun for Cin vs. Bos (NL)	1–0
1945	Sept. 9	H (2nd game)	Dick Fowler for Phi vs. St. L (AL)	1–0
1946	Apr. 23	H	Ed Head for Bkn vs. Bos (NL)	5–0
	Apr. 30	A	2 Bob Feller for Cle vs. NY (AL)	1–0
1947	June 18	H	Ewell Blackwell for Cin vs. Bos (NL)	6–0
	July 10	H (1st game)	Don Black for Cle vs. Phi (AL)	3–0
	Sept. 3	H	Bill McCahan for Phi vs. Was (AL)	3–0
1948	June 30	A	Bob Lemon for Cle vs. Det (AL)	2–0
	Sept. 9	A	Rex Barney for Bkn vs. NY (NL)	2–0
1950	Aug. 11	H	Vern Bickford for Bos vs. Bkn (NL)	7–0
1951	May 6	A (2nd game)	Cliff Chambers for Pit vs. Bos (NL)	3–0
	July 1	A (1st game)	3 Bob Feller for Cle vs. Det (AL)	2–1
	July 12	A	Allie Reynolds for NY vs. Cle (AL)	1–0
	Sept. 28	H (1st game)	2 Allie Reynolds for NY vs. Bos (AL)	8–0

Year	Date	H/A	Pitcher/Teams	Score
1952	May 15	H	Virgil Trucks for Det vs. Was (AL)	1–0
	June 19	H	Carl Erskine for Bkn vs. Chi (NL)	5–0
	Aug. 25	A	2 Virgil Trucks for Det vs. NY (AL)	1–0
1953	May 6	H	Bobo Holloman for St. L vs. Phi (AL)	6–0
1954	June 12	H	Jim Wilson for Mil vs. Phi (NL)	2–0
1955	May 12	H	Sam Jones for Chi vs. Pit (NL)	4–0
1956	May 12	H	2 Carl Erskine for Bkn vs. NY (NL)	3–0
	July 14	H	Mel Parnell for Bos vs. Chi (AL)	4–0
	Sept. 25	H	Sal Maglie for Bkn vs. Phi (NL)	5–0
	Oct. 8	H	**Don Larsen** for NY vs. Bkn World Series Game	2–0
1957	Aug. 20	H (2nd game)	Bob Keegan for Chi vs. Was (AL)	6–0
1958	July 20	A (1st game)	Jim Bunning for Det vs. Bos (AL)	3–0
	Sept. 20	H	Hoyt Wilhelm for Bal vs. NY (AL)	1–0
1959	May 26	A	**Harvey Haddix** for Pit vs. Mil (NL) Perfect game for 12 innings, lost in 13th on 1 hit.	0–1
1960	May 15	H (2nd game)	Don Cardwell for Chi vs. St. L (NL)	4–0
	Aug. 18	H	Lew Burdette for Mil vs. Phi (NL)	1–0
	Sept. 16	H	Warren Spahn for Mil vs. Phi (NL)	4–0
1961	Apr. 28	H	2 Warren Spahn for Mil vs. SF (NL)	1–0
1962	May 5	H	Bo Belinsky for LA vs. Bal (AL)	2–0
	June 26	H	Earl Wilson for Bos vs. LA (AL)	2–0
	June 30	H	Sandy Koufax for LA vs. NY (NL)	5–0
	Aug. 1	A	Bill Monboquette for Bos vs. Chi (AL)	1–0
	Aug. 26	H	Jack Kralick for Min vs. KC (AL)	1–0
1963	May 11	H	2 Sandy Koufax for LA vs. SF (NL)	8–0
	May 17	H	Don Nottebart for Hous vs. Phi (NL)	4–1
	June 15	H	Juan Marichal for SF vs. Hou (NL)	1–0
1964	Apr. 23	H	Ken Johnson for Hou vs. Cin (NL)	0–1
	June 4	A	3 Sandy Koufax for LA vs. Phi (NL)	3–0
	June 21	A (1st game)	2 **Jim Bunning** for Phi vs. NY (NL)	6–0
1965	June 14	H	Jim Maloney for Cin vs. NY (NL) no-hitter for 10 innings, lost in 11th on 2 hits.	0–1
	Aug. 19	A (1st game)	2 Jim Maloney for Cin vs. Chi (NL)	1–0
	Sept. 9	H	4 **Sandy Koufax** for LA vs. Chi (NL)	1–0
	Sept. 16	H	Dave Morehead for Bos vs. Cle (AL)	2–0
1966	June 10	H	Sonny Siebert for Cle vs. Was (AL)	2–0
1967	June 18	H	Don Wilson for Hous vs. Atl (NL)	2–0
	Aug. 25	A (2nd game)	2 Dean Chance for Min vs. Cle (AL)	2–1
	Sept. 10	H (1st game)	Joel Horlen for Chi vs. Det (AL)	6–0
1968	Apr. 27	H	Tom Phoebus for Bal vs. Bos (AL)	6–0
	May 8	H	**Catfish Hunter** for Oak vs. Min (AL)	4–0
	July 29	A (2nd game)	George Culver for Cin vs. Phi (NL)	6–1
	Sept. 17		Gaylord Perry for SF vs. St. L (NL)	1–0
	Sept. 18	A	Ray Washburn for St. L vs. SF (NL)	2–0

Year	Date	H/A	Pitcher/Teams	Score
1969	Apr. 17	A	Bill Stoneman for Mont vs. Phi (NL)	7–0
	Apr. 30	H	3 Jim Maloney for Cin vs. Hou (NL)	10–0
	May 1	A	2 Don Wilson for Hou vs. Cin (NL)	4–0
	Aug. 13	H	Jim Palmer for Bal vs. Oak (AL)	8–0
	Aug. 19	H	Ken Holtzman for Chi vs. Atl (NL)	3–0
	Sept. 20	A	Bob Moose for Pit vs. NY (NL)	4–0
1970	June 12	A (1st game)	Dock Ellis for Pit vs. San D (NL)	2–0
	July 3	H	Clyde Wright for Cal vs. Oak (AL)	4–0
	July 20	H	Bill Singer for LA vs. Phi (NL)	5–0
	Sept. 21	H	Vida Blue for Oak vs. Min (AL)	6–0
1971	June 3	H	2 Ken Holtzman for Chi vs. Cin (NL)	1–0
	June 23	A	Rick Wise for Phi vs. Cin (NL)	4–0
	Aug. 14	A	Bob Gibson for St. L vs. Pit (NL)	11–0
1972	Apr. 16	H	Burt Hooton for Chi vs. Phi (NL)	1–0
	Sept. 2	H	Milt Pappas for Chi vs. San D (NL)	3–0
	Oct. 2	H	Bill Stoneman for Mont vs. NY (NL)	7–0
1973	Apr. 27	A	Steve Busby for KC vs. Det (AL)	3–0
	May 15	A	Nolan Ryan for Cal vs. KC (AL)	3–0
	July 15	A	2 Nolan Ryan for Cal vs. Det (AL)	6–0
	July 30	A	Jim Bibby for Tex vs. Oak (AL)	6–0
	Aug. 5	H	Phil Niekro for Atl vs. San D (NL)	9–0
1974	June 19	A	Steve Busby for KC vs. Mil (AL)	2–0
	July 20	H	Dick Bosman for Clev vs. Oak (AL)	4–0
	Sept. 28	H	Nolan Ryan for Cal vs. Min (AL)	4–0
1975	June 1	H	Nolan Ryan for Cal vs. Balt (AL)	1–0
	Aug. 24	H	Ed Halicki for SF vs. NY (NL)	6–0
	Sept. 28	H	Vida Blue, Glen Abbott, Paul Lindblad and Rollie Fingers for Oakland vs. Cal (AL)	5–0

Combination No-hitters

Year	Date	H/A	Pitcher/Teams	Score
1956	May 26	A	Johnny Klippstein-7 innings Hersh Freeman-1 inning Joe Black-1.2 innings; for Cin vs. Mil (NL) no-hitter for 9.2 innings, lost in 11th on 3 hits.	1–2
1967	Apr. 30	H (1st game)	Steve Barber-8.2 innings; for Bal vs. Det (AL) Stu Miller-1 inning	1–2

BOX SCORES

May 9, 1901   Chicago at Cleveland

CHICAGO	ab	b	p	a	e
Hoy, cf	3	0	6	0	0
Jones, rf	4	0	3	0	0
Mertes, 2b	3	1	2	2	0
Isbell, 1b	4	0	11	0	0
Hartman, 3b	4	1	1	2	0
Shugart, ss	4	0	2	4	0
McFarland, lf	4	0	3	0	0
Sullivan, c	4	0	2	0	0
Katoll, p	3	0	0	3	0
Totals	33	2	30	11	0

CLEVELAND	ab	b	p	a	e
Pickering, rf	4	2	2	0	0
McCarthy, lf	3	0	2	0	0
Genins, cf	4	1	4	0	0
Lachance, 1b	4	1	15	1	0
Bradley, 3b	4	0	1	1	0
Beck, 2b	3	0	3	2	1
Shay, ss	4	0	0	6	0
Woods, c	4	2	2	0	0
Moore, p	3	0	1	3	1
* Yeager	1	0	0	0	0
Totals	34	6	30	13	2

* Batted for Moore in tenth.
No hits made by Chicago until the tenth.

```
Chicago.....................  0 0 0 2 0 0 0 0 0 2 — 4
Cleveland..................  0 0 2 0 0 0 0 0 0 0 — 2
```

Two-base hit—Pickering. Stolen base—Isbell. Bases on balls—Off Moore 1, off Katoll 1. Left on bases—Cleveland 6, Chicago 1. Umpires—Sheridan and Mannasau.

July 15, 1901   New York at St. Louis

NEW YORK	ab	b	p	a	e
Van Ha'n, cf	5	2	1	0	1
Selbach, lf	4	2	1	0	0
McBride, rf	3	1	1	0	0
Davis, 3b	3	1	0	3	0
Ganzel, 1b	4	0	14	1	0
Hickman, ss	4	2	2	6	0
Strang, 2b	4	2	1	2	0
Warner, c	3	0	5	1	0
Mathewson, p	4	0	2	3	0
Totals	34	10	27	16	1

ST. LOUIS	ab	b	p	a	e
Burkett, lf	3	0	0	0	0
Donovan, rf	4	0	2	0	0
Schriver, 1b	3	0	10	3	0
Padden, 2b	2	0	3	5	0
Wallace, ss	3	0	4	3	1
Kruger, 3b	3	0	2	2	0
Ryan, c	3	0	4	1	0
Nichols, cf	3	0	0	0	0
Sudhoff, p	3	0	2	3	0
Totals	27	0	27	17	1

```
New York ..................  2 2 0 0 0 0 0 1 0 — 5
St. Louis .....................  0 0 0 0 0 0 0 0 0 — 0
```

Left on bases—New York 4, St. Louis 3. Bases on balls—Off Mathewson 4, off Sudhoff 2. Struck out—By Mathewson 4, by Sudhoff 3. Stolen base—Van Haltren. Umpire—Dwyer.

Sept. 20, 1902   Detroit at Chicago

DETROIT	ab	r	b	p	a	e
Harley, lf	4	0	0	2	0	0
Elberfeld, ss	3	0	0	3	2	2
Barrett, cf	4	0	0	1	0	0
McAlli'r, 3b	3	0	0	0	3	1
Yeager, 2b	2	0	0	3	4	0
Lepine, rf	3	0	0	0	0	0
O'Conn'l, 1b	3	0	0	12	0	0
McGuire, c	3	0	0	3	1	0
Egan, p	3	0	0	0	4	0
Totals	28	0	0	24	14	3

CHICAGO	ab	r	b	p	a	e
Strang, 3b	4	1	2	2	4	0
Jones, cf	4	0	0	4	0	0
Green, rf	4	1	1	2	0	0
Davis, ss	4	1	2	0	5	1
Mertes, lf	4	0	0	2	0	0
Daly, 2b	4	0	1	1	0	0
Isbel, 1b	3	0	1	13	1	0
McFarla'd, c	3	0	1	2	0	0
Callahan, p	3	0	0	1	4	0
Totals	33	3	8	27	14	1

```
Detroit ........................  0 0 0 0 0 0 0 0 0 — 0
Chicago........................  3 0 0 0 0 0 0 0 0 — 3
```

Left on bases—Chicago 4, Detroit 1. Two-base hit—Isbel. Three-base hit—Davis. Sacrifice hit—Isbel. Stolen bases—Strang, Green. Double play—Eagan, Elberfeld, O'Connell. Struck out—By Callahan 2. Passed ball—McFarland. First on balls—Off Callahan 2, Egan 2. Umpires—Caruthers and Sheridan. Time—1.20.

Sept. 14, 1903 New York at St. Louis

NEW YORK	ab	r	b	p	a	b
Browne, rf	3	1	1	0	0	0
Bresna'n, cf	3	1	1	0	0	0
McGann, 1b	3	0	0	4	0	0
Mertes, lf	2	1	0	0	0	0
Babb, ss	1	1	0	3	2	0
Lauder, 3b	2	0	1	0	0	0
Gilbert, 2b	3	0	0	1	2	0
Warner, c	3	1	1	7	0	0
Ames, p	2	0	0	0	0	0
Total	22	5	4	15	4	0

ST. LOUIS	ab	r	b	p	a	b
Dunlea'y, rf	2	0	0	0	0	0
Smoot, cf	1	0	0	0	0	0
Brain, ss	2	0	0	2	2	0
Burke, 3b	2	0	0	0	2	0
Barclay, lf	2	0	0	1	0	0
Ryan, c	2	0	0	3	0	0
Demont, 2b	1	0	0	3	0	3
Murphy, 1b	0	0	0	3	0	1
Hackett, 1b	1	0	0	3	0	1
O'Neill, p	1	0	0	0	3	0
Total	14	0	0	15	7	5

```
New York ................... 3 1 0 0 1 — 5
St. Louis ...................  0 0 0 0 0 — 0
```

Two-base hit—Bresnahae. Sacrifice hits—Babb, Lauder. DP—Gilbert, McGann. BB—Off O'Neill 2 Ames 2. SO—By O'Neill 2 Ames 7. LOB—St. Louis 1, NY 6 T—1:04 U—Moran & Johnstone. A—1,895.

Sept. 18, 1903 Philadelphia at Chicago

PHILADELPHIA	ab	r	h	p	a	e
Thomas, cf	3	0	1	4	0	0
Hallman, 2b	5	2	1	2	3	1
Wolverton, 3b	4	2	2	1	2	0
Barry, lf	5	3	3	1	0	0
Titus, rf	4	2	2	1	0	0
Douglas, 1b	5	1	3	13	0	0
Hulswitt, ss	4	0	1	1	5	3
Zimmer, c	4	0	1	4	1	0
Fraser, p	3	0	0	0	2	0
Totals	37	10	14	27	13	4

CHICAGO	ab	r	h	p	a	e
Slagle, cf	3	0	0	0	0	1
McCarthy, lf	4	0	0	1	0	1
Chance, 1b	2	0	0	12	0	0
Jones, rf	4	0	0	0	0	0
Tinker, ss	4	0	0	2	5	0
Kling, c	4	0	0	5	5	1
Evers, 2b	3	0	0	5	5	0
Casey, 3b	2	0	0	2	3	0
Graham, p	2	0	0	0	3	0
Currie, p	1	0	0	0	1	0
Totals	29	0	0	27	22	3

```
Philadelphia ............... 4 0 0 0 2 0 1 0 3 — 10
Chicago ....................... 0 0 0 0 0 0 0 0 0 —  0
```

Left on bases—Chicago 7, Philadelphia 7. Two-base hits—Zimmer, Barry. Double plays—Kling, Casey; Zimmer, Wolverton; Fraser, Hulswitt, Douglas. Sacrifice hit—Titus. Stolen bases—Chance 2. Struck out—By Graham 4, Fraser 4. First base on balls—Off Graham 3, Fraser 5. Hit by pitcher—Wolverton. Time— 1:40. Umpires—Emslie, and Moran. Attendance—2,000.

May 5, 1904 Philadelphia at Boston

PHILADELPHIA	ab	h	po	a	e
Hartsel, lf	1	0	0	0	0
Hoffman, lf	2	0	2	1	0
Pick'ing, cf	3	0	1	0	0
Davis, 1b	3	0	5	0	1
L. Cross, 3b	3	0	4	1	0
Seybold, rf	3	0	2	0	0
Murphy, 2b	3	0	1	2	0
M. Cross, ss	3	0	2	3	0
Schreck, c	3	0	7	0	0
Waddell, p	3	0	0	1	0
Totals	27	0	24	8	1

BOSTON	ab	h	po	a	e
D'ugh'ty, lf	4	1	1	0	0
Collins, 3b	4	2	2	0	0
Stahl, cf	4	1	3	0	0
Fre'man, rf	4	1	2	0	0
Parent, ss	4	2	1	4	0
LaCh'ce, 1b	3	1	9	0	0
Ferris, 2b	3	1	10	3	0
Criger, c	3	1	9	0	0
Young, p	3	0	0	2	0
Totals	32	10	27	9	0

```
Philadelphia ............... 0 0 0 0 0 0 0 0 0 — 0
Boston ......................... 0 0 0 0 1 2 0 x — 3
```

Two-Base Hits—Collins, Criger. Three-Base Hits—Stahl, Freeman, Ferris. Sacrifice Hit—La Chance. Double Plays—Hoffman and Schreck, L. Cross and Davis. Struck Out—By Young, 8; by Waddell, 6. Time—1:25. Umpire—Dwyer. Attendance—10,267.

June 11, 1904   Chicago at New York

CHICAGO	r	h	p	a	e	NEW YORK	r	h	p	a	e
Slagle, lf	0	0	2	1	0	Bresn'n, cf	0	0	4	0	0
Casey, 3b	0	2	1	3	1	Browne, rf	0	0	1	0	0
Chance, 1b	1	3	15	3	0	Devlin, 3b	0	0	0	4	0
Kling, c	0	0	10	0	0	McGann, 1b	0	0	18	1	0
Jones, rf	0	2	2	0	0	Mertes, lf	0	1	4	0	0
Evers, 2b	0	2	3	7	0	Dahlen, ss	0	0	4	6	0
Tinker, ss	0	1	0	3	1	Gilbert, 2b	0	0	2	4	0
Wil'ms, cf	0	0	1	0	0	Warner, c	0	0	3	4	0
Wicker, p	0	0	2	2	0	McGinnity, p	0	0	0	6	0
Totals	1	10	36	19	2	Totals	0	1	36	25	0

```
Chicago ...... 0 0 0 0 0 0 0 0 0 0 0 1 — 1
New York .... 0 0 0 0 0 0 0 0 0 0 0 0 — 0
```

First base on errors—New York, 2. Left on bases—New York, 3; Chicago, 5. First base on balls—Off Wicker, 1. Struck out—By McGinnity, 2; by Wicker, 10; Two-base hit—Evers—Sacrifice hits—Evers (2). Stolen bases—Browne, Deviln, Tinker. Double plays—Gilbert, Dahlen and McGann. Umpires—Emslie and O'Day. Time—2 hours and 15 minutes. Attendance 38,805.

August 17, 1904   Boston at Chicago

BOSTON	ab	h	po	a	e	CHICAGO	ab	h	po	a	e
Selbach, lf	4	2	0	0	0	Green, rf	3	0	0	0	0
Parent, ss	4	2	0	4	0	Jones, cf	3	0	1	0	0
Stahl, cf	3	1	5	0	0	Callahan, lf	3	0	1	0	0
Collins, 3b	5	2	1	2	0	Davis, ss	2	0	2	2	1
Freeman, lf	3	1	2	0	0	L. Tan'ill, 3b	3	0	2	2	0
LaChan'e, 1b	4	0	12	0	0	Isbell, 1b	3	0	10	3	0
Ferris, 2b	4	1	1	5	0	Dundon, 2b	3	0	1	3	0
Farrell, c	2	0	6	0	0	Sullivan, c	3	0	7	2	0
J. Tan'ill, p	3	1	0	2	0	Altrock, p	1	0	2	2	0
Total	32	10	27	13	0	Walsh, p	2	0	1	3	0
						Totals	26	0	27	17	1

```
Boston ......................... 1 0 3 0 0 0 0 0 2 — 6
Chicago ....................... 0 0 0 0 0 0 0 0 0 — 0
```

Base Hits—Off Altrock, 6, in three innings; off Walsh, 4 in six innings. Left on Bases—Chicago, 2; Boston, 7. Two-Base Hits—Stahl, Selbach. Three-Base Hit—Collins. Sacrifice Hits—Jones, Parent, Farrell. Double Plays—Altrock, Sullivan, Dundon and Altrock; Davis and Bell. Struck Out—By Walsh, 4; by Tannehill, 4. Bases on Balls—Off Altrock, 2; off Walsh 5; off Tannehill, 1. Wild Pitch—Walsh. Hit by Ball—Green. Time 1:36. Umpire—Sheridan. Attendance 10,500.

June 13, 1905   New York at Chicago

NEW YORK	ab	r	bh	tb	po	a	e	CHICAGO	ab	r	bh	tb	po	a	e
Donlin, cf	4	0	1	1	3	0	0	Slagle, cf	4	0	0	0	3	0	0
Browne, rf	4	0	1	1	1	1	0	Schulte, lf	3	0	0	0	1	0	0
McGann, 1b	4	1	1	1	14	0	0	Maloney, rf	3	0	0	0	5	0	0
Mertes, lf	4	0	1	1	3	0	0	Chance, 1b	3	0	0	0	8	0	0
Dahlen, ss	4	0	1	2	3	1	Tinker, ss	3	0	0	0	3	4	1
Devlin, 3b	1	0	0	0	0	1	0	Evers, 2b	3	0	0	0	2	2	0
Gilbert, 2b	3	0	0	0	1	5	1	Casey, 3b	3	0	0	0	1	2	0
Bowerman, c	3	0	0	0	3	0	0	Kling, c	3	0	0	0	4	2	1
Mathewson, p	3	0	0	0	4	0	Brown, p	3	0	0	0	0	0	0
Totals	30	1	5	5	27	14	2	Totals	28	0	0	0	27	10	2

```
New York ..................... 0 0 0 0 0 0 0 1 — 1
Chicago ....................... 0 0 0 0 0 0 0 0 0 — 0
```

Left on bases—Chicago 1. New York 4. Stolen bases, Schulte, Dahlen. Double play—Browne and McGann. Struck out—By Brown 3, by Mathewson 2. Bases on balls—Off Brown 2. Balk—Brown. Time—1h. 25m. Umpires—Bauswine and Emslie. Attendance—9000.

July 22, 1905 Philadelphia at St. Louis

PHILADELPHIA	ab	r	bh	tb	po	a	e
Hartsel, lf	3	1	1	2	0	0	0
Hoffman, cf	4	2	2	4	4	0	0
Davis, 1b	4	2	3	6	11	1	0
Cross, 3b	5	1	3	4	1	2	0
Seybold, rf	3	0	1	2	2	0	0
Murphy, 2b	4	0	0	0	3	2	0
Knight, ss	4	0	0	0	2	2	0
Barton, c	4	0	0	0	2	3	1
Henley, p	4	0	0	0	2	4	0
Totals	35	6	10	18	27	14	1

ST. LOUIS	ab	r	bh	tb	po	a	e
Stone, lf	4	0	0	0	3	0	0
Starr, 2b	2	0	0	0	1	4	0
Van Zant, rf	3	0	0	0	0	0	0
Wallace, ss	3	0	0	0	1	7	0
Koehler, cf	3	0	0	0	0	0	1
Jones, 1b	3	0	0	0	14	0	0
Gleason, 3b	1	0	0	0	0	0	0
Roth, c	3	0	0	0	8	2	0
Pelty, p	3	0	0	0	0	2	0
Totals	23	0	0	0	27	15	1

```
Philadelphia............... 2 0 2 0 1 0 1 0 0 — 6
St. Louis..................... 0 0 0 0 0 0 0 0 0 — 0
```

Two base hits—Cross, Seybold. Davis, Hartsel. Two-base hits—Davis. Hoffman. Stolen bases—Hoffman 2, Murphy. Bases on balls—Off Pelty 5, off Henley 3. Struck out—By Pelty 5, by Henley 2. Left on bases—St. Louis 1, Philadelphia 7. Time—1h. 40m. Umpire—O'Loughlin.

Sept. 6, 1905 Chicago at Detroit

CHICAGO	ab	h	po	a	e
Green, rf	4	1	2	0	0
Isbell, cf	5	2	4	0	0
Davis, ss	5	0	0	1	0
Callahan, lf	5	2	1	0	0
Donohue, 1b	4	1	5	1	0
McFarl'nd, c	5	2	11	0	0
Rohe 2b	5	1	1	3	0
Tann'hill, 3b	4	1	2	1	0
Smith, p	4	2	1	0	0
Totals	41	12	27	6	0

DETROIT	ab	h	po	a	e
McIntyre, lf	3	0	3	0	0
Lindsay, 1b	4	0	10	2	1
Schaefer, 2b	2	0	1	1	0
Lowe, 2b	2	0	2	1	0
Crawf'rd, rf	2	0	1	0	0
Cobb, cf	2	0	0	0	0
O'ughlin, 3b	3	0	1	3	1
O'Leary, ss	3	0	4	4	3
Warner, c	0	0	2	0	0
Doran, c	3	0	2	0	0
Wiggs, p	0	0	0	1	0
Disch, p	3	0	1	2	0
Totals	27	0	27	14	5

```
Chicago....................... 8 1 0 0 1 0 5 0 0 — 15
Detroit....................... 0 0 0 0 0 0 0 0 0 — 0
```

Hits—Off Wiggs, 1 in one inning; off Disch, 11 in eight innings. Two-Base Hits—McFarland. Smith, Green. Three-Base Hit—Callahan. Sacrifice Hit—Davis. Stolen Base—Isbell. Bases on Balls—Off Wiggs, 5; off Disch, 1; off Smith, 3. Hit with Ball—By Disch, 1. Left on Bases—Detroit. 3; Chicago, 7. Struck Out—By Wiggs, 2; by Disch, 2; by Smith, 8. Time—1:43. Umpires—O'Loughlin and McCarthy.

Sept. 27, 1905 Chicago at Boston

CHICAGO	ab	h	po	a	e
Jones, cf	3	0	2	0	0
Isbell, 2b	3	0	4	4	0
Davis, ss	3	0	3	4	1
Calla'n, lf	3	0	1	1	0
Dono'e, 1b	3	0	11	0	0
Green, rf	3	0	0	0	0
Rohe, 3b	2	0	1	0	0
Sullivan, c	3	0	2	0	0
Owen, p	3	0	0	4	0
Totals	26	0	24	13	1

BOSTON	ab	h	po	a	e
Parent, ss	4	0	2	1	0
Stahl, cf	4	1	3	0	0
Ungl'b, 3b	2	0	3	1	0
Burkett, lf	3	2	2	0	0
Free'n, 1b	2	0	7	0	0
Selbach, rf	3	1	1	0	0
Ferris, 2b	3	2	3	1	0
Armb'er, c	3	0	6	1	0
Dineen, p	3	0	0	1	0
Totals	27	6	27	5	0

```
Chicago....................... 0 0 0 0 0 0 0 0 0 — 0
Boston....................... 0 0 0 1 0 0 1 0 x — 2
```

Two-Base Hit—Stahl. Three-Base Hits—Selbach. Ferris. Sacrifice Hits—Isbell, Unglaub, Freeman. Double Play—Isbell. Davis and Donohue. Hit by Pitched Ball—By Dineen, Rohe. Struck Out—By Owen, 2; by Dineen, 6. First Base on Balls—Off Dineen, 2. Time—1:30. Umpire—Connolly.

May 1, 1906   Philadelphia at Brooklyn

PHILADELPHIA	ab	r	bh	tb	po	a	e
Thomas, cf........	4	2	2	2	1	0	0
Ward, 3b...........	5	2	4	6	0	2	0
Magee, rf..........	4	1	1	1	0	0	0
Titus, lf..............	4	1	2	2	2	0	0
Bransfield, 1b...	4	0	1	1	7	1	0
Doolin, ss.........	2	0	0	0	1	3	1
Gleason, 2b......	4	0	1	1	2	2	0
Dooin, c............	4	0	0	0	11	0	0
Lush, p..............	4	0	0	0	3	1	0
Totals	35	6	11	13	27	9	1

BROOKLYN	ab	r	bh	tb	po	a	e
Lumley, rf.........	4	0	0	0	3	0	0
Maloney, cf.......	3	0	0	0	3	0	0
Casey, 3b..........	4	0	0	0	2	3	2
Jordan, 1b..........	4	0	0	0	6	1	0
Batch, lf	2	0	0	0	1	0	0
Lewis, ss...........	2	0	0	0	1	0	0
Hummel, 2b......	3	0	0	0	4	2	0
Bergen, c	3	0	0	0	6	3	1
Eason, p............	2	0	0	0	1	2	1
* McIntyre........	1	0	0	0	0	0	0
Knolls, p	0	0	0	0	0	0	1
Totals	28	0	0	0	27	11	5

* Batted for Eason in eighth inning.

```
Philadelphia................ 2  0  0  1  0  0  0  2  1 — 6
Brooklyn..................... 0  0  0  0  0  0  0  0  0 — 0
```

Three-base hit—Ward. Hits—Off Eason 9, in eight innings; off Knolls 2, in one inning. Sacrifice hits—Doolin. Casey, Stolen base—Titus. Left on bases—Philadelphia 6. Brooklyn 4. First base on balls—Off Eason 3, off Knolls 1, off Lush 3. First base on errors—Philadelphia 2, Brooklyn 1. Struck out—By Eason 1, by Knolls 1, by Lush 11. Time—1h. 45m. Umpire—O'Day.

July 20, 1906   Brooklyn at St. Louis

BROOKLYN	ab	r	bh	tb	po	a	e
Maloney, cf.......	4	0	1	1	0	0	0
Casey, 3b..........	4	0	0	0	1	1	0
Lumley, rf.........	4	0	1	1	3	0	0
Jordan, 1b.........	3	1	2	3	9	0	0
Alperman, 2b.....	1	0	0	0	2	3	0
McCarthy, lf.....	3	0	1	1	2	0	0
Lewis, ss...........	3	1	2	2	2	2	1
Ritter, c.............	3	0	2	2	8	2	0
Eason, p............	3	0	1	1	0	1	0
Totals	28	2	10	11	27	9	1

ST. LOUIS	ab	r	bh	tb	po	a	e
Burch, cf...........	3	0	0	0	0	0	0
Bennett, 2b.......	4	0	0	0	1	4	0
Mertes, lf..........	3	0	0	0	2	1	0
Grady, c.............	2	0	0	0	2	3	0
Noonan, 1b........	3	0	0	0	14	3	1
J. Marshall, rf...	3	0	0	0	1	0	0
Hostetter, 3b	3	0	0	0	0	0	0
McBride, ss	3	0	0	0	7	5	0
Thompson, p....	2	0	0	0	0	6	0
* Murray	1	0	0	0	0	0	0
	27	0	0	0	27	22	1

* Batted for Thompson in ninth.

```
Brooklyn..................... 0  2  0  0  0  0  0  0  0 — 2
St. Louis ..................... 0  0  0  0  0  0  0  0  0 — 0
```

Two-base hit—Jordan. Sacrifice hits—Alperman 2. Double play—Thompson. McBride and Noonan. Wild Pitch—Thompson. First base on balls—Off Thompson 1, off Eason 3. Struck out—By Eason 5, by Thompson 1. Left on bases—St. Louis 3, Brcoklyn 2. Time 1h. 35m. Umpire—Carpenter.

August 1, 1906 Brooklyn at Pittsburgh

PITTSBURGH	r	h	p	a	e
Leach, lf	0	0	1	0	0
B'mont, cf	0	0	2	0	0
Ganley, rf	1	1	1	0	0
Wagner, ss	0	1	6	8	0
Nealon, 1b	0	1	17	2	0
Sh'han, 3b	0	0	1	4	0
Ritchey, 2b	0	1	5	7	0
Phelps, c	0	0	6	1	0
Liefield, p	0	0	0	4	0
Totals	1	4	39	26	0

BROOKLYN	r	h	p	a	e
Maloney, cf	0	0	1	0	0
Casey, 3b	0	1	1	2	0
Lumley, rf	0	1	2	0	0
Jordan, 1b	0	1	14	0	0
Alperm'n, 2b	0	2	2	3	1
McCarthy, lf	0	2	1	0	0
Lewis, ss	0	1	5	5	0
Bergen, c	0	0	13	1	0
McIntire, p	0	1	0	4	0
Totals	0	9	39	15	1

Brooklyn 0 0 0 0 0 0 0 0 0 0 0 0 0 — 0
Pittsburgh 0 0 0 0 0 0 0 0 0 0 0 0 1 — 1

First base on error—Pittsburgh. Left on bases—Pittsburgh 8: Brooklyn, 9. First base on balls—Off McIntire, 1: off Liefield, 2. Struck out—By McIntire, 8; by Liefield, 5. Two base hits—Lumley, Wagner. Sacrifice hits—Maloney, McCarthy, Bergen. Stolen bases—Casey, Lewis. Double plays—McIntire, Lewis and Jordan; Alperman, Lewis and Jordan; Wagner, Ritchey and Nealon. Hit by pitcher—By Liefield, 1. Umpire—Johnstone. Time—2 hours and 10 minutes. Attendance—3,000.

May 8, 1907 Cincinnati at Boston

CINCINNATI	ab	r	b	p	a	e
Huggins, 2b	4	0	0	5	4	2
Kane, 3b	4	0	0	0	3	1
Davis, cf	4	0	0	3	0	0
Lobert, ss	3	0	0	1	2	0
Cannell, 1b	2	0	0	10	2	0
Mitchell, rf	3	0	0	1	0	1
Kruger, lf	3	0	0	0	0	0
Schlei, c	2	0	0	3	2	0
Mason, p	2	0	0	1	3	0
Totals	27	0	0	24	16	4

BOSTON	ab	r	b	p	a	e
Bates, rf	3	1	1	1	0	0
Tenney, 1b	2	2	0	12	0	0
Beaum't, cf	4	1	2	3	0	0
Howard, 2b	3	0	0	2	3	0
Bridwell, ss	3	1	1	0	4	0
Burke, lf	4	0	1	2	0	0
Brain, 3b	3	0	1	2	3	1
Brown, c	3	1	1	5	0	0
Pfeffer, p	3	0	1	0	2	0
Totals	28	6	8	27	12	1

Cincinnati 0 0 0 0 0 0 0 0 0 — 0
Boston 0 0 1 1 2 0 0 2 x — 6

Two-base hit—Pfeffer. Sacrifice hits—Tenney, Howard, Mason, Huggins. Stolen bases—Bridwell, Ganzel. Left on bases—Boston 4, Cincinnati 4. First on balls—Off Pfeffer 1, Mason 3. Hit by pitcher—Ganzel, Bridwell. Struck out—By Pfeffer 3. Mason 1. Umpire—Emslie. Time—1:45. Attendance—2696.

Sept. 20, 1907 Brooklyn at Pittsburgh

BROOKLYN	ab	r	b	p	a	e
Casey, 3b	3	0	0	0	3	0
Lewis, ss	3	0	0	3	4	0
Jordan, 1b	3	0	0	12	0	0
Hummel, 2b	4	0	0	1	3	0
Batch, lf	4	1	0	3	0	0
Burch, rf	2	0	0	1	0	0
Maloney, cf	2	0	0	0	0	0
Bergen, c	3	0	0	0	0	0
Stricklett, p	3	0	0	0	2	0
Totals	27	1	0	24	12	0

PITTSBURGH	ab	r	b	p	a	e
Hallman, rf	4	0	0	2	0	0
Leach, cf	4	0	0	1	0	0
Clarke, lf	4	0	2	0	0	0
Wagner, ss	3	1	0	3	3	1
Abbat'o, 2b	3	0	0	0	4	0
Swaci'a, 1b	2	1	0	14	0	0
Storke, 3b	0	0	0	1	2	0
Gibson, c	2	0	0	6	0	0
Maddox, p	3	0	0	0	1	1
Totals	25	2	2	27	10	2

Brooklyn 0 0 0 1 0 0 0 0 0 — 1
Pittsburgh 0 0 0 1 0 1 0 x — 2

Two-base hit—Clarke. Sacrifice hits—Storke, Gibson, Maloney. First on balls—Off Maddox 3, Stricklett 4. Hit by pitcher—Jordan. Struck out—By Maddox 5. Left on bases—Pittsburgh 5, Brooklyn 4. First on errors—Brooklyn 2. Time—1:30. Umpire—Klem. Attendance—2380.

June 30, 1908   Boston at New York

BOSTON	ab	r	b	p	a	e
Thoney, lf	0	0	0	0	0	0
Cravath, lf	5	0	1	4	0	0
Sullivan, cf	5	1	1	1	0	0
McCon'l, 2b	2	2	2	2	4	0
Gessler, rf	3	0	1	2	0	0
Laporte, 3b	4	0	2	2	2	0
Unglaub, 1b	4	2	2	13	0	0
Wagner, ss	4	2	1	0	3	0
Criger, c	3	0	0	3	2	0
Young, p	5	1	3	0	1	0
Totals	35	8	13	27	12	0

NEW YORK	ab	r	b	p	a	e
Niles, 2b	2	0	0	3	6	0
Keeler, rf	3	0	0	2	1	1
Moriar'y, 1b	3	0	0	10	1	1
Hemphill, cf	3	0	0	0	0	0
Ball, ss	3	0	0	3	3	0
Stahl, lf	3	0	0	2	1	0
Conroy, 3b	3	0	0	0	1	0
Blair, c	3	0	0	7	2	0
Manning, p	0	0	0	0	2	0
Newton, p	1	0	0	0	1	1
Lake, p	2	0	0	0	0	0
Totals	26	0	0	27	18	3

```
Boston...................... 1 1 2 1 0 1 0 0 2 — 8
New York ................ 0 0 0 0 0 0 0 0 0 — 0
```

Hits—Off Manning 3 in 1 2-3 innings. Newton 3 in 2-3 inning, Lake 7 in 5 2-3 innings. Sacrifice hits—McConnell 2, Criger 2. Stolen base—McConnell. Double play—Stahl, Blair. Left on bases—Boston 11. First on balls—Off Manning 3, Newton 1, Lake 1, Young 1. First on errors—Boston 2. Hit by pitcher—By Manning 1. Newton 1. Struck out—By Manning 1, Newton 1, Lake 4, Young 2. Time—2h. Umpire—O'Loughlin. Attendance—1500.

July 4, 1908   Philadelphia at New York

PHILLIES	ab	h	o	a	e
Grant, 3b	4	0	3	4	1
Knabe, 2b	4	0	1	4	0
Titus, rf	4	0	1	0	0
Magee, lf	4	0	2	0	0
Bransfield, 1b	3	0	14	0	0
Osborne, cf	3	0	2	0	0
Doolin, ss	1	0	2	2	0
Dooin, c	3	0	1	1	0
McQuillen, p	2	0	0	3	0
Courtney, ss.	2	0	1	3	1
Totals	30	0*27	17	3

NEW YORK	ab	h	o	a	e
Tenney, 1b	4	2	14	1	0
Doyle, 2b	3	0	0	1	0
Bresnahan, c	4	0	5	1	0
Donlin, rf	3	1	4	0	0
Seymour, cf	4	1	0	0	0
Devlin, 3b	4	2	0	0	0
Shannon, lf	2	0	3	0	0
Bridwell, ss	4	2	3	7	0
Wiltse, p	1	0	1	4	0
Totals	29	8	30	14	0

* None out when winning run was made.

```
Philadelphia .......... 0 0 0 0 0 0 0 0 0 0 — 0
New York ............... 0 0 0 0 0 0 0 0 0 1 — 1
```

Stolen base—Donlin. Double plays—Knabe and Bransfield; Grant and Bransfield. Hit by pitcher—By Wiltse 1. Struck out—By Wiltse 5, by McQuillen 1.

Sept. 5, 1908   Boston at Brooklyn

BOSTON	ab	h	o	a	e
Browne, rf	3	0	0	0	0
*Bowerman	1	0	0	0	0
Bates, lf	3	0	3	1	1
†Smith	1	0	0	0	0
Keeley, cf	3	0	0	0	0
McGann, 1b	3	0	14	0	1
Dahlen, ss	3	0	2	3	0
Sweeney, 3b	3	0	1	1	1
Graham, c	3	0	2	1	0
Hannifan, 2b	3	0	2	4	0
Flaherty, p	2	0	0	5	1
‡Ritchey	1	0	0	0	0
Totals	29	0	24	15	4

BROOKLYN	ab	h	o	a	e
Burch, cf	4	1	2	0	0
Lumley, rf	4	1	1	0	1
Hummel, lf	4	0	0	0	0
Jordan, 1b	3	3	7	0	0
Alperman, 2b	3	2	0	4	0
Lewis, ss	2	0	1	0	1
Sheehan, 3b	3	0	0	0	1
Bergen, c	4	1	15	1	0
Rucker, p	4	0	1	2	0
Totals	31	8	27	7	3

* Batted for Browne in ninth.
† Batted for Bates in ninth.
‡ Batted for Flaherty in ninth.

```
Boston..........................  0 0 0 0 0 0 0 0 0 — 0
Brooklyn.....................  0 4 0 0 0 0 0 2 * — 6
```

Two-base hit—Bergen. Home run—Jordan. Double plays—Rucker and Jordan; Bates, Graham and Sweeney. Bases on balls—Off Flaherty 2. Hit by pitcher—By Flaherty 1. Struck out—By Rucker 14, by Flaherty 2. Umpire—Johnstone.

Sept. 18, 1908   Boston at Cleveland

BOSTON	ab	r	b	p	a	e
Niles, 2b	4	0	0	2	1	0
Lord, 3b	4	0	0	0	2	0
Speaker, cf	3	0	0	0	0	0
Gessler, rf	1	1	0	1	0	1
Thoney, lf	2	0	0	2	0	0
Wagner, ss	3	0	0	4	7	1
Stahl, 1b	3	0	0	9	0	0
Donohoe, c	3	0	0	5	1	1
Arellanes, p	3	0	0	1	1	0
Totals	26	1	0	24	12	3

CLEVELAND	ab	r	b	p	a	e
Goode, rf	4	1	1	0	0	0
Bradley, 3b	4	0	0	1	1	1
Hinch'n, lf	4	0	0	1	0	0
Lajoie, 2b	4	1	1	3	7	1
Stovall, 1b	3	0	1	16	2	0
Bemis, c	3	0	1	2	1	0
Birmi'm, cf	3	0	0	2	0	0
Perring, ss	3	0	0	1	2	0
Rhoades, p	3	0	1	1	7	0
Totals	31	2	5	27	19	2

```
Boston..........................  0 1 0 0 0 0 0 0 0 — 1
Cleveland.....................  0 0 0 1 0 0 0 1 x — 2
```

First on errors—Boston 2, Cleveland 2. Three-base hits—Rhoades, Lajoie. Sacrifice hits—Thoney 2, Gessler 2. First on balls—Off Rhoades 2. Hit by pitched ball—Rhoades 1. Left on bases—Cleveland 5, Boston 5. Struck out—By Rhoades 2. Arellanes 5. Wild pitches—Rhoades, Arellanes 1. Time—1:39. Umpire—Connolly. Attendance—6950.

Sept. 20, 1908 Philadelphia at Chicago

ATHLETICS	ab	r	b	p	a	e
Nicholls, ss	4	0	0	1	2	0
Oldring, lf	4	0	0	3	0	0
Murphy, 1b	3	0	0	12	0	0
Coombs, cf	3	0	0	0	0	0
Seybold, rf	3	0	0	1	0	0
Manusch, 3b	2	0	0	1	4	1
Barr, 2b	3	0	0	2	2	1
Lapp, c	3	0	0	5	1	0
Plank, p	3	0	0	0	1	0
Totals	28	0	0	*25	10	2

CHICAGO	ab	r	b	p	a	e
Hahn, rf	4	0	1	1	0	0
Jones, cf	4	0	0	3	0	0
Isbell, 1b	3	1	2	14	0	1
Anderson, lf	4	0	0	3	0	0
Davis, 2b	3	0	0	2	2	0
Parent, ss	4	0	0	1	2	0
Sullivan, c	3	0	1	3	0	0
Tanne'l, 3b	3	0	0	0	5	0
Smith, p	3	0	0	0	5	0
Totals	31	1	4	27	14	1

* One out when winning run was scored.

```
Athletics .................. 0 0 0 0 0 0 0 0 0 — 0
Chicago .................... 0 0 0 0 0 0 0 0 1 — 1
```

Left on bases—Chicago 5. Athletics 2. Stolen bases—Isbell, Davis. Double play—Murphy, unassisted. First on balls—Off Smith 1, Plank 1. Struck out—By Smith 2, Plank 5. Hit by pitcher—By Plank 1. Passed ball—Lapp. Wild pitch—Plank. Umpires—Fagan and O'Loughlin. Time—1.31. Attendance—14,000.

October 2, 1908 Chicago at Cleveland

CHICAGO	ab	r	h	o	a	e
Hahn, rf	3	0	0	1	0	0
Jones, cf	3	0	0	0	0	0
Isbell, 1b	3	0	0	7	1	1
Dougherty, lf	3	0	0	0	0	0
Davis, 2b	3	0	0	1	0	0
Parent, ss	3	0	0	0	3	0
Schreck, c	2	0	0	12	1	0
Shaw, c	0	0	0	2	0	0
*White	1	0	0	0	0	0
Tannehill, 3b	2	0	0	0	0	0
†Donohue	1	0	0	0	0	0
Walsh, p	2	0	0	1	3	0
‡Anderson	1	0	0	0	0	0
Totals	27	0	0	24	8	1

CLEVELAND	ab	r	h	o	a	e
Goode, rf	4	0	0	1	0	0
Bradley, 3b	4	0	0	0	1	0
Hinchman, lf	3	0	0	3	0	0
Lajoie, 2b	3	0	1	2	8	0
Stovall, 1b	3	0	0	16	0	0
N. Clarke, c	3	0	0	4	1	0
Birmingham, cf	3	1	2	0	0	0
Perring, ss	2	0	1	1	1	0
Joss, p	3	0	0	0	5	0
Totals	28	1	4	27	16	0

* Batted for Shaw in ninth.
† Batted for Tannehill in 9th.
‡ Batted for Walsh in ninth.

```
Chicago .................... 0 0 0 0 0 0 0 0 0 — 0
Cleveland .................. 0 0 1 0 0 0 0 0 x — 1
```

Stolen bases—Birmingham 2, Lajoie, Perring. First base on balls—Off Walsh 1. Left on bases—Cleveland 4. Struck out—by Joss 3, Walsh 15. Wild Pitch—Walsh. Time—1:29. Umpires—Connolly and O'Loughlin. Attendance—10,598.

April 15, 1909   Brooklyn at New York

BROOKLYN	ab	h	p	a	e
Burch, lf	6	1	5	0	0
Alper'an, 2b	6	2	2	11	0
Hummel, ss	5	0	3	3	0
Sebring, cf	5	0	3	1	0
Lumley, rf	5	1	1	0	0
Jordan, 1b	4	1	19	0	0
Lennox, 3b	4	1	1	2	0
Bergen, c	5	1	5	2	0
Wilhelm, p	5	0	0	4	0
Totals	45	7	39	23	0

NEW YORK	ab	h	p	a	e
Herzog, lf	6	2	0	0	0
Fletcher, 2b	5	0	0	7	1
*McCor'ick	1	0	0	0	0
Murray, rf	5	0	0	1	0
Tenney, 1b	5	0	24	1	0
O'Hara, cf	3	0	0	0	0
Devlin, 3b	2	0	0	0	0
Bridwell, ss	4	0	4	7	0
Schlei, c	4	1	10	1	1
Ames, p	4	0	1	9	0
†Myers	1	1	0	0	0
Totals	40	4	39	26	2

* Batted for Fletcher in the thirteenth inning.
† Batted for Ames in the thirteenth inning.

```
Brooklyn   0 0 0 0 0 0 0 0 0 0 0 0 3 — 3
New York   0 0 0 0 0 0 0 0 0 0 0 0 0 — 0
```

Runs—Brooklyn—Lumley, 1; Jordan, 1; Lennox, 1. First base on error—Brooklyn. Left on bases—Brooklyn, 4; New York, 8. First base on balls—Off Wilhelm, 7; off Ames, 2. Struck out—By Wilhelm, 4; by Ames, 10. Three base hit—Lumley. Two base hits—Alperman (2), Jordan. Stolen bases—Burch, O'Hara. Double play—Fletcher, Bridwell and Tenney. Umpires—Johnstone and Cusack. Time—2 hours and 20 minutes. Attendance—30,000.

April 20, 1910   Cleveland at Chicago

CLEVELAND	ab	r	b	p	a	e
Krueger, lf	4	1	2	1	0	0
Bradley, 3b	4	0	1	0	4	1
Turner, 2b	4	0	2	0	2	0
Lajole, 1b	3	0	0	19	0	0
Lord, rf	4	0	1	2	0	0
Clarke, c	3	0	1	3	2	0
Birmi'm, cf	3	0	0	0	0	0
Ball, ss	3	0	0	2	3	0
Joss, p	3	0	0	0	10	0
Totals	31	1	7	27	21	1

CHICAGO	ab	r	b	p	a	e
Hahn, rf	4	0	0	1	0	0
Zeider, 2b	4	0	0	3	1	0
Gandil, 1b	3	0	0	12	0	0
Burrows, lf	3	0	0	1	0	0
Parent, cf	2	0	0	0	0	0
Purtell, 3b	2	0	0	1	4	0
Blackb'n, ss	3	0	0	2	2	0
Payne, c	3	0	0	7	1	0
White, p	2	0	0	0	6	0
Totals	26	0	0	27	14	0

```
Cleveland   0 0 0 0 0 1 0 0 0 — 1
Chicago     0 0 0 0 0 0 0 0 0 — 0
```

Two-base hit—Krueger. Sacrifice hit—Purtell. Stolen bases—Bradley, Turner, Double play—Payne Gandil. Left on bases— Chicago 2. Cleveland 6. First on balls —Off White 2, Joss 2. Hit by pitcher—By White 1. Struck out—By White 4. Joss 2. Time—1:40. Umpires—Perrine and O'Loughlin. Attendance—5000.

May 12, 1910   Cleveland at Philadelphia

ATHLETICS	ab	r	b	p	a	e
Hartsel, lf	4	0	1	4	0	0
Oldring, cf	4	0	0	3	0	0
Collins, 2b	3	0	0	1	1	0
Baker, 3b	4	2	2	3	2	0
Davis, 1b	3	0	1	9	0	0
Murphy, rf	4	1	2	2	0	0
Barry, ss	3	0	2	0	4	0
Thomas, c	3	0	0	6	1	0
Bender, p	3	1	1	0	1	0
Totals	31	4	9	27	9	0

CLEVELAND	ab	r	b	p	a	e
Graney, cf	3	0	0	4	0	0
Krueger, lf	3	0	0	2	1	0
Turner, ss	2	0	0	2	1	1
Lajoie, 2b	3	0	0	3	1	0
Stovall, 1b	3	0	0	9	3	0
Easterly, c	3	0	0	3	0	0
Lord, rf	3	0	0	0	0	0
Bradley, 3b	3	0	0	0	1	1
Lincke, p	2	0	0	1	6	2
*Flick	1	0	0	0	0	0
Totals	26	0	0	24	13	4

* Batted for Lincke in ninth inning.

Cleveland	0	0	0	0	0	0	0	0	0 —	0
Athletics	0	1	0	1	0	1	0	1	1 x —	4

Two-base hit—Murphy. Three-base hit—Hartsel. Sacrifice hit—Davis. Struck out—By Lincke 2, Bender 4. Left on bases—Athletics 5. First on balls—Off Lincke 1, Bender 1. Time—1.36. Umpires—Dineen and Connolly. Attendance—2500.

August 30, 1910   Cleveland at New York

CLEVELAND	ab	r	b	p	a	e
Turner, 3b	4	1	0	0	3	0
Thomas'n, rf	5	1	1	2	0	0
Niles, lf	5	1	2	2	0	0
Lajoie, 2b	5	1	2	3	2	0
Stovall, 1b	5	0	1	13	1	0
Birmin'm, cf	4	0	0	4	0	0
Ball, ss	4	0	0	2	0	0
Land, c	4	0	0	6	3	0
Kaler, p	4	1	1	1	5	0
Totals	40	5	7	33	13	0

NEW YORK	ab	r	b	p	a	e
Daniels, lf	5	0	1	3	0	0
Wolter, rf	4	0	0	2	0	0
Chase, 1b	4	0	0	13	1	0
Knight, ss	3	0	1	1	3	0
Laporte, 2b	3	0	0	1	2	0
Cree, cf	4	0	1	3	0	0
Austin, 3b	2	0	0	2	4	1
Criger, c	4	0	0	8	0	0
Hughes, p	3	0	0	0	2	0
*Roach	1	0	0	0	0	0
Totals	33	0	3	33	17	1

* Batted for Hughes in eleventh inning.

Cleveland	0	0	0	0	0	0	0	0	0	0	5 —	5
New York	0	0	0	0	0	0	0	0	0	0	0 —	0

Sacrifice hits—Austin, Laporte. Stolen base—Lajoie. Left on bases—Cleveland 3, New York 4. First on error—Cleveland. First on balls—Off Kaler 2. Hughes 1. Struck out—By Kaler 6, Hughes 7. Umpires—Egan and O'Loughlin. Time—1.58. Attendance—12,000.

July 29, 1911   St. Louis at Boston

ST. LOUIS

	ab	r	h	o	a
Shotten, cf	4	0	0	1	0
Austin, 3b	4	0	0	1	4
Sch'zer, rf	3	0	0	1	0
Laporte, 2b	8	0	0	3	2
Hogan, lf	1	0	0	1	0
Stephens, c	2	0	0	4	2
Block, 1b	3	0	0	10	2
Wallace, ss	3	0	0	1	2
Lake, p	1	0	0	2	3
*Criss	1	0	0	0	0
Totals	25	0	0	24	15

BOSTON

	ab	r	h	o	a
Hooper, rf	4	0	0	0	0
Engle, 1b	4	0	2	8	1
Speaker, cf	3	1	1	2	0
Wagner, 2b	4	1	0	0	2
Carri'n, c	4	1	1	14	0
Gardner, 3b	4	1	1	0	2
Riggert, lf	3	0	1	1	0
Yerkes, ss	3	1	1	1	1
Wood, p	3	0	0	1	2
Totals	32	5	7	27	8

* Batted for Lake in ninth.

```
St. Louis ..................... 0 0 0 0 0 0 0 0 0 — 0
Boston ....................... 0 1 0 0 1 2 0 1 x — 5
```

Errors—St. Louis, Laporte, Stephens, Block, Wallace; Boston, none. Two-base hit—Engle. Three-base hit—Gardner. Home run—Speaker. Sacrifice hit—Stephens. Stolen base—Gardner. Double plays—Yerkes to Engle; Austin to Laporte to Block. Left on bases—Boston 5, St. Louis 2. First base on balls—Off Wood 2, off Lake 2. First base on errors—Boston 3. Hit by pitcher—by Wood (Hogan). Struck out—By Wood 12, by Lake 4. Time—1:48. Umpire—O'Loughlin.

August 27, 1911   Boston at Chicago

BOSTON

	ab	h	o	a	e
Henricks'n, rf	1	0	0	0	0
Riggert, rf	3	0	0	0	0
Speaker, cf	1	0	0	0	0
Williams, 1b	2	0	6	0	1
Engle, 1b-cf	2	0	4	1	1
Lewis, lf	3	0	3	0	0
Gardner, 3b	3	0	1	5	0
Carrigan, c	3	0	4	0	0
Wagner, 2b	3	0	1	0	0
Yerkes, ss	3	0	4	3	0
Collins, p	2	0	1	1	0
*Nunamaker	1	0	0	0	0
Totals	37	0	24	10	2

CHICAGO

	ab	h	o	a	e
McIntyre, rf	5	1	3	0	0
Lord, 3b	3	1	0	3	0
Callahan, lf	4	1	0	0	0
Bodie, cf	4	2	1	0	0
McConnell, 2b	4	1	0	5	0
Tannehill, ss	4	2	0	3	0
Mullen, 1b	3	0	17	0	0
Block, c	4	2	6	4	0
Walsh, p	4	1	0	2	0
Totals	35	11	27	17	0

* Batted for Collins in ninth.

```
Boston ....................... 0 0 0 0 0 0 0 0 0 — 0
Chicago ...................... 3 0 0 0 0 0 1 1 x — 5
```

Two-base hits—McConnell, Lord, Tannehill. Three-base hits—McIntyre, Tannehill. Bases on balls—Off Walsh 1. Struck out—By Walsh 8, by Collins 1. Wild pitch—Collins. Umpires—Evans and Mullen.

July 4, 1912   St. Louis at Detroit

ST. LOUIS	ab	r	b	p	a	e
Shotten, cf	1	0	0	4	1	0
Jantzen, rf	3	0	0	1	0	0
Kutina, 1b	4	0	0	7	1	0
Pratt, ss	4	0	0	3	4	1
Laporte, 2b	3	0	0	2	1	0
Austin, 3b	1	0	0	3	1	0
Hogan, lf	2	0	0	1	0	0
Compton, lf	1	0	0	0	0	0
Stephens, c	3	0	0	3	4	2
Adams, p	1	0	0	0	1	0
Hamilton, p	1	0	0	0	0	0
Mitchell, p	0	0	0	0	0	0
*Stovall	1	0	0	0	0	0
Totals	25	0	0	24	13	3

DETROIT	ab	r	b	p	a	e
Vitt, 3b	5	1	0	0	0	0
Bush, ss	3	1	1	4	1	0
Cobb, cf	4	1	3	6	0	0
Crawford, rf	3	1	1	2	0	0
Delaha'y, lf	3	1	1	0	0	0
Moriarty, 1b	4	0	1	6	1	0
Louden, 2b	3	2	3	1	3	1
Stanage, c	4	0	1	7	1	0
Mullin, p	4	0	3	1	3	0
Totals	33	7	14	27	9	1

* Batted for Hamilton in eighth inning.

```
St. Louis ..................... 0 0 0 0 0 0 0 0 0 — 0
Detroit ....................... 1 1 1 0 0 0 0 4 x — 7
```

Two-base hits—Delahanty, Mullin. Stolen bases—Vitt, Louden, Shotten, Austin. Sacrifice hit—Jantzen. Sacrifice fly—Delahanty. Struck out—By Mullin 5, Adams 1. First on balls—Off Mullin 5, Adams 1, Hamilton 1. Double plays—Mullen, Moriarty, Bush; Shatten, Pratt, Stephens; Stephens, Kutina. Stephens; Pratt, Laporte. First on errors—Detroit 2, St. Louis 1, Left on bases—Detroit 6, St. Louis 4. Hits—Off Adams 6 in 4 innings, Hamilton 2 in 3 innings, Mitchell 6 in 1 inning. Hit by pitcher—By Adams 1. Time—2.05. Umpires—Dineen and Sheridan.

August 30, 1912   St. Louis at Detroit

ST. LOUIS	ab	r	h	o	a
Shotten, cf	4	0	0	4	0
Compton, lf	5	0	2	3	0
Williams, r	5	0	1	0	0
Pratt, 2b	4	1	1	1	3
Kutina, 1b	4	1	1	16	0
Austin, 3b	3	0	2	1	3
Smowtry, s	4	0	0	1	3
Alex'der, c	3	1	2	0	0
Hamilt'n, p	1	1	0	1	3
Totals	33	5	9	27	12

DETROIT	ab	r	h	o	a
Jones, lf	4	0	0	0	0
Bush, ss	4	0	0	5	4
Cobb, cf	2	1	0	2	0
Crawford, r	4	0	0	0	0
Corriden, 2	3	0	0	3	5
Moriarty, 1	3	0	0	10	0
Vitt, 3b	3	0	0	2	2
Stanage, c	3	0	0	5	2
Dubuc, p	3	0	0	0	1
Totals	29	1	0	27	14

```
St. Louis ..................... 1 0 2 1 0 0 0 1 0 — 5
Detroit ....................... 0 0 0 1 0 0 0 0 0 — 1
```

Errors—St. Louis 2, Pratt. Austin; Detroit 3, Corridon 2, Dubuc. Two-base hits—Compton, Williams, Kutina, Alexander. Three-base hit—Austin. Sacrifice fly—Alexander. Sacrifice hit —Hamilton. Stolen bases—Shotten, Austin. Left on bases—St. Louis, 7; Detroit, 3. First base on balls—Off Dubuc, 4; off Hamilton, 2. First base on errors—Detroit, 2; St. Louis, 2. Struck out—By Dubuc, 5. Time—1:35. Umpires—O'Loughlin and Westervelt.

Sept. 6, 1912   New York at Philadelphia

NEW YORK	ab	r	b	p	a	e
Devore, lf...............	1	0	0	2	0	0
Becker, lf, rf...........	2	0	1	2	0	0
Doyle, 2b...............	5	0	2	0	2	0
Snodgr's, cf............	3	0	0	2	0	0
Murray, rf, lf.........	4	0	2	4	0	0
Merkle, 1b.............	4	0	2	7	0	1
Herzog, 3b.............	3	1	0	1	1	0
Wilson, c................	1	1	1	3	1	0
Fletcher, ss............	4	1	2	5	1	1
Tesreau, p..............	3	0	1	1	1	0
Totals...........	30	3	11	27	6	2

PHILADELPHIA	ab	r	b	p	a	e
Paskert, cf............	3	0	0	3	0	0
Mangus, lf............	4	0	0	2	0	0
Miller, rf...............	4	0	0	0	0	0
Luderus, 1b..........	3	0	0	4	2	0
Walsh, 2b..............	3	0	0	4	3	2
Doolan, ss.............	3	0	0	5	4	0
Dodge, 3b..............	2	0	0	0	2	0
Killifer, c..............	3	0	0	8	3	2
Rixey, p................	1	0	0	0	2	0
Nicholson, p.........	0	0	0	0	0	0
Nelson, p................	0	0	0	0	1	0
*Magee..................	1	0	0	0	0	0
†Cravath.................	1	0	0	0	0	0
Totals...........	28	0	0	‡26	17	4

* Batted for Rixey in sixth inning.
† Batted for Nicholson in eighth inning.
‡ Merkle out, hit by batted ball.

```
New York ................... 0 0 2 1 0 0 0 0 0 — 3
Philadelphia ............... 0 0 0 0 0 0 0 0 0 — 0
```

Left on bases—New York 11. Philadelphia 3. Struck out—By Rixey 4. Nelson 1. Tesreau 2. Double play—Paskert. Killifer. First on errors—Philadelphia 2. New York 1. First on balls—Off Rixey 4, Nicholson 2, Nelson 1, Tesreau 2. Hits—Off Rixey 8 in 6 innings, Nicholson 2 in 2 innings. Nelson 1 in 1 inning. Wild pitch —Tesreau. Passed balls—Killifer 2. Sacrifice hits—Wilson, Tesreau. Stolen bases— Merkle, Herzog. Time—1.55. Umpires—Klem and Orth.

May 14, 1914   Chicago at Washington

CHICAGO	ab	r	b	p	a	e
Demmitt, rf............	4	0	1	1	0	0
Berger, ss...............	4	0	0	2	1	0
Chase, 1b...............	4	0	1	17	1	0
Collins, lf...............	4	0	0	1	0	0
Bodie, cf................	4	0	1	2	0	0
Alcock, 3b.............	3	0	0	0	0	0
Blackb'n, 2b...........	4	0	0	2	8	2
Schalk, c................	3	0	0	2	1	1
Scott, p..................	3	0	0	0	5	0
Totals...........	33	0	3	*27	16	3

WASHINGTON	ab	r	b	p	a	e
Moeller, rf.............	4	0	0	6	0	0
Foster, 3b..............	4	0	0	0	1	1
Milan, cf...............	4	0	0	3	1	0
Gandil, 1b..............	4	1	1	14	2	0
Shanks, lf..............	4	0	1	0	0	0
Morgan, 2b............	3	0	0	0	7	1
McBride, ss............	2	0	0	2	5	0
Henry, c................	2	0	0	3	0	0
Avers, p.................	3	0	0	2	0	0
Totals...........	30	1	2	30	16	2

* None out when winning run was scored.

```
Chicago .................. 0 0 0 0 0 0 0 0 0 — 0
Washington ............ 0 0 0 0 0 0 0 0 1 — 1
```

Two-base hit—Shanks. Three-base hit—Chase. Stolen bases—Collins, McBride. Double play—Morgan. McBride, Gandil. Left on bases—Chicago 4, Washington 4. First on balls—Off Scott 3, Ayers 1. First on errors—Chicago 2, Washington 2. Struck out—By Scott 2, Ayers 1. Time—2.00. Umpires—Dineen and Connolly.

May 31, 1914   Cleveland at Chicago

CLEVELAND	ab	r	b	p	a	e
Wood, 1b	3	1	0	8	2	0
Bisland, ss	4	0	0	3	5	1
Graney, lf	2	0	0	1	0	1
Jackson, rf	3	0	0	0	0	0
Lajole, 2b	3	0	0	3	1	1
Turner, 3b	3	0	0	4	3	0
Birmin'm, cf	3	0	0	1	0	0
O'Neil, c	3	0	0	4	1	0
Bowman, p	1	0	0	0	2	0
Blanding, p	1	0	0	0	2	0
*Lelivelt	1	0	0	0	0	0
Totals	27	1	0	24	16	3

CHICAGO	ab	r	b	p	a	e
Weaver, ss	4	1	3	2	4	1
Chase, 1b	3	3	1	16	1	0
Demmitt, lf	4	2	3	1	0	0
Collins, rf	3	0	2	1	0	0
Bodie, cf	4	0	1	0	0	0
Schalk, c	4	0	1	4	2	0
Alcock, 3b	4	0	1	1	0	1
Berger, 2b	4	0	1	2	2	1
Benz, p	4	0	0	0	6	0
Totals	34	6	13	27	15	3

* Batted for Blanding in ninth inning.

```
Cleveland ..................... 0 0 0 1 0 0 0 0 0 — 1
Chicago ....................... 1 0 2 0 0 0 3 0 x — 6
```

Two-base hits—Collins, Berger, Chase. Hits—Off Bowman 4 in 3 innings, Blanding 9 in 5 innings. Stolen bases—Demmitt, Collins. Double plays—Bowman, Turner, Wood; Berger, Chase; Weaver, Chase; Weaver, Berger, Chase. Left on bases—Cleveland 1, Chicago 6. First on balls—Off Bowman 2, Benz 2. Struck out—By Benz 6, Bowman 1, Blanding 2. Time—1.45. Umpires—Egan and Evans.

Sept. 9, 1914   Philadelphia at Boston

PHILADELPHIA	ab	r	b	p	a	e
Lobert, 3b	4	0	0	3	2	0
Becker, lf	3	0	0	0	0	0
Magee, 1b	4	0	0	4	1	0
Hilley, rf	4	0	2	0	0	0
Byrne, 2b	3	0	0	3	0	0
Paskert, cf	1	0	0	5	0	1
Martin, ss	2	0	0	3	3	0
Burns, c	3	0	0	4	0	0
Tineup, p	1	0	0	0	0	0
Rixey, p	0	0	0	0	1	0
Oeschger, p	0	0	0	0	0	0
*Cravath	1	0	0	0	0	0
†Killifer	1	0	0	0	0	0
Totals	27	0	0	24	7	1

BOSTON	ab	r	b	p	a	e
Moran, cf	2	0	0	0	0	0
Mann, cf	2	1	2	1	0	0
Evers, 2b	4	0	0	2	2	0
Connolly, lf	2	0	0	0	0	0
Cather, lf	2	0	0	0	0	0
Whitted, rf	4	1	2	1	0	0
Schmidt, 1b	4	0	1	14	0	0
Smith, 3b	4	2	2	2	3	2
Maranv'e, ss	3	1	1	3	2	0
Gowdy, c	4	1	1	4	1	0
Davis, p	4	1	3	0	3	0
Totals	35	7	12	27	11	2

* Batted for Tineup in fifth inning.
† Batted for Rixey in eighth inning.

```
Philadelphia ................. 0 0 0 0 0 0 0 0 0 — 0
Boston ....................... 0 2 0 2 0 0 1 2 x — 7
```

Hits—Off Tineup 5 in 4 innings, Rixey 4 in 3 innings, Oeschger 3 in 1 inning. Three-base hit—Mann. Sacrifice hit—Evers. Stolen base—Whitted. Double plays—Maranville, Evers, Schmidt 2. Left on bases—Boston 7, Philadelphia 5. First on balls—Off Tineup 2, Davis 5. First on errors—Philadelphia 2. Struck out—By Rixey 3, Davis 4. Time—2.00. Umpires—Eason and Quigley.

April 15, 1915   Brooklyn at New York

BROOKLYN

	ab	r	b	p	a	e
Schultz, 3b	4	0	0	1	3	0
Myers, cf	4	0	0	3	0	0
Wheat, lf	3	0	0	1	1	0
Cutshaw, 2b	3	0	0	3	3	0
Hummel, 1b	3	0	0	11	0	0
Stengel, rf	1	0	0	0	0	0
*McCarty	1	0	0	0	0	0
Zimme'n, rf	0	0	0	0	0	0
Getz, ss	3	0	0	2	0	2
Miller, c	3	0	0	2	2	0
Rucker, p	2	0	0	1	3	0
†Egan	1	0	0	0	0	0
Ragan, p	0	0	0	0	1	0
Totals	28	0	0	24	13	2

NEW YORK

	ab	r	b	p	a	e
Snodgrass, cf	2	0	1	1	0	0
Doyle, 2b	4	0	1	2	1	0
Lobert, 3b	4	1	2	2	3	0
Fletcher, ss	4	0	0	0	5	1
Burns, lf	4	0	1	1	0	0
Merkle, 1b	4	1	1	17	0	0
Thorpe, rf	2	0	0	1	0	0
Myers, c	3	0	1	3	0	0
Marquard, p	3	0	1	0	6	0
Totals	30	2	8	27	15	1

* Batted for Stengel in seventh inning.
† Batted for Rucker in eighth inning.

```
Brooklyn ....................  0 0 0 0 0 0 0 0 0 — 0
New York ..................   0 0 0 1 0 0 1 0 x — 2
```

First on errors—New York 1, Brooklyn 1. Two-base hit—Burns. Stolen base—Snodgrass. Left on bases—New York 7, Brooklyn 1. First on balls—Off Marquard 2, Rucker 3. Struck out—By Marquard 2, Rucker 1, Ragan 1. Wild pitch—Rucker. Hits—Off Rucker 8 in 7 innings, Ragan 0 in 1 inning. Umpires—Rigler and Hart. Time 1.21.

August 31, 1915   Chicago at New York

CHICAGO

	ab	r	b	p	a	e
Goode, rf	3	1	0	0	0	0
Fisher, ss	4	0	2	0	2	1
Schulte, lf	4	0	0	1	0	0
Zimme'n, 2b	4	0	1	1	4	0
Saier, 1b	4	0	0	14	2	0
Williams, cf	4	1	2	1	0	0
Phelan, 3b	4	0	0	0	1	0
Archer, c	4	0	0	8	3	0
Lavender, p	3	0	1	2	4	0
Totals	34	3	6	27	16	1

NEW YORK

	ab	r	b	p	a	e
Burns, lf	4	0	0	0	0	0
Grant, 3b	4	0	0	4	5	0
Robertson, rf	3	0	0	2	0	0
Doyle, 2b	3	0	0	2	2	0
Merkle, cf	2	0	0	1	0	0
Fletcher, ss	3	0	0	2	3	1
Brainerd, 1b	3	0	0	10	1	0
Dooin, c	2	0	0	5	1	0
Schang, c	1	0	0	1	0	0
Schauer, p	2	0	0	0	2	0
*Myers	1	0	0	0	0	0
Totals	28	0	0	27	14	1

* Batted for Schauer in ninth inning.

```
Chicago ......................  0 0 0 1 1 0 0 0 0 — 2
New York ..................   0 0 0 0 0 0 0 0 0 — 0
```

Two-base hits—Williams, Lavender. Home run—Williams. Stolen base—Phelan. Earned runs—Chicago 2. Left on bases—New York 2, Chicago 6. First on errors—New York 1, Chicago 1. First on balls—Off Schauer 1, Lavender 1. Struck out—By Lavender 8, Schauer 2. Time—1.41. Umpires—Klem and Emslie.

June 16, 1916   Pittsburgh at Boston

PITTSBURGH	ab	h	o	a	e
Carey, cf	4	0	2	0	0
Johnston, 1b	4	0	7	0	0
Wagner, ss	3	0	6	3	0
Hinchman, rf	2	0	0	0	0
Schultz, 3b	3	0	1	3	0
Barney, lf	3	0	0	0	0
Viox, 2b	3	0	0	1	0
Schmidt, c	3	0	7	6	0
Kantlehner, p	2	0	1	1	1
Harmon, p	0	0	0	1	0
*Costello	1	0	0	0	0
Totals	28	0	24	15	1

BOSTON	ab	h	o	a	e
Mar'ville, ss	1	0	4	1	0
Snodg'ss, cf	4	3	0	0	0
Wilhoit, rf	4	0	5	0	0
Magee, lf	3	1	2	0	0
Koney, 1b	3	1	5	0	0
Smith, 3b	3	0	0	0	1
Egan, 2b	3	1	1	1	0
Tragressor, c	0	0	0	0	0
Gowdy, c	3	1	9	0	0
Hughes, p	3	0	1	1	0
Totals	27	7	27	3	1

* Batted for Kantlehner in eighth.

Pittsburgh	0	0	0	0	0	0	0	0	0 —	0
Boston	1	0	0	0	0	0	0	1	x —	2

Two-base hit—Gowdy. Stolen bases—Wagner, Maranville, Snodgrass. Bases on balls—Off Kantlehner 2, off Harmon 1, off Hughes 2. Hits—Off Kantlehner 6 in 7 innings. Struck out—By Kantlehner 5, by Harmon 2, by Hughes 7. Umpires—Klem and Emslie.

June 21, 1916   New York at Boston

NEW YORK	ab	r	h	o	a
Gilhooley, r	4	0	0	5	0
High, lf	3	0	0	2	0
P'ck'p'gh, s	3	0	0	2	2
Pipp, 1b	3	0	0	6	0
Baker, 3b	3	0	0	0	1
Magee, cf	2	0	0	5	0
Gedeen, 2b	3	0	0	1	2
Nuna'ker, c	2	0	0	3	2
Shawkey, p	1	0	0	0	1
*Caldwell	1	0	0	0	0
Totals	25	0	0	24	8

BOSTON	ab	r	h	o	a
Hooper, rf	4	1	3	3	0
Janvrin, 2b	3	1	2	1	1
Lewis, lf	3	0	2	3	0
H'blitz'l, 1b	3	0	0	6	1
Walker, cf	3	0	0	5	0
Gardner, 3b	3	0	0	3	0
Scott, ss	3	0	1	1	0
Carrigan, c	3	0	0	4	2
Foster, p	3	0	0	1	3
Totals	28	2	8	27	7

* Batted for Shawkey in ninth.

New York	0	0	0	0	0	0	0	0	0 —	0
Boston	1	0	0	0	1	0	0	0	x —	2

Errors—Boston, 0; New York, 0. Two-base hit—Hooper. Three-base hit—Janvrin. Sacrifice hits—Janvrin, Shawkey. Sacrifice fly—Lewis. Left on bases—Boston 4, New York 2. Bases on balls—Off Foster 3. Hits and earned runs—Off Foster, no hits and no runs in 9 innings; off Shawkey, 8 hits and 2 runs in 8 innings. Struck out—By Foster 3, by Shawkey 2. Umpires—Hildebrand and O'Loughlin. Time—1:31.

August 26, 1916 Cleveland at Philadelphia

INDIANS

	ab	r	h	o	a	e
Graney, lf	3	0	0	1	0	0
Turner, 3b	2	0	0	2	1	0
Speaker, cf	3	0	0	2	1	0
Roth, rf	3	0	0	2	0	0
Wamby, ss	3	0	0	4	0	0
Gandil, 1b	3	0	0	6	1	0
Chapman, 2b	3	0	0	0	2	0
O'Neill, c	3	0	0	6	3	0
Coveleskie, p	1	0	0	1	1	0
Coumbe, p	0	0	0	0	1	0
*Moeller	1	0	0	0	0	0
†Coleman	1	0	0	0	0	0
Totals	26	0	0	24	10	0

ATHLETICS

	ab	r	h	o	a	e
Witt, ss	4	1	2	1	2	0
Walsh, rf	3	0	1	3	0	0
Strunk, cf	4	1	1	2	0	0
Schang, lf	3	1	3	3	0	0
Lajoie, 2b	3	0	1	0	1	0
McInnis, 1b	3	0	1	9	0	0
Pick, 3b	3	0	1	2	3	0
Picinich, c	3	1	1	7	0	0
Bush, p	3	1	1	0	1	0
Totals	29	5	12	27	7	0

* Batted for Coveleskie in sixth.
† Batted for Coumbe in ninth.

Cleveland	0 0 0 0 0 0 0 0 0	—	0
Philadelphia	0 1 0 1 3 0 0 0 x	—	5

Two-base hits—Picinich, Bush. Three-base hits—Schang, Witt, Lajoie. Sacrifice hits—Turner, Walsh. Bases on balls—Off Coveleskie 1, off Bush 1. Struck out—By Coveleskie 2, by Coumbe 1, by Bush, 8. Seven hits, 5 runs off Coveleskie in 5 innings. Passed ball—O'Neil. Umpires—Connolly and Chill. Attendance—3,000.

August 30, 1916 St. Louis at Boston

ST. LOUIS

	ab	r	h	o	a
Shotton, lf	4	0	0	2	1
Miller, rf	2	0	0	3	0
Tobin, rf	1	0	0	0	0
Sisler, 1b	3	0	0	5	2
Pratt, 2b	3	0	0	3	1
Marsans, cf	3	0	0	4	0
Severeid, c	2	0	0	4	1
Austin, 3b	3	0	0	1	1
Lavan, ss	3	0	0	1	2
Weilman, p	2	0	0	1	1
*Rumler	1	0	0	0	0
†Hartley	0	0	0	0	0
Totals	27	0	0	24	9

BOSTON

	ab	r	h	o	a
Hooper, rf	3	0	2	4	0
McNally, 2b	4	0	0	1	2
Lewis, lf	4	0	1	6	0
Gainer, 1b	4	0	1	8	0
Walker, cf	4	2	2	2	0
Gardner, 3b	3	2	2	1	2
Scott, ss	2	0	0	2	4
Carrigan, c	3	0	1	3	0
Leonard, p	2	0	1	0	0
Totals	29	4	10	27	8

* Batted for Miller in seventh.
† Batted for Weilman in ninth.

St. Louis	0 0 0 0 0 0 0 0 0	—	0
Boston	0 2 0 0 0 2 0 0 x	—	4

Errors—St. Louis, 0; Boston, 0. Two-base hits—Hooper, Walker, Gardner. Three-base hit—Walker. Stolen bases—Lewis, Hooper. Sacrifice hits—Scott, Hooper. Double play—Austin to Sisler to Severeid. Left on bases—St. Louis 2, Boston 4. Bases on balls—Off Weilman 1, off Leonard 2. Hits and earned runs—Off Weilman, 10 hits and 4 runs in 8 innings. Struck out—By Weilman 2, by Leonard 3. Passed ball—Severeid. Umpires—Owens and Hildebrand. Time—1:35.

May 2, 1917   Cincinnati at Chicago

CINCINNATI (N.)	ab	r	h	o	a	e
Groh, 3b	1	0	0	2	2	0
*Getz	1	0	0	2	1	0
Kopf, ss	4	1	1	1	4	0
Neale, cf	4	0	0	1	0	0
Chase, 1b	4	0	0	12	0	0
Thorpe, rf	4	0	1	1	0	0
Shean, 2b	3	0	0	3	2	0
Cueto, lf	3	0	0	5	0	0
Huhn, c	3	0	0	3	0	0
Toney, p	3	0	0	0	1	0
Totals	30	1	2	30	10	0

CHICAGO (N.)	ab	r	h	o	a	e
Zeider, ss	4	0	0	1	0	1
Wolter, rf	4	0	0	0	0	0
Doyle, 2b	4	0	0	5	4	0
Merkle, 1b	4	0	0	7	1	0
Williams, cf	2	0	0	2	0	1
Mann, lf	3	0	0	0	0	0
Wilson, c	3	0	0	14	1	0
Deal, 3b	3	0	0	1	0	0
Vaughn, p	3	0	0	0	3	0
Totals	30	0	0	30	9	2

* Batted for Groh in the seventh inning.

Cincinnati .... 0 0 0 0 0 0 0 0 0 1 — 1
Chicago .... 0 0 0 0 0 0 0 0 0 0 — 0

Stolen base—Chase. Double plays—Doyle, Merkle and Zeider; Vaughn, Doyle and Merkle. Left on bases—Chicago, 2; Cincinnati, 1. First base on errors—Cincinnati, 2. Bases on balls—Off Toney, 2; off Vaughn, 2. Earned runs—Off Vaughn, 0 in 10 innings; off Toney, 0 in 10 innings. Struck out—By Vaughn, 10; by Toney, 3. Umpires—Messrs. Orth and Rigler. Time of game—1 hour and 50 minutes.

May 5, 1917   Chicago at St. Louis

CHICAGO	ab	h	o	a	e
J. Collins, rf	4	0	1	0	0
Weaver, 3b	4	0	0	1	0
E. Collins, 2b	4	0	3	3	0
Jackson, lf	2	0	1	0	0
Felsch, cf	4	0	1	0	0
Gandil, 1b	3	0	7	1	0
Risberg, ss	2	0	3	3	1
Schalk, c	3	0	7	2	0
Cicotte, p	1	0	1	3	0
Totals	27	0	24	13	1

ST. LOUIS	ab	h	o	a	e
Shotton, lf	4	0	2	0	0
Austin, 3b	4	1	0	3	0
Sisler, 1b	4	1	13	0	0
Severeid, c	3	0	1	0	0
Jacobson, rf	3	0	4	0	0
Marsans, cf	2	1	1	0	0
Johnson, 2b	2	0	3	4	1
Lavan, ss	3	2	3	5	1
Koob, p	2	0	0	3	0
Totals	27	5	27	15	2

Chicago .... 0 0 0 0 0 0 0 0 0 — 0
St. Louis .... 0 0 0 0 0 1 0 0 x — 1

Two-base hit—Marsans. Double plays—Koob, Johnson and Sisler; Austin Johnson and Sisler, Bases on balls—Off Koob 5, off Cicotte 2. Struck out—By Koob 2, by Cicotte 3. Umpires—Nallin and Evans.

Appendix

May 6, 1917 Chicago at St. Louis

CHICAGO

	ab	r	h	o	a
Liebold, rf	3	0	0	1	0
Weaver, 3b	2	0	0	3	5
E. Collins, 2b	3	0	0	3	2
Jackson, lf	2	0	0	1	0
Felsch, cf	3	0	0	1	0
Grandil, 1b	3	0	0	10	2
Risberg, ss	2	0	0	1	3
Schalk, c	2	0	0	4	2
Benz, p	2	0	0	0	3
*Murphy	1	0	0	0	0
Totals	23	0	0	24	17

ST. LOUIS

	ab	r	h	o	a
Shotton, lf	4	0	0	1	0
Austin, 3b	4	0	1	1	1
Sisler, 1b	3	2	3	7	2
Jacobson, rf	4	0	2	1	0
Marsans, cf	4	0	0	3	0
Johnson, 2b	3	1	1	2	0
Severeid, c	3	0	0	7	2
Lavan, ss	3	0	1	4	3
Groom, p	2	0	0	1	1
Totals	30	3	8	27	9

* Batted for Benz in 9th inning.

```
Chicago........................ 0 0 0 0 0 0 0 0 0 — 0
St. Louis...................... 1 1 0 0 0 0 0 1 x — 3
```

Errors—Chicago, Risberg 2; St. Louis, 0. Two-base hits—Jacobson, Johnson. Stolen bases—Austin, Sisler. Sacrifice hits—Groom, Sisler, Schalk. Double play—Severeid to Lavan to Sisler. Left on bases—Chicago 1, St. Louis 5. First base on errors—St. Louis 2. Bases on balls—Off Groom 3. Hits and earned runs—Off Benz, 8 hits, 3 runs in 8 innings; off Groom, no hits, no runs in 9 innings. Hit by pitcher—By Groom (Weaver). Struck out—By Benz 2, by Groom 4. Umpires—Nallin and Evans. Time—1:21.

May 14, 1917 Chicago at St. Louis

CHICAGO

	ab	h	o	a	e
Leibold, rf	4	1	0	0	0
Risberg, ss	5	2	3	2	0
E. Collins, 2b	3	2	1	3	0
Jackson, lf	4	1	5	0	0
Felsch, cf	4	2	4	0	0
Gandil, 1b	5	0	5	0	1
Weaver, 3b	4	0	3	1	0
Schalk, c	4	1	6	0	0
Cicotte, p	3	1	0	0	0
Totals	36	10	27	6	1

ST. LOUIS

	ab	h	o	a	e
Shotton, lf	2	0	1	0	0
Miller, rf	3	0	2	0	0
Sisler, 1b	4	0	10	1	1
Pratt, 2b	4	0	2	2	0
Marsans, cf	3	0	6	0	0
Austin, 3b	3	0	3	1	0
Lavan, ss	2	0	0	2	2
Hale, c	2	0	3	3	1
Hartley, c	0	0	0	0	0
Hamilton, p	0	0	0	0	0
Rogers, p	2	0	0	1	1
Park, p	0	0	0	0	0
Pennington, p	0	0	0	0	0
*Paulette	1	0	0	0	0
†Jacobson	1	0	0	0	0
Totals	27	0	27	10	5

* Batted for Hale in eighth.
† Batted for Rogers in eighth.

```
Chicago........................ 1 7 0 1 0 2 0 0 0 — 11
St. Louis...................... 0 0 0 0 0 0 0 0 0 — 0
```

Two-base hits—Jackson, Schalk, Risberg. Double play—E. Collins, Risberg and Gandil. Stolen bases—Shotton, Felsch. Hit by pitcher—By Hamilton 1, by Cicotte 1. Wild pitch—Park. Bases on balls—Off Hamilton 1, off Rogers 3, off Cicotte 3. Struck out—By Cicotte 5, by Rogers 2. Hits—Off Hamilton 3 in 1 inning, off Park 4 in 0 innings, off Rogers 2 in 7 innings. Umpires—O'Loughlin and Hildebrand.

April 24, 1917 New York at Boston

NEW YORK	ab	r	h	o	a
Gilhooley, rf	4	0	1	1	0
High, lf	3	0	0	2	0
Miller, lf	1	0	0	0	0
Maisel, 2b	3	0	1	5	7
Pipp, 1b	2	0	0	12	2
Aragon, 3b	4	1	1	1	4
Magee, cf	4	0	2	1	0
Peck'p'gh, s	3	1	2	2	4
Nunmaker, c	4	0	1	3	1
Mogridge, p	3	0	0	0	1
*Bauman	1	0	0	0	0
Totals	32	2	8	27	19

BOSTON	ab	r	h	o	a
Hooper, rf	4	0	0	3	0
Barry, 2b	3	1	0	0	1
Gainer, 1b	4	0	0	10	0
Lewis, lf	3	0	0	1	0
Walker, cf	2	0	0	2	2
Gardner, 3b	1	0	0	1	2
McNally, 3b	0	0	0	1	2
Scott, ss	3	0	0	0	0
Cady, c	3	0	0	9	0
Leonard, p	3	0	0	0	3
†Walsh	0	0	0	0	0
Totals	26	1	0	27	10

* Batted for High in 7th.
† Batted for Gardner in 7th.

```
New York ............... 0 0 0 0 0 1 0 0 1 — 2
Boston ................. 0 0 0 0 0 0 1 0 0 — 1
```

Errors—New York, Maisel, Peckinpaugh 2; Boston, Lewis, Gardner, McNally, Cady. Two-base hit—Aragon. Stolen bases—Maisel, Peckinpaugh. Sacrifice hits—Peckinpaugh, Mogridge, Pipp, Walker, Lewis. Sacrifice fly—Walsh. Left on bases—New York 9, Boston 4. First base on errors—New York 2, Boston 2. Bases on balls—Off Mogridge 3, off Leonard 3. Earned runs—Off Mogridge none in 9 innings, off Leonard 2 in 9 innings. Struck out—By Mogridge 3, by Leonard 6. Umpires—Connolly and McCormick. Time—2:01.

June 23, 1917 Washington at Boston

WASHINGTON	a	r	h	o	a
Morgan, 2	2	0	0	4	2
Foster, 3	3	0	0	1	3
Leonard, 3	0	0	0	0	1
Milan, cf	3	0	0	1	0
Rice, rf	3	0	0	3	0
Gharrity, 1	0	0	0	0	0
Judge, 1	3	0	0	11	1
Jamieson, lf	3	0	0	0	0
Shanks, s	3	0	0	1	2
Henry, c	3	0	0	1	0
Ayres, p	2	0	0	2	8
*Menoskey	1	0	0	0	0
Totals	26	0	0	24	17

BOSTON	a	r	h	o	a
Hooper, rf	4	0	1	0	0
Barry, 2	4	0	2	1	
Hoblitzell, 1	4	0	0	12	2
Gardner, 3	4	1	1	2	1
Lewis, lf	4	0	3	2	0
Walker, cf	3	1	1	4	0
Scott, s	3	0	0	1	5
Thomas, c	0	0	0	0	0
Agnew, c	3	1	3	2	1
Ruth, p	0	0	0	0	0
Shore, p	2	1	0	2	6
Totals	31	4	9	27	16

* Batted for Ayers in ninth.

```
Washington ............... 0 0 0 0 0 0 0 0 0 — 0
Boston ................... 0 1 0 0 0 0 3 0 x — 4
```

Errors—Foster 2, Rice. Two-base hits—Walker, Agnew. Sacrifice hits—Walker, Shore, Scott. Double plays—Ayres to Foster to Judge; Ayres to Judge. Left on bases—Boston 6. First base on errors—Boston 3. First base on balls—Off Ruth 1. Hits and earned runs—Off Ruth no hits, no runs in no inning (none out in first); off Shore no hits, no runs in 9 innings; off Ayres 9 hits, 2 runs in 8 innings. Struck out—By Shore 2. Umpires—Owen, McCormick and Dineen. Time—1:40.

June 23, 1918   Boston at Detroit

BOSTON	a	r	h	o	a
Hooper, rf	4	1	1	4	0
Shean, 2	4	0	0	2	1
Ruth, cf	5	1	1	3	0
Whiteman, lf	4	0	1	1	0
McInnis, 1	3	1	1	7	0
Thomas, 3	3	1	1	1	2
Scott, s	4	1	2	3	4
Schang, c	4	0	1	6	0
Leonard, p	4	0	0	0	1
Totals	35	5	8	27	8

DETROIT	a	r	h	o	a
Bush, s	4	0	0	2	3
Young, 2	3	0	0	4	1
Veach, lf	2	0	0	0	0
Heilmann, rf	3	0	0	0	0
Dyer, 1	3	0	0	8	2
Walker, cf	3	0	0	3	1
Vitt, 3	3	0	0	2	2
Yelle, c	3	0	0	7	1
Dauss, p	1	0	0	0	1
Cunningh'm, p	0	0	0	1	1
*Spencer	1	0	0	0	0
†Cobb	1	0	0	0	0
Totals	27	0	0	27	12

* Batted for Dauss in sixth.
† Batted for Cunningham in ninth.

Boston.......................... 1 0 0 1 1 2 0 0 0 — 5
Detroit........................ 0 0 0 0 0 0 0 0 0 — 0

Errors—Young 2. Two-base hit—Whiteman. Three-base hit—Hooper. Home run—Ruth. Stolen bases—Whiteman, Hooper, McInnis. Sacrifice hit—Thomas. Double play—Yelle and Vitt. Left on bases—Boston 7, Detroit 1, First base on errors—Boston 2. First base on balls—Off Leonard 1, off Dauss 2, off Cunningham 1. Hits—Off Dauss 8 in 6 innings; off Cunningham none in 3 innings. Struck out—By Dauss 5, by Cunningham 2, by Leonard 4. Wild pitch—Dauss. Losing pitcher—Dauss. Umpires—Dinneen and Connelly.

May 11, 1919   St. Louis at Cincinnati

ST. LOUIS	ab	h	o	a	e
Shotton, lf	4	0	3	0	0
Smith, cf	3	0	2	0	0
Stock, 3b	3	0	2	0	1
Hornsby, ss	2	0	1	4	0
Cruise, rf, 1b	2	0	3	0	0
Paulette, 1b	2	0	6	0	0
Schultz, rf	0	0	0	0	0
Miller, 2b	3	0	5	1	1
Snyder, c	3	0	2	5	1
May, p	2	0	0	1	0
*Heathcote	1	0	0	0	0
Totals	25	0	24	11	3

CINCINNATI	ab	h	o	a	e
Rath, 2b	1	0	0	2	0
Neale, cf	3	1	3	0	0
Groh, 3b	3	1	1	0	0
Magee, lf	4	0	0	0	0
Daubert, 1b	4	2	8	0	0
Kopf, ss	2	0	3	0	0
Cueto, rf	4	2	2	0	0
Rariden, c	3	1	10	3	0
Eller, p	4	1	0	4	0
Totals	28	8	27	9	0

* Batted for May in ninth.

St. Louis...................... 0 0 0 0 0 0 0 0 0 — 0
Cincinnati.................... 0 0 0 2 4 0 0 0 x — 6

Stolen bases—Groh 2, Daubert, Kopf, Cueto. Double plays—Rariden and Groh; Miller and Paulette, Bases on balls—Off Eller 3, off May 6. Hit by pitcher—By May 2. Struck out—By Eller 8, by May 2. Wild pitch—May.

Sept. 10, 1919   Cleveland at New York

CLEVELAND	ab	h	o	a	e
Graney, lf	3	0	3	0	0
Chapman, ss	2	1	1	6	0
Speaker, cf	3	1	3	0	0
Harris, 1b	3	2	11	0	0
Gardner, 3b	4	1	0	2	0
Wambs'gs, 2b	4	0	1	0	1
Smith, rf	4	0	2	0	0
O'Neill, c	3	0	6	1	0
Caldwell, p	4	1	0	1	0
Totals	30	6	27	10	1

NEW YORK	ab	h	o	a	e
Fewster, rf	4	0	3	0	0
Peck'gh, ss	4	0	4	4	0
Baker, 3b	3	0	0	2	0
Pipp, 1b	3	0	13	2	0
Pratt, 2b	3	0	0	3	0
Lewis, lf	3	0	1	0	0
Bodle, cf	3	0	2	0	0
Hannah, c	2	0	2	0	0
Mays, p	2	0	2	4	0
*Vick	1	0	0	0	0
Totals	27	0	27	15	0

* Batted for Mays in the ninth.

Cleveland	2	0	0	0	0	1	0	0	0	—	3
New York	0	0	0	0	0	0	0	0	0	—	0

Two-base hits—Harris, Caldwell. Home run—Harris. Bases on balls—Off Mays 3, off Caldwell 1. Hit by pitcher—By Mays 1. Struck out—By Mays 2, by Caldwell 5.

July 1, 1920   Washington at Boston

WASHINGTON	a	r	h	o	a
Judge, 1	4	0	1	2	1
Milan, lf	4	0	0	3	0
Rice, cf	3	0	1	3	0
Roth, rf	4	1	0	0	0
Shanks, 3	4	0	3	1	1
Shannon, s	3	0	0	1	0
Harris, 2	2	0	1	0	2
Picinich, c	3	0	11	4	0
Johnson, p	2	0	0	3	0
Totals	29	1	7	27	4

BOSTON	a	r	h	o	a
Hooper, rf	4	0	0	1	0
McNally, 2	3	0	0	1	3
Menosky, lf	3	0	2	0	0
Schang, cf	3	0	0	0	1
McInnis, 1	3	0	0	10	1
Foster, 3	3	0	0	2	4
Scott, s	3	0	0	4	3
Walters, c	2	0	0	7	3
Harper, p	2	0	0	0	1
*Karr	1	0	0	0	0
†Eibel	1	0	0	0	0
Totals	28	0	0	27	16

* Batted for Walters in ninth.
† Batted for Harper in ninth.

Washington	0	0	0	0	0	0	1	0	0	—	1
Boston	0	0	0	0	0	0	0	0	0	—	0

Errors—Harris, Harper. Stolen base—Rice. Double play—Walters to McNally. Left on bases—Washington 4, Boston 1. Bases on balls—Off Harper 1. Hit by pitcher—By Harper (Rice, Harris). Struck out—By Johnson 10, by Harper 7. Umpires—Chill and Moriarity. Time—1:46.

April 30, 1922   Chicago at Detroit

CHICAGO	a	r	h	o	a
Mulligar, s	4	0	1	0	0
McClellan, 3	3	0	1	1	3
Collins, 2	3	0	1	4	3
Hooper, rf	3	1	0	3	0
Mostil, lf	4	1	1	3	0
Strunk, cf	3	0	0	0	0
Sheely, 1	4	0	2	9	0
Schalk, p	4	0	1	7	1
Robertson, p	4	0	0	0	1
Totals	32	3	7	27	8

DETROIT	a	r	h	o	a
Blue, 1	3	0	0	11	3
Cutshaw, 2	3	0	0	2	3
Cobb, c	3	0	0	1	0
Veach, lf	3	0	0	2	0
Heilmann, rf	3	0	0	1	0
Jones, 3	3	0	0	1	5
Rigney, s	2	0	0	2	1
Manion, c	3	0	0	7	1
Pillette, p	2	0	0	0	3
*Clark	1	0	0	0	0
†Bassler	1	0	0	0	0
Totals	27	0	0	27	16

* Batted for Rigney in the ninth.
† Batted for Pillette in the ninth.

```
Chicago.......................  0 2 0 0 0 0 0 0 0 — 2
Detroit.......................  0 0 0 0 0 0 0 0 0 — 0
```

Error—Blue. Two-base hits—Mulligan, Sheely. Sacrifice hits—McClellan, Collins, Strunk. Left on bases—Chicago 8. Bases on balls—Off Pillette 2. Struck out—By Pillette 5, by Robertson 6. Umpires—Nallin and Evans. Time—1:55. Attendance 25,000.

May 7, 1922   Philadelphia at New York

PHILADELPHIA	a	r	h	o	a
Lebourv'u, lf	3	0	0	2	0
Rapp, 3	3	0	0	0	1
Walker, rf	3	0	0	1	0
Williams, cf	2	0	0	3	0
Parkinson, 2	3	0	0	1	6
Fletcher, s	3	0	0	4	3
Leslie, 1	2	0	0	12	0
*King	1	0	0	0	0
Henline, c	2	0	0	1	2
†Lee	1	0	0	0	0
Meadows, p	0	0	0	0	0
G. Smith, p	2	2	0	0	0
‡Wrightst'ne	1	0	0	0	0
Totals	26	0	0	24	14

NEW YORK	a	r	h	o	a
Bancroft, s	2	1	1	1	5
Rawlings, 2	4	0	0	0	7
Groh, 3	4	1	2	1	0
Young, rf	4	2	2	0	0
Meusel, lf	4	0	1	1	0
Kelly, 1	4	1	3	16	0
Shinners, cf	3	0	0	3	0
E. Smith, c	3	0	0	5	1
J. Barnes, p	2	1	0	0	2
Totals	30	6	9	27	15

* Batted for Leslie in the ninth inning.
† Batted for Henline in the ninth inning.
‡ Batted for G. Smith in the ninth inning.

```
Philadelphia.................  0 0 0 0 0 0 0 0 0 — 0
New York....................  2 3 0 0 1 0 0 0 x — 6
```

Two-base hits—Kelly 2. Stolen bases—Young 2. Double plays—Rawlings, Bancroft and Kelly; Fletcher, Parkinson and Leslie. Left on bases—New York 4. Bases on balls—Off Meadows 2, off Barnes 1. Struck out—By Barnes 5. Hits—Off Meadows, 4 in 1 1-3 innings; off G. Smith, 5 in 6 2-3 innings. Hit by pitcher—By Meadows (Shinners); by G. Smith (Bancroft). Losing pitcher—Meadows. Umpires—Hart, O'Day and Emslie. Time—1:37.

Sept. 4, 1923   New York at Philadelphia

NEW YORK	a	r	h	o	a
Witt, cf	4	0	1	6	0
Dugan, 3	4	0	1	2	5
Ruth, lf	4	0	1	2	0
Pipp, 1	4	0	0	13	0
Meusel, rf	4	0	2	1	0
Ward, 2	4	0	0	1	5
Hofmann, c	3	1	1	2	0
Scott, s	4	1	1	0	3
Jones, p	3	0	0	0	0
Totals	34	2	7	27	13

PHILADELPHIA	a	r	h	o	a
Matthews, cf	4	0	0	4	0
Galloway, s	3	0	0	1	1
Hale, 3	3	0	0	0	4
Hauser, 1	3	0	0	10	0
Miller, lf	3	0	0	5	0
Welch, rf	3	0	0	3	1
Dykes, 2	3	0	0	2	4
Perkins, c	3	0	0	2	0
Hasty, p	2	0	0	0	1
*McGowan	1	0	0	0	0
Totals	28	0	0	27	11

* Batted for Hasty in ninth.

New York	0	0	0	2	0	0	0	0	0 —	2		
Philadelphia	0	0	0	0	0	0	0	0	0 —	0		

Errors—Scott, Dykes. Two-base hit—Meusel. Double play—Welch and Perkins. Left on bases—New York 6, Philadelphia 2. Bases on balls—Off Jones 1, off Hasty 1. Struck out—By Hasty 1. Umpires—Dinneen, Ormsby and Moriarty. Time—1:23

Sept. 7, 1923   Boston at Philadelphia

BOSTON	a	r	h	o	a
Mitchell, s	5	0	0	5	4
Picinich, c	5	1	1	2	0
Reichle, cf	4	0	1	1	0
Flagstead, rf	3	1	3	1	0
J. Harris, 1	5	1	1	15	0
Shanks, 3	5	1	1	0	2
Menosky, lf	2	0	0	3	1
McMillan, 2	4	0	0	0	8
Ehmke, p	4	0	2	0	3
Totals	37	4	9	27	18

PHILADELPHIA	a	r	h	o	a
Matthews, cf	4	0	0	3	0
Galloway, s	3	0	0	1	2
Perkins, c	3	0	0	6	0
Hauser, 1	2	0	0	14	0
Miller, lf	3	0	0	1	0
Welch, rf	3	0	0	1	0
Dykes, 3	3	0	0	1	2
Scheer, 2	3	0	0	0	2
B. Harris, p	2	0	0	0	4
*McGowan	1	0	0	0	0
Totals	27	0	0	27	10

* Batted for B. Harris in ninth.

Boston	1	0	0	0	0	0	0	3	0 —	4	
Philadelphia	0	0	0	0	0	0	0	0	0 —	0	

Errors—Menosky, Galloway. Two-base hit—Shanks. Double play—Mitchell and J. Harris. Left on bases—Boston 11, Philadelphia 1. Bases on balls—Off Ehmke 1, off B. Harris 5. Struck out—By Ehmke 1, by B. Harris 6. Wild pitch—B. Harris. Balk—B. Harris. Passed ball—Perkins. Umpires—Dinneen, Ormsby and Moriarity. Time—1:34.

July 17, 1924   Boston at St. Louis

BOSTON

	ab	r	bh	tb	po	a	e
Felix, cf.............	4	0	0	0	3	0	1
Cunningham, lf	3	0	0	0	4	0	0
Stengel, rf.........	4	0	0	0	1	0	0
McInnis, 1b......	3	0	0	0	9	1	0
Padgett, 2b.......	3	0	0	0	2	3	1
Nerney, 3b........	3	0	0	0	1	1	0
R. Smith, ss	3	0	0	0	0	2	0
O'Neil, c	3	0	0	0	3	0	0
McNamara, p....	0	0	0	0	1	4	0
John Cooney, p.	0	0	0	0	0	0	0
*Gibson.............	1	0	0	0	0	0	0
Totals	27	0	0	0	24	11	2

ST. LOUIS

	ab	r	h	po	a
J. Smith, rf..................	5	0	2	3	0
Holm, cf......................	4	1	1	4	0
Hornsby, 2b	4	1	3	1	4
Bottomley, 1b.............	4	1	1	9	0
Blades, lf	4	0	0	3	0
Torporcer, 3b.............	2	1	0	0	0
Gonzales, c.................	4	0	2	5	0
J. Cooney, ss	4	0	2	2	2
Haines, p....................	3	1	1	0	3
Totals........	34	5	12	27	9

* Batted for McNamara in eighth.

Boston............................ 0 0 0 0 0 0 0 0 0 — 0
St. Louis...................... 1 0 1 0 3 0 0 0 x — 5

Two-base hit, J. Smith. Sacrifices, Haines, Holm. Double play, Tierney, Padgett and McInnis. Left on base, Boston 3, St. Louis 9. Base on balls, by McNamara, by Haines 3. Struck out, by Cooney 2, by Haines 5. Hits, off McNamara, 12 in 7 innings; off Cooney, 0 in 1 inning. Hit by pitcher, by McNamara, Toporcer. Wild pitch, McNamara. Losing pitcher, McNamara. Time, 1h. 43m. Umpires, O'Day, Sweeney and Quigley. Attendance—13,000.

Sept. 13, 1925   Philadelphia at Brooklyn

PHILADELPHIA

	a	r	h	o	a
Sand, s.........................	1	0	0	2	1
*Wright'e.....................	1	0	0	0	0
Metz, s	0	0	0	1	1
†Kimmick	1	0	0	0	0
Leach, cf......................	4	0	0	3	0
Williams, rf.................	3	0	0	2	0
Harper, lf	3	0	0	3	0
Hawks, 1......................	3	1	0	3	0
Huber, 3	3	0	0	1	2
Friberg, 2	2	0	0	4	0
Wilson, c.....................	2	0	0	0	0
Wendell, c...................	1	0	0	5	2
C. Mitchell, p..............	0	0	0	0	0
Decatur, p	1	0	0	0	0
Betts, p	1	0	0	0	1
‡Fonseca	1	0	0	0	0
Totals................	27	1	0	24	7

BROOKLYN

	a	r	h	o	a
J. Mitchell, s	5	2	3	1	2
Stock, 2........................	4	3	2	1	2
Johnston, lf..................	4	2	3	3	0
Cox, rf.........................	5	1	4	2	0
Brown, cf.....................	4	0	0	3	0
Hargreaves, 1..............	4	1	1	6	2
Tierney, 3.....................	3	0	1	0	0
Deberry, c	3	1	1	9	0
Vance, p.......................	4	0	0	2	1
Totals..............	36	10	15	27	7

* Batted for Sand in sixth.
† Batted for Metz in ninth.
‡ Batted for Betts in ninth.

Philadelphia................ 0 1 0 0 0 0 0 0 0 — 1
Brooklyn...................... 4 0 0 4 0 1 1 0 x — 10

Errors—Friberg, Sand, Johnston 2, Hargreaves. Two-base hits—J. Mitchell, Cox. Three-base hit—Johnson. Stolen bases—J. Mitchell, Stock, Johnston, Cox, Hargreaves. Sacrifices—Friberg, Deberry. Double plays—Huber and Sand; Wendell and Friberg. Left on bases—Philadelphia 1, Brooklyn 6. Bases on balls —Off Decatur 2, off Betts 1, off Vance 1. Struck out—By Betts 4, by Vance 9. Passed balls—Deberry, Wilson. Hits—Off C. Mitchell 3 (none out in first); off Decatur 7 in 4 innings; off Betts 5 in 4 innings. Losing pitcher—C. Mitchell. Umpires—Pfirman, Wilson and O'Day. Time—1:45.

August 21, 1926   Chicago at Boston

CHICAGO	ab	r	bh	tb	po	a	e
Mostil, cf............	5	1	4	5	2	0	0
Morehart, 2b.....	3	1	1	1	0	3	0
Sheely, 1b.........	4	1	2	2	9	2	0
Falk, lf..............	3	0	0	0	1	0	0
Barrett, rf.........	5	0	2	3	5	0	0
Hunnefield, ss..	4	0	1	1	4	3	1
Kamm, 3b	4	2	2	2	2	2	0
Grabowski, c....	3	1	0	0	2	0	0
Lyons, p............	4	0	1	1	2	2	0
Totals	35	6	13	15	27	12	1

BOSTON	ab	r	bh	tb	po	a	e
Tobin, rf............	3	0	0	0	2	1	0
Rigney, ss	3	0	0	0	3	1	0
Jacobson, cf......	3	0	0	0	2	0	0
Rosenthal, lf.....	3	0	0	0	3	0	1
Regan, 2b..........	3	0	0	0	3	0	1
Todt, 1b............	3	0	0	0	8	0	0
Haney, 3b	3	0	0	0	1	5	0
Gaston, c..........	2	0	0	0	5	1	0
*Bratche............	1	0	0	0	0	0	0
Stokes, c...........	0	0	0	0	0	0	0
Harriss, p..........	1	0	0	0	0	3	0
†Shaner............	1	0	0	0	0	0	0
Russell, p.........	0	0	0	0	0	1	0
‡Bischoff..........	1	0	0	0	0	0	0
Totals	27	0	0	0	27	12	2

* Batted for Gaston in eighth.
† Batted for Harriss in sixth.
‡ Batted for Russell in ninth.

```
Chicago........................ 0 1 0 0 2 2 1 0 0 — 6
Boston.......................... 0 0 0 0 0 0 0 0 0 — 0
```

Two-base hits, Barrett, Mostil. Hits, off Harriss, 10 in 6 innings; off Russell, 3 in 3 innings. First base on errors, Boston. Left on base, Chicago 9, Boston 2. Stolen bases, Mostil, Hunnefield. Sacrifice hits, Morehart, Rigney, Sheely. Sacrifice fly, Hunnefield. Base on balls, by Lyons, by Harriss 3, by Russell. Struck out, by Lyons 2, by Harriss, by Russell. Wild pitches. Harriss. Losing pitcher, Harriss. Time, 1h. 50m. Umpire-in-chief. McGowan. Umpires on bases, Connolly and Rowland. Attendance, 7000.

May 8, 1929   Pittsburgh at New York

PITTSBURGH	ab	bh	po	a
Adams, 2............................	3	0	1	2
L. Waner, cf.......................	3	0	2	0
P. Waner, r........................	4	0	3	0
Traynor, 3..........................	3	0	0	1
Stoner, 3............................	0	0	0	1
Grantham, lf.......................	1	0	2	0
Com'r'sky, lf......................	2	0	0	0
Sheely, 1............................	3	0	8	1
Bartell, s............................	3	0	2	2
Hargre'ves, c	3	0	6	0
Petty, p..............................	0	0	0	1
Fussell, p............................	1	0	0	0
Kremer, p...........................	1	0	0	2
*Riconda...........................	1	0	0	0
Totals......................	28	0	24	10

NEW YORK	ab	bh	po	a
Roush, cf............................	5	1	1	0
Cohen, 2............................	5	3	1	2
Lindstrom, 3.......................	4	0	6	0
Ott, rf................................	3	2	2	0
Terry, 1..............................	4	1	13	1
Jackson, s...........................	4	1	2	5
Fullis, lf.............................	4	2	2	0
O'Farrell, c	4	2	5	0
Hubbell, p..........................	3	0	1	2
Totals......................	36	12	27	16

* Batted for Kremer in ninth.

```
Pittsburgh................... 0 0 0 0 0 0 0 0 0 — 0
New York .................... 2 2 2 0 0 5 0 0 x — 11
```

Runs, Roush, Cohen 2, Lindstrom, Ott 3, O'Farrell 2, Hubbell, Fullis. Errors, Jackson 2, Fullis, Traynor, Sheely. Runs batted in, Ott 4, Fullis 2, Hubbell, Cohen 2, Roush 2. Two-base hit, O'Farrell. Three-base hits, O'Farrell, Roush. Home runs, Ott 2, Fullis, Cohen. Sacrifices, L. Waner, Hubbell. Double play, Hubbell, Jackson and Terry. Left on bases, New York 3, Pittsburgh 3. Base on balls, by Hubbell, by Fussell. Struck out, by Hubbell 4, by Kremer 6. Hits, off Petty, 3 in 1¹/₂ inning; off Fussell, 3 in 1¹/₃ inning; off Kremer, 6 in 5¹/₃ innings. Losing pitcher, Petty. Time, 1h 35m. Umpires, Moran, McLaughlin and Quigley.

April 29, 1931   St. Louis at Cleveland

ST. LOUIS	ab	bh	po	a
Levey, s	2	0	0	0
Burns, 3	4	0	6	3
Goslin, lf	3	0	7	0
Kress, r	4	0	1	0
Schulte, cf	4	0	1	0
Storti, 3	3	0	1	2
Melillo, 2	3	0	3	3
R. Ferrell, c	3	0	2	0
Gray, p	2	0	3	2
*Waddey	1	0	0	0
Stiles, p	0	0	0	0
Totals	29	0	24	10

CLEVELAND	ab	bh	po	a
Burnett, 3	4	2	1	3
Fonseca, 1	4	1	12	0
Averill, cf	5	2	1	0
Hodapp, 2	4	1	2	3
Vosmik, lf	4	1	1	0
Falk, r	4	0	0	0
Hunnefield, s	4	2	2	3
Sewell, c	3	2	8	0
W. Ferrell, p	4	2	0	2
Totals	36	13	27	11

* Batted for Gray in eighth.

St. Louis .... 0 0 0 0 0 0 0 0 0 — 0
Cleveland .... 0 1 1 2 0 0 2 3 x — 9

Runs, Burnett 2, Averill, Hunnefield 2, Sewell 2, W. Ferrell 2. Errors, Hunnefield 3. Runs batted in, W. Ferrell 4, Averill 2, Hodapp, Sewell, Fonseca. Two-base hits, Hunnefield, Vosmik, W. Ferrell. Home runs, W. Ferrell, Averill. Sacrifice, Fonseca. Double play, Burnett and Fonseca. Left on base, St. Louis 5, Cleveland 6. Base on balls, by Ferrell 3, by Stiles 2. Struck out, by Ferrell 8, by Gray. Hits, off Gray, 10 in 7 innings; off Stiles, 3 in 1 inning. Losing pitcher, Gray. Time, 1h 45m. Umpires, Heisel, Moriarity and Hildebrand.

August 8, 1931   Boston at Washington

BOSTON	ab	r	bh	tb	po	a	e
Rothrock, lf	4	0	0	0	0	0	0
Rhyne, ss	4	0	0	0	1	7	0
Pickering, 2b	1	0	0	0	6	2	0
Webb, rf	4	0	0	0	0	0	0
Sweeney, 1b	1	0	0	0	14	2	0
Miller, 3b	3	0	0	0	0	1	0
Oliver, cf	3	0	0	0	1	0	0
Berry, c	3	0	0	0	1	0	0
Moore, p	3	0	0	0	1	5	0
Totals	26	0	0	0	24	17	0

WASHINGTON	ab	r	bh	tb	po	a	e
Myer, 2b	4	1	1	3	2	0	0
Rice, rf	4	2	3	3	0	0	0
Manush, lf	4	1	2	2	3	0	0
Cronin, ss	4	1	1	1	3	4	0
West, cf	4	0	1	1	3	0	0
Bluege, 3b	4	0	0	0	0	1	0
Kuhel, 1b	3	0	2	3	8	0	0
Spencer, c	2	0	0	0	8	1	0
Burke, p	4	0	0	0	0	1	0
Totals	33	5	10	13	27	7	0

Boston .... 0 0 0 0 0 0 0 0 0 — 0
Washington .... 1 0 1 0 0 0 0 3 x — 5

Runs batted in, Cronin 2, Rice, West, Spencer. Two-base hit, Kuhel. Three-base hit, Myer. Sacrifice hit, Spencer. Left on bases, Boston 4, Washington 7. Base on balls, by Moore 2, by Burke 5. Struck out, by Moore, by Burke 8. Time, 1h 35m. Umpires, Moriarity, Nallin and Van Graflau.

Sept. 18, 1934 Boston at St. Louis

BOSTON	ab	r	h	o	a	e
Bishop, 2b	3	1	0	1	4	0
Werber, 3b	4	0	0	2	4	1
Almada, cf	5	0	0	2	0	1
Johnson, lf	4	1	1	2	0	0
Graham, rf	4	0	0	2	1	0
R. Ferrell, c	1	0	0	1	0	0
Hinkle, c	3	0	0	4	0	0
Morgan, 1b	2	0	0	15	0	0
Lary, ss	4	0	0	1	2	0
W. Ferrell, p	1	0	0	0	0	0
Walberg, p	3	0	0	0	5	0
Totals	34	2	1	30	16	2

BROWNS	ab	r	h	o	a	e
Clift, 3b	4	0	1	2	2	0
Garms, lf	4	0	2	4	0	0
Burns, 1b	5	0	1	7	0	0
Pepper, cf	5	0	1	4	0	1
Campbell, rf	4	0	1	1	0	0
Mellilo, 2b	4	0	0	1	2	1
Hemsley, c	5	1	2	10	1	0
Strange, ss	2	0	1	0	2	1
Newsom, p	4	0	0	1	3	0
*Bejma	1	0	1	0	0	0
Totals	38	1	10	30	10	3

* Batted for Campbell in tenth inning.

Club..	1	2	3	4	5	6	7	8	9	10		
Boston	0	1	0	0	0	0	0	0	1	—	2	
Browns	0	0	0	0	0	1	0	0	0	—	1	

Two-base hits—Grams, Bejma. Runs batted in—Lary, Johnson, Strange. Sacrifice hit—Garms. Stolen bases—Clift, Burns. Passed ball—Hinkle. Base on balls—Off W. Ferrell, 1; off Newsom, 7; off Walberg, 3. Struck out—By W. Ferrell, 1; by Newsom, 9; by Walberg, 4. Pitching record—Off W. Ferrell, no hits no runs in 1 inning; off Walberg, 10 hits 1 run in 9 innings. Left on bases—St. Louis, 12, Boston, 9. Umpires—Kolls and Geisel. Winning pitcher—Walberg. Time of game—2:22:00.

Sept. 21, 1934 St. Louis at Brooklyn

ST. LOUIS	ab	bh	po	a
Martin, 3	4	1	0	1
Rothrock, r	4	0	1	0
Frisch, 2	4	0	1	3
Medwick, lf	4	2	6	0
Collins, 1	4	1	9	1
DeLancey, c	4	1	7	0
Orsatti, cf	3	0	1	0
Durocher, s	3	0	1	3
P. Dean, p	3	2	1	2
Totals	33	7	27	10

BROOKLYN	ab	bh	po	a
Boyle, r	4	0	2	0
Frey, s	3	0	4	3
Koen'ke, cf	2	0	1	1
Leslie, 1	3	0	10	1
Cuccin'lo, 3	3	0	3	0
Freder'k, lf	3	0	2	0
Jordan, 2	3	0	1	6
Lopez, c	2	0	3	1
*Bucher	1	0	0	0
Benge, p	2	0	1	1
†McCarthy	1	0	0	0
Totals	27	0	27	13

* Batted for Lopez in ninth.
† Batted for Benge in ninth.

St. Louis	0	0	0	0	0	1	1	0	1	—	3
Brooklyn	0	0	0	0	0	0	0	0	0	—	0

Runs, Medwick 2, P. Dean. Error, Jordan. Runs batted in, Martin, Collins 2. Two-base hits, P. Dean, Martin, Medwick. Three-base hit, Medwick. Left on base, St. Louis 3, Brooklyn. Base on balls, off P. Dean. Struck out, by Benge, by P. Dean 6. Time, 1h 38m. Umpires, Klem, Sears and Rigler.

August 31, 1935   Cleveland at Chicago

CLEVELAND

	ab	bh	po	a
Galatzer, r	4	0	1	0
Averill, cf	3	0	3	0
Vosmik, lf	3	0	2	0
Trosky, 1	3	0	13	0
Hale, 3	3	0	1	5
Knick'er, s	3	0	0	2
Phillips, c	2	0	2	1
Hughes, 2	2	0	2	3
Hudlin, p	2	0	0	2
*Carson	1	0	0	0
Totals	26	0	24	13

CHICAGO

	ab	bh	po	a
Conlan, cf	5	1	4	0
Simmons, lf	4	1	5	0
Piet, 2	4	0	1	4
Appling, s	3	1	1	2
Bonura, 1	4	3	8	2
Dykes, 3	4	2	1	1
Wash'ton, r	4	1	2	0
Sewell, c	1	0	5	0
Kennedy, p	4	1	0	1
Totals	33	10	27	10

* Batted for Hudlin in ninth.

Cleveland...............   0 0 0 0 0 0 0 0 0 — 0
Chicago.................   1 0 0 1 0 3 0 0 x — 5

Runs, Conlan, Dykes, Bonura 2, Sewell. Error, Phillips. Runs batted in, Appling, Dykes, Kennedy 3. Two-base hit, Bonura. Three-base hit, Kennedy. Stolen base, Hughes. Double plays, Knickerbocker, Hughes and Trosky; Dykes, Piet and Bonura. Left on bases, Cleveland 3, Chicago 8. Base on balls, off Hudlin 4, off Kennedy 4. Struck out, by Kennedy 5. Time, 1h 41m. Umpires, Summers and Owens.

June 1, 1937   St. Louis at Chicago

ST. LOUIS

	ab	r	h	o	a
Davis, 1b	4	0	0	5	0
West, cf	4	0	0	3	0
Vosmik, lf	3	0	0	2	1
Bell, rf	3	0	0	1	0
Clift, 3b	3	0	0	1	2
Knick'ker, ss	3	0	0	1	4
Hemsley, c	2	0	0	6	1
Carey, 2b	3	0	0	5	2
Hogsett, p	0	0	0	0	0
Van Atta, p	1	0	0	0	0
*Bottomley	1	0	0	0	0
Totals	27	0	0	24	9

CHICAGO

	ab	r	h	o	a
Radcliff, lf	2	1	0	3	0
Kreevich, cf	5	2	3	4	0
Walker, rf	4	2	2	1	0
Bonura, 1b	4	0	1	12	0
Appling, ss	4	0	2	1	4
Hayes, 2b	4	0	0	1	3
Piet, 3b	3	0	1	0	1
Sewell, c	2	2	1	5	0
Dietrich, p	3	1	0	0	1
Totals	31	8	10	27	9

* Batted for Van Atta in ninth.

St. Louis................   0 0 0 0 0 0 0 0 0 — 0
Chicago.................   3 0 0 2 0 0 0 3 x — 8

Errors—Vosmik, Hemsley, Piet. Runs batted in—Walker 3, Sewell, Kreevich 3, Appling. Two-base hits—Kreevich, Walker, Sewell. Stolen bases—Piet, Kreevich. Double plays—Knickerbocker, Carey and Davis; Appling, Hayes and Bonura. Bases on balls—Off Hogsett 5, off Van Atta 4, off Dietrich 2. Struck out—By Dietrich 5, by Van Atta 6. Hits—Off Hogsett 2 in 1 inning (none out in second). Wild pitch—Van Atta. Losing pitcher—Hogsett. Umpires—Hubbard, Dinncen and Quinn. Attendance 1500.

June 11, 1938   Boston at Cincinnati

BOSTON (N.)	ab	r	h	po	a	e
G. Moore, rf............	1	0	0	2	0	0
Fletcher, 1b............	1	0	0	5	0	0
*Mueller................	1	0	0	0	0	0
C'oney, 1b, rf.........	3	0	0	4	0	0
DiM'ggio, cf..........	3	0	0	1	0	0
Cuc'ello, 2b..........	2	0	0	1	3	1
R. Reis, lf.............	3	0	0	3	0	0
English, 3b...........	2	0	0	0	2	0
Riddle, c...............	3	0	0	5	0	0
Warstler, ss..........	2	0	0	3	3	0
†Kahle.................	1	0	0	0	0	0
M'Fayden, p.........	2	0	0	0	0	0
‡Maggert..............	1	0	0	0	0	0
Total	25	0	0	24	8	1

CINCINNATI (N.)	ab	r	h	po	a	e
Frey, 2b.................	4	0	0	1	2	0
Berger, lf...............	3	2	1	2	0	0
Goodman, rf..........	3	0	0	0	0	0
McC'ick, 1b..........	4	0	1	14	1	0
Lombardi, c	4	1	2	5	2	0
Craft, cf	3	0	0	3	0	0
Riggs, 3b..............	3	0	1	0	5	0
Myers, ss..............	3	0	0	1	2	0
V. Meer, p.............	3	0	1	1	2	0
Total	30	3	6	27	14	0

* Batted for Fletcher in ninth.
† Batted for Warstler in ninth.
‡ Batted for MacFayden in ninth.

```
Boston.................... 0 0 0 0 0 0 0 0 0 — 0
Cincinnati.............. 0 0 0 1 0 2 0 0 x — 3
```

Runs batted in—Goodman, Lombardi 2. Three-base hits—Berger, Riggs. Home run—Lombardi. Double plays—Cuccinello, Warstler and Cooney; Lombardi and McCormick. Left on bases—Boston 1, Cincinnati 5. Bases on balls—Off MacFayden 1, Vander Meer 3. Struck out—By MacFayden 4, Vander Meer 4. Hit by pitcher—By MacFayden (Goodman). Umpires—Magerkurth, Parker and Moran. Time of game—1:48.

June 15, 1938   Cincinnati at Brooklyn

CINCINNATI	ab	r	h	po	a	e
Frey, 2b.................	5	0	1	2	2	0
Berger, lf...............	5	1	3	1	0	0
Goodman, rf..........	3	2	1	3	0	0
McC'mick, 1b.........	5	1	1	9	1	0
Lombardi, c	3	1	0	9	0	0
Craft, cf	5	0	3	1	0	0
Riggs, 3b..............	4	0	1	0	3	0
Myers, ss..............	4	0	0	0	1	0
V. Meer, p.............	4	1	1	2	4	0
Total	38	6	11	27	11	0

BROOKLYN	ab	r	h	po	a	e
Cuyler, rf..............	2	0	0	1	0	0
Coscarart, 2b.........	2	0	0	1	2	0
*Brack..................	1	0	0	0	0	0
Hudson, 2b............	1	0	0	1	0	0
Hassett, lf............	4	0	0	3	0	0
Phelps, c	3	0	0	9	0	0
†Rosen..................	0	0	0	0	0	0
Lavagetto, 3b.........	2	0	0	0	2	2
Camilli, 1b............	1	0	0	7	0	0
Koy, cf	4	0	0	4	0	0
Durocher, ss	4	0	0	1	2	0
Butcher, p.............	0	0	0	0	1	0
Pressnell, p............	2	0	0	0	0	0
Hamlin, p..............	0	0	0	0	1	0
‡English................	1	0	0	0	0	0
Tamulis, p.............	0	0	0	0	0	0
Total	27	0	0	27	8	2

* Batted for Coscarat in sixth.
† Ran for Phelps in ninth.
‡ Batted for Hamlin in eighth.

```
Cincinnati.................. 0 0 4 0 0 0 1 1 0 — 6
Brooklyn.................... 0 0 0 0 0 0 0 0 0 — 0
```

Runs batted in—McCormick 3, Riggs, Craft, Berger. Two-base hit—Berger. Three-base hit—Berger. Home run—McCormick. Stolen base—Goodman. Left on bases—Cincinnati 9, Brooklyn 8. Bases on balls—Off Butcher 3, Vander Meer 8, Hamlin 1. Struck out—By Butcher 1, Pressnell 3, Vander Meer 7, Hamlin 3. Hits—Off Butcher 5 in 2 2-3, Hamlin 2 in 1 2-3, Pressnell 4 in 3 2-3, Tamulis 0 in 1. Losing pitcher—Butcher. Umpires—Stewart, Stark and Barr. Time of game—2:22. Attendance 40,000.

August 27, 1938 Cleveland at New York

CLEVELAND	ab	r	h	o	a
Lary, ss	2	0	0	3	3
†Pytlak	1	0	0	0	0
Campbell, rf	3	0	0	2	0
Heath, lf	3	0	0	3	0
Averill, cf	2	0	0	1	0
Weatherly, cf	1	0	0	0	0
Trosky, 1b	3	0	0	6	0
Hemsley, c	3	0	0	8	0
Keltner, 3b	3	0	0	0	3
Hale, 2b	3	0	0	1	0
Humphries, p	1	0	0	0	0
Galehouse, p	1	0	0	0	0
*Solters	1	0	0	0	0
Totals	27	0	0	24	6

NEW YORK	ab	r	h	o	a
Crosetti, ss	4	1	0	1	2
Rolfe, 3b	5	2	2	2	0
Henrich, rf	5	2	3	1	0
DiMaggio, cf	5	2	1	0	0
Gehrig, 1b	4	3	2	6	1
Selkirk, lf	5	1	2	4	0
Gordon, 2b	4	2	3	1	5
Glenn, c	4	0	0	9	0
Pearson, p	3	0	0	3	0
Totals	39	13	13	27	8

* Batted for Galehouse in ninth.
† Batted for Lary in ninth.

Cleveland	0	0	0	0	0	0	0	0	0	—	0
New York	5	0	2	3	0	2	1	0	x	—	13

Errors—Lary 2. Runs batted in—Henrich 4, Gordon 6, Selkirk 2, Glenn. Three-base hit—Gordon. Home runs—Henrich 2, Gordon 2. Bases on balls—Off Humphries 3, off Pearson 2, off Galehouse 1. Struck out—By Humphries 3, by Pearson 7, by Galehouse 5. Hits—Off Humphries 9 in 4 innings. Losing pitcher—Humphries. Umpires—Kolls, Hubbard and Rue.

April 16, 1940 Cleveland at Chicago

CLEVELAND	ab	r	h	o	a	e
Boudreau, ss	3	0	0	1	2	0
Weatherly, cf	4	0	1	2	0	1
Chapman, rf	3	0	0	6	0	0
Trosky, 1b	4	0	0	8	0	0
Heath, lf	4	1	1	0	0	0
Keltner, 3b	4	0	1	0	2	0
Hemsley, c	4	0	2	8	0	0
Mack, 2b	4	0	1	2	3	0
Feller, p	3	0	0	0	0	0
Totals	33	1	6	27	7	1

CHICAGO	ab	r	h	o	a	e
Kennedy, 3b	4	0	0	1	2	0
Kuhel, 1b	3	0	0	11	0	0
Kreevich, cf	3	0	0	3	0	0
Solters, lf	4	0	0	2	0	0
Appling, ss	3	0	0	0	2	0
Wright, rf	4	0	0	3	0	0
McNair, 2b	3	0	0	2	2	1
Tresch, c	2	0	0	5	0	0
Smith, p	1	0	0	0	2	0
*Rosenthal	1	0	0	0	0	0
Brown, p	0	0	0	0	1	0
Totals	28	0	0	27	9	1

* Batted for Smith in eighth.

Cleveland	0	0	0	1	0	0	0	0	0	—	1
Chicago	0	0	0	0	0	0	0	0	0	—	0

Run batted in—Hemsley. Two-base hit—Mack. Three-base hit—Hemsley. Stolen base—Kuhel. Double play—Kuhel (unassisted). Left on bases—Cleveland 7, Chicago 6. Bases on balls—Feller 5, Smith 2. Struck out—Feller 8. Smith 5. Hits—Smith, 6 in 8; Brown, none in 1. Umpires—Geisel, McGowan and Kolls. Time—2:24.

April 30, 1940 Brooklyn at Cincinnati

BROOKLYN	ab	r	h	o	a
Walker, cf	4	1	0	4	0
Cosc'art, 2b	4	1	2	1	3
Vosmik, lf	4	0	1	2	0
Lavag'to, 3b	4	0	2	1	4
Camilli, 1b	4	0	0	9	0
Cul'bine, rf	3	0	0	3	0
Franks, c	3	1	0	6	1
Reese, ss	4	0	0	1	2
Carleton, p	2	0	0	0	0
Totals	32	3	5	27	10

CINCINNATI	ab	r	h	o	a
Werber, 3b	2	0	0	1	1
Frey, 2b	4	0	0	2	3
Goodman, rf	4	0	0	2	0
F. McCor'k, 1b	3	0	0	10	1
Lombardi, e	3	0	0	5	0
Craft, cf	3	0	0	3	0
M. McCor'k, lf	3	0	0	1	0
Joost, ss	3	0	0	2	2
Turner, p	2	0	0	1	1
*Berger	1	0	0	0	0
Moore, p	0	0	0	0	0
Totals	28	0	0	27	8

* Batted for Turner in eighth.

Brooklyn	0	0	0	0	3	0	0	0	0	—	3
Cincinnati	0	0	0	0	0	0	0	0	0	—	0

Errors—Coscarart, Lavagetto, Reese. Runs batted in—Coscarart 3. Two-base hit —Vosmik. Home run—Coscarart. Bases on balls—Off Carleton 2, off Turner 2, off Moore 1. Struck out—By Carleton 4, by Turner 2, by Moore 1. Hits—Off Turner 4 in 8 innings. Losing pitcher—Turner. Umpires—Stewart, Magerkurth and Barr.

August 30, 1941 St. Louis at Cincinnati

ST. LOUIS	ab	r	h	o	a
J. Brown, 3b	3	1	1	3	2
Hopp, cf	5	1	1	1	0
Padgett, lf	4	0	0	1	0
Mize, 1b	3	0	0	9	0
Crabtree, rf	2	0	1	1	0
W. Cooper, c	3	0	1	4	1
Crespi, 2b	3	0	0	3	2
Marion, ss	4	0	0	5	5
Warneke, p	4	0	1	0	0
Totals	31	2	5	27	10

CINCINNATI	ab	r	h	o	a
Werber, 3b	4	0	0	2	2
M. McCor'k, lf	3	0	0	2	0
Frey, 2b	2	0	0	2	4
F. McCor'k, 1b	3	0	0	7	0
Gleeson, rf	3	0	0	4	0
Lombardi, c	3	0	0	3	1
Craft, cf	3	0	0	3	0
Joost, ss	2	0	0	4	3
*Waner	1	0	0	0	0
E. Riddle, p	2	0	0	0	0
†Koy	1	0	0	0	0
Totals	27	0	0	27	10

* Batted for Joost in ninth.
† Batted for E. Riddle in ninth.

St. Louis	0	0	0	0	0	0	2	0	0	—	2
Cincinnati	0	0	0	0	0	0	0	0	0	—	0

Errors—Craft, Joost, J. Brown, Crespi. Double plays—W. Cooper and Marion; Crespi, Marion and Mize; Frey, Joost and F. McCormick. Bases on balls—Off Warneke 1, off E. Riddle 5. Struck out—By Warneke 2, by E. Riddle 2. Umpires— Conlan, Goetz and Reardon.

April 27, 1944 Brooklyn at Boston

BROOKLYN	ab	r	h	o	a	e
P. Waner, rf............	2	0	0	5	0	0
Walker, lf..............	4	0	0	3	0	0
Olmo, 2b................	3	0	0	2	3	0
Galan, cf................	3	0	0	4	0	0
Schultz, 1b............	3	0	0	6	1	0
English, 3b............	3	0	0	1	2	0
Hart, ss.................	3	0	0	0	3	2
Owen, c..................	3	0	0	2	0	0
Ostermueller, p.....	2	0	0	1	0	0
*Bordagaray...........	1	0	0	0	0	0
Totals...........	27	0	0	24	9	2

BOSTON	ab	r	h	o	a	e
Ryan, 3b................	4	1	2	1	3	0
Holmes, cf.............	4	0	0	2	0	0
Workman, rf..........	3	0	1	2	0	0
Ross, lf.................	3	0	0	2	0	0
Clemens, lf...........	0	0	0	0	0	0
Masi, c..................	3	0	0	7	0	0
Etchison, 1b..........	3	0	1	10	0	0
Wietelmann, ss......	3	0	0	1	1	0
Shemo, 2b.............	3	0	1	2	4	0
Tobin, p................	3	1	1	0	1	0
Totals...........	29	2	5	27	9	0

* Batted for Ostermueller in ninth.

```
Brooklyn......................  0 0 0 0 0 0 0 0 0 — 0
Boston.........................  0 0 1 0 0 0 0 1 x — 2
```

Runs batted in—Workman, Tobin. Two-base hits—Ryan 2. Home run—Tobin. Double play—Hart, Olmo and Schultz. Bases on balls—Off Tobin 2, off Ostermueller 2. Struck out—By Tobin 6, by Ostermueller 2. Umpires—Stewart, Jorda and Magerkurth.

May 15, 1944 Boston at Cincinnati

BOSTON	ab	r	h	o	a	e
Holmes, cf.............	4	0	0	3	0	0
Macon, 1b..............	3	0	0	12	0	1
Ross, lf.................	3	0	0	0	0	0
Workman, rf..........	3	0	0	2	0	0
Masi, c..................	3	0	0	2	1	0
Ryan, 2b...............	3	0	0	3	3	0
Phillips, 3b............	3	0	0	0	5	0
Wietelmann, ss......	2	0	0	2	5	1
*Hofferth...............	1	0	0	0	0	0
Tobin, p................	2	0	0	0	3	0
Totals...........	27	0	0	24	17	2

CINCINNATI	ab	r	h	o	a	e
Clay, cf.................	4	0	0	2	0	0
Williams, 2b...........	3	0	0	2	1	0
Walker, rf.............	3	0	0	2	0	0
McCormick, 1b......	3	0	0	8	0	0
Tipton, lf..............	3	0	2	5	0	0
Miller, ss..............	3	0	0	4	3	0
Alene, 3b..............	3	1	1	0	0	0
Mueller, c.............	3	0	0	4	0	0
Shoun, p...............	3	0	2	0	3	0
Totals...........	28	1	5	27	7	0

* Batted for Wietelmann in ninth.

```
Boston.........................  0 0 0 0 0 0 0 0 0 — 0
Cincinnati...................  0 0 0 0 1 0 0 0 x — 1
```

Run batted in—Aleno. Two-base hit—Shoun. Home run—Aleno. Stolen base—Miller. Double play—Tobin, Ryan and Macon. Base on balls—Off Shoun 1. Struck out—By Tobin 2, by Shoun 1. Umpires—Reardon and Goetz.

June 22, 1944   Philadelphia at Boston

PHILADELPHIA	ab	r	h	o	a	e
Hamrick, ss	1	0	0	2	2	0
Adams, cf	2	0	0	0	0	0
Lupien, 1b	1	0	0	8	1	0
Wasdell, lf	2	0	0	0	0	0
Northey, rf	2	0	0	0	0	0
Cieslak, 3b	2	0	0	1	1	1
Finley, c	2	0	0	3	1	0
Mullen, 2b	2	0	0	1	1	0
R. Barrett, p	1	0	0	0	1	0
Mussill, p	0	0	0	0	1	0
Totals	15	0	0	15	8	1

BOSTON	ab	r	h	o	a	e
Holmes, cf	3	3	2	3	0	0
Ryan, 2b	2	1	1	1	1	0
Workman, rf	2	0	1	2	0	0
Nieman, lf	3	1	2	0	0	0
Etchison, 1b	3	1	2	6	0	0
Masi, c	2	0	0	1	0	0
Wietelmann, ss	2	0	0	1	1	0
Phillips, 3b	2	0	0	1	1	0
Tobin, p	2	1	1	0	2	0
Totals	21	7	9	15	5	0

```
Philadelphia ................................... 0 0 0 0 0 — 0
Boston .............................................. 3 0 1 0 3 — 7
```

Game called on account of darkness.

Runs batted in—Holmes 2, Nieman 3, Ryan, Etchison. Two-base hits—Tobin, Holmes. Home runs—Holmes, Nieman. Bases on balls—Off Tobin 2. Struck out— By R. Barrett 2, by Tobin 1. Hits—Off R. Barrett 6 in 4 innings, off Mussill 3 in 1 inning. Losing pitcher—R. Barrett. Umpires—Sears, Conlan and Barr.

Sept. 9, 1945   St. Louis at Philadelphia

BROWNS	ab	r	h	rbi	o	a	e
Byrnes, cf	3	0	0	0	3	0	0
Finney, 1b	3	0	0	0	7	1	0
Moore, rf	2	0	0	0	5	0	0
Laabs, lf	3	0	0	0	2	0	0
Christman, 3b	3	0	0	0	2	1	1
Stephens, ss	2	0	0	0	2	2	0
Mancuso, c	3	0	0	0	2	0	0
Gutteridge, 2b	2	0	0	0	1	3	0
Miller, p	3	0	0	0	0	1	0
Totals	24	0	0	0	*24	8	1

ATHLETICS	ab	r	h	rbi	o	a	e
Smith, lf	4	0	0	0	2	0	0
Peck, rf	4	1	1	0	1	0	0
Hall, 2b	3	0	1	1	3	2	0
Estalella, cf	3	0	0	0	2	0	0
Siebert, 1b	3	0	2	0	8	0	0
Kell, 3b	3	0	0	0	0	3	0
Rosar, c	3	0	0	0	7	1	0
Brancato, ss	3	0	0	0	4	3	0
Fowler, p	3	0	1	0	0	2	0
Totals	29	1	5	1	27	11	0

* None out in 9th when winning run scored.

```
St. Louis ....................... 0 0 0 0 0 0 0 0 0 — 0
Athletics ....................... 0 0 0 0 0 0 0 0 1 — 1
```

Two-base hit—Fowler. Three-base hit—Peck. Sacrifice—Moore. Double plays —Hall and Siebert; Finney, Stephens and Finney; Hall, Brancato and Siebert. Left on bases—St. Louis 2; Athletics 5. Base on balls—Off Fowler 4; Miller 1. Struck out—By Fowler 6; Miller 1. Umpires—Pipgras, Rommel and Weafer. Time—1:15.

April 23, 1946   Boston at Brooklyn

BOSTON	ab	r	h	o	a	e
Ryan, 2b	3	0	0	2	1	0
Hopp, cf	4	0	0	3	0	0
Holmes, rf	3	0	0	3	0	0
Sanders, 1b	3	0	0	4	1	0
Rowell, lf	3	0	0	3	0	0
Masi, c	2	0	0	4	1	0
Roberge, 3b	3	0	0	2	3	0
Wietelmann, ss	2	0	0	2	0	0
Cooper, p	2	0	0	1	1	0
*Workman	0	0	0	0	0	0
Totals	25	0	0	24	7	0

BROOKLYN	ab	r	h	o	a	e
Whitman, lf	4	1	1	2	0	0
Herman, 2b	2	2	1	1	4	0
Reiser, 3b	4	1	2	2	3	0
Walker, rf	3	0	2	0	0	0
Stevens, 1b	4	0	1	13	1	0
Furillo, cf	4	0	0	4	0	0
Anderson, c	4	1	2	2	1	0
Reese, ss	4	0	0	2	6	1
Head, p	3	0	1	1	2	0
Totals	32	5	10	27	17	1

* Batted for Cooper in ninth.

Boston	0	0	0	0	0	0	0	0	0	—	0
Brooklyn	0	0	2	0	2	1	0	0	x	—	5

Two-base hit—Stevens. Home run—Anderson. Sacrifice—Masi. Double plays—Herman, Reese and Stevens; Anderson and Stevens. Left on bases—Boston 2, Brooklyn 6. Bases on balls—Off Cooper 3, Head 3. Struck out—By Cooper 4, Head 2. Umpires—Pinelli, Ballanfante and Barlick. Time of game—1:45. Attendance—30,287.

April 30, 1946   Cleveland at New York

CLEVELAND	ab	h	p	a
Case, lf	4	2	1	0
Lemon, cf	4	1	1	0
Edwards, rf	2	0	0	0
Fleming, 1b	3	1	9	0
Keltner, 3b	1	0	0	3
Boudr'u, ss	3	0	0	4
Hayes, c	4	2	12	1
Mack, 2b	3	1	4	2
Feller, p	4	0	0	1
Totals	28	7	27	11

NEW YORK	ab	h	p	a
Rizzuto, ss	3	0	5	5
Stirnw'ss, 3b	3	0	1	2
Henrich, rf	1	0	0	0
DiMaggio, cf	4	0	1	0
Keller, lf	3	0	3	0
Etten, 1b	3	0	8	0
Gordon, 2b	3	0	3	3
Dickey, c	2	0	6	3
Bevens, p	3	0	0	2
Totals	25	0	27	15

Cleveland	0	0	0	0	0	0	0	1	—	1
New York	0	0	0	0	0	0	0	0	—	0

Runs—Hayes. Errors—Fleming, Keltner. Runs batted in—Hayes. Home run—Hayes. Stolen bases—Case, Henrich. Bases on balls—Off Bevens, 5; Feller, 5. Struck out—By Bevens, 5; Feller, 11. Attendance—37,144.

June 18, 1947   Boston at Cincinnati

BOSTON (N.)	ab	r	h	po	a
Holmes, rf	3	0	0	3	0
Hopp, cf	2	0	0	3	0
Rowell, lf	4	0	0	0	0
R. Elliott, 3b	3	0	0	1	1
Torgeson, 1b	3	0	0	8	3
Masi, c	2	0	0	2	1
Sisti, ss	2	0	0	3	4
Ryan, 2b	0	0	0	0	0
Lanfranconi, p	2	0	0	0	1
*McCormick	1	0	0	0	0
Karl, p	0	0	0	0	0
Totals	25	0	0	24	11

CINCINNATI (N.)	ab	r	h	po	a
Baumholtz, rf	5	2	4	3	0
Zientara, 2b	3	0	1	2	2
Hatton, 3b	1	2	1	1	4
Young, 1b	5	2	2	9	1
Haas, cf	4	0	0	3	0
Galan, lf	5	0	2	4	0
Miller, ss	5	0	0	2	1
Lamanno, c	3	0	1	3	1
Blackwell, p	4	0	1	0	2
Totals	35	6	12	27	11

* Batted for Lanfranconi in eighth.

Boston	0	0	0	0	0	0	0	0	0	—	0
Cincinnati	3	0	0	0	0	0	0	3	x	—	6

Errors—Sisti 2. Runs batted in—Young 6. Home runs—Young 2. Sacrifices—Hopp, Zientara 2. Double plays—Miller to Zientara, Ryan to Sisti to Torgeson. Left on bases—Boston 3, Cincinnati 13. Bases on balls—Off Blackwell 4, Wright 3, Lanfranconi 1, Karl 1. Strikeouts—Blackwell 3, Wright 1. Hits—Off Wright, 3 in 1⅓ innings; Lanfranconi, 6 in 5⅔; Karl, 3 in 1. Hit by pitcher—By Wright (Haas). Losing pitcher—Wright. Umpires—Barlick, Gore and Pinelli. Time—1:51. Attendance—18,137.

July 10, 1947   Philadelphia at Cleveland

ATHLETICS	ab	r	h	rbi	sh	sb	o	a	e
Joost, ss	3	0	0	0	0	0	2	3	0
McCosky, lf	2	0	0	0	0	0	2	0	0
Valo, rf	2	0	0	0	0	0	0	0	0
Binks, rf	2	0	0	0	0	0	2	0	0
Fain, 1b	2	0	0	0	0	0	6	1	0
Chapman, cf	4	0	0	0	0	0	1	0	0
Rosar, c	2	0	0	0	0	0	4	0	0
Suder, 2b	3	0	0	0	0	0	6	1	0
Majeski, 2b	3	0	0	0	0	0	1	2	0
McCahan, p	3	0	0	0	0	0	0	3	0
Totals	26	0	0	0	0	0	24	10	0

INDIANS	ab	r	h	rbi	sh	sb	o	a	e
Metkovich, cf	4	0	1	1	0	0	3	0	0
Mitchell, lf	4	0	2	0	0	0	2	0	0
Edwards, rf	3	0	0	0	0	0	1	0	0
Boudreau, ss	4	0	2	0	0	0	0	1	0
Robinson, 1b	4	1	1	0	0	0	12	0	0
Gordon, 2b	4	1	1	0	0	0	2	6	0
Keltner, 3b	3	0	0	0	0	0	2	0	0
Hegan, c	3	1	1	1	0	0	6	0	0
Black, p	2	0	2	1	1	0	1	3	0
Totals	31	3	10	3	1	0	27	12	0

Philadelphia	0	0	0	0	0	0	0	0	0	—	0
Cleveland	0	3	0	0	0	0	0	0	x	—	3

Double plays—Boudreau, Gordon and Robinson; McCahan, Joost and Fain; Majeski, Suder and Fain. Left on bases—Athletics, 5; Cleveland, 6. Bases on balls —Off Black, 1; McCahan, 1. Struck out—By Black, 5; McCahan, 2. Umpires—Rommel, Passarella, McKinley and Boyer. Time of game—1:43.

Sept. 3, 1947 Washington at Philadelphia

WASHINGTON	ab	r	h	o	a	e
Yost, 3b	3	0	0	1	0	0
Lewis, rf	3	0	0	3	0	0
Robertson, lf	3	0	0	0	0	0
Vernon, 1b	3	0	0	9	2	0
Spence, cf	8	0	0	1	0	0
Priddy, 2b	3	0	0	2	4	0
Mancuso, c	3	0	0	4	1	0
Sullivan, ss	2	0	0	3	6	0
Scarborough, p	2	0	0	1	1	0
*Wynn	1	0	0	0	0	0
†Grace	1	0	0	0	0	0
‡Travis	1	0	0	0	0	0
Totals	28	0	0	24	14	0

PHILADELPHIA	ab	r	h	o	a	e
McCosky, lf	4	1	2	2	0	0
Joost, ss	2	0	0	3	3	0
Valo, rf	4	0	2	2	0	0
Binks, rf	0	0	0	0	0	0
Fain, 1b	2	1	0	10	0	1
Rosar, c	4	0	1	2	0	0
Majeski, 3b	3	0	1	3	2	0
Suder, 2b	4	0	0	0	4	0
Chapman, cf	4	0	2	5	0	0
McCahan, p	3	1	1	0	0	0
Totals	30	3	9	27	9	1

* Popped up for Sullivan in ninth.
† Grounded out for Scarborough in ninth.
‡ Fanned for Yost in ninth.

Washington	0	0	0	0	0	0	0	0	0	—	0
Philadelphia	0	1	0	0	0	0	2	0	x	—	3

Runs batted in—Chapman, Valo (2). Two-base hits—McCosky, Valo. Double plays—Priddy, Sullivan and Vernon (2); Sullivan, Priddy and Vernon. Left on base—Washington 1, Philadelphia 8. Bases on balls—Off Scarborough 4. Struck out—By McCahan 2. Hit by pitcher—By Scarborough 1. Umpires—Passarella, Boyer and Rommel. Attendance—2,816. Time of game—1:26.

June 30, 1948 Cleveland at Detroit

CLEVELAND (A.)	ab	r	h	tb	po	a	e
Mitchell, lf	4	1	2	2	4	0	0
Berardino, 1b	4	0	1	1	11	2	0
Boudreau, ss	4	1	1	2	0	1	0
Edwards, rf	4	0	0	0	1	0	0
Kennedy, rf	0	0	0	0	0	0	0
Judnich, cf	4	0	1	1	3	0	0
Gordon, 2b	4	0	0	0	1	2	0
Keltner, 3b	2	0	0	0	0	4	0
Hegan, c	3	0	0	0	5	0	0
Lemon, p	3	0	0	0	2	4	0
Totals	32	2	5	6	27	13	0

DETROIT (A.)	ab	r	h	tb	po	a	e
Lipon, ss	3	0	0	0	1	4	1
†Wertz	1	0	0	0	0	0	0
Mayo, 2b	4	0	0	0	2	4	0
Kell, 3b	3	0	0	0	0	2	1
Wakefield, lf	2	0	0	0	4	0	0
Evers, cf	3	0	0	0	3	0	0
Mullin, rf	3	0	0	0	2	0	0
Vico, 1b	2	0	0	0	14	0	0
Swift, c	2	0	0	0	1	0	0
*Hutchinson	1	0	0	0	0	0	0
Wagner, c	0	0	0	0	0	0	0
Houtteman, p	3	0	0	0	0	4	0
Totals	27	0	0	0	27	14	2

* Flied out for Swift in eighth.
† Grounded out for Lipon in ninth.

Cleveland	2	0	0	0	0	0	0	0	0	—	2
Detroit	0	0	0	0	0	0	0	0	0	—	0

Runs batted in—Boudreau, Edwards. Two-base hit—Boudreau. Stolen base—Mitchell. Left on base—Cleveland 4; Detroit 3. Bases on balls—Off Lemon 3 (Kell, Wakefield, Vico), off Houtteman 2 (Keltner). Struck out—By Lemon 4 (Mayo, Evers, Swift, Houtteman), by Houtteman 1 (Keltner). Umpires—Hubbard, Paparella and McGowan. Time of game—1:33. Attendance—49,628.

Sept. 9, 1948 Brooklyn at New York

BROOKLYN	ab	r	h	tb	po	a	e
Cox, 3b............	3	1	0	0	0	1	0
Robinson, 2b....	4	0	0	0	0	1	1
Reiser, lf..........	3	0	0	0	1	0	0
Shuba, lf	0	0	0	0	0	0	0
Edwards, c........	4	0	2	2	8	0	0
Furillo, cf.........	4	1	3	3	4	0	0
Reese, ss..........	4	0	1	2	3	5	0
Hodges, 1b.......	4	0	0	0	10	0	0
Hermanski, rf...	3	0	0	0	1	0	0
Barney, p..........	3	0	0	0	0	2	1
Totals	32	2	6	7	27	9	2

NEW YORK	ab	r	h	tb	po	a	e
Lohrke, 2b........	3	0	0	0	5	1	1
Lockman, cf......	4	0	0	0	2	0	0
Gordon, 3b	3	0	0	0	0	3	0
Mize, 1b...........	2	0	0	0	9	1	0
Marshall, rf.......	3	0	0	0	2	0	0
Mueller, lf........	3	0	0	0	3	0	0
Cooper, c..........	3	0	0	0	4	1	0
Kerr, ss.............	2	0	0	0	2	4	0
*Frey.................	1	0	0	0	0	0	0
Rhawn, ss	0	0	0	0	0	0	0
Kennedy, p.......	2	0	0	0	0	1	0
†Lafata	1	0	0	0	0	0	0
Totals	27	0	0	0	27	11	1

* Bounced out for Kerr in eighth.
† Struck out for Kennedy in ninth.

Brooklyn.....................	0 1 1 0 0 0 0 0 0 —	2
New York	0 0 0 0 0 0 0 0 0 —	0

Runs batted in—Hodges, Furillo. Two-base hit—Reese. Stolen bases—Reese, Hermanski. Left on bases—New York 2, Brooklyn 6. Double plays—Robinson, Reese and Hodges; Barney, Reese and Hodges; Kerr, Lohrke and Mize. Bases on balls—Off Barney 2 (Lohrke, Mize), off Kennedy 3 (Cox, Reiser, Hermanski). Struck out—By Kennedy 3 (Hodges, Barney 2), by Barney 4 (Marshall, Mueller, Kennedy, Lafata). Umpires—Pinelli, Gore and Robb. Time—2:06. Attendance—36,324.

August 11, 1950 Brooklyn at Boston

BROOKLYN	ab	r	h	tb	o	a	e
Reese, ss...........	4	0	0	0	2	2	0
Hermanski, lf ...	2	0	0	0	0	0	0
Snider, cf.........	4	0	0	0	3	0	1
Robinson, 2b....	3	0	0	0	2	4	0
Furillo, rf.........	3	0	0	0	4	0	0
Hodges, 1b.......	3	0	0	0	4	2	0
Campanella, c ..	2	0	0	0	7	0	0
Cox, 3b.............	3	0	0	0	1	1	0
Erskine, p.........	0	0	0	0	1	0	1
Hatten, p..........	1	0	0	0	0	0	1
*Abrams...........	1	0	0	0	0	0	0
Bankhead, p	0	0	0	0	0	2	0
†Russell	0	0	0	0	0	0	0
Totals	26	0	0	0	24	11	3

BOSTON	ab	r	h	tb	o	a	e
Hartsfield, 2b ...	5	1	2	2	1	3	0
Jethroe, cf.........	4	1	2	2	2	0	0
Torgeson, 1b....	4	2	1	1	12	0	0
Elliott, 3b	5	2	3	4	2	3	0
Cooper, c..........	4	1	2	4	4	0	0
Gordon, lf.........	3	0	2	2	1	0	0
Marshall, rf.......	2	0	0	0	2	0	0
Kerr, ss.............	4	0	0	0	3	5	0
Bickford, p........	4	0	1	1	0	1	0
Totals	35	7	12	14	27	12	0

* Flied out for Hatten in sixth.
† Walked for Bankhead in ninth.

Brooklyn......................	0 0 0 0 0 0 0 0 0 —	0
Boston........................	3 1 0 0 1 0 2 0 x —	7

Runs batted in—Elliott 2, Cooper 2, Gordon 2, Jethroe. Two-base hits—Elliott, Cooper. Double play—Kerr to Torgeson. Left on bases—Brooklyn 3, Boston 9. Bases on balls—Off Bickford 4, off Erskine 1, off Hatten 2, off Bankhead 2. Struck out—By Bickford 3, by Erskine 4, Hatten 2, by Bankhead 2. Pitching record—Off Erskine 5 hits, 4 runs in 1⅔ innings; off Hatten, 3 hits, 1 run in 3½ innings; off Bankhead, 4 hits, 2 runs in 3 innings. Losing pitcher—Erskine. Umpires—Goetz, Dascoli and Jorda. Time of game—2:05. Attendance—29,008.

May 6, 1951 Pittsburgh at Boston

PITTSBURGH	ab	r	h	tb	o	a	e
Dillinger, 3b	5	0	1	1	0	1	0
Metkovich, cf	4	2	3	5	2	0	0
Bell, rf	4	0	1	1	2	0	0
Kiner, 1b	5	0	1	2	11	0	0
Westlake, lf	4	1	0	0	2	0	0
Strickland, ss	2	0	0	0	1	5	0
Basgall, 2b	3	0	1	1	4	2	0
Fitz Gerald, c	4	0	1	1	5	1	0
Chambers, p	4	0	1	1	0	2	0
Totals	35	3	9	12	27	11	0

BOSTON	ab	r	h	tb	o	a	e
Hartsfield, 2b	1	0	0	0	3	3	0
Jethroe, cf	4	0	0	0	3	0	0
Torgeson, 1b	1	0	0	0	9	0	0
Elliott, 3b	4	0	0	0	1	3	0
Gordon, rf	3	0	0	0	4	0	0
Cooper, c	4	0	0	0	4	0	0
Olmo, lf	4	0	0	0	2	0	0
Kerr, ss	2	0	0	0	1	4	0
Estock, p	0	0	0	0	0	0	1
*Marquez	1	0	0	0	0	0	0
Nichols, p	0	0	0	0	0	0	0
Totals	24	0	0	0	27	10	1

* Fanned for Estock in eighth.

```
Pittsburgh.................... 1 0 0 0 0 1 0 1 0 — 3
Boston........................ 0 0 0 0 0 0 0 0 0 — 0
```

Runs batted in—Bell, Chambers, Basgall. Two-base hits—Metkovich 2, Kiner. Stolen base—Bell. Sacrifices—Estock, Hartsfield, Strickland. Double plays—Basgall and Kiner; Elliott, Hartsfield and Torgeson. Left on bases—Pittsburgh 11, Boston 7. Bases on balls—Off Estock 5, off Chambers 8. Struck out—By Estock 2, by Chambers 4. Pitching records—Off Estock 8 hits, 3 runs in 8 innings, off Nichols 1 hit, 0 runs in 1 inning. Wild pitch—Chambers. Winning pitcher—Chambers (3-2). Losing pitcher—Estock (0-1). Umpires—Dascoli, Goetz and Jorda. Time of game—2:01. Attendance—15,492.

July 1, 1951 Detroit at Cleveland

DETROIT	ab	r	h	o	a
Lipon, ss	3	1	0	1	3
*Hutch'n	1	0	0	0	0
Berry, ss	0	0	0	0	0
Priddy, 2b	3	0	0	2	1
†Keller	1	0	0	0	0
Kell, 3b	4	0	0	1	1
Wertz, rf	3	0	0	1	0
Evers, lf	3	0	0	5	0
Kry'ski, 1b	3	0	0	8	1
Ginsberg, c	3	0	0	3	1
Groth, cf	2	0	0	2	0
Cain, p	2	0	0	1	1
Totals	28	1	0	24	8

CLEVELAND	ab	r	h	o	a
Mitchell, lf	3	1	1	3	0
Avila, 2b	4	0	1	0	3
Chapman, cf	4	0	1	1	0
‡Neilsen	0	1	0	0	0
Doby, cf	0	0	0	0	0
Easter, 1b	4	0	1	13	0
Simpson, 1b	0	0	0	0	0
Rosen, 3b	4	0	0	0	4
Kennedy, rf	4	0	0	3	0
Boone, ss	2	0	0	2	5
Hegan, c	3	0	2	5	0
Feller, p	2	0	0	0	0
Totals	30	2	6	27	12

* Flied out for Lipon in 8th.
† Flied out for Priddy in 9th.
‡ Ran for Chapman in 8th.

```
Detroit......................... 0 0 0 1 0 0 0 0 0 — 1
Cleveland.................... 1 0 0 0 0 0 0 1 x — 2
```

Errors—Boone, Feller. Runs batted in—Easter 2, Kell. Three-base hit—Chapman. Stolen base—Lipon. Left on bases—Detroit 3, Cleveland 7. Bases on balls—Cain 3, Feller 3. Strikeouts—Cain, 3; Feller, 5. Winner—Feller (11-2). Loser—Cain (6-6). Umpires—Berry, Napp, Hurley and Passarella. Time—2:05.

July 12, 1951   New York at Cleveland

NEW YORK	ab	r	h	o	a	e
Mantle, rf.............	3	0	1	0	0	0
Rizzuto, ss............	4	0	0	0	4	1
Collins, 1b............	4	0	0	9	1	0
Berra, c.................	4	0	1	4	1	0
Woodling, cf.........	4	1	1	2	0	0
Bauer, lf................	3	0	0	7	0	0
McDougald, 3b......	3	0	1	1	2	0
Coleman, 2b..........	3	0	0	4	5	0
Reynolds, p...........	2	0	0	0	0	0
Totals...........	30	1	4	27	13	1

CLEVELAND	ab	r	h	o	a	e
Mitchell, lf............	4	0	0	0	0	0
Avila, 2b................	4	0	0	3	4	0
Doby, cf.................	1	0	0	0	0	0
Chapman, cf..........	1	0	0	1	0	0
Easter, 1b.............	2	0	0	12	0	0
Rosen, 3b..............	3	0	0	1	1	0
Simpson, rf............	2	0	0	3	0	0
Boone, ss...............	3	0	0	1	1	0
Hegan, c................	3	0	0	6	0	0
Feller, p.................	2	0	0	0	1	0
*Lemon..................	1	0	0	0	0	0
Totals...........	26	0	0	27	7	0

* Struck out for Feller in ninth.

```
New York....................  0 0 0 0 0 0 1 0 0 — 1
Cleveland....................  0 0 0 0 0 0 0 0 0 — 0
```

RBI—Woodling. 2B—Mantle. HR—Woodling. DP—Rizzuto, Coleman and Collins; Berra, Coleman and Collins; Boone, Avila and Easter. LOB—New York 5; Cleveland 2. BB—Reynolds 3; Feller 3. SO—Reynolds 4, Feller 3. Winner—Reynolds (10-5). Loser—Feller (12-3). U—McGowan, McKinley, Hurley and Honochick. T—2:12. A—39,195.

Sept. 28, 1951   Boston at New York

BOSTON	ab	r	h	o	a	e
D. DiMaggio, cf....	2	0	0	2	0	1
Pesky, 2b...............	4	0	0	1	2	0
Williams, lf...........	3	0	0	3	0	0
Vollmer, rf............	2	0	0	0	0	1
Goodman, 1b........	3	0	0	12	0	0
Boudreau, ss.........	3	0	0	0	1	0
Hatfield, 3b...........	3	0	0	3	2	1
Robinson, c...........	3	0	0	3	0	0
Parnell, p..............	1	0	0	0	2	0
Scarborough, p......	1	0	0	0	1	0
Taylor, p................	0	0	0	0	2	0
*Maxwell................	1	0	0	0	0	0
Totals...........	26	0	0	24	10	3

NEW YORK	ab	r	h	o	a	e
Rizzuto, ss.............	5	1	1	1	2	0
Coleman, 2b..........	3	2	1	2	3	0
Bauer, rf................	4	0	1	5	0	0
J. DiMaggio, cf......	4	0	1	0	0	0
McDougald, 3b......	3	1	1	0	1	0
Berra, c.................	4	0	1	9	1	1
Woodling, lf...........	4	2	2	2	0	0
Collins, 1b............	4	2	2	8	0	0
Reynolds, p...........	3	0	0	0	1	0
Totals...........	34	8	10	27	8	1

* Grounded out for Taylor in ninth.

```
Boston...........................  0 0 0 0 0 0 0 0 0 — 0
New York.......................  2 0 2 1 0 2 0 1 x — 8
```

RBI—Bauer, Berra, McDougald, Coleman, Collins 2, Woodling. 2B—Collins. HR—Collins, Woodling. SB—Coleman. SH—Reynolds. DP—Hatfield and Goodman; Rizzuto and Collins. LOB—Boston 3, New York 5. BB—Off Parnell 2, Reynolds 4. SO—By Parnell 2, Reynolds 9. H—Off Parnell, 5 in 3; Scarborough, 3 in 3; Taylor, 2 in 2. Winner—Reynolds (17-8). Loser—Parnell (18-11). U—Hubbard, McGowan, Berry and Hurley. T—2:12. A—39,038.

May 15, 1952 Washington at Detroit

WASHINGTON	ab	r	h	tb	o	a	e
Yost, 3b	3	0	0	0	2	1	0
Busby, cf	3	0	0	0	3	0	0
Jensen, rf	4	0	0	0	2	0	0
Vernon, 1b	4	0	0	0	9	0	0
Runnels, ss	3	0	0	0	3	3	0
Coan, lf	3	0	0	0	2	0	0
Marsh, 2b	3	0	0	0	1	2	0
Kluttz, c	2	0	0	0	4	2	0
Porterfield, p	3	0	0	0	0	0	0
Totals	28	0	0	0*26	8	0	

DETROIT	ab	r	h	tb	o	a	e
Lipon, ss	4	0	0	0	1	4	0
Kell, 3b	3	0	1	1	1	2	0
Mullin, lf	4	0	0	0	3	0	0
Wertz, rf	3	1	2	6	1	0	0
Souchock, 1b	3	0	0	0	9	0	0
Ginsberg, c	3	0	0	0	7	0	0
Groth, cf	3	0	0	0	5	0	0
Priddy, 2b	3	0	0	0	0	1	3
Trucks, p	3	0	1	1	0	0	0
Totals	29	1	4	8	27	7	3

* Two out when winning run scored.

Washington	0	0	0	0	0	0	0	0	0 —	0
Detroit	0	0	0	0	0	0	0	1 —		1

Run batted in—Wertz. Two-base hit—Wertz. Home run—Wertz. Left on bases—Washington 4, Detroit 4. Bases on balls—Off Trucks 1 (Kluttz), off Porterfield 2 (Kell, Wertz). Struck out—By Trucks 7 (Yost 2, Busby, Vernon, Runnels, Coan, Kluttz), by Porterfield 5 (Souchock, Ginsberg, Groth, Priddy, Trucks). Hit by pitcher —By Trucks 2 (Yost, Busby). Earned run—Off Porterfield 1. Winning pitcher—Trucks (1-2). Losing pitcher—Porterfield (3-4). Umpires—Honochick, Duffy, Summers and McKinley. Time of game—1:32. Attendance—2,215. Official scorer—Leo Macdonell.

June 19, 1952 Chicago at Brooklyn

CHICAGO	ab	r	h	tb	o	a	e
Miksis, ss	4	0	0	0	4	6	0
Addis, cf	3	0	0	0	1	0	0
Hermanski, rf	3	0	0	0	2	0	0
Sauer, lf	3	0	0	0	2	0	0
Atwell, c	3	0	0	0	2	1	1
Fondy, 1b	3	0	0	0	12	1	0
Jackson, 3b	3	0	0	0	1	3	0
Ramazzotti, 2b	3	0	0	0	0	0	0
Hacker, p	0	0	0	0	0	0	0
Ramsdell, p	1	0	0	0	0	0	0
*Cavarretta	1	0	0	0	0	0	0
Totals	27	0	0	0	24	11	1

BROOKLYN	ab	r	h	tb	o	a	e
Morgan, 3b	4	0	0	0	0	4	0
Reese, ss	4	2	2	2	2	3	0
Robinson, 2b	3	0	0	0	0	5	0
Campanella, c	4	1	2	5	2	0	0
Furillo, rf	4	1	1	4	3	0	0
Snider, cf	3	0	0	0	1	0	0
Hodges, 1b	3	0	0	0	16	2	0
Pafko, lf	3	1	2	5	1	0	0
Erskine, p	3	0	0	0	2	4	0
Totals	31	5	7	16	27	18	0

* Flied out for Ramsdell in ninth.

Chicago	0	0	0	0	0	0	0	0	0 —	0
Brooklyn	3	1	0	0	0	0	1	x —		5

Runs batted in—Campanella 3, Furillo, Pafko. Home runs—Campanella, Furillo, Pafko. Stolen bases—Reese 2. Bases on balls—Off Erskine 1 (Ramsdell), off Ramsdell 1 (Robinson). Struck out—By Erskine 1 (Fondy), by Hacker 1 (Morgan), by Ramsdell 2 (Snider, Hodges). Left on bases—Chicago 1, Brooklyn 3. Pitching records—Off Hacker 4 hits, 4 runs, 4 earned in 1⅓ innings; off Ramsdell 6 hits, 1 run, 1 earned in 6⅔ innings. Winning pitcher—Erskine (6-1). Losing pitcher—Hacker (4-2). Umpires—Conlan, Stewart, Guglielmo and Gore. Time of game—1:48. Attendance—7,732. Official scorer—Harold Rosenthal.

August 25, 1952 Detroit at New York

DETROIT

	ab	r	h	tb	o	a	e
Groth, cf	4	0	0	0	2	0	0
Pesky, ss	4	0	0	0	3	2	1
Hatfield, 3b	3	0	1	1	2	0	0
Dropo, 1b	4	1	2	3	5	3	0
Souchock, rf	4	0	1	1	3	0	0
Delsing, lf	4	0	0	0	2	1	0
Batts, c	2	0	1	1	6	2	1
Federoff, 2b	3	0	0	0	1	0	0
Trucks, p	2	0	0	0	4	2	0
Totals	30	1	5	6	27	11	2

NEW YORK

	ab	r	h	tb	o	a	e
Mantle, cf	3	0	0	0	3	0	0
Collins, 1b	4	0	0	0	10	1	0
Bauer, rf	4	0	0	0	0	1	0
Berra, c	3	0	0	0	7	0	0
Woodling, lf	3	0	0	0	3	0	0
Babe, 3b	3	0	0	0	3	2	0
Martin, 2b	3	0	0	0	1	4	0
Rizzuto, ss	2	0	0	0	0	5	0
*Mize	1	0	0	0	0	0	0
Brideweser, ss..	0	0	0	0	0	0	0
Miller, p	1	0	0	0	0	1	0
†Noren	1	0	0	0	0	0	0
Scarborough, p.	0	0	0	0	0	0	0
Totals	28	0	0	0	27	14	0

* Fouled out for Rizzuto in eighth.
† Flied out for Miller in eighth.

Detroit	0 0 0 0 0 0 1 0 0 —	1
New York	0 0 0 0 0 0 0 0 0 —	0

Run batted in—Souchock. Two-base hit—Dropo. Sacrifice—Miller. Double play—Babe, Martin and Collins. Left on bases—Detroit 6, New York 3. Bases on balls—Off Trucks 1 (Mantle), off Miller 2 (Hatfield, Trucks). Struck out—By Trucks 8 (Mantle 2, Collins, Bauer 2, Woodling, Babe, Martin), by Miller 7 (Groth, Pesky 3, Hatfield 2, Delsing). Hit by pitcher—By Miller 1 (Batts). Pitching records—Off Miller 4 hits, 1 run, 1 earned in 8 innings; off Scarborough 1 hit, 0 runs in 1 inning. Winning pitcher—Trucks (5-15). Losing pitcher—Miller (3-5). Umpires—Robb, Grieve, Honochick and Passarella. Time of game—2:03. Attendance—13,442. Official scorer—John Drebinger.

May 6, 1953 Philadelphia at St. Louis

PHILADELPHIA

	ab	r	h	o	a	e
Joost, ss	3	0	0	3	3	0
Philley, cf	4	0	0	0	0	0
Babe, 3b	3	0	0	1	6	0
Robinson, 1b	4	0	0	8	0	0
Clark, rf	3	0	0	2	0	0
Zernial, lf	3	0	0	1	0	0
Michaels, 2b	3	0	0	5	3	1
Astroth, c	1	0	0	4	2	0
Martin, p	1	0	0	0	0	0
*Hamilton	1	0	0	0	0	0
Scheib, p	0	0	0	0	1	0
†Valo	0	0	0	0	0	0
‡De Maestri	0	0	0	0	0	0
Totals	26	0	0	24	15	1

ST. LOUIS

	ab	r	h	o	a	e
Groth, cf	5	0	2	4	0	0
Hunter, ss	5	1	2	1	4	0
Dyck, lf	3	1	1	1	0	0
Elliott, 3b	4	0	2	1	0	0
Wertz, rf	3	0	1	3	0	0
Moss, c	5	2	2	3	0	0
Sievers, 1b	3	1	1	12	0	0
Young, 2b	2	1	0	1	7	0
Holloman, p	3	0	2	1	1	1
Totals	33	6	13	27	12	1

* Struck out for Martin in sixth.
† Walked for Scheib in ninth.
‡ Ran for Valo in ninth.

Philadelphia	0 0 0 0 0 0 0 0 0 —	0
St. Louis	0 1 1 0 1 1 2 0 x —	6

Pitchers	ip	h	r	er	bb	so
Holloman (W. 1-1)	9	0	0	0	5	3
Martin (L. 1-1)	5	7	3	2	4	2
Scheib	3	6	3	3	3	1

RBI—Holloman 3, Dyck, Wertz, Groth. 2B—Moss 2, Hunter, Wertz, Elliott. SH—Holloman. DP—Young and Sievers; Babe, Michaels and Robinson; Michaels, Joost and Robinson; Young, Hunter and Sievers. LOB—Philadelphia, 4; St. Louis, 12. HP—By Scheib (Young). U—Duffy, Grieve, Passarella and Napp. T—2:09. A—2,473.

June 12, 1954 Philadelphia at Milwaukee

PHILADELPHIA

	ab	r	h	tb	po	a	e
Jones, 3b	4	0	0	0	3	2	0
Ashburn, cf	1	0	0	0	0	0	0
Schell, cf	2	0	0	0	1	0	0
Torgeson, 1b	3	0	0	0	7	2	0
Ennis, lf	3	0	0	0	2	0	0
Hamner, 2b	3	0	0	0	3	1	0
Burgess, c	1	0	0	0	4	1	0
Wyrostek, rf	3	0	0	0	3	0	0
Morgan, ss	3	0	0	0	0	3	0
Roberts, p	2	0	0	0	1	2	0
*Clark	1	0	0	0	0	0	0
Totals	26	0	0	0	24	11	0

MILWAUKEE

	ab	r	h	tb	po	a	e
Bruton, cf	4	0	2	2	2	0	0
Logan, ss	3	1	1	4	2	2	0
Aaron, lf	4	0	1	1	4	0	0
Mathews, 3b	3	0	0	0	0	2	0
Adcock, 1b	3	0	0	0	9	0	0
Pafko, rf	3	0	0	0	2	0	0
O'Connell, 2b	3	0	1	1	2	1	0
Crandall, c	3	1	1	4	6	1	0
Wilson, p	3	0	1	2	0	2	0
Totals	29	2	7	14	27	8	0

* Struck out for Roberts in ninth.

Philadelphia	0	0	0	0	0	0	0	0	0	— 0
Milwaukee	1	0	0	0	1	0	0	0	x	— 2

Runs batted in—Logan, Crandall. Two-base hit—Wilson. Home runs—Logan, Crandall. Sacrifice hit—Logan. Stolen base—Bruton. Bases on balls—Off Wilson 2 (Burgess 2). Struck out—By Wilson 6 (Wyrostek 2, Roberts 2, Morgan, Clark), by Roberts 3 (Aaron 2, Adcock). Caught stealing—By Crandall (Burgess), by Burgess (Aaron). Double play—Crandall and Logan. Earned runs—Off Roberts 2. Winning pitcher—Wilson (2-0). Losing pitcher—Roberts (7-7). Umpires—Pinelli, Boggess and Engeln. Time of game—1:40. Attendance—28,218. Official scorer—Sam Levy.

May 12, 1955 Pittsburgh at Chicago

PITTSBURGH

	ab	r	h	tb	o	a	e
Saffell, cf	3	0	0	0	4	0	0
Groat, ss	4	0	0	0	3	2	0
Clemente, rf	4	0	0	0	1	0	0
Thomas, lf	4	0	0	0	1	0	0
Long, 1b	0	0	0	0	5	1	0
G. Freese, 3b	3	0	0	0	0	1	0
Atwell, c	2	0	0	0	4	2	0
E. Freese, 2b	2	0	0	0	5	2	0
N. King, p	0	0	0	0	0	0	0
*Montemayor	1	0	0	0	0	0	0
Law, p	1	0	0	0	1	3	0
†Ward	0	0	0	0	0	0	0
‡Mejias	0	0	0	0	0	0	0
Totals	24	0	0	0	24	11	0

CHICAGO

	ab	r	h	tb	o	a	e
Miksis, cf	4	0	2	3	3	0	0
Baker, 2b	3	1	1	1	2	3	0
Speake, lf	5	0	1	1	1	0	0
J. King, lf	0	0	0	0	0	0	0
Jackson, 3b	4	0	2	2	3	4	0
T. Tappe, rf	5	2	2	6	1	0	0
Banks, ss	4	0	3	5	1	3	0
Fondy, 1b	4	1	2	2	9	2	0
McCullough, c	4	0	0	0	6	1	0
Jones, p	4	0	2	2	1	1	0
Totals	37	4	15	22	27	14	0

* Struck out for N. King in third.
† Walked for Law in ninth.
‡ Ran for Ward in ninth.

Pittsburgh	0	0	0	0	0	0	0	0	0	— 0
Chicago	1	1	0	0	1	0	1	0	x	— 4

Runs batted in—T. Tappe 2, Miksis, Banks. Two-base hits—T. Tappe, Miksis. Three-base hits—Banks. Home runs—T. Tappe. Stolen bases—Fondy, Miksis, Baker. Sacrifice hits—Miksis, Baker. Double plays—Banks, Baker and Fondy; Jackson and Fondy. Left on base—Pittsburgh 4, Chicago 13. Bases on balls—Off N. King 1, off Law 1, off Jones 7. Struck out—By N. King 2, by Law 2, by Jones 6. Hits—Off N. King 5 in 2 innings, off Law 10 in 6 innings. Runs and earned runs—Off N. King 2-2, off Law 2-2. Wild pitch—Jones. Winning pitcher—Jones (4-3). Losing pitcher—N. King (1-1). Umpires—Gore, Donatelli, Dixon and Conlan. Time of game—2:38. Attendance—2,918.

May 12, 1956 New York at Brooklyn

NEW YORK	ab	r	h	tb	o	a	e
Lockman, lf	4	0	0	0	1	1	0
Dark, ss	3	0	0	0	1	0	0
Mays, cf	2	0	0	0	7	1	0
Rhodes, rf	3	0	0	0	2	0	0
Spencer, 2b	3	0	0	0	1	0	0
White, 1b	3	0	0	0	5	0	0
Castleman, 3b	2	0	0	0	1	0	0
*Mueller	1	0	0	0	0	0	0
Thompson, 3b	0	0	0	0	0	1	0
Katt, c	3	0	0	0	6	0	0
Worthington, p	2	0	0	0	0	3	0
Grissom, p	0	0	0	0	0	0	0
†Wilson	1	0	0	0	0	0	0
Totals	27	0	0	0	24	6	0

BROOKLYN	ab	r	h	tb	o	a	e
Gilliam, 2b	4	0	1	1	0	1	0
Reese, ss	3	2	1	1	0	1	0
Snider, cf	3	1	2	3	0	0	0
Campanella, c	4	0	1	1	4	1	0
Hodges, 1b	3	0	0	0	13	1	0
Robinson, 3b	2	0	0	0	2	2	0
Amoros, lf	4	0	0	0	2	0	0
Furillo, rf	2	0	0	0	2	0	0
Erskine, p	4	0	1	2	1	3	0
Totals	29	3	6	8	27	9	0

* Lined out for Castleman in eighth.
† Fouled out for Grissom in ninth.

New York	0 0 0	0 0 0	0 0 0 — 0
Brooklyn	0 0 1	0 0 0	2 0 x — 3

Runs batted in—Robinson, Snider, Campanella. Two-base hits—Erskine, Snider. Left on base—New York 2, Brooklyn 9. Bases on balls—Erskine 2, Worthington 7. Strikeouts—Erskine 3, Worthington 4. Hits—Worthington 6 in 6⅓ innings; Grissom 0 in 1⅔ innings. Runs and earned runs—Worthington 3-3. Winning pitcher—Erskine (2-2). Losing pitcher—Worthington (1-3). Umpires—Donatelli, Boggess, Gorman and Pinelli. Time of game—2:10. Attendance—17,395.

May 26, 1956 Cincinnati at Milwaukee

CINCINNATI	ab	r	h	tb	o	a	e
Temple, 2b	2	0	0	0	2	2	0
§Bailey	1	0	0	0	0	0	0
Bridges, 2b-lf	1	0	0	0	0	0	0
Robinson, lf	2	0	1	1	3	0	0
*Crowe	1	0	0	0	0	0	0
Palys, lf	0	0	0	0	2	0	0
Freeman, p	0	0	0	0	0	0	0
‖Thurman	1	0	0	0	0	0	0
Black, p	1	0	0	0	0	0	0
Bell, cf	5	0	1	2	3	0	0
Kluszewski, 1b	4	0	1	1	5	1	0
¶Dyck, 1b	1	1	1	1	4	0	0
Post, rf	3	0	1	2	3	0	0
Jablonski, 3b	5	0	0	0	1	2	0
Burgess, c	4	0	2	2	5	1	0
McMillan, ss	2	0	0	0	3	1	0
Klippstein, p	2	0	0	0	0	2	0
‡Frazier, lf	2	0	0	0	0	0	0
Grammas, 2b	0	0	0	0	0	0	0
Totals	37	1	7	9**	31	9	0

MILWAUKEE	ab	r	h	tb	o	a	e
O'Connell, 2b	3	0	0	0	1	3	0
†Covington	1	0	0	0	0	0	0
Dittmer, 2b	1	0	1	2	1	2	0
Logan, ss	4	0	0	0	2	4	0
Mathews, 3b	5	0	0	0	0	0	0
Aaron, rf	4	2	1	3	0	0	0
Thomson, lf	2	0	0	0	4	0	0
#Tanner	0	0	0	0	0	0	0
Bruton, cf	2	0	0	0	6	0	0
Torre, 1b	4	0	1	1	14	1	1
Crandall, c	2	0	0	0	5	1	0
Crone, p	2	0	0	0	0	2	0
Totals	30	2	3	6	33	13	1

* Flied out for Robinson in sixth.
† Struck out for O'Connell in seventh.
‡ Grounded out for Klippstein in eighth.
§ Grounded out for Temple in eighth.
‖ Grounded out for Freeman in ninth.
¶ Ran for Kluszewski in ninth.
# Purposely walked for Thomson in eleventh.
** One out when winning run scored.

```
Cincinnati........  0 0 0 0 0 0 0 0 1 0 0 — 1
Milwaukee........  0 1 0 0 0 0 0 0 0 1 — 2
```

Runs batted in—Post, Torre 2. Two-base hits—Bell, Post, Dittmer. Three-base hit—Aaron. Sacrifice hits—McMillan, Crone, Bruton. Sacrifice fly—Torre. Double plays—Kluszewski and McMillan; O'Connell, Logan and Torre. Left on base—Cincinnati 8, Milwaukee 10. Bases on balls—Crone 4, Klippstein 7, Black 2. Strike-outs—Crone 4, Klippstein 4, Black 1. Hits—Klippstein 0 in 7 innings, Freeman 0 in 1 inning, Black 3 in 2⅓ innings. Runs and earned runs—Crone 1-1, Klippstein 1-1, Black 1-1. Hit by pitcher—Klippstein (Aaron). Winning pitcher—Crone (3-1). Losing pitcher—Black (2-2). Umpires—Secory, Landes, Goetz and Dascoli. Time of game—2:39. Attendance—22,936.

July 14, 1956   Chicago at Boston

CHICAGO	ab	r	h	tb	o	a	e
Rivera, rf	3	0	0	0	0	0	0
†Dropo	1	0	0	0	0	0	0
Fox, 2b	3	0	0	0	3	6	0
Minoso, lf	3	0	0	0	3	1	0
Philley, 1b	3	0	0	0	12	0	0
Doby, cf	2	0	0	0	2	0	0
Lollar, c	3	0	0	0	2	0	0
Esposito, 3b	2	0	0	0	1	3	0
Aparicio, ss	3	0	0	0	1	5	0
McDonald, p	2	0	0	0	0	1	0
LaPalme, p	0	0	0	0	0	1	0
*Phillips	1	0	0	0	0	0	0
Totals	26	0	0	0	24	17	0

BOSTON	ab	r	h	tb	o	a	e
Goodman, 2b	4	1	1	2	3	6	0
Klaus, 3b	4	1	2	3	2	4	0
Williams, lf	3	1	2	2	0	0	0
Stephens, lf	0	0	0	0	0	0	0
Vernon, 1b	4	0	1	1	11	0	0
Jensen, rf	3	0	0	0	1	0	0
Piersall, cf	3	1	1	2	4	0	0
White, c	3	0	0	0	4	1	0
Buddin, ss	2	0	1	1	1	3	1
Parnell, p	2	0	0	0	1	1	0
Totals	28	4	8	11	27	15	1

* Hit into force play for LaPalme in ninth.
† Grounded out for Rivera in ninth.

Chicago	0	0	0	0	0	0	0	0	0	—	0
Boston	0	0	0	2	0	1	1	0	x	—	4

Runs batted in—Vernon, Klaus, Buddin. Two-base hits—Klaus, Goodman, Piersall. Sacrifice hit—Parnell. Double plays—Buddin, Goodman and Vernon; White and Goodman; Minoso and Esposito; Esposito, Fox and Philley, 2. Left on base—Chicago 1, Boston 3. Bases on balls—Parnell 2, McDonald 1. Strikeouts—Parnell 4, McDonald 1, LaPalme 1. Hits—McDonald 5 in 5 innings (pitched to two batters in sixth), LaPalme 3 in 3 innings. Runs and earned runs—McDonald 3-3, LaPalme 1-1. Hit by pitcher—McDonald (Buddin). Wild pitch—McDonald. Winning pitcher—Parnell (3-2). Losing pitcher—McDonald (0-1). Umpires—Summers, McKinley, Flaherty and Rice. Time of game—1:52. Attendance—14,542.

Sept. 25, 1956   Philadelphia at Brooklyn

PHILADELPHIA	ab	r	h	tb	o	a	e
Ashburn, cf	3	0	0	0	2	0	0
Blaylock, 1b	4	0	0	0	7	3	0
Lopata, c	3	0	0	0	6	2	1
Ennis, lf	3	0	0	0	0	0	0
Jones, 3b	2	0	0	0	1	0	0
Valo, rf	3	0	0	0	2	0	0
Hemus, 2b	3	0	0	0	3	1	0
Kazanski, 2b	0	0	0	0	1	0	0
Smalley, ss	2	0	0	0	2	4	0
†Baumholtz	1	0	0	0	0	0	0
Meyer, p	0	0	0	0	0	0	1
R. Miller, p	0	0	0	0	0	2	0
*Bouchee	1	0	0	0	0	0	0
Sanford, p	0	0	0	0	0	0	0
‡Haddix	1	0	0	0	0	0	0
Totals	26	0	0	0	24	12	2

BROOKLYN	ab	r	h	tb	o	a	e
Gilliam, 2b	3	1	1	1	2	4	0
Reese, ss	3	0	0	0	2	3	0
Snider, cf	2	1	0	0	1	0	0
Robinson, 3b	2	1	1	2	0	3	0
Amoros, lf	4	0	0	0	4	0	0
Hodges, 1b	2	1	1	1	14	1	0
Furillo, rf	3	0	0	0	0	0	0
Campanella, c	2	1	1	4	4	0	0
Maglie, p	3	0	0	0	0	1	0
Totals	24	5	4	8	27	12	0

* Struck out for R. Miller in sixth.
† Fouled out for Smalley in ninth.
‡ Struck out for Sanford in ninth.

Philadelphia	0	0	0	0	0	0	0	0	0	—	0
Brooklyn	0	3	2	0	0	0	0	0	x	—	5

Runs batted in—Furillo, Campanella 2. Two-base hit—Robinson. Home run—Campanella. Sacrifice hits—Reese, Robinson. Double plays—R. Miller, Lopata and Blaylock; Lopata and Hemus; Blaylock and Hemus; Hodges, Reese and Hodges. Left on base—Philadelphia 2, Brooklyn 4. Bases on balls—Maglie 2, Meyer 3, R. Miller 1, Sanford 3. Strikeouts—Maglie 3, R. Miller 2, Sanford 2. Hits—Meyer 3 in 2⅓, R. Miller 0 in 2⅔, Sanford 1 in 3. Runs and earned runs—Meyer 5-3. Hit by pitcher—Maglie (Ashburn). Winning pitcher—Maglie (12-5). Losing pitcher—Meyer (7-11). Umpires—Dixon, Donatelli, Gorman and Pinelli. Time of game—2:07. Attendance—15,204.

October 8, 1956 Brooklyn at New York: World Series

BROOKLYN (N.)

	ab	r	h	o	a	e
Gilliam, 2b	3	0	0	2	0	0
Reese, ss	3	0	0	4	2	0
Snider, cf	3	0	0	1	0	0
Robinson, 3b	3	0	0	2	4	0
Hodges, 1b	3	0	0	5	1	0
Amoros, lf	3	0	0	3	0	0
Furillo, rf	3	0	0	0	0	0
Campanella, c	3	0	0	7	2	0
Maglie, p	2	0	0	0	1	0
*Mitchell	1	0	0	0	0	0
Totals	27	0	0	24	10	0

NEW YORK (A.)

	ab	r	h	o	a	e
Bauer, rf	4	0	1	4	0	0
Collins, 1b	4	0	1	7	0	0
Mantle, cf	3	1	1	4	0	0
Berra, c	3	0	0	7	0	0
Slaughter, lf	2	0	0	1	0	0
Martin, 2b	3	0	1	3	4	0
McDougald, ss	2	0	0	0	2	0
Carey, 3b	3	1	1	1	1	0
Larsen, p	2	0	0	0	1	0
Totals	26	2	5	27	8	0

* Called out on strikes for Maglie in ninth.

```
Brooklyn ................ 0 0 0 0 0 0 0 0 0 — 0
New York ................ 0 0 0 1 0 1 0 0 x — 2
```

Runs batted in—Mantle, Bauer. Home run—Mantle. Sacrifice hit—Larsen. Double plays—Reese and Hodges; Hodges, Campanella, Robinson, Campanella and Robinson. Left on bases—Brooklyn 0, New York 3. Earned runs—New York 2, Brooklyn 0. Bases on balls—Off Maglie 2. Struck out—By Larsen 7, by Maglie 5. Winning pitcher—Larsen. Losing pitcher—Maglie. Umpires—Pinelli (N. L.), Soar (A. L.), Boggess (N. L.), Napp (A. L.), Gorman (N. L.), Runge (A. L.). Time—2:06. Attendance—64,519.

August 20, 1957 Washington at Chicago

WASHINGTON

	ab	r	h	tb	o	a	e
Yost, 3b	4	0	0	0	2	0	0
Plews, 2b	3	0	0	0	3	3	0
Sievers, lf	3	0	0	0	1	0	0
Schult, rf	3	0	0	0	2	0	0
Runnels, 1b	3	0	0	0	8	0	0
Berberet, c	2	0	0	0	3	0	0
Usher, cf	3	0	0	0	3	0	0
Bridges, ss	2	0	0	0	2	3	0
†Lemon	1	0	0	0	0	0	0
Stobbs, p	1	0	0	0	0	2	0
*Throneberry	0	0	0	0	0	0	0
Black, p	0	0	0	0	0	0	0
‡Becquer	1	0	0	0	0	0	0
Totals	26	0	0	0	24	8	0

CHICAGO

	ab	r	h	tb	o	a	e
Aparicio, ss	5	1	2	2	1	5	0
Fox, 2b	4	1	2	2	1	4	0
Minoso, lf	5	1	2	4	3	0	0
Dropo, 1b	3	1	2	2	15	0	0
Doby, cf	4	1	1	4	4	0	0
Lollar, c	5	0	2	3	3	0	0
Rivera, rf	3	0	0	0	0	0	0
Phillips, 3b	4	1	2	3	0	3	0
Keegan, p	4	0	1	1	0	2	0
Totals	37	6	14	21	27	14	0

* Walked for Stobbs in sixth.
† Grounded out for Bridges in ninth.
‡ Struck out for Black in ninth.

```
Washington ............... 0 0 0 0 0 0 0 0 0 — 0
Chicago .................. 0 0 5 0 1 0 0 0 x — 6
```

Runs batted in—Minoso 2, Dropo, Doby 2, Keegan. Two-base hits—Minoso 2, Lollar, Phillips. Home run—Doby. Double play—Keegan, Fox and Dropo. Left on bases—Washington 1, Chicago 12. Bases on balls—Off Stobbs 3, off Black 1, off Keegan 2. Struck out—By Stobbs 1, by Keegan 1. Hits—Off Stobbs 12 in 5 innings, off Black 2 in 3 innings. Runs and earned runs—Stobbs 6-6, Black 0-0. Hit by pitcher—By Stobbs 1 (Fox). Winning pitcher Keegan (8-6). Losing pitcher—Stobbs (6-16). Umpires—Stevens, Napp, Rice and Rommel. Time of game—1:55. Attendance—22,815.

July 20, 1958   Detroit at Boston

DETROIT	ab	r	h	tb	po	a	e
Kuenn, cf	4	0	2	3	3	0	0
Martin, ss	4	0	1	1	1	1	0
Kaline, rf	4	0	0	0	4	0	0
Harris, 1b	4	1	1	3	5	0	0
Zernial, lf	4	1	2	3	0	0	0
‡Groth, lf	0	0	0	0	0	0	0
F. Bolling, 2b	4	0	0	0	1	0	0
Virgil, 3b	4	0	1	1	0	3	0
Wilson, c	4	1	1	1	13	0	0
Bunning, p	3	0	1	1	0	0	0
Totals	35	3	9	13	27	4	0

BOSTON	ab	r	h	tb	po	a	e
Stephens, cf	2	0	0	0	0	0	1
Runnels, 2b	1	0	0	0	1	2	0
Lepcio, 2b	3	0	0	0	2	3	0
Williams, lf	4	0	0	0	1	0	0
Malzone, 3b	3	0	0	0	2	1	0
Jensen, rf	2	0	0	0	3	0	0
Gernert, 1b	3	0	0	0	9	0	0
Berberet, c	3	0	0	0	7	0	0
Consolo, ss	3	0	0	0	2	4	0
Sullivan, p	1	0	0	0	0	1	0
*Keough	1	0	0	0	0	0	0
Byerly, p	0	0	0	0	0	0	0
†Klaus	1	0	0	0	0	0	0
Bowsfield, p	0	0	0	0	0	0	0
Totals	27	0	0	0	27	11	1

* Struck out for Sullivan in sixth.
† Struck out for Byerly in eighth.
‡ Ran for Zernial in ninth.

```
Detroit ........................ 0 0 0 0 3 0 0 0 0 — 3
Boston ......................... 0 0 0 0 0 0 0 0 0 — 0
```

Runs batted in—Kuenn, Zernial, Wilson. Two-base hits—Zernial, Kuenn. Three-base hit—Harris. Double play—Consolo, Runnels and Gernert. Left on bases —Detroit 5, Boston 3. Bases on balls—Off Bunning 2 (Stephens 2). Struck out—By Bunning 12 (Lepcio 3, Berberet 3, Consolo 2, Stephens, Malzone, Keough, Klaus), by Sullivan 4 (Wilson, Martin, Kaline, Virgil), by Byerly 2 (Bolling, Kaline). Hits— Off Sullivan 6 in 6 innings, off Byerly 2 in 2 innings, off Bowsfield 1 in 1 inning. Runs and earned runs—Sullivan 3-3, Byerly 0-0, Bowsfield 0-0. Hit by pitcher—By Bunning 1 (Jensen). Winning pitcher—Bunning (8-6). Losing pitcher—Sullivan (8-3). Umpires—Umont, Summers, Honochick and Soar. Time of game—2:02. Attendance—29,529.

Sept. 20, 1958   New York at Baltimore

NEW YORK	ab	r	h	tb	po	a	e
Bauer, rf	4	0	0	0	4	0	0
Lumpe, ss	2	0	0	0	3	2	0
Mantle, cf	3	0	0	0	2	0	0
Skowron, 3b	3	0	0	0	0	1	1
Siebern, lf	3	0	0	0	4	1	0
Howard, c	3	0	0	0	6	0	0
Throneberry, 1b	2	0	0	0	3	0	0
*Berra, 1b	1	0	0	0	1	0	0
Richardson, 2b	2	0	0	0	1	1	0
Larsen, p	2	0	0	0	0	0	0
Shantz, p	0	0	0	0	0	0	0
†Slaughter	1	0	0	0	0	0	0
Totals	26	0	0	0	24	5	1

BALTIMORE	ab	r	h	tb	po	a	e
Williams, 3b-lf	4	0	1	2	1	0	0
Boyd, 1b	4	0	1	1	6	0	0
Woodling, rf	2	0	0	0	2	0	0
Busby, cf	1	0	1	1	1	0	0
Nieman, lf	3	0	0	0	2	0	0
Robinson, 3b	1	0	0	0	0	0	0
Triandos, c	3	1	1	4	8	2	0
Tasby, cf-rf	3	0	0	0	4	0	0
Gardner, 2b	3	0	0	0	2	2	0
Castleman, ss	2	0	1	1	1	1	0
Miranda, ss	0	0	0	0	0	0	0
Wilhelm, p	3	0	0	0	0	2	0
Totals	29	1	5	9	27	7	0

* Grounded out for Throneberry in eighth.
† Flied out for Shantz in ninth.

```
New York ..................... 0 0 0 0 0 0 0 0 0 — 0
Baltimore ..................... 0 0 0 0 0 0 1 0 x — 1
```

Run batted in—Triandos. Two-base hit—Williams. Home run—Triandos. Left on bases—New York 1, Baltimore 6. Bases on balls—Off Wilhelm 2 (Richardson, Lumpe), off Larsen 2 (Castleman, Woodling). Struck out—By Wilhelm 8 (Bauer 2, Howard 2, Lumpe, Mantle, Siebern, Throneberry), by Larsen 2 (Nieman, Tasby), by Shantz 2 (Tasby, Boyd). Hits—Off Larsen 1 in 6 innings, off Shantz 4 in 2 innings. Runs and earned runs—Larsen 0-0, Shantz 1-1. Passed ball—Triandos. Winning pitcher—Wilhelm (3-10). Losing pitcher—Shantz (7-6). Umpires— Paparella, Chylak, Tabacchi and Stewart. Time of game—1:48. Attendance—18,192 (10,941 paid).

May 26, 1959   Pittsburgh at Milwaukee

PITTSBURGH	ab	r	h	tb	po	a	e
Schofield, ss	6	0	3	3	2	4	0
Virdon, cf	6	0	1	1	8	0	0
Burgess, c	5	0	0	0	8	0	0
Nelson, 1b	5	0	2	2	14	0	0
Skinner, lf	5	0	1	1	4	0	0
Mazeroski, 2b...	5	0	1	1	1	1	0
Hoak, 3b	5	0	2	2	0	6	1
Mejias, rf	3	0	1	1	1	0	0
*Stuart	1	0	0	0	0	0	0
Christopher, rf..	1	0	0	0	0	0	0
Haddix, p	5	0	1	1	0	2	0
Totals	47	0	12	12‡	38	13	1

MILWAUKEE	ab	r	h	tb	po	a	e
O'Brien, 2b	3	0	0	0	2	5	0
†Rice	1	0	0	0	0	0	0
Mantilla, 2b	1	1	0	0	1	2	0
Mathews, 3b......	4	0	0	0	2	3	0
Aaron, rf	4	0	0	0	1	0	0
Adcock, 1b........	5	0	1	2	17	3	0
Covington, lf	4	0	0	0	4	0	0
Crandall, c........	4	0	0	0	2	1	0
Pafko, cf	4	0	0	0	6	0	0
Logan, ss..........	4	0	0	0	3	5	0
Burdette, p	4	0	0	0	1	3	0
Totals	38	1	1	2	39	22	0

* Flied out for Mejias in tenth.
† Flied out for O'Brien in tenth.
‡ Two out when game ended.

```
Pittsburgh 0 0 0 0 0 0 0 0 0 0 0 0 0 — 0
Milwaukee  0 0 0 0 0 0 0 0 0 0 0 0 1 — 1
```

Run batted in—Adcock. Two-base hit—Adcock. Sacrifice hit—Mathews. Double plays—Adcock, Logan and Adcock; Mathews, O'Brien and Adcock; Adcock and Logan. Left on bases—Pittsburgh 8, Milwaukee 1. Bases on balls—Off Haddix 1 (Aaron). Struck out—By Haddix 8 (Adcock 2, Burdette 3, O'Brien, Mathews, Pafko), by Burdette 2 (Mazeroski, Hoak). Runs and earned runs—Haddix 1-0, Burdette 0-0. Winning pitcher—Burdette (8-2). Losing pitcher—Haddix (3-3). Umpires—Smith, Dascoli, Secory and Dixon. Time of game—2:54. Attendance—19,194.

May 15, 1960   St. Louis at Chicago

ST. LOUIS	ab	r	h	tb	po	a	e
Cunningham, rf	4	0	0	0	1	0	0
Grammas, ss	1	0	0	0	2	4	0
*Shannon, 2b.....	1	0	0	0	0	0	0
White, 1b-cf......	3	0	0	0	10	0	0
Boyer, 3b	3	0	0	0	2	4	0
Spencer, 2b-ss..	3	0	0	0	2	2	0
Wagner, lf	3	0	0	0	0	0	0
Flood, cf	2	0	0	0	1	0	0
†Musial, 1b.......	1	0	0	0	2	0	0
Smith, c............	2	0	0	0	4	2	0
‡Sawatski..........	1	0	0	0	0	0	0
McDaniel, p	2	0	0	0	0	2	0
‖Crowe...............	1	0	0	0	0	0	0
Totals	27	0	0	0	24	14	0

CHICAGO	ab	r	h	tb	po	a	e
Ashburn, cf	3	1	2	3	2	0	0
Altman, rf..........	4	0	1	1	3	0	0
Bouchee, 1b	4	0	0	0	11	0	0
Banks, ss..........	4	1	1	4	0	3	0
Moryn, lf..........	3	0	0	0	4	0	0
Thomas, 3b.......	3	1	1	1	0	1	0
Zimmer, 3b.......	0	0	0	0	0	0	0
Rice, c..............	3	0	1	1	7	0	0
Kindall, 2b........	3	1	1	1	0	4	0
Cardwell, p.......	3	0	0	0	0	2	0
Totals	30	4	7	11	27	10	0

* Flied out for Grammas in seventh.
† Struck out for Flood in eighth.
‡ Lined out for Smith in ninth.
‖ Flied out for McDaniel in ninth.

```
St. Louis ..................... 0 0 0 0 0 0 0 0 0 — 0
Chicago........................ 0 0 0 0 1 2 1 0 x — 4
```

Runs batted in—Ashburn, Banks 2, Kindall. Two-base hit—Ashburn. Home run—Banks. Stolen base—Kindall. Left on bases—St. Louis 1, Chicago 4. Bases on balls—Off McDaniel 2 (Ashburn, Moryn), off Cardwell 1 (Grammas). Struck out—By McDaniel 5 (Altman, Moryn, Kindall, Cardwell 2), by Cardwell 7 (Boyer 2, Spencer, Flood, Musial, Smith, McDaniel). Runs and earned runs—McDaniel 4-4. Wild pitch—McDaniel 1. Winning pitcher—Cardwell (2-2). Losing pitcher—McDaniel (1-2). Umpires—Venzon, Dascoli, Secory and Crawford. Time—1:46. Attendance—33,543.

August 18, 1960   Philadelphia at Milwaukee

PHILADELPHIA	ab	r	h	tb	po	a	e
Callison, rf	3	0	0	0	4	0	0
Taylor, 2b	3	0	0	0	2	5	0
Curry, lf	3	0	0	0	1	0	0
Herrera, 1b	3	0	0	0	9	0	2
Gonzalez, cf	2	0	0	0	1	0	0
Walls, 3b	3	0	0	0	0	3	0
Malkmus, 3b	0	0	0	0	0	0	0
Coker, c	3	0	0	0	6	0	0
Amaro, ss	2	0	0	0	1	2	0
*Walters	1	0	0	0	0	0	0
Conley, p	2	0	0	0	0	3	0
†Smith	1	0	0	0	0	0	0
Totals	26	0	0	0	24	13	2

MILWAUKEE	ab	r	h	tb	po	a	e
Bruton, cf	4	0	2	3	4	0	0
Crandall, c	4	0	2	2	3	0	0
Mathews, 3b	4	0	1	1	0	4	0
Aaron, rf	4	0	1	1	0	0	0
Covington, lf	3	0	1	1	0	0	0
Spangler, lf	0	0	0	0	0	0	0
Roach, 2b	3	0	1	1	0	3	0
Cottier, 2b	0	0	0	0	0	0	0
Adcock, 1b	3	0	0	0	18	2	0
Logan, ss	3	0	0	0	1	7	0
Burdette, p	3	1	2	3	1	3	0
Totals	31	1	10	12	27	19	0

* Grounded out for Amaro in ninth.
† Flied out for Conley in ninth.

Philadelphia	0 0 0	0 0 0	0 0 0 — 0
Milwaukee	0 0 0	0 0 0	0 1 x — 1

Run batted in—Bruton. Two-base hits—Burdette, Bruton. Double plays—Conley, Taylor and Herrera; Mathews, Adcock and Logan. Left on bases—Milwaukee 6, Philadelphia 0. Bases on balls—None. Struck out—By Conley 6 (Bruton, Mathews, Aaron, Covington, Roach, Burdette), by Burdette 3 (Taylor, Gonzalez, Conley). Runs and earned runs—Off Conley 1-1. Hit by pitcher—By Burdette (Gonzalez). Winning pitcher—Burdette (14-7). Losing pitcher—Conley (7-10). Umpires—Jackowski, Landes, Pelekoudas and Barlick. Time—2:10. Attendance—16,338.

Sept. 16, 1960   Philadelphia at Milwaukee

PHILADELPHIA	ab	r	h	tb	po	a	e
Callison, lf	3	0	0	0	1	0	0
§Del Greco	1	0	0	0	0	0	0
Malkmus, 2b	4	0	0	0	4	6	0
Walters, rf	2	0	0	0	4	0	0
Herrera, 1b	3	0	0	0	9	1	0
Gonzalez, cf	3	0	0	0	4	0	0
Neeman, c	2	0	0	0	2	1	0
Woods, 3b	2	0	0	0	0	0	0
*Taylor	1	0	0	0	0	0	0
Lepcio, 3b	0	0	0	0	0	0	0
Amaro, ss	2	0	0	0	0	2	0
†Walls	1	0	0	0	0	0	0
Koppe, ss	0	0	0	0	0	0	0
Buzhardt, p	2	0	0	0	0	2	0
‡Smith	1	0	0	0	0	0	0
Totals	27	0	0	0	24	12	0

MILWAUKEE	ab	r	h	tb	po	a	e
Bruton, cf	3	1	2	2	4	0	0
Crandall, c	4	0	2	2	15	0	0
Mathews, 3b	4	0	2	2	0	1	0
Aaron, rf	3	1	1	1	0	0	0
Dark, lf	4	1	1	3	1	0	0
Adcock, 1b	2	0	1	1	4	1	0
Logan, ss	3	0	0	0	1	2	0
Cottier, 2b	3	0	0	0	0	0	0
Spahn, p	3	1	1	1	1	2	0
Totals	29	4	10	12	27	6	0

* Struck out for Woods in eighth.
† Struck out for Amaro in eighth.
‡ Struck out for Buzhardt in ninth.
§ Struck out for Callison in ninth.

Philadelphia	0 0 0	0 0 0	0 0 0 — 0
Milwaukee	0 0 0	2 1 0	1 0 x — 4

Runs batted in—Crandall, Mathews, Dark, Adcock. Three-base hit—Dark. Stolen base—Bruton. Sacrifice hit—Logan. Sacrifice fly—Adcock. Double plays—Amaro, Malkmus and Herrera 2. Left on bases—Philadelphia 2, Milwaukee 6. Bases on balls—Off Buzhardt 3 (Bruton, Aaron, Adcock), off Spahn 2 (Walters, Neeman). Struck out—By Buzhardt 1 (Logan), by Spahn 15 (Callison, Del Greco, Walters, Herrera 2. Gonzalez 3, Neeman, Woods 2, Taylor, Walls, Buzhardt, Smith). Runs and earned runs—off Buzhardt 4-4. Winning pitcher—Spahn (20-9). Losing pitcher—Buzhardt (4-16). Umpires—Gorman, Smith, Sudol and Boggess. Time—2:02. Attendance—6,117.

April 28, 1961   San Francisco at Milwaukee

SAN FRANCISCO

	ab	r	h	tb	po	a	e
Hiller, 2b	2	0	0	0	2	0	0
Kuenn, 3b	3	0	0	0	1	0	0
Mays, cf	3	0	0	0	4	0	0
McCovey, 1b	2	0	0	0	3	1	1
Cepeda, lf	3	0	0	0	2	0	0
F. Alou, rf	3	0	0	0	1	0	0
Bailey, c	3	0	0	0	11	0	0
Pagan, ss	2	0	0	0	0	1	0
*M. Alou	1	0	0	0	0	0	0
Jones, p	2	0	0	0	0	0	0
†Amalfitano	1	0	0	0	0	0	0
Totals	25	0	0	0	24	2	1

MILWAUKEE

	ab	r	h	tb	po	a	e
McMillan, ss	3	0	0	0	3	6	0
Bolling, 2b	3	1	2	2	2	0	0
Mathews, 3b	3	0	0	0	1	0	0
Aaron, cf	3	0	1	1	1	0	0
Roach, lf	4	0	1	1	1	0	0
Spangler, lf	0	0	0	0	0	0	0
Adcock, 1b	3	0	1	1	10	0	0
Lau, c	2	0	0	0	5	0	1
DeMerit, rf	4	0	0	0	4	0	0
Spahn, p	4	0	0	0	0	5	0
Totals	29	1	5	5	27	11	1

* Grounded out for Pagan in ninth.
† Grounded out for Jones in ninth.

```
San Francisco .............  0 0 0 0 0 0 0 0 0 — 0
Milwaukee ................  1 0 0 0 0 0 0 0 x — 1
```

Run batted in—Aaron. Sacrifice hit—McMillan. Double plays—Spahn, McMillan and Adcock 2. Passed balls—Bailey 2. Left on bases—San Francisco 0, Milwaukee 11. Bases on balls—Off Jones 5 (Mathews, Aaron, Adcock, Lau 2), off Spahn 2 (Hiller, McCovey). Strikeouts—By Jones 10 (McMillan, Mathews, Aaron, Roach, Lau, DeMerit 3, Spahn), by Spahn 5 (Mays 2, McCovey, Bailey, Jones). Runs and earned runs—Jones 1-0. HP—Jones (Bolling). Winning pitcher—Spahn (2-1). Losing pitcher—Jones (2-1). Umpires Donatelli, Burkhart, Pelekoudas, Forman and Conlan. Time—2:16. Attendance—8,518.

May 5, 1962   Baltimore at Los Angeles

ORIOLES

	ab	r	h	rbi
Temple, 2b	4	0	0	0
Williams, lf	4	0	0	0
B. Rob'son, 2b	4	0	0	0
Gentile, 1b	2	0	0	0
Brandt, cf	3	0	0	0
Triandos, c	2	0	0	0
Nicholson, rf	4	0	0	0
Hansen, ss	3	0	0	0
Barber, p	1	0	0	0
†Breeding	1	0	0	0
Stock, p	0	0	0	0
Totals	28	0	0	0

ANGELS

	ab	r	h	rbi
Pearson, cf	4	0	0	0
Moran, 2b	4	1	2	0
Wagner, rf	4	0	2	0
Bilko, 1b	4	0	0	0
Torres, 3b	3	0	0	0
Averill, lf	2	1	1	0
*L. Thomas, lf	0	0	0	0
Rodgers, c	3	0	1	0
Koppe, ss	3	0	0	1
Belinsky, p	2	0	0	0
Totals	29	2	6	1

* Ran for Averill in sixth.
† Struck out for Barber in seventh.

```
Baltimore .................  0 0 0 0 0 0 0 0 0 — 0
Los Angeles ...............  1 1 0 0 0 0 0 0 x — 2
```

E—Torres. PO-A—Baltimore 24-13, Los Angeles 27-10. LOB—Baltimore 7, Los Angeles 5. 2B—Wagner, Rodgers. S—Belinsky.

PITCHING

	ip	h	r	er	bb	so
Barber (L, 3-1)	6	6	2	2	1	6
Stock	2	0	0	0	0	1
Belinsky (W, 4-0)	9	0	0	4	9	

HBP—By Belinsky (Gentile, Barber). WP—Belinsky. U—Schwarts, Berry, Honochick, Smith. T—2:00. A—15,886.

June 26, 1962   Los Angeles at Boston

LOS ANGELES	ab	r	h	tb	po	a	e
Pearson, cf	4	0	0	0	3	0	0
Moran, 2b	3	0	0	0	2	1	0
Wagner, rf	4	0	0	0	0	0	0
L. Thomas, 1b	3	0	0	0	5	0	1
Rodgers, c	3	0	0	0	11	0	0
Averill, lf	2	0	0	0	1	0	0
Yost, 3b	2	0	0	0	2	1	0
Koppe, ss	3	0	0	0	0	3	0
Belinsky, p	2	0	0	0	0	0	0
*Burgess	1	0	0	0	0	0	0
Chance, p	0	0	0	0	0	0	0
Totals	27	0	0	0	24	5	1

BOSTON	ab	r	h	tb	po	a	e
Gardner, 2b	4	0	0	0	1	4	0
Geiger, cf	4	0	0	0	2	0	0
Yastrzemski, lf	4	0	0	0	3	0	0
Malzone, 3b	3	1	1	1	1	1	0
Runnels, 1b	3	0	2	2	8	0	0
Tillman, c	4	0	0	0	6	0	0
Hardy, rf	3	0	1	1	4	0	0
Bressoud, ss	2	0	0	0	2	0	0
Wilson, p	3	1	1	4	0	1	0
Totals	30	2	5	8	27	6	0

* Lined out for Belinsky in eighth.

```
Los Angeles ............... 0 0 0 0 0 0 0 0 0 — 0
Boston ..................... 0 0 1 1 0 0 0 0 x — 2
```

Runs batted in—Hardy, Wilson. Home run—Wilson. Left on bases—Los Angeles 4, Boston 7. Bases on balls—Off Belinsky 3 (Bressoud, Malzone, Runnels), off Wilson 4 (Averill, Moran, L. Thomas, Yost). Strikeouts—By Belinsky 10 (Tillman 2, Geiger 2, Wilson 2, Bressoud, Gardner, Hardy, Yastrzemski), by Chance 1 (Tillman), by Wilson 5 (Averill, Belinsky, Moran, Wagner, Yost). Runs and earned runs—Belinsky 2-1. Hits—Off Belinsky 3 in 7 innings, off Chance 2 in 1 inning. Winning pitcher—Wilson (6-2). Losing pitcher—Belinsky (7-3). Umpires—Schwarts, Berry, Honochick and Smith. Time—2:24. Attendance—14,002.

June 30, 1962   New York at Los Angeles

NEW YORK	ab	r	h	tb	po	a	e
Ashburn, lf	3	0	0	0	3	0	0
Kanehl, 3b	4	0	0	0	0	0	0
Mantilla, 2b	3	0	0	0	4	1	0
Thomas, 1b	2	0	0	0	5	1	0
Cook, rf	3	0	0	0	1	0	0
Hickman, cf	3	0	0	0	3	0	0
Chacon, ss	2	0	0	0	1	1	0
Cannizzaro, c	3	0	0	0	7	1	0
R. L. Miller, p	0	0	0	0	0	0	0
Daviault, p	2	0	0	0	0	0	0
*Woodling	0	0	0	0	0	0	0
†Christopher	0	0	0	0	0	0	0
Totals	25	0	0	0	24	4	0

LOS ANGELES	ab	r	h	tb	po	a	e
Wills, ss	5	0	1	1	0	4	0
Gilliam, 3b	3	0	1	1	0	3	0
W. Davis, cf	4	1	2	4	3	0	0
T. Davis, lf	4	1	2	2	2	0	0
Fairly, 1b-rf	3	1	0	0	4	0	0
Howard, rf	3	2	2	5	0	0	0
Harkness, 1b	0	0	0	0	0	0	0
Roseboro, c	3	0	1	2	13	0	0
Burright, 2b	4	0	2	2	5	2	0
Koufax, p	4	0	0	0	0	0	0
Totals	33	5	11	17	27	9	0

* Walked for Daviault in ninth.
† Ran for Woodling in ninth.

```
New York ................... 0 0 0 0 0 0 0 0 0 — 0
Los Angeles ............... 4 0 0 0 0 0 1 0 x — 5
```

Runs batted in—T. Davis, Howard 2, Roseboro 2. Two-base hit—Roseboro. Three-base hit—W. Davis. Home run—Howard. Stolen bases—T. Davis, W. Davis, Wills. Double plays—Gilliam, Burright and Fairly; Thomas and Chacon. Left on bases—New York 3, Los Angeles 10. Bases on balls—Off Miller 1 (Fairly), off Daviault 5 (Gilliam 2, W. Davis, Howard, Roseboro), off Koufax 5 (Ashburn, Mantilla, Thomas, Chacon, Woodling). Strikeouts—By Daviault 7 (Koufax 3, T. Davis, Fairly, Roseboro, Burright), by Koufax 13 (Kanehl 2, Cook 2, Chacon 2, Cannizzaro 2, Daviault 2, Hickman, Ashburn, Mantilla). Runs and earned runs—Miller 4-4, Daviault 1-1. Hits—Off Miller 5 in ⅔ inning, off Daviault 6 in 7⅓ innings. Wild pitch—Daviault. Winning pitcher—Koufax (11-4). Losing pitcher—Miller (0-6). Umpires—Steiner, Boggess, Landes and Smith. Time—2:46. Attendance—29,797.

August 1, 1962   Boston at Chicago

BOSTON	ab	r	h	tb	po	a	e
Gardner, 2b	5	0	1	1	1	1	0
Geiger, cf	2	0	0	0	2	0	0
Yastrzemski, lf..	3	0	0	0	2	0	0
Pagliaroni, c	4	1	1	1	8	0	0
Runnels, 1b	4	0	2	2	8	0	0
Clinton, rf	4	0	3	3	3	0	0
Malzone, 3b	3	0	0	0	1	2	0
Bressoud, ss	4	0	0	0	2	3	0
Monbouquette,p	3	0	1	1	0	1	0
Totals	32	1	8	8	27	7	0

CHICAGO	ab	r	h	tb	po	a	e
Aparicio, ss	4	0	0	0	3	1	0
Sadowski, 2b	3	0	0	0	3	4	0
Cunningham,1b	3	0	0	0	6	0	0
Robinson, rf	3	0	0	0	2	0	0
Maxwell, lf	3	0	0	0	3	0	0
A. Smith, 3b	3	0	0	0	1	0	0
Landis, cf	3	0	0	0	3	0	0
Lollar, c	3	0	0	0	6	1	0
Wynn, p	2	0	0	0	0	4	0
*Fox	1	0	0	0	0	0	0
Totals	28	0	0	0	27	10	0

* Grounded out for Wynn in ninth.

```
Boston............................ 0 0 0 0 0 0 0 1 0 — 1
Chicago.......................... 0 0 0 0 0 0 0 0 0 — 0
```

Run batted in—Clinton. Stolen base—Geiger. Sacrifice hit—Geiger. Double play—Wynn, Sadowski and Cunningham. Left on bases—Boston 9, Chicago 1. Bases on balls—Off Monbouquette 1 (A. Smith), off Wynn 4 (Geiger, Malzone, Monbouquette, Yastrzemski). Strikeouts—By Monbouquette 7 (Landis 2, Sadowski 2, Aparicio, Lollar, A. Smith), by Wynn 5 (Yastrzemski 2, Gardner, Monbouquette, Runnels). Runs and earned runs—Wynn 1-1. Winning pitcher—Monbouquette (9-10). Losing pitcher—Wynn (5-8). Umpires—McKinley, Chylak, Umont and Stewart. Time—2:24. Attendance—17,185.

August 26, 1962   Kansas City at Minnesota

KANSAS CITY	ab	r	h	tb	po	a	e
Del Greco, cf	4	0	0	0	2	0	0
Charles, 3b	3	0	0	0	0	4	0
Lumpe, 2b	3	0	0	0	3	3	0
Siebern, 1b	3	0	0	0	9	0	0
Cimoli, rf	3	0	0	0	1	0	0
Jimenez, lf	3	0	0	0	2	0	1
Causey, ss	3	0	0	0	2	3	0
Bryan, c	2	0	0	0	5	1	0
*Alusik	0	0	0	0	0	0	0
†Howser	0	0	0	0	0	0	0
Fischer, p	2	0	0	0	0	0	0
‡Consolo	1	0	0	0	0	0	0
Totals	27	0	0	0	24	11	1

MINNESOTA	ab	r	h	tb	po	a	e
Green, cf-lf	3	0	0	0	1	0	0
Power, 1b	4	0	2	2	14	3	0
Rollins, 3b	4	0	0	0	1	2	0
Killebrew, lf	4	0	0	0	0	0	0
Tuttle, cf	0	0	0	0	2	0	0
Allison, rf	4	0	0	0	3	0	0
Battey, c	3	0	1	1	3	0	0
Allen, 2b	3	1	3	3	0	4	0
Versalles, ss	2	0	1	1	0	1	0
Kralick, p	2	0	1	1	3	3	0
Totals	29	1	8	8	27	13	0

* Walked for Bryan in ninth.
† Ran for Alusik in ninth.
‡ Fouled out for Fischer in ninth.

```
Kansas City ................. 0 0 0 0 0 0 0 0 0 — 0
Minnesota..................... 0 0 0 0 0 0 1 0 x — 1
```

Run batted in—Green. Sacrifice hits—Versalles, Kralick. Sacrifice fly—Green. Left on bases—Kansas City 1, Minnesota 7. Base on balls—Off Kralick 1 (Alusik). Strikeouts—By Fischer 6 (Allison 4, Green, Tuttle), by Kralick 3 (Charles, Bryan, Siebern). Runs and earned runs—Fischer 1-1. Winning pitcher—Kralick (10-8). Losing pitcher Fischer (4-6). Umpires—Honochick, Schwarts, Salerno and Berry. Time—1:45. Attendance—23,224.

May 11, 1963   San Francisco at Los Angeles

SAN FRANCISCO	ab	r	h	tb	po	a	e
Kuenn, lf............	4	0	0	0	0	0	0
F. Alou, rf.........	3	0	0	0	0	0	0
Mays, cf............	3	0	0	0	1	0	0
Cepeda, 1b........	3	0	0	0	11	0	0
Bailey, c...........	2	0	0	0	9	0	0
Davenport, 3b ..	3	0	0	0	0	2	0
Amalfitano, 2b..	3	0	0	0	1	0	0
Pagan, ss..........	3	0	0	0	2	5	0
Marichal, p......	2	0	0	0	1	2	0
Pregenzer, p.....	0	0	0	0	0	1	0
*McCovey.........	0	0	0	0	0	0	0
Totals	26	0	0	0	24	11	0

LOS ANGELES	ab	r	h	tb	po	a	e
W. Davis, cf......	5	1	0	0	4	0	0
Gilliam, 2b-3b..	3	2	2	2	2	0	0
Fairly, 1b.........	5	0	3	4	10	0	0
T. Davis, 3b-lf..	4	1	1	1	1	1	0
Moon, lf............	3	2	2	5	0	0	0
Oliver, 2b	1	0	0	0	1	2	0
Howard, rf........	3	0	0	0	3	0	0
Roseboro, c.......	4	0	2	2	5	0	0
Tracewski, ss....	4	1	2	2	1	4	0
Koufax, p...........	3	1	0	0	0	2	0
Totals	35	8	12	16	27	9	0

* Walked for Pregenzer in ninth.

```
San Francisco.............. 0 0 0 0 0 0 0 0 0 — 0
Los Angeles ............... 0 1 0 0 0 3 0 4 x — 8
```

Runs batted in—Fairly 3, Moon 2, Roseboro 2. Two-base hit—Fairly. Home run —Moon. Stolen base—Gilliam. Double plays—Pregenzer, Pagan and Cepeda; Tracewski, Oliver and Fairly. Left on bases—San Francisco 1, Los Angeles 8. Bases on balls—Off Marichal 1 (Howard), off Pregenzer 4 (Gilliam 2, T. Davis, Koufax), off Koufax 2 (Bailey, McCovey). Strikeouts—By Marichal 5 (W. Davis 2, Koufax 2, Howard), by Pregenzer 1 (Koufax), by Koufax 4 (Pagan 2, F. Alou, Marichal). Runs and earned runs—Marichal 4-4, Pregenzer 4-4. Hits—Off Marichal 9 in 5⅓ innings; off Pregenzer 3 in 2⅔ innings. Balk—Pregenzer. Winning pitcher—Koufax (4-1). Losing pitcher—Marichal (4-3). Umpires—Walsh, Conlan, Burkhart and Pelekoudas. Time—2:13. Attendance—49,807.

May 17, 1963   Philadelphia at Houston

PHILADELPHIA	ab	r	h	tb	po	a	e
Taylor, 2b.........	3	0	0	0	1	0	0
Callison, rf.......	4	0	0	0	2	0	0
Gonzalez, cf......	4	0	0	0	4	0	0
Covington, lf	4	0	0	0	0	0	0
Demeter, 1b-3b	3	1	0	0	5	6	0
Dalrymple, c	1	0	0	0	7	0	0
Hoak, 3b...........	1	0	0	0	0	0	0
†Sievers, 1b......	1	0	0	0	2	0	0
Wine, ss...........	2	0	0	0	2	3	0
Hamilton, p......	2	0	0	0	1	1	0
‡Klaus	1	0	0	0	0	0	0
Duren, p...........	0	0	0	0	0	0	0
Totals	26	1	0	0	24	10	0

HOUSTON	ab	r	h	tb	po	a	e
Temple, 3b.......	4	0	1	1	0	2	0
Aspromonte, 3b	0	0	0	0	0	0	0
Spangler, lf.......	4	1	0	0	3	0	0
Warwick, rf.......	4	1	4	9	1	0	0
Staub, 1b..........	2	0	1	1	4	0	0
*Runnels, 1b	1	1	0	0	4	0	0
Goss, cf.............	4	1	1	4	6	0	0
Bateman, c.......	3	0	0	0	8	0	0
Lillis, 2b..........	3	0	0	0	0	1	0
Hartman, ss	3	0	0	0	1	2	1
Nottebart, p......	3	0	0	0	0	1	0
Totals	31	4	7	15	27	6	1

* Ran for Staub in sixth.
† Flied out for Hoak in seventh.
‡ Grounded out for Hamilton in eighth.

```
Philadelphia................ 0 0 0 0 1 0 0 0 0 — 1
Houston....................... 1 0 0 0 0 3 0 0 x — 4
```

Runs batted in—Hoak, Warwick, Goss 3. Three-base hit—Warwick. Home runs —Warwick, Goss. Sacrifice hit—Dalrymple. Sacrifice fly—Hoak. Left on bases— Philadelphia 3, Houston 4. Bases on balls—Off Duren 1 (Runnels), off Nottebart 3 (Taylor, Dalrymple, Wine). Strikeouts—By Hamilton 5 (Temple 2, Nottebart 2, Staub), by Duren 2 (Spangler, Goss), by Nottebart 8 (Hamilton 2, Taylor, Callison, Gonzalez, Covington, Demeter, Hoak). Runs and earned runs—Hamilton 4-4, Nottebart 1-0. Hits—Off Hamilton 6 in 7 innings, off Duren 1 in 1 inning. Winning pitcher—Nottebart (5-1). Losing pitcher—Hamilton (2-1). Umpires—Vargo, Harvey, Weyer and Barlick. Time—2:12. Attendance—8,223.

June 15, 1963 Houston at San Francisco

HOUSTON

	ab	r	h	tb	po	a	e
Fazio, 2b	3	0	0	0	1	1	0
‡Runnels	1	0	0	0	0	0	0
Davis, cf	4	0	0	0	0	0	0
Aspromonte, 3b	2	0	0	0	1	1	0
Warwick, rf	3	0	0	0	2	0	0
Staub, 1b	3	0	0	0	6	0	0
Spangler, lf	2	0	0	0	2	0	0
Lillis, ss	3	0	0	0	4	2	0
Bateman, c	3	0	0	0	8	1	0
Drott, p	2	0	0	0	0	0	0
†Temple	1	0	0	0	0	0	0
Totals	27	0	0	0	24	5	0

SAN FRANCISCO

	ab	r	h	tb	po	a	e
Hiller, 2b	3	0	1	2	2	0	0
F. Alou, rf	4	0	0	0	1	0	0
Mays, cf	3	0	1	1	3	0	0
McCovey, lf	2	0	0	0	2	0	0
Cepeda, 1b	3	0	0	0	11	0	0
Bailey, c	3	0	0	0	5	0	0
Davenport, 3b	3	1	1	2	1	4	0
Pagan, ss	1	0	0	0	2	1	0
*M. Alou	1	0	0	0	0	0	0
Bowman, ss	0	0	0	0	0	0	0
Marichal, p	3	0	0	0	0	1	0
Totals	26	1	3	5	27	6	0

* Called out on strikes for Pagan in eighth.
† Fouled out for Drott in ninth.
‡ Struck out for Fazio in ninth.

Houston .... 0 0 0 0 0 0 0 0 0 — 0
San Francisco .... 0 0 0 0 0 0 0 1 x — 1

Run batted in—Hiller. Two-base hits—Davenport, Hiller. Double play—Bateman and Lillis. Left on bases—Houston 2, San Francisco 4. Bases on balls—Off Drott 3 (Hiller, McCovey, Pagan), off Marichal 2 (Aspromonte, Spangler). Strikeouts—By Drott 7 (F. Alou 2, McCovey 2, Cepeda, Bailey, M. Alou), by Marichal 5 (Davis 2, Fazio, Runnels, Drott). Runs and earned runs—Drott 1-1. Winning pitcher—Marichal (10-3). Losing pitcher—Drott (2-4). Umpires—Sudol, Forman, Gorman and Landes. Time—1:41. Attendance—18,869.

April 23, 1964 Cincinnati at Houston

CINCINNATI

	ab	r	h	tb	po	a	e
Rose, 2b	4	1	0	0	3	2	0
Ruiz, 3b	4	0	0	0	1	4	0
Pinson, cf	3	0	0	0	0	0	0
*Keough, cf	0	0	0	0	0	0	0
Robinson, rf	4	0	0	0	1	0	0
D. Johnson, 1b	3	0	0	0	8	0	1
Skinner, lf	2	0	0	0	5	0	0
Edwards, c	3	0	0	0	7	1	0
Cardenas, ss	3	0	0	0	2	0	1
Nuxhall, p	3	0	0	0	0	0	0
Totals	29	1	0	0	27	7	2

HOUSTON

	ab	r	h	tb	po	a	e
Kasko, ss	4	0	0	0	2	0	0
Fox, 2b	4	0	2	2	1	4	1
Runnels, 1b	3	0	1	1	12	0	0
†Lillis	0	0	0	0	0	0	0
Weekly, rf	4	0	0	0	1	0	0
Aspromonte, 3b	3	0	1	1	0	4	0
Wynn, lf	3	0	1	2	1	0	0
Beauchamp, cf	3	0	0	0	1	0	0
Grote, c	3	0	0	0	9	0	0
K. Johnson, p	3	0	0	0	0	3	1
Totals	30	0	5	6	27	11	2

* Ran for Pinson in ninth.
† Ran for Runnels in ninth.

Cincinnati .... 0 0 0 0 0 0 0 0 1 — 1
Houston .... 0 0 0 0 0 0 0 0 0 — 0

Runs batted in—None. Two-base hit—Wynn. Double plays—Cardenas and D. Johnson; Ruiz, Rose and D. Johnson; Cardenas, Ruiz and Cardenas. Left on bases—Cincinnati 3, Houston 4. Bases on balls—Off Nuxhall 1 (Runnels), off K. Johnson 2 (Pinson, Skinner). Strikeouts—By Nuxhall 6 (Kasko, Weekly, Aspromonte, Grote, Beauchamp 2), by K. Johnson 9 (Rose, Ruiz, Robinson 2, Johnson 2, Skinner, Cardenas, Nuxhall). Runs and earned runs—K. Johnson 1-0. Winning pitcher—Nuxhall (1-1). Losing pitcher—K. Johnson (2-1). Umpires—Donatelli, Landes, Steiner and Barlick. Time—1:56. Attendance—5,426.

June 4, 1964 Los Angeles at Philadelphia

LOS ANGELES	ab	r	h	tb	po	a	e
W. Davis, cf......	4	0	0	0	1	0	0
Wills, ss...........	4	0	1	1	0	2	0
Gilliam, 3b.......	4	1	1	1	0	3	0
T. Davis, lf.......	4	1	2	2	1	.0	0
Howard, rf.........	3	1	1	4	1	0	0
Fairly, 1b.........	1	0	0		3	0	0
McMullen, 1b..	3	0	1	1	7	0	0
Parker, rf..........	1	0	1	2	1	0	0
Camilli, c.........	4	0	0	0	12	1	0
Tracewski, 2b...	3	0	1	2	1	0	0
Koufax, p..........	3	0	1	1	0	2	0
Totals.....	34	3	9	14	27	8	0

PHILADELPHIA	ab	r	h	tb	po	a	e
Rojas, cf...........	3	0	0	0	1	0	0
Callison, rf........	3	0	0	0	2	0	0
Allen, 3b..........	2	0	0	0	1	0	1
Cater, lf............	3	0	0	0	1	1	0
Triandos, c........	3	0	0	0	6	0	0
Sievers, 1b........	3	0	0	0	12	0	0
Taylor, 2b.........	3	0	0	0	2	2	0
Amaro, ss..........	3	0	0	0	2	8	0
Short, p.............	2	0	0	0	0	2	0
Roebuck, p	0	0	0	0	0	0	0
Culp, p..............	0	0	0	0	0	0	0
*Wine...............	1	0	0	0	0	0	0
Totals.....	26	0	0	0	27	13	1

* Struck out for Culp in ninth.

Los Angeles................ 0 0 0 0 0 0 3 0 0 — 3
Philadelphia.............. 0 0 0 0 0 0 0 0 0 — 0

Runs batted in—Howard 3. Two-base hits—Tracewski, Parker. Home run—Howard. Double play—Taylor, Amaro and Sievers. Left on bases—Los Angeles 4, Philadelphia 0. Bases on balls—Off Koufax 1 (Allen). Strikeouts—By Koufax 12 (Callison, Allen, Carter, Triandos 2, Sievers, Taylor 2, Amaro, Short 2, Wine), by Short 4 (Howard, Camilli, Koufax, Wills), by Culp 2 (Gilliam, T. Davis). Runs and earned runs—Short 3-3. Hits—Off Short 8 in 6⅔ innings, off Roebuck 0 in ⅓ inning, off Culp 1 in 2 innings. Winning pitcher—Koufax (6-4). Losing pitcher—Short (3-3). Umpires—Vargo, Forman, Jackowski and Crawford. Time—1:55. Attendance—29,709.

June 21, 1964 Philadelphia at New York

PHILADELPHIA	ab	r	h	tb	po	a	e
Briggs, cf...........	4	1	0	0	2	0	0
Herrnstein, 1b..	4	0	0	0	7	0	0
Callison, rf........	4	1	2	5	1	0	0
Allen, 3b..........	3	0	1	1	0	2	0
Covington, lf	2	0	0	1	0	0	0
*Wine, ss	1	1	0	0	2	1	0
T. Taylor, 2b	3	2	1	1	0	3	0
Rojas, ss-lf........	3	0	1	1	3	0	0
Triandos, c........	4	1	2	3	11	1	0
Bunning, p........	4	0	1	2	0	0	0
Totals.....	32	6	8	13	27	7	0

NEW YORK	ab	r	h	tb	po	a	e
Hickman, cf......	3	0	0	0	2	0	0
Hunt, 2b	3	0	0	0	3	2	0
Kranepool, 1b...	3	0	0	0	8	1	0
Christopher, rf..	3	0	0	0	4	0	0
Gonder, c..........	3	0	0	0	6	2	0
R. Taylor, lf	3	0	0	0	1	0	0
C. Smith, ss	3	0	0	0	2	1	0
Samuel, 3b........	2	0	0	0	0	1	0
‡Altman	1	0	0	0	0	0	0
Stallard, p.........	1	0	0	0	2	0	0
Wakefield, p.....	0	0	0	0	0	0	0
†Kanehl.............	1	0	0	0	0	0	0
Sturdivant, p.....	0	0	0	0	1	0	0
‖Stephenson......	1	0	0	0	0	0	0
Totals.....	27	0	0	0	27	9	0

* Ran for Covington in sixth.
† Grounded out for Wakefield in sixth.
‡ Struck out for Samuel in ninth.
‖ Struck out for Sturdivant in ninth.

Philadelphia................ 1 1 0 0 0 4 0 0 0 — 6
New York .... 0 0 0 0 0 0 0 0 0 — 0

Runs batted in—Callison, Allen, Triandos 2, Bunning 2. Two-base hits—Triandos, Bunning. Home run—Callison. Sacrifices—Herrnstein, Rojas. Left on bases—Philadelphia 5, New York 0. Bases on balls—Off Stallard 4 (Briggs, T. Taylor, Allen, Covington). Strikeouts—By Bunning 10 (Hickman 3, C. Smith, Hunt, Kranepool, Christopher, R. Taylor, Altman, Stephenson), by Stallard 3 (Callison, Herrnstein, Allen), by Sturdivant 3 (Rojas, Triandos, Briggs). Runs and earned runs—Stallard 6-6. Hits—Off Stallard 7 in 5⅔ innings, off Wakefield 0 in ⅓ inning, off Sturdivant 1 in 3 innings. Wild pitch—Stallard. Winning pitcher—Bunning (7-2). Losing pitcher—Stallard (4-3). Umpires—Sudol, Pryor, Secory and Burkhart. Time—2:19. Attendance—32,026.

June 14, 1965 New York at Cincinnati

NEW YORK

	ab	r	h	tb	po	a	e
Cowan, cf.........	4	0	0	0	0	0	0
Hickman, lf......	0	0	0	0	1	0	0
Hiller, 2b.........	4	0	0	0	1	2	0
Smith, 3b.........	4	0	0	0	0	5	0
Kranepool, 1b...	3	0	0	0	20	1	0
Lewis, rf.........	4	1	1	4	2	0	0
Swoboda, lf......	4	0	0	0	1	0	0
Klaus, 2b..........	0	0	0	0	0	0	0
McMillan, ss.....	4	0	1	1	1	4	1
Cannizzaro, c....	2	0	0	0	2	2	1
*Gonder, c........	2	0	0	0	2	1	0
Lary, p	2	0	0	0	3	5	0
†Christopher....	1	0	0	0	0	0	0
Bearnarth, p......	0	0	0	0	0	0	0
Totals	34	1	2	5	33	20	2

CINCINNATI

	ab	r	h	tb	po	a	e
Harper, lf..........	4	0	1	1	1	0	0
Rose, 2b............	4	0	0	0	2	2	0
Pinson, cf..........	5	0	1	1	2	0	0
Robinson, rf......	4	0	1	1	3	0	0
Coleman, 1b.....	5	0	1	1	8	0	0
Johnson, 3b......	4	0	0	0	0	2	0
Edwards, c........	4	0	2	2	17	0	0
‡Ruiz.................	0	0	0	0	0	0	0
Pavletich, c......	0	0	0	0	0	0	0
Cardenas, ss	2	0	1	1	2	3	0
Maloney, p	4	0	0	0	0	1	0
Totals	36	0	7	7	33	8	0

* Flied out for Cannizzaro in ninth.
† Struck out for Lary in ninth.
‡ Ran for Edwards in tenth.

New York......... 0 0 0 0 0 0 0 0 0 0 1 — 1
Cincinnati......... 0 0 0 0 0 0 0 0 0 0 0 — 0

Run batted in—Lewis. Home run—Lewis. Sacrifice hits—Cardenas 2. Stolen base—Harper. Double plays—Rose, Cardenas and Coleman; Cardenas and Coleman; Hiller and Kranepool. Left on bases—New York 1, Cincinnati 8. Bases on balls—Off Maloney 1 (Kranepool), off Bearnarth 1 (Robinson), off Lary 1 (Rose). Strikeouts—By Maloney 18 (Cowan 3, Smith 3, Kranepool, Lewis 3, Swoboda 3, McMillan 2, Cannizzaro, Gonder, Lary), by Lary 3 (Coleman, Johnson, Maloney), by Bearnarth 1 (Pinson). Hits—Off Lary 5 in 8 innings, off Bearnarth 2 in 3 innings. Runs and earned runs—Off Maloney 1-1. Hit by pitcher—By Lary (Harper). Passed ball—Cannizzaro. Wild pitch—Maloney. Winning pitcher—Bearnarth (2-1). Losing pitcher—Maloney (5-3). Umpires—Steiner, Barlick, Donatelli and Landes. Time of game—2:50. Attendance—5,989.

August 19, 1965 Cincinnati at Chicago

CINCINNATI

	ab	r	h	tb	po	a	e
Harper, lf..........	5	0	1	1	1	0	0
Rose, 2b............	5	0	1	1	6	3	0
Pinson, cf..........	3	0	2	2	2	0	0
Robinson, rf......	4	0	2	4	0	0	0
Coleman, 1b.....	4	0	0	0	6	0	0
Keough, 1b.......	0	0	0	0	1	0	0
Johnson, 3b......	4	0	0	0	0	1	0
Edwards, c........	4	0	0	0	12	0	0
Cardenas, ss	4	1	1	4	2	4	0
Maloney, p........	4	0	2	2	0	2	0
Totals	37	1	9	14	30	10	0

CHICAGO

	ab	r	h	tb	po	a	e
Landrum, cf......	4	0	0	0	2	0	0
Clemens, lf.......	3	0	0	0	1	0	0
Williams, rf.......	4	0	0	0	1	0	0
Banks, 1b..........	5	0	0	0	14	3	1
Santo, 3b...........	3	0	0	0	1	4	0
Bailey, c............	2	0	0	0	5	1	0
Beckert, 2b.......	2	0	0	0	2	3	0
Kessinger, ss.....	2	0	0	0	2	5	0
*Stewart, ss......	1	0	0	0	0	1	0
Jackson, p.........	2	0	0	0	2	1	0
Totals	28	0	0	0	30	18	1

* Flied out for Kessinger in ninth.

Cincinnati.............. 0 0 0 0 0 0 0 0 1 — 1
Chicago................. 0 0 0 0 0 0 0 0 0 — 0

Run batted in—Cardenas. Three-base hit—Robinson. Home run—Cardenas. Sacrifice hits—Pinson, Landrum. Double plays—Cardenas, Rose and Keough; Kessinger and Banks. Left on bases—Cincinnati 7, Chicago 10. Bases on balls—Off Maloney 10 (Clemens 2, Williams, Bailey 2, Beckert 2, Kessinger, Jackson 2). Strikeouts—By Maloney 12 (Landrum 2, Clemens 2, Banks, Santo, Bailey, Beckert, Kessinger 2, Jackson 2), by Jackson 5 (Harper 2, Johnson, Edwards, Maloney). Runs and earned runs—Off Jackson 1-1. Hit by pitcher—By Maloney (Santo). Winning pitcher—Maloney (14-6). Losing pitcher—Jackson (11-15). Umpires—Steiner, Barlick, Donatelli and Landes. Time of game—2:51. Attendance—11,342.

Sept. 9, 1965   Chicago at Los Angeles

CHICAGO	ab	r	h	tb	po	a	e
Young, cf	3	0	0	0	5	0	0
Beckert, 2b	3	0	0	0	1	1	0
Williams, rf	3	0	0	0	0	0	0
Santo, 3b	3	0	0	0	1	2	0
Banks, 1b	3	0	0	0	13	0	0
Browne, lf	3	0	0	0	1	0	0
Krug, c	3	0	0	0	3	0	1
Kessinger, ss	2	0	0	0	0	2	0
*Amalfitano	1	0	0	0	0	0	0
Hendley, p	2	0	0	0	0	5	0
†Kuenn	1	0	0	0	0	0	0
Totals	27	0	0	0	24	10	1

LOS ANGELES	ab	r	h	tb	po	a	e
Wills, ss	3	0	0	0	0	2	0
Gilliam, 3b	3	0	0	0	0	1	0
W. Davis, cf	3	0	0	0	2	0	0
Johnson, lf	2	1	1	2	2	0	0
Fairly, rf	2	0	0	0	3	0	0
Lefebvre, 2b	3	0	0	0	1	0	0
Tracewski, 2b	0	0	0	0	0	0	0
Parker, 1b	3	0	0	0	4	0	0
Torborg, c	3	0	0	0	15	0	0
Koufax, p	2	0	0	0	0	0	0
Totals	24	1	1	2	27	3	0

* Struck out for Kessinger in ninth.
† Struck out for Hendley in ninth.

Chicago	0	0	0	0	0	0	0	0	0 —	0
Los Angeles	0	0	0	0	1	0	0	0	x —	1

Run batted in—None. Two-base hit—Johnson. Sacrifice hit—Fairly. Stolen base—Johnson. Left on bases—Los Angeles 1. Chicago 0. Bases on balls—Off Hendley 1 (Johnson). Strikeouts—By Koufax 14 (Young, Beckert, Williams 2, Santo, Banks 3, Browne, Krug, Amalfitano, Hendley 2, Kuenn), by Hendley 3 (Lefebvre 2, Koufax). Runs and earned runs—Off Hendley 1-0. Winning pitcher—Koufax (22-7). Losing pitcher—Hendley (2-3). Umpires—Vargo, Pelekoudas, Jackowski and Pryor. Time of game—1:43. Attendance—29,139.

Sept. 16, 1965   Cleveland at Boston

CLEVELAND	ab	r	h	tb	po	a	e
Howser, ss	3	0	0	0	1	1	0
‖Davalillo	1	0	0	0	0	0	0
Alvis, 3b	3	0	0	0	0	0	0
Wagner, lf	3	0	0	0	2	0	0
Colavito, rf	2	0	0	0	2	0	0
Whitfield, 1b	3	0	0	0	4	2	0
Hinton, cf	3	0	0	0	1	0	0
Gonzalez, 2b	2	0	0	0	1	2	0
*Davis	1	0	0	0	0	0	0
Moran, 2b	0	0	0	0	0	0	0
Sims, c	2	0	0	0	12	0	0
†Brown	1	0	0	0	0	0	0
Tiant, p	2	0	0	0	1	0	0
‡Clinton	1	0	0	0	0	0	0
Totals	27	0	0	0	24	5	0

BOSTON	ab	r	h	tb	po	a	e
Gosger, cf	4	1	2	2	4	0	0
Jones, 3b	4	0	2	4	0	3	0
Yastrzemski, lf	4	0	0	0	1	0	0
Conigliaro, cf	3	0	0	0	1	0	0
Thomas, 1b	3	1	1	4	10	2	0
Mantilla, 2b	3	0	0	0	1	0	0
Bressoud, ss	3	0	1	1	1	5	0
Tillman, c	3	0	0	0	9	0	0
Morehead, p	3	0	0	0	2	1	0
Totals	30	2	6	11	27	12	0

* Flied out for Gonzalez in eighth.
† Lined out for Sims in ninth.
‡ Flied out for Tiant in ninth.
‖ Grounded out for Howser in ninth.

Cleveland	0	0	0	0	0	0	0	0	0 —	0
Boston	0	0	0	0	0	1	1	0	x —	2

Runs batted in—Jones, Thomas. Three-base hit—Jones. Home run—Thomas. Stolen base—Jones. Left on bases—Boston 4, Cleveland 1. Bases on balls—Off Morehead 1 (Colavito). Strikeouts—By Morehead 8 (Alvis 2, Whitfield, Hinton 2, Gonzalez, Sims, Tiant), by Tiant 11 (Gosger 2, Yastrzemski 3. Conigliaro 2, Bressoud, Morehead 3). Runs and earned runs—Off Tiant 2-2. Winning pitcher—Morehead (10-16). Losing pitcher—Tiant (11-11). Umpires—Runge, Salerno, Stewart and Paparella. Time of game—2:00. Attendance—1,247.

June 10, 1966   Washington at Cleveland

WASHINGTON

	ab	r	h	tb	po	a	e
Blasingame, 2b.	4	0	0	0	2	1	0
Saverine, 3b-ss.	4	0	0	0	1	3	0
King, rf.............	3	0	0	0	1	0	0
Howard, lf........	3	0	0	0	1	0	0
Nen, 1b.............	2	0	0	0	8	0	0
Lock, cf.............	3	0	0	0	4	0	0
Casanova, c.......	3	0	0	0	4	0	0
Brinkman, ss.....	2	0	0	0	1	2	1
*Chance............	1	0	0	0	0	0	0
McMullen, 3b ..	0	0	0	0	0	0	0
Ortega, p...........	2	0	0	0	2	1	0
†Valentine........	1	0	0	0	0	0	0
Totals	28	0	0	0	24	7	1

CLEVELAND

	ab	r	h	tb	po	a	e
Davalillo, cf......	3	1	0	0	1	0	0
Salmon, ss.........	4	0	2	2	0	2	1
Wagner, lf.........	4	1	1	4	1	0	0
Landis, rf...........	0	0	0	0	0	0	0
Alvis, 3b............	3	0	1	1	3	0	0
Whitfield, 1b	3	0	1	1	11	1	0
Colavito, rf........	3	0	0	0	0	0	0
Hinton, lf...........	0	0	0	0	1	0	0
Howser, 2b........	3	0	0	0	0	4	0
Azcue, c............	3	0	0	0	8	0	0
Siebert, p..........	3	0	0	0	2	1	0
Totals	29	2	5	8	27	8	1

* Struck out for Brinkman in eighth.
† Grounded out for Ortega in ninth.

```
Washington ................  0  0  0  0  0  0  0  0  0 — 0
Cleveland ...................  1  0  1  0  0  0  0  0  x — 2
```

Runs batted in—Salmon, Wagner. Home run—Wagner. Left on bases—Washington 2, Cleveland 5. Bases on balls—Off Ortega 2 (Davalillo, Alvis), off Siebert 1 (Nen). Strikeouts—By Ortega 5 (Davalillo, Salmon, Whitfield, Howser, Siebert), by Siebert 7 (King, Howard, Lock, Brinkman 2, Chance, Ortega). Runs and earned runs—Ortega 2-2, Siebert 0-0. Winning pitcher—Siebert (5-3), Losing pitcher—Ortega (5-3). Umpires—Honochick, Umont, Neudecker and Kinnamon. Time of game—2:13. Attendance—10,469.

April 30, 1967   Detroit at Baltimore

DETROIT

	ab	r	h	rbi
McAu'fe, 2b......................	3	0	0	0
Horton, ph	1	0	0	0
Lumpe, 2b.......................	0	0	0	0
Stanley, cf.......................	2	0	0	0
Wert, 2b	3	0	0	0
Kaline, rf.........................	4	0	0	0
Northrup, lf......................	4	0	0	0
Freehan, c.......................	1	0	0	0
Cash, 1b..........................	1	0	0	0
Tr'ski, ph-ss.....................	0	1	0	0
Oyler, ss..........................	2	0	0	0
Wood, ph-1b.....................	0	1	0	0
Wilson, p.........................	3	0	0	0
Gladding, p......................	0	0	0	0
Totals......................	24	2	0	0

BALTIMORE

	ab	r	h	rbi
Aparicio, ss	3	0	0	1
Snyder, cf........................	4	0	0	0
F. Ro'son, rf.....................	4	0	1	0
B. R'son, 3b.....................	3	0	0	0
Epstein, 1b	4	0	0	0
Blefary, lf........................	2	1	0	0
Held, 2b..........................	2	0	0	0
Haney, c..........................	0	0	0	0
Etcheba'n, c.....................	2	0	1	0
Lau, ph...........................	0	0	0	0
Belanger, 2b.....................	0	0	0	0
Barber, p.........................	1	0	0	0
S. Mil'r, p........................	0	0	0	0
Totals......................	25	1	2	1

```
Detroit......................  0  0  0  0  0  0  0  2 — 2
Baltimore..................  0  0  0  0  0  0  1  0 — 1
```

DETROIT

	ip	h	r	er	bb	so
Wilson (W. 2-2)......	8	2	1	1	4	4
Gladding (Save 2) .	1	0	0	0	0	1

BALTIMORE

	ip	h	r	er	bb	so
Barber (L. 2-1).......8²/₃	0	2	1	10	3
S. Miller.................. ¹/₃	0	0	0	0	0

E—Kaline, Belanger, Barber. DP—Detroit 1. Baltimore 1. LOB—Detorit 11, Baltimore 4. SB—Freehan, F. Robinson. SH—Cash, Oyler, Wilson, Barber, Held. SF—Aparicio. HBP—By Barber (McAuliffe, Freehan). WP—Barber. U—Stevens, Stewart, Valentine and Springstead. T—2:38. A—26,884.

June 18, 1967 Atlanta at Houston

ATLANTA	ab	r	h	rbi
Alou, lf	4	0	0	0
Fr'cona, 1b	4	0	0	0
Aaron, rf	3	0	0	0
Jones, cf	3	0	0	0
delaHoz, 3b	3	0	0	0
Menke, ss	1	0	0	0
Uecker, c	2	0	0	0
Carty, ph	1	0	0	0
Martinez, c	0	0	0	0
W'dward, 2b	2	0	0	0
Lau, ph	1	0	0	0
Hern'dez, p	0	0	0	0
Niekro, p	2	0	0	0
Boyer, ph-3b	1	0	0	0
Totals	27	0	0	0

HOUSTON	ab	r	h	rbi
Gotay, 2b	4	0	1	0
Jackson, ss	3	1	3	0
Lillis, ss	1	0	0	0
Wynn, cf	4	1	2	1
Staub, rf	4	0	1	0
Mathews, 1b	3	0	0	1
Landis, lf	3	0	1	0
Aspro'nte, 3b	2	0	0	0
Adlesh, c	3	0	0	0
Wilson, p	3	0	0	0
Totals	30	2	8	2

```
Atlanta ..................... 0 0 0 0 0 0 0 0 0 — 0
Houston .................... 0 0 0 2 0 0 0 0 x — 2
```

ATLANTA	ip	h	r	er	bb	so
Niekro (L. 2-3)	7	8	2	2	2	5
Hernandez	1	0	0	0	0	2

HOUSTON	ip	h	r	er	bb	so
Wilson (W. 4-3)	9	0	0	0	3	15

E—None. DP—Atlanta 1. LOB—Atlanta 3, Houston 6. 2B—Wynn 2, Gotay. PB—Uecker 2. U—Secory, Burkhart, Vargo and Williams. T—2:31. A—19,199.

August 25, 1967 Minnesota at Cleveland

MINNESOTA	ab	r	h	rbi
Carew, 2b	5	0	1	0
Uhl'nder, cf	4	0	1	0
Tovar, 3b	4	1	1	0
Oliva, rf	3	1	2	0
Killeb'w, 1b	3	0	2	1
Val'spino, lf	4	0	0	0
Zim'rman, c	3	0	0	0
Hern'dez, ss	3	0	0	0
Reese, ph	1	0	0	0
Versalles, ss	0	0	0	0
Chance, p	3	0	0	0
Totals	33	2	7	1

CLEVELAND	ab	r	h	rbi
Maye, lf	2	1	0	0
Davalillo, cf	3	0	0	0
Hinton, rf	3	0	0	0
Horton, 1b	4	0	0	0
Alvis, 3b	3	0	0	0
Azcue, c	3	0	0	0
Fuller, 2b	1	0	0	0
Whitf'ld, ph	1	0	0	0
Gonzalez, 2b	0	0	0	0
Brown, ss	3	0	0	0
Siebert, p	2	0	0	0
Wagner, ph	1	0	0	0
Culver, p	0	0	0	0
Totals	26	1	0	0

```
Minnesota ................... 0 1 0 0 0 1 0 0 0 — 2
Cleveland ................... 1 0 0 0 0 0 0 0 0 — 1
```

MINNESOTA	ip	h	r	er	bb	so
Chance (W. 17-9)	9	0	1	1	5	9

CLEVELAND	ip	h	r	er	bb	so
Siebert (L. 6-11)	8	7	2	2	2	7
Culver	1	0	0	0	1	0

E—Tovar. DP—Minnesota 2, Cleveland 1. LOB—Minnesota 8, Cleveland 3. 2B—Carew. HBP—By Siebert (Chance). WP—Chance, Culver. Balk—Siebert. U—Napp, Umont, Kinnamon and Valentine. T—2:48. A—10,519.

Sept. 10, 1967   Detroit at Chicago

DETROIT	ab	r	h	rbi
McAu'fe, ss	4	0	0	0
Cash, 1b	3	0	0	0
Kaline, rf	3	0	0	0
Horton, lf	3	0	0	0
Mathews, 3b	3	0	0	0
Northrup, cf	3	0	0	0
Freehan, c	1	0	0	0
Dobson, p	0	0	0	0
Brown, ph	1	0	0	0
Marshall, p	0	0	0	0
Lumpe, 2b	3	0	0	0
Sparma, p	0	0	0	0
Podres, p	0	0	0	0
Match'k, ph	1	0	0	0
W'k'sham, p	0	0	0	0
Heath, c	2	0	0	0
Totals	27	0	0	0

CHICAGO	ab	r	h	rbi
Agee, cf	3	1	1	0
Buford, 3b	3	0	1	0
Voss, rf	4	1	0	0
Boyer, 1b	4	1	1	0
Nash, 1b	0	0	0	0
Ward, lf	3	1	1	1
Bradford, lf	1	0	0	0
Causey, 2b	4	2	2	2
J. C. M'in, c	4	0	1	1
Hansen, ss	3	0	0	0
Horlen, p	2	0	1	1
Totals	31	6	8	5

Detroit	0	0	0	0	0	0	0	0	0	—	0
Chicago	5	0	0	0	0	0	0	1	x	—	6

DETROIT	ip	h	r	er	bb	so
Sparma (L. 14-9)	1/3	4	5	3	0	1
Podres	1⅔	1	0	0	1	0
Wickersham	3	1	0	0	0	0
Dobson	2	0	0	0	2	2
Marshall	1	2	1	0	0	0

CHICAGO	ip	h	r	er	bb	so
Horlen (W. 16-6)	9	0	0	0	0	4

E—Sparma, Boyer. DP—Detroit 1, Chicago 1. LOB—Detroit 1, Chicago 5. 3B—Causey. SB—Agee 2, Buford. HBP—By Horlen (Freehan), by Wickersham (Horlen). WP—Dobson. PB—Heath. U—Stevens, Stewart, DiMuro and Neudecker. T—2:17. A—26,625.

April 27, 1968   Boston at Baltimore

BOSTON	ab	r	h	rbi
Andrews, 2b	2	0	0	0
Jones, 2b	2	0	0	0
Foy, 3b	3	0	0	0
Yastr'ski, lf	2	0	0	0
Smith, cf	3	0	0	0
Lahoud, rf	3	0	0	0
Scott, 1b	3	0	0	0
Petroc'li, ss	3	0	0	0
Howard, c	1	0	0	0
Oliver, c	1	0	0	0
Wasle'ski, p	1	0	0	0
Tartab'l, ph	1	0	0	0
Rog'burk, p	0	0	0	0
Siebern, ph	1	0	0	0
Totals	26	0	0	0

BALTIMORE	ab	r	h	rbi
Blair, cf	5	1	1	0
Motton, lf	4	1	1	0
Blefary, c	3	1	1	0
B. R'son, 3b	3	1	1	3
Powell, 1b	3	0	1	0
Johnson, 2b	4	1	3	2
May, rf	4	0	0	0
Belanger, ss	4	0	0	0
Pho'bus, p	4	1	2	1
Totals	34	6	10	6

Boston	0	0	0	0	0	0	0	0	0	—	0
Baltimore	0	0	4	0	1	0	0	1	x	—	6

BOSTON	ip	h	r	er	bb	so
Waslewski (L. 2-1)	5	8	5	1	2	3
Roggenburk	3	2	1	1	0	1

BALTIMORE	ip	h	r	er	bb	so
Phoebus (W. 3-1)	9	0	0	0	3	9

E—Scott, Petrocelli. DP—Boston 1. LOB—Boston 2, Baltimore 7. 2B—B. Robinson, Johnson. SH—Blefary. WP—Phoebus, Waslewski 2. U—Honochick, Umont, Valentine and Ashford. T—2:26. A—3,147.

May 8, 1968   Minnesota at Oakland

MINNESOTA	ab	r	h	rbi
Tovar, 3b	3	0	0	0
Carew, 2b	3	0	0	0
Kil'brew, 1b	3	0	0	0
Oliva, rf	3	0	0	0
Uhl'nder, cf	3	0	0	0
Allison, lf	3	0	0	0
Hern'dez, ss	2	0	0	0
Roseb'o, ph	1	0	0	0
Look, c	3	0	0	0
Boswell, p	2	0	0	0
Per'noski, p	0	0	0	0
Reese, ph	1	0	0	0
Totals	27	0	0	0

OAKLAND	ab	r	h	rbi
Camp'eris, ss	4	0	2	0
Jackson, rf	4	0	0	0
Bando, 3b	3	0	1	0
Webster, 1b	4	1	2	0
Don'son, 2b	3	0	0	0
Pagliaroni, c	3	1	0	0
Monday, cf	3	2	2	0
Rudi, lf	3	0	0	0
Robinson, ph	0	0	0	0
Cater, ph	0	0	0	1
Hersh'ger, lf	0	0	0	0
Hunter, p	4	0	3	3
Totals	31	4	10	4

Minnesota.................. 0 0 0 0 0 0 0 0 0 — 0
Oakland .... 0 0 0 0 0 0 1 3 x — 4

MINNESOTA	ip	h	r	er	bb	so
Boswell (L. 3-3)	7²/₃	9	4	4	4	6
Perranoski	¹/₃	1	0	0	1	0

OAKLAND	ip	h	r	er	bb	so
Hunter (W. 3-2)	9	0	0	0	0	11

E—Boswell. DP—Minnesota 2. LOB—Minnesota 0, Oakland 9. 2B—Hunter, Monday. SB—Campaneris. HBP—By Boswell (Donaldson). WP—Boswell 2. U—Napp, Salerno, Haller and Neudecker. T—2:28. A—6,298.

July 29, 1968   Cincinnati at Philadelphia

CINCINNATI	ab	r	h	rbi
Rose, cf	5	2	2	0
Helms, 2b	5	1	2	0
Johnson, lf	4	2	3	2
May, rf	4	0	1	0
Perez, 3b	4	1	0	0
Pav'tich, 1b	4	0	2	2
Corrales, c	5	0	2	2
W'dward, ss	5	0	0	0
Culver, p	4	0	0	0
Totals	40	6	12	6

PHILADELPHIA	ab	r	h	rbi
Taylor, 3b	3	0	0	0
Pena, ss	4	0	0	0
Callison, rf	3	0	0	0
Allen, lf	3	1	0	0
White, 1b	4	0	0	0
Lock, cf	3	0	0	0
Rojas, 2b	3	0	0	1
Dalrymple, c	3	0	0	0
Short, p	0	0	0	0
Wagner, p	1	0	0	0
Gonzalez, ph	0	0	0	0
Farrell, p	0	0	0	0
Totals	27	1	0	1

Cincinnati.................. 0 0 3 3 0 0 0 0 0 — 6
Philadelphia............... 0 1 0 0 0 0 0 0 0 — 1

CINCINNATI	ip	h	r	er	bb	so
Culver (W. 9-9)	9	0	1	0	5	4

PHILADELPHIA	ip	h	r	er	bb	so
Short (L. 9-11)	3²/₃	9	6	6	3	4
Wagner	4¹/₃	2	0	0	0	3
Farrell	1	1	0	0	0	1

E—Perez, Corrales, Woodward, Taylor. LOB—Cincinnati 11, Philadelphia 6. 2B—Johnson 2. SB—Johnson. SF—Rojas. HBP—By Wagner (Johnson). U—Jackowski, Secory, Burkhart and Wendelstedt. T—2:43. A—14,083.

Sept. 17, 1968   St. Louis at San Francisco

ST. LOUIS	ab	r	h	rbi
Tolan, lf	4	0	0	0
Flood, cf	4	0	0	0
Maris, rf	3	0	0	0
Cepeda, 1b	3	0	0	0
McCarver, c	3	0	0	0
Shannon, 3b	2	0	0	0
Gagliano, 2b	2	0	0	0
Maxvill, ss	2	0	0	0
Edwards, ph	1	0	0	0
Schofield, ss	0	0	0	0
Gibson, p	2	0	0	0
Brock, ph	1	0	0	0
Totals	27	0	0	0

SAN FRANCISCO	ab	r	h	rbi
Bonds, cf-rf	3	0	1	0
Hunt, 2b	3	1	1	1
Cline, lf	3	0	1	0
McCovey, 1b	3	0	0	0
Hart, 3b	3	0	0	0
Davenp't, 3b	0	0	0	0
Marshall, rf	2	0	0	0
Mays, cf	1	0	0	0
Dietz, c	2	0	0	0
Lanier, ss	3	0	1	0
Perry, p	3	0	0	0
Totals	26	1	4	1

St. Louis .... 0 0 0 0 0 0 0 0 0 — 0
San Francisco............. 1 0 0 0 0 0 0 0 x — 1

ST. LOUIS	ip	h	r	er	bb	so
Gibson (L. 21-8)	8	4	1	1	2	10

SAN FRANCISCO	ip	h	r	er	bb	so
Perry (W. 15-14)	9	0	0	0	2	9

E—None. DP—St. Louis 1. LOB—St. Louis 2, San Francisco 4. 2B—Lanier, Bonds. HR—Hunt. SB—Bonds. SH—Hunt. U—Wendelstedt, Jackowski, Secory and Burkhart. T—1:40. A—9,546.

Sept. 18, 1968   St. Louis at San Francisco

ST. LOUIS	ab	r	h	rbi
Brock, lf	4	0	0	0
Flood, cf	4	0	2	1
Tolan, rf	4	0	1	0
Cepeda, 1b	3	1	1	0
Edwards, c	4	0	0	0
Shannon, 3b	4	0	2	1
Gagliano, 2b	3	0	0	0
Schofield, ss	3	1	1	0
Wash'n, p	2	0	0	0
Totals	31	2	7	2

SAN FRANCISCO	ab	r	h	rbi
Bonds, rf	4	0	0	0
Hunt, 2b	3	0	0	0
Mays, cf	3	0	0	0
McCovey, 1b	3	0	0	0
Hart, 3b	3	0	0	0
Dietz, c	2	0	0	0
Cline, lf	3	0	0	0
Lanier, ss	2	0	0	0
Schroder, ph	1	0	0	0
Mason, ss	0	0	0	0
Bolin, p	2	0	0	0
Marshall, ph	0	0	0	0
Linzy, p	0	0	0	0
Totals	26	0	0	0

St. Louis .... 0 0 0 0 0 0 1 1 0 — 2
San Francisco............. 0 0 0 0 0 0 0 0 0 — 0

ST. LOUIS	ip	h	r	er	bb	so
Washburn (W. 13-7)	9	0	0	0	5	8

SAN FRANCISCO	ip	h	r	er	bb	so
Bolin (L. 9-5)	8	7	2	2	2	6
Linzy	1	0	0	0	0	0

E—Lanier. DP—St. Louis 1, San Francisco 1. LOB—St. Louis 5, San Francisco 4. 2B—Shannon, Schofield. SH—Washburn. U—Jackowski, Secory, Burkhart and Wendelstedt. T—2:19. A—4,703.

April 17, 1969   Montreal at Philadelphia

MONTREAL	ab	r	h	rbi	e
Bosch, cf	4	1	0	0	0
Wills, ss	5	1	1	0	0
Staub, rf	5	2	4	3	0
Jones, lf	4	0	0	0	0
Bailey, 1b	1	0	1	0	0
Cline, 1b	3	0	2	1	0
Bateman, c	4	0	1	0	0
Laboy, 3b	5	2	4	1	0
Sutherland, 2b	3	0	0	0	0
Stoneman, p	3	1	0	0	0
Totals	37	7	13	5	0

PHILADELPHIA	ab	r	h	rbi	e
Taylor, 2b	3	0	0	0	1
Stone, lf	4	0	0	0	0
Briggs, 1b	3	0	0	0	0
D. Johnson, 3b	4	0	0	0	1
Callison, rf	2	0	0	0	0
Money, ss	3	0	0	0	0
Hisle, cf	2	0	0	0	1
Ryan, c	3	0	0	0	0
Wilson, p	0	0	0	0	0
Farrell, p	0	0	0	0	0
J. Johnson, p	2	0	0	0	0
Roznovsky, ph-c	0	0	0	0	0
Totals	26	0	0	0	3

```
Montreal ........................  0 0 1 1 0 2 0 0 3 — 7
Philadelphia ................  0 0 0 0 0 0 0 0 0 — 0
```

MONTREAL	ip	h	r	er	bb	so
Stoneman (W. 1-2)	9	0	0	0	5	8

PHILADELPHIA	ip	h	r	er	bb	so
J. Johnson (L. 0-2)	8	11	4	3	3	7
Wilson	0*	2	3	3	1	0
Farrell	1	0	0	0	1	3

* Pitched to four batters in ninth.

Double plays—Montreal 1, Philadelphia 2. Left on bases—Montreal 9, Philadelphia 4. Two-base hits—Bailey, Staub 3. Home run—Staub. Stolen base—D. Johnson. Sacrifice hit—Bosch. Wild pitch—J. Johnson. Balk—Farrell. Umpires—Gorman, Landes, Williams and Colosi. Time of game—2:24. Attendance—6,494.

April 30, 1969   Houston at Cincinnati

HOUSTON	ab	r	h	rbi	e
Morgan, 2b	3	0	0	0	0
Alou, lf	4	0	0	0	0
Wynn, cf	2	0	0	0	0
Rader, 3b	3	0	0	0	0
Miller, rf	3	0	0	0	0
Menke, ss	2	0	0	0	1
Blefary, 1b	3	0	0	0	1
Edwards, c	3	0	0	0	0
Blasingame, p	1	0	0	0	0
Ray, p	0	0	0	0	0
Geronimo, ph	1	0	0	0	0
Guinn, p	0	0	0	0	0
Geiger, ph	1	0	0	0	0
Coombs, p	0	0	0	0	0
Totals	26	0	0	0	2

CINCINNATI	ab	r	h	rbi	e
Rose, cf	4	2	0	0	0
Tolan, rf	5	0	3	4	0
Johnson, lf	3	1	1	0	0
Savage, lf	0	0	0	0	0
Perez, 3b	4	0	1	0	0
Bench, c	3	1	1	0	0
May, 1b	3	1	0	1	0
Helms, 2b	4	2	1	0	0
Chaney, ss	4	1	1	2	0
Maloney, p	3	2	1	1	0
Totals	33	10	9	8	0

```
Houston .......................  0 0 0 0 0 0 0 0 0 —  0
Cincinnati ...................  1 0 0 7 0 0 0 2 x — 10
```

HOUSTON	ip	h	r	er	bb	so
Blasingame (L.0-5)	3²/₃	3	7	6	3	2
Ray	1¹/₃	2	1	1	1	1
Guinn	2	2	0	0	0	3
Coombs	1	2	2	2	0	1

CINCINNATI	ip	h	r	er	bb	so
Maloney (W. 3-0)	9	0	0	0	5	13

Double plays—Houston 1, Cincinnati 1. Left on bases—Houston 4, Cincinnati 6. Two-base hit—Maloney. Three-base hit—Tolan. Hit by ｐitcher—By Blasingame (Johnson, May), by Coombs (Johnson). Wild pitches—Blasingame, Ray. Umpires—Venzon, Secory, Pryor and Davidson. Time of game—2:28. Attendance—3,898.

May 1, 1969   Houston at Cincinnati

HOUSTON	ab	r	h	rbi	e
Morgan, 2b	3	1	1	0	0
Alou, lf	5	0	0	0	0
Wynn, cf	4	1	1	0	0
Rader, 3b	5	1	1	1	0
Menke, ss	4	0	2	2	0
Miller, rf	4	0	0	0	0
Blefary, 1b	3	1	2	0	0
Bryant, c	4	0	2	0	1
Wilson, p	2	0	0	1	0
Totals	34	4	9	4	1

CINCINNATI	ab	r	h	rbi	e
Rose, cf	2	0	0	0	0
Tolan, rf	4	0	0	0	1
Johnson, lf	4	0	0	0	0
Perez, 3b	4	0	0	0	0
Bench, c	2	0	0	0	0
Whitfield, 1b	2	0	0	0	0
Helms, 2b	4	0	0	0	1
Chaney, ss	2	0	0	0	0
Carroll, p	0	0	0	0	0
Stewart, ph-ss	0	0	0	0	0
Merritt, p	1	0	0	0	0
Ruiz, ss	1	0	0	0	0
Beauchamp, ph	1	0	0	0	0
Noriega, p	0	0	0	0	0
Totals	27	0	0	0	2

```
Houston ..................... 0 0 0 1 2 0 0 1 0 — 4
Cincinnati ................. 0 0 0 0 0 0 0 0 0 — 0
```

HOUSTON	ip	h	r	er	bb	so
Wilson (W. 2-3)	9	0	0	0	6	13

CINCINNATI	ip	h	r	er	bb	so
Merritt (L. 1-2)	5²/₃	6	3	3	3	3
Carroll	2¹/₃	3	1	1	0	1
Noriega	1	0	0	0	1	2

Double play—Cincinnati 1. Left on bases—Houston 10, Cincinnati 7. Two-base hit—Menke. Three-base hit—Blefary. Home run—Rader. Stolen base—Bench. Sacrifice hit—Morgan. Sacrifice fly—Wilson. Hit by pitcher—By Merritt (Wilson), by Wilson (Bench). Umpires—Venzon, Secory, Pryor and Davidson. Time of game—2:32. Attendance—4,042.

August 13, 1969   Oakland at Baltimore

OAKLAND	ab	r	h	rbi	e
Campaneris, ss	4	0	0	0	0
Tartabull, cf	4	0	0	0	0
Jackson, rf	1	0	0	0	0
Bando, 3b	4	0	0	0	0
Cater, 1b	4	0	0	0	0
Green, 2b	2	0	0	0	0
Reynolds, lf	3	0	0	0	0
Duncan, c	2	0	0	0	0
Kubiak, ph	1	0	0	0	0
Haney, c	1	0	0	0	0
Dobson, p	1	0	0	0	0
Webster, ph	1	0	0	0	0
Blue, p	0	0	0	0	0
Lauzerique, p	0	0	0	0	0
Johnson, ph	1	0	0	0	0
Roland, p	0	0	0	0	0
Totals	29	0	0	0	0

BALTIMORE	ab	r	h	rbi	e
Buford, 2b	4	2	3	2	0
Blair, cf	4	0	0	1	1
F. Robinson, rf	4	1	1	1	0
Powell, 1b	4	1	1	0	0
B. Robinson, 3b	4	1	1	3	0
Hendricks, c	2	1	1	0	0
Rettenmund, lf	3	1	0	0	0
Floyd, ss	2	0	1	0	1
Palmer, p	3	1	2	1	0
Totals	30	8	10	8	2

```
Oakland ..................... 0 0 0 0 0 0 0 0 0 — 0
Baltimore ................. 1 0 0 2 0 0 5 0 x — 8
```

OAKLAND	ip	h	r	er	bb	so
Dobson (L. 13-9)	4	6	3	3	4	3
Blue	2¹/₃	3	4	4	1	3
Lauzerique	²/₃	1	1	1	2	0
Roland	1	0	0	0	0	0

BALTIMORE	ip	h	r	er	bb	so
Palmer (W. 11-2)	9	0	0	0	6	3

Double play—Oakland 1. Left on bases—Oakland 8, Baltimore 7. Two-base hit—Palmer. Three-base hit—Buford. Home run—B. Robinson. Stolen base—Buford. Sacrifice hit—Floyd. Sacrifice fly—Blair. Umpires—DiMuro, Neudecker, Chylak and O'Donnell. Time of game—2:22. Attendance—16,826.

August, 19, 1969   Atlanta at Chicago

ATLANTA	ab	r	h	rbi	e
Alou, cf	4	0	0	0	0
Millan, 2b	4	0	0	0	0
H. Aaron, rf	4	0	0	0	0
Carty, lf	2	0	0	0	0
Cepeda, 1b	3	0	0	0	0
Boyer, 3b	3	0	0	0	0
Didier, c	2	0	0	0	0
Garrido, ss	2	0	0	0	0
Niekro, p	2	0	0	0	0
T. Aaron, ph	1	0	0	0	0
Neibauer, p	0	0	0	0	0
Totals	27	0	0	0	0

CHICAGO	ab	r	h	rbi	e
Kessinger, ss	4	1	2	0	0
Beckert, 2b	4	1	1	0	0
Williams, lf	4	0	0	0	0
Santo, 3b	4	1	1	3	0
Banks, 1b	3	0	0	0	0
Hickman, rf	3	0	0	0	0
Heath, c	2	0	0	0	0
G. Oliver, c	0	0	0	0	0
Young, cf	2	0	1	0	0
Holtzman, p	3	0	0	0	0
Totals	29	3	5	3	0

Atlanta	0	0	0	0	0	0	0	0	0	—	0
Chicago	3	0	0	0	0	0	0	0	x	—	3

ATLANTA	ip	h	r	er	bb	so
Niekro (L. 16-11)	7	5	3	3	2	4
Neibauer	1	0	0	0	0	0

CHICAGO	ip	h	r	er	bb	so
Holtzman (W. 14-7)	9	0	0	0	3	0

Left on bases—Atlanta 3, Chicago 4. Home run—Santo. Umpires—Stello, Donatelli, Steiner and Engel. Time of game—2:00. Attendance—37,514.

Sept. 20, 1969   Pittsburgh at New York

PITTSBURGH	ab	r	h	rbi	e
Alou, cf	5	0	1	0	0
Cash, 2b	2	1	0	0	0
Stargell, lf	4	1	1	0	0
Jeter, lf	0	0	0	0	0
Clemente, rf	3	1	0	0	0
Oliver, 1b	3	0	1	0	0
Sanguillen, c	4	1	2	1	0
Hebner, 3b	4	0	1	0	0
Patek, ss	4	0	0	0	0
Moose, p	3	0	0	0	0
Totals	32	4	6	1	0

NEW YORK	ab	r	h	rbi	e
Agee, cf	4	0	0	0	0
Garrett, 3b	4	0	0	0	0
Shamsky, lf	4	0	0	0	0
Boswell, 2b	3	0	0	0	0
Kranepool, 1b	2	0	0	0	0
Swoboda, rf	2	0	0	0	0
Martin, c	3	0	0	0	0
Harrelson, ss	3	0	0	0	0
Gentry, p	1	0	0	0	0
Gosger, ph	1	0	0	0	0
McGraw, p	0	0	0	0	0
Gaspar, ph	0	0	0	0	0
Totals	27	0	0	0	0

Pittsburgh	0	0	0	3	0	0	0	0	1	—	4
New York	0	0	0	0	0	0	0	0	0	—	0

PITTSBURGH	ip	h	r	er	bb	so
Moose (W. 12-3)	9	0	0	0	3	6

NEW YORK	ip	h	r	er	bb	so
Gentry (L. 11-12)	6	4	3	3	3	2
McGraw	3	2	1	1	1	3

Left on bases—Pittsburgh 6, New York 3. Stolen bases—Cash, Stargell. Hit by pitcher—By Gentry (Oliver). Wild pitches—Gentry 2, McGraw. Umpires—Donatelli, Steiner, Engel and Stella. Time of game—2:08. Attendance—38,874.

June 12, 1970   Pittsburgh at San Diego

PITTSBURGH

	ab	r	h	rbi	e
Alou, cf	4	0	0	0	0
Alley, ss	4	0	1	0	0
Clemente, rf	4	0	0	0	0
Robertson, 3b	3	0	0	0	0
Pagan, 3b	1	0	0	0	0
Stargell, lf	3	2	2	2	0
May, c	3	0	0	0	0
Oliver, 1b	3	0	2	0	0
Mazeroski, 2b	3	0	0	0	0
Ellis, p	3	0	0	0	0
Totals	31	2	5	2	0

SAN DIEGO

	ab	r	h	rbi	e
Campbell, 2b	3	0	0	0	0
Huntz, 3b	1	0	0	0	0
Ferrara, lf	4	0	0	0	0
Colbert, 1b	2	0	0	0	0
Brown, rf	3	0	0	0	0
Murrell, cf	3	0	0	0	0
Cannizzaro, c	3	0	0	0	0
Dean, ss	3	0	0	0	0
Kelly, ph	1	0	0	0	0
Roberts, p	2	0	0	0	0
Webster, ph	1	0	0	0	0
Herbel, p	0	0	0	0	0
Spiezio, ph	1	0	0	0	0
Totals	27	0	0	0	

Pittsburgh	0	1	0	0	0	0	1	0	0	—	2
San Diego	0	0	0	0	0	0	0	0	0	—	0

PITTSBURGH

	ip	h	r	er	bb	so
Ellis (W. 5-4)	9	0	0	0	8	6

SAN DIEGO

	ip	h	r	er	bb	so
Roberts (L. 4-3)	7	5	2	2	0	7
Herbel	2	0	0	0	0	0

Left on bases—Pittsburgh 2, San Diego 9. Home runs—Stargell 2 (12). Stolen bases—Murrell, Campbell, Colbert. Hit by pitcher—By Ellis (Murrell). Umpires—Venzon, Secory, Engel and Wendelstedt. Time of game—2:13. Attendance 9,903.

July 3, 1970   Oakland at California

OAKLAND

	ab	r	h	rbi	e
Campaneris, ss	4	0	0	0	0
Alou, rf	4	0	0	0	0
Jackson, cf	3	0	0	0	0
Bando, 3b	2	0	0	0	0
Davis, lf	3	0	0	0	0
Rudi, 1b	3	0	0	0	0
Duncan, c	2	0	0	0	0
Green, 2b	3	0	0	0	0
Dobson, p	1	0	0	0	0
LaRussa, ph	1	0	0	0	0
Roland, p	0	0	0	0	0
Fernandez, ph	0	0	0	0	0
Tartabull, pr	0	0	0	0	0
Totals	26	0	0	0	0

CALIFORNIA

	ab	r	h	rbi	e
Alomar, 2b	4	0	0	0	0
Repoz, rf	3	1	1	0	0
Fregosi, ss	4	0	0	1	0
Johnson, lf	3	1	1	0	0
Tatum, lf	0	0	0	0	0
Spencer, 1b	3	1	1	0	0
McMullen, 3b	3	1	1	3	0
Azcue, c	3	0	1	0	0
Johnstone, cf	3	0	0	0	0
Wright, p	3	0	0	0	0
Totals	29	4	5	4	0

Oakland	0	0	0	0	0	0	0	0	0	—	0
California	1	0	0	3	0	0	0	0	x	—	4

OAKLAND

	ip	h	r	er	bb	so
Dobson (L. 7-9)	5	4	4	4	2	2
Roland	3	1	0	0	0	2

CALIFORNIA

	ip	h	r	er	bb	so
Wright (W. 12-5)	9	0	0	0	3	1

Double play—California 1. Left on bases—Oakland 2, California 3. Two-base hit—Spencer. Three-base hit—Repoz. Home run—McMullen (9). Umpires—Napp, Rice, Springstead and Barnett. Time of game—1:51. Attendance—12,131.

July 20, 1970   Philadelphia at Los Angeles

PHILADELPHIA	ab	r	h	rbi	e
Doyle, 2b	4	0	0	0	0
Gamble, rf	1	0	0	0	0
Browne, rf	2	0	0	0	0
Money, 3b	3	0	0	0	1
Johnson, 1b	3	0	0	0	0
Briggs, lf	3	0	0	0	0
Hisle, cf	3	0	0	0	0
Bowa, ss	3	0	0	0	1
Ryan, c	3	0	0	0	0
Fryman, p	1	0	0	0	0
Palmer, p	1	0	0	0	0
Harmon, ph	1	0	0	0	0
Totals	28	0	0	0	2

LOS ANGELES	ab	r	h	rbi	e
Grabarkewitz, ss	4	1	1	0	0
Sizemore, lf	4	1	1	0	0
Wills, 3b	0	0	0	0	0
Davis, cf	3	1	1	1	0
Parker, 1b	4	1	2	1	0
Lefebvre, 2b	4	0	3	1	0
Garvey, 3b	4	1	0	0	0
Joshua, lf	0	0	0	0	0
Russell, rf	4	0	2	2	0
Torborg, c	4	0	1	0	0
Singer, p	4	0	0	0	2
Totals	35	5	11	5	2

Philadelphia	0	0	0	0	0	0	0	0	0	—	0
Los Angeles	2	0	1	0	2	0	0	0	x	—	5

PHILADELPHIA	ip	h	r	er	bb	so
Fryman (L. 6-6)	4²/₃	5	5	0	3	
Palmer	3¹/₃	1	0	0	0	5

LOS ANGELES	ip	h	r	er	bb	so
Singer (W. 7-3)	9	0	0	0	0	10

Left on bases—Philadelphia 2, Los Angeles 7. Two-base hits—Parker, Russell. Stolen bases—Davis, Parker. Sacrifice fly—Davis. Hit by pitcher—By Singer (Gamble). Umpires—Sudol, Steiner, Williams and Colosi. Time of game—2:10. Attendance—12,454.

Sept. 21, 1970   Minnesota at Oakland

MINNESOTA	ab	r	h	rbi	e
Tovar, cf-lf	4	0	0	0	0
Cardenas, ss	3	0	0	0	0
Killebrew, 1b	2	0	0	0	0
Oliva, rf	3	0	0	0	0
Alyea, lf	3	0	0	0	0
Holt, cf	0	0	0	0	0
Renick, 3b	3	0	0	0	0
Mitterwald, c	3	0	0	0	0
Thompson, 2b	3	0	0	0	1
Perry, p	2	0	0	0	0
Allison, ph	1	0	0	0	0
Totals	27	0	0	0	1

OAKLAND	ab	r	h	rbi	e
Campaneris, ss	5	2	2	3	0
Rudi, lf	2	0	1	0	0
Hovley, cf	2	0	1	0	0
Alou, rf-lf	4	0	1	0	0
Mincher, 1b	3	1	2	0	0
Bando, 3b	3	1	1	0	0
Jackson, cf-rf	3	0	0	0	0
Tenace, c	2	1	0	0	0
Green, 2b	4	1	1	1	0
Blue, p	2	0	0	0	0
Totals	30	6	9	4	0

Minnesota	0	0	0	0	0	0	0	0	0	—	0
Oakland	1	0	0	0	0	0	0	5	x	—	6

MINNESOTA	ip	h	r	er	bb	so
Perry (L. 23-12)	8	9	6	2	5	3

OAKLAND	ip	h	r	er	bb	so
Blue (W. 2-0)	9	0	0	0	1	9

Double play—Minnesota 1. Left on bases—Minnesota 1, Oakland 8. Two-base hit—Alou. Three-base hit—Campaneris. Home run—Campaneris (21). Sacrifice hit —Blue. Hit by pitcher—By Perry (Mincher, Bando). Umpires—Napp, Rice, Springstead and Barnett. Time of game—2:21. Attendance—4,284.

June 3, 1971   Chicago at Cincinnati

CHICAGO

	ab	r	h	bi
Kessinger, ss	4	0	1	0
Beckert, 2b	4	0	2	1
B. Williams, lf	4	0	1	0
Santo, 3b	4	0	0	0
Pepitone, 1b	4	0	1	0
B. Davis, cf	4	0	0	0
Callison, rf	3	0	1	0
D. Breeden, c	3	0	0	0
Holtzman, p	3	1	0	0
Total	33	1	6	1

CINCINNATI

	ab	r	h	bi
McRae, lf	3	0	0	0
Helms, 2b	4	0	0	0
L. May, 1b	3	0	0	0
Bench, c	3	0	0	0
T. Perez, 3b	3	0	0	0
Foster, cf	3	0	0	0
Bradford, rf	1	0	0	0
Concepcn, ss	3	0	0	0
Nolan, p	2	0	0	0
Ferrara, ph	1	0	0	0
Gibbon, p	0	0	0	0
Total	26	0	0	0

```
Chicago.................... 0 0 1 0 0 0 0 0 0 — 1
Cincinnati................. 0 0 0 0 0 0 0 0 0 — 0
```

CHICAGO

	ip	h	r	er	bb	so
Holtzman (W, 3-6).	9	0	0	0	4	6

CINCINNATI

	ip	h	r	er	bb	so
Nolan (L, 3-6)	8	5	1	0	0	3
Gibbon	1	1	0	0	0	0

E—T. Perez. DP—Chicago 1. LOB—Chicago 5, Cincinnati 3. SB—Kessinger, McRae. WP—Holtzman. T—1:55. A—11,751.

June 23, 1971   Philadelphia at Cincinnati

PHILADELPHIA

	ab	r	h	rbi	e
Harmon, 2b	4	0	0	0	0
Bowa, ss	4	0	0	0	0
McCarver, c	3	0	2	0	0
Johnson, 1b	2	0	0	0	0
Lis, lf	2	1	0	0	0
Stone, lf	1	0	0	0	0
Montanez, cf	4	0	1	0	0
Freed, rf	4	1	1	1	0
Vukovich, 3b	4	0	1	0	0
Wise, p	4	2	2	3	0
Totals	32	4	7	4	0

CINCINNATI

	ab	r	h	rbi	e
Rose, rf	4	0	0	0	0
Foster, cf	3	0	0	0	0
May, 1b	3	0	0	0	0
Bench, c	3	0	0	0	0
Perez, 3b	3	0	0	0	0
McRae, lf	3	0	0	0	0
Granger, p	0	0	0	0	0
Helms, 2b	3	0	0	0	0
Concepcion, ss	1	0	0	0	0
Stewart, ph	1	0	0	0	0
Grimsley, p	1	0	0	0	0
Carbo, ph	1	0	0	0	0
Carroll, p	0	0	0	0	0
Cline, lf	1	0	0	0	0
Totals	27	0	0	0	0

```
Philadelphia................ 0 1 0 0 2 0 0 1 0 — 4
Cincinnati................... 0 0 0 0 0 0 0 0 0 — 0
```

PHILADELPHIA

	ip	h	r	er	bb	so
Wise (W. 8-4)	9	0	0	0	1	3

CINCINNATI

	ip	h	r	er	bb	so
Grimsley (L. 4-3)	6	4	3	3	2	1
Carroll	2	2	1	1	1	1
Granger	1	1	0	0	0	1

Double plays—Cincinnati 2. Left on bases—Philadelphia 5, Cincinnati 1. Two-base hits—Montanez, Freed. Home runs—Wise 2 (4). Hit by pitcher—By Grimsley (Lis). Umpires—Dale, Gorman, Pelekoudas and Harvey. Time of game—1:53. Attendance—13,329.

August 14, 1971   St. Louis at Pittsburgh

ST. LOUIS	ab	r	h	rbi	e
Alou, 1b	4	1	0	0	0
Sizemore, lf	6	0	2	0	0
Cruz, cf	6	1	1	0	0
Torre, 3b	6	2	4	1	0
Simmons, c	6	3	4	1	0
Hague, rf	3	3	2	3	0
Kubiak, 2b	4	1	2	2	0
Maxvill, ss	3	0	0	1	0
Gibson, p	4	0	1	3	0
Totals	42	11	16	11	0

PITTSBURGH	ab	r	h	rbi	e
Cash, 3b	4	0	0	0	0
Davalillo, rf	4	0	0	0	0
Oliver, cf	4	0	0	0	0
Stargell, lf	3	0	0	0	0
May, c	3	0	0	0	0
Robertson, 1b	2	0	0	0	0
Mazeroski, 2b	3	0	0	0	1
Hernandez, ss	2	0	0	0	0
Johnson, p	0	0	0	0	0
Moose, p	1	0	0	0	1
Sands, ph	1	0	0	0	0
Veale, p	0	0	0	0	0
Clines, ph	1	0	0	0	0
Briles, p	0	0	0	0	0
Totals	28	0	0	0	2

```
St. Louis .................... 5 0 0 0 3 0 0 3 0 — 11
Pittsburgh.................. 0 0 0 0 0 0 0 0 0 — 0
```

ST. LOUIS	ip	h	r	er	bb	so
Gibson (W. 11-10)	9	0	0	0	3	10

PITTSBURGH	ip	h	r	er	bb	so
Johnson (L. 7-8)	1/3	4	5	5	1	0
Moose	4 2/3	6	3	3	2	0
Veale	3	5	3	3	3	0
Briles	1	1	0	0	0	0

Double play—Pittsburgh 1. Left on bases—St. Louis 12. Pittsburgh 4. Two-base hits—Simmons, Kubiak. Home run—Hague (11). Sacrifice fly—Gibson. Wild pitch—Gibson. Umpires—Wendelstedt, Olsen, Gorman and Pelekoudas. Time of game—2:22. Attendance—30,678.

April 16, 1972   Philadelphia at Chicago

PHILADELPHIA	ab	r	h	rbi	e
Bowa, ss	3	0	0	0	0
McCarver, c	4	0	0	0	1
Montanez, cf	2	0	0	0	0
Johnson, 1b	4	0	0	0	0
Luzinski, lf	3	0	0	0	0
Money, 3b	1	0	0	0	0
Anderson, rf	2	0	0	0	0
Doyle, 2b	3	0	0	0	0
Brandon, p	0	0	0	0	0
Reynolds, p	0	0	0	0	0
Selma, p	1	0	0	0	0
Stone, ph	0	0	0	0	0
Short, p	0	0	0	0	0
Harmon, 2b	1	0	0	0	0
Totals	24	0	0	0	1

CHICAGO	ab	r	h	rbi	e
Cardenal, rf	5	1	2	0	0
Beckert, 2b	4	0	1	1	0
Williams, lf	5	1	3	0	0
Pepitone, 1b	5	1	2	0	0
Santo, 3b	5	1	3	0	0
Monday, cf	2	0	0	0	0
Kessinger, ss	3	0	0	0	0
Hundley, c	2	0	1	2	0
Hooton, p	4	0	0	0	0
Totals	35	4	12	3	0

```
Philadelphia................ 0 0 0 0 0 0 0 0 0 — 0
Chicago....................... 0 0 0 1 0 0 2 1 x — 4
```

PHILADELPHIA	ip	h	r	er	bb	so
Selma (L. 0-1)	5	6	1	0	4	0
Short	1 2/3	4	2	2	1	2
Brandon	1/3*	2	1	1	0	0
Reynolds	1	0	0	0	0	0

CHICAGO	ip	h	r	er	bb	so
Hooton (W. 1-0)	9	0	0	0	7	7

* Pitched to two batters in eighth.

Double plays—Philadelphia 1, Chicago 1. Left on bases—Philadelphia 5, Chicago 13. Two-base hit—Santo. Three-base hit—Cardenal. Sacrifice hits—Kessinger, Bowa. Umpires—Pryor, Wendelstedt, Froemming and Vargo. Time of game—2:33. Attendance—9,583.

Sept. 2, 1972 San Diego at Chicago

SAN DIEGO	ab	r	h	rbi	e
Hernandez, ss	3	0	0	0	1
Jestadt, ph	1	0	0	0	0
Roberts, lf	3	0	0	0	0
Lee, 3b	3	0	0	0	0
Colbert, 1b	3	0	0	0	0
Gaston, rf	3	0	0	0	0
Thomas, 2b	3	0	0	0	0
Jeter, cf	3	0	0	0	0
Kendall, c	3	0	0	0	0
Caldwell, p	2	0	0	0	0
Severinsen, p	0	0	0	0	0
Stahl, ph	0	0	0	0	0
Totals	27	0	0	0	1

CHICAGO	ab	r	h	rbi	e
Kessinger, ss	5	1	2	3	0
Cardenal, rf	4	1	2	1	0
Williams, lf	4	1	2	0	0
Santo, 3b	3	1	0	0	0
Hickman, 1b	4	1	3	1	0
Fanzone, 2b	3	1	0	1	0
Hundley, c	4	1	2	0	0
North, cf	4	1	2	1	0
Pappas, p	4	0	0	0	0
Totals	35	8	13	7	0

San Diego	0	0	0	0	0	0	0	0	0	—	0
Chicago	2	0	2	0	0	0	0	4	x	—	8

SAN DIEGO	ip	h	r	er	bb	so
Caldwell (L. 6-8)	7²/₃	13	8	6	2	4
Severinsen	¹/₃	0	0	0	0	0

CHICAGO	ip	h	r	er	bb	so
Pappas (W. 12-7)	9	0	0	0	1	6

Double plays—San Diego 3. Left on bases—San Diego 1, Chicago 6. Two-base hits—Hickman, Kessinger. Hit by pitcher—By Caldwell (Santo). Umpires—Froemming, Donatelli, Landes and Davidson. Time of game—2:03. Attendance—11,144.

October 2, 1972 New York at Montreal

NEW YORK	ab	h	r	rbi	e
Barnes, 2b	3	0	0	0	0
Fregosi, 3b	3	0	0	0	0
Milner, lf	2	0	0	0	0
Kranepool, 1b	4	0	0	0	1
Sudakis, c	3	0	0	0	0
Schneck, cf	3	0	0	0	0
Hahn, rf	3	0	0	0	0
Martinez, ss	3	0	0	0	0
McAndrew, p	1	0	0	0	0
Strom, p	0	0	0	0	0
Marshall, ph	1	0	0	0	0
Rauch, p	0	0	0	0	0
Garrett, ph	1	0	0	0	0
Sadecki, p	0	0	0	0	0
Totals	27	0	0	0	1

MONTREAL	ab	r	h	rbi	e
Hunt, 2b	4	3	2	0	0
McCarver, c	4	1	2	0	0
Singleton, lf	4	1	2	2	0
Fairly, 1b	4	1	2	1	0
Fairey, rf	3	1	1	0	0
Day, cf	4	0	1	3	0
Foli, ss	4	0	0	0	0
Laboy, 3b	3	0	0	0	0
Stoneman, p	3	0	0	0	1
Totals	33	7	10	6	1

New York	0	0	0	0	0	0	0	0	0	—	0
Montreal	2	0	4	1	0	0	0	0	x	—	7

NEW YORK	ip	h	r	er	bb	so
McAn'w (L. 11-8)	2¹/₃	6	6	6	1	2
Strom	1²/₃	3	1	1	0	1
Rauch	3	1	0	0	0	3
Sadecki	1	0	0	0	1	0

MONTREAL	ip	h	r	er	bb	so
Sto'man (W. 12-14)	9	0	0	0	7	9

Double plays—New York 1, Montreal 1. Left on bases—New York 7, Montreal 6. Two-base hits—Hunt, Fairly. Three-base hit—Day. Home run—Fairly (16). Sacrifice hit—Stoneman. Hit by pitcher—By McAndrew (Hunt). Wild pitch—McAndrew. Umpires—Burkhart, Weyer, Olsen and McSherry. Time of game—2:14. Attendance—7,184.

April 27, 1973　Kansas City at Detroit

KANSAS CITY	ab	r	h	rbi	e	DETROIT	ab	r	h	rbi	e
Patek, ss	4	0	0	0	0	Northrup, rf	4	0	0	0	0
Hovley, dh	4	0	1	0	0	Rodriguez, 3b	3	0	0	0	1
McRae, dh	1	0	0	0	0	Sims, ph	0	0	0	0	0
Otis, cf	4	1	1	1	0	Reese, lf	3	0	0	0	0
Mayberry, 1b	3	0	0	0	0	Freehan, c	2	0	0	0	0
Paniella, lf	4	0	2	0	0	G. Brown, dh	3	0	0	0	0
Kirkpatrick, rf	4	2	3	1	0	Cash, 1b	1	0	0	0	1
Rojas, 2b	3	0	1	0	0	McAuliffe, 2b	3	0	0	0	0
Schaal, 3b	4	0	0	0	0	Stanley, cf	3	0	0	0	0
Healy, c	4	0	0	0	0	Brinkman, ss	3	0	0	0	0
Busby, p	0	0	0	0	0	Perry, p	0	0	0	0	0
						Scherman, p	0	0	0	0	0
Totals	35	3	8	2	0	Totals	25	0	0	0	2

Kansas City .... 0 0 0 0 1 0 0 1 1 — 3
Detroit .... 0 0 0 0 0 0 0 0 0 — 0

KANSAS CITY	ip	h	r	er	bb	so	DETROIT	ip	h	r	er	bb	so
Busby (W. 2-2)	9	0	0	0	6	4	Perry (L. 2-2)	8²/₃	8	3	2	2	2
							Scherman	¹/₃	0	0	0	0	0

Double plays—Kansas City 2, Detroit 1. Left on bases—Kansas City 8. Detroit 4. Home runs—Kirkpatrick (3), Otis (4). Sacrifice hit—Rojas. Wild pitch—Busby. Passed balls—Healy, Freehan. Umpires—Rice, Goetz, Maloney and Evans. Time—2:18. Attendance—16,345.

May 15, 1973　California at Kansas City

CALIFORNIA	ab	r	h	rbi	e	KANSAS CITY	ab	r	h	rbi	e
Pinson, lf	5	1	2	0	0	Patek, ss	4	0	0	0	0
Alomar, 2b	4	0	0	0	0	Hovley, rf	3	0	0	0	0
Valentine, cf	4	0	1	0	0	Otis, cf	4	0	0	0	0
Robinson, dh	3	1	1	0	0	Mayberry, 1b	3	0	0	0	0
Oliver, rf	4	1	2	2	0	Rojas, 2b	3	0	0	0	0
Berry, rf	0	0	0	0	0	Kirkpatrick, dh-c	3	0	0	0	0
Gallagher, 3b	4	0	2	1	0	Piniella, lf	3	0	0	0	0
Spencer, 1b	4	0	1	0	0	Schaal, 3b	2	0	0	0	0
Meoli, ss	4	0	1	0	0	Taylor, c	1	0	0	0	0
Torborg, c	4	0	1	0	0	Hopkins, ph	1	0	0	0	0
Ryan, p	0	0	0	0	0	Dal Canton, p	0	0	0	0	0
						Garber, p	0	0	0	0	0
Totals	36	3	11	3	0	Totals	27	0	0	0	0

California .... 2 0 0 0 0 1 0 0 0 — 3
Kansas City .... 0 0 0 0 0 0 0 0 0 — 0

CALIFORNIA	ip	h	r	er	bb	so	KANSAS CITY	ip	h	r	er	bb	so
Ryan (W. 5-3)	9	0	0	0	3	12	Dal Cant'n (L. 2-2)	5²/₃	8	3	3	1	0
							Garber	3¹/₃	3	0	0	0	0

DP—Kansas City 1. LOB—California 8, Kansas City 3. HR—Oliver (4). SB—Hovley. SH—Alomar. U—Evans, Rice, Goetz and Maloney. T—2:20. A—12,205.

July 15, 1973 California at Detroit

CALIFORNIA	ab	r	h	rbi	e
Alomar, 2b	5	0	2	0	0
Pinson, rf	4	0	0	1	0
McCraw, lf	2	0	0	0	0
Llenas, ph	1	0	1	2	0
Stanton, pr-lf	0	1	0	0	0
Epstein, 1b	3	1	1	0	0
Oliver, dh	3	1	1	1	0
Berry, cf	3	0	0	0	0
Gallagher, 3b	4	0	2	2	0
Meoli, ss	4	1	1	0	0
Kusnyer, c	3	2	1	0	0
Ryan, p	0	0	0	0	0
Totals	32	6	9	6	0

DETROIT	ab	r	h	rbi	e
Northrup, lf	4	0	0	0	0
Stanely, cf	3	0	0	0	0
G. Brown, dh	2	0	0	0	0
Cash, 1b	4	0	0	0	0
Sims, c	3	0	0	0	0
McAuliffe, 2b	3	0	0	0	0
Sharon, rf	2	0	0	0	0
Rodriguez, 3b	3	0	0	0	0
Brinkman, ss	3	0	0	0	0
Perry, p	0	0	0	0	0
Scherman, p	0	0	0	0	0
Miller, p	0	0	0	0	0
Farmer, p	0	0	0	0	0
Totals	27	0	0	0	0

```
California.............. 0 0 1 0 0 0 0 5 0 — 6
Detroit................. 0 0 0 0 0 0 0 0 0 — 0
```

CALIFORNIA	ip	h	r	er	bb	so
Ryan 11-11	9	0	0	0	4	17

DETROIT	ip	h	r	er	bb	so
Perry 9-9	7⅓	5	3	3	3	2
Scherman	⅓	0	0	0	0	0
Miller	0*	2	3	3	1	0
Farmer	1⅓	2	0	0	1	0

* Faced three batters in eighth.

DP—Detroit 2. LOB—Calif. 5, Det. 4. 2B—Epstein, Meoli. SF—Pinson. U—Luciano, Phillips and Haller. Time—2:21. Attendance—41,411.

July 30, 1973 Texas at Oakland

TEXAS	ab	r	h	rbi	e
Nelson, 2b	4	0	2	0	0
Harris, cf-rf	2	1	0	0	0
Fregosi, ss	4	1	0	0	0
Mackanin, ss	0	0	0	0	0
A. Johnson, dh	4	1	2	0	0
Burroughs, lf	4	1	2	4	0
Maddox, pr-cf	0	1	0	0	0
Sudakis, 3b	3	1	1	1	0
Spencer, 1b	4	0	1	1	0
Grieve, rf-lf	4	0	1	0	0
Billings, c	4	0	0	0	0
Bibby, p	0	0	0	0	0
Totals	33	6	9	6	0

OAKLAND	ab	r	h	rbi	e
Campaneris, ss	3	0	0	0	0
North, cf	4	0	0	0	0
Bando, 3b	3	0	0	0	0
Jackson, rf	2	0	0	0	1
D. Johnson, dh	3	0	0	0	0
Tenace, 1b-c	3	0	0	0	0
Conigliaro, lf	3	0	0	0	0
Fosse, c	2	0	0	0	0
Johnstone, ph	1	0	0	0	0
Hegan, 1b	0	0	0	0	0
Kubiak, 2b	3	0	0	0	1
Blue, p	0	0	0	0	0
Totals	27	0	0	0	2

```
Texas.......................... 5 0 0 0 0 0 0 0 1 — 6
Oakland...................... 0 0 0 0 0 0 0 0 0 — 0
```

TEXAS	ip	h	r	er	bb	so
Bibby (W. 5-4)	9	0	0	0	6	13

OAKLAND	ip	h	r	er	bb	so
Blue (L. 9-7)	9	9	6	5	1	5

Double plays—Oakland 2. Left on bases—Texas 3, Oakland 6. Home runs—Burroughs (17), Sudakis (7). Stolen base—Bando. Sacrifice hits—Harris, Sudakis. Umpires—Frantz, Phillips, Umont and Barnett. Time—2:10. Attendance—21,606.

August 5, 1973   San Diego at Atlanta

SAN DIEGO	ab	r	h	rbi	e
Anderson, ss	3	0	0	0	0
Grubb, cf	4	0	0	0	0
Roberts, 3b	4	0	0	0	1
Colbert, 1b	3	0	0	0	0
Gaston, rf	4	0	0	0	0
Locklear, lf	3	0	0	0	0
Kendall, c	2	0	0	0	0
Corrales, c	0	0	0	0	0
R. Morales, 2b	3	0	0	0	0
Arlin, p	1	0	0	0	0
Romo, p	1	0	0	0	0
Winfield, ph	1	0	0	0	0
Ross, p	0	0	0	0	0
Totals	29	0	0	0	1

ATLANTA	ab	r	h	rbi	e
Garr, rf	3	3	3	0	0
Jackson, rf	2	1	1	0	0
Lum, lf	4	1	1	1	0
Evans, 3b	0	2	0	1	1
Baker, cf	5	1	2	2	0
Johnson, 2b	3	0	1	0	0
Goggin, 2b	0	0	0	1	0
Tepedino, 1b	4	0	2	2	0
Perez, ss	4	0	1	0	1
Casanova, c	4	1	1	1	0
Niekro, p	3	0	0	0	0
Totals	32	9	12	8	2

```
San Diego....................  0 0 0 0 0 0 0 0 0 — 0
Atlanta .......................  1 0 2 1 0 4 0 1 x — 9
```

SAN DIEGO	ip	h	r	er	bb	so
Arlin (L. 6-10)	2*	5	3	3	2	1
Romo	5	6	5	2	5	2
Ross	1	1	1	0	1	0

ATLANTA	ip	h	r	er	bb	so
Niekro (W. 11-5)	9	0	0	0	3	4

* Pitched to four batters in third.

Double plays—San Diego 2. Left on bases—San Diego 5, Atlanta 9. Two-base hits—Garr 2. Home runs—Casanova (4). Stolen bases—Garr, Jackson. Sacrifice flies —Evans, Goggin. Passed balls—Kendall, Corrales. Umpires—Tata, Vargo, Pryor and Froemming. Time—2:26. Attendance—8,748.

June 19, 1974   Kansas City at Milwaukee

KANSAS CITY	ab	r	h	rbi	e
Patek, ss	4	0	2	0	0
Rojas, 2b	4	0	1	0	0
Otis, cf	4	0	1	0	0
Mayberry, 1b	3	1	0	0	0
McRae, dh	4	0	1	0	0
Wohlford, lf	4	1	1	0	0
Cowens, rf	3	0	0	0	0
Brett, 3b	3	0	1	1	0
Healy, c	3	0	0	0	0
Busby, p	0	0	0	0	0
Totals	32	2	7	1	0

MILWAUKEE	ab	r	h	rbi	e
Money, 3b	4	0	0	0	0
Yount, ss	3	0	0	0	1
May, lf	3	0	0	0	0
Scott, 1b	2	0	0	0	0
Briggs, lf	3	0	0	0	0
Porter, c	3	0	0	0	1
Hansen, dh	3	0	0	0	0
Coluccio, cf	3	0	0	0	0
Johnson, 2b	3	0	0	0	0
Wright, p	0	0	0	0	0
Totals	27	0	0	0	2

```
Kansas City .................  0 1 0 1 0 0 0 0 0 — 2
Milwaukee ...................  0 0 0 0 0 0 0 0 0 — 0
```

KANSAS CITY	ip	h	r	er	bb	so
Busby (W. 9-6)	9	0	0	0	1	3

MILWAUKEE	ip	h	r	er	bb	so
Wright (L. 5-9)	9	7	2	1	2	2

DP—Milwaukee 2. LOB—Kansas City 5, Milwaukee 1. U—Brinkman, Bremigan, Chylak and McCoy. T—2:03. A—9,019.

July 20, 1974 Oakland at Cleveland

OAKLAND	ab	r	h	bi
North, cf	4	0	0	0
Campnris, ss	3	0	0	0
Bando, 3b	3	0	0	0
R. Jackson, rf	3	0	0	0
Rudi, lf	3	0	0	0
C. Whntg, dh	3	0	0	0
Bourque, 1b	3	0	0	0
D. Green, 2b	3	0	0	0
Haney, c	2	0	0	0
J. Alou, ph	1	0	0	0
Hamilton, p	0	0	0	0
Odom, p	0	0	0	0
Knowles, p	0	0	0	0
Total	28	0	0	0

CLEVELAND	ab	r	h	bi
Lowenstn, lf	3	0	0	0
R. Torres, lf	0	0	0	0
Duffy, ss	4	0	0	0
Hendrick, cf	3	0	1	0
Spikes, rf	3	0	0	0
Ellis, c	3	1	1	0
B. Bell, 3b	3	1	2	1
McCraw, 1b	3	1	1	1
Lis, dh	2	1	1	2
Gamble, dh	1	0	0	0
Brohamr, 2b	2	0	1	0
Bosman, p	0	0	0	0
Total	27	4	7	4

```
Oakland.................... 0 0 0 0 0 0 0 0 0 — 0
Cleveland................. 0 0 2 2 0 0 0 0 x — 4
```

OAKLAND	ip	h	r	er	bb	so
Hamilton (L, 6-3)	3⅓	5	4	4	0	4
Odom	3⅔	1	0	0	1	1
Knowles	1	1	0	0	0	0

CLEVELAND	ip	h	r	er	bb	so
Bosman (W, 2-0)	9	0	0	0	0	4

E—Bosman. DP—Oakland 2. LOB—Oakland 1, Cleveland 1. 2B—B. Bell. HR—Lis (2). HBP—By Hamilton (Brohamer). T—1:56. A—24,302.

Sept. 28, 1974 Minnesota at California

MINNESOTA	ab	r	h	rbi	e
Brye, cf	2	0	0	0	0
Carew, 2b	2	0	0	0	0
Braun, 3b	3	0	0	0	1
Darwin, rf	4	0	0	0	0
Oliva, dh	3	0	0	0	0
Hisle, lf	3	0	0	0	0
Bourque, 1b	3	0	0	0	0
Killebrew, ph	0	0	0	0	0
Terrell, pr	0	0	0	0	0
Gomez, ss	2	0	0	0	1
Soderholm, ss	2	0	0	0	0
Borgmann, c	3	0	0	0	0
Decker, p	0	0	0	0	0
Butler, p	0	0	0	0	0
Totals	27	0	0	0	2

CALIFORNIA	ab	r	h	rbi	e
Nettles, cf	4	1	2	3	0
Doyle, 2b	4	0	1	0	0
Bochte, 1b	3	0	0	1	0
Lahoud, dh	4	0	1	0	0
Stanton, rf	4	0	1	0	0
Chalk, 3b	2	1	0	0	0
Balaz, lf	2	1	1	0	0
Meoli, ss	2	1	1	0	0
Egan, c	2	0	0	0	0
Ryan, p	0	0	0	0	0
Totals	27	4	7	4	0

```
Minnesota................... 0 0 0 0 0 0 0 0 0 — 0
California................... 0 0 2 2 0 0 0 0 x — 4
```

MINNESOTA	ip	h	r	er	bb	so
Decker (L. 16-14)	2⅔	4	2	1	0	1
Butler	5⅓	3	2	1	3	8

CALIFORNIA	ip	h	r	er	bb	so
Ryan (W. 22-16)	9	0	0	0	8	15

LOB—Minnesota 8, California 4. 2B—Meoli. SB—Nettles. SH—Egan. SF—Bochte. U—Haller, Kunkel, Anthony and Rodriguez. T—2:22. A—10,872.

June 1, 1975 Baltimore at California

BALTIMORE (A.)	ab	r	h	bi
Singleton, rf	4	0	0	0
Shopay, cf	3	0	0	0
Bumbry, lf	4	0	0	0
Baylor, dh	2	0	0	0
T. Davis, dh	2	0	0	0
Grich, 2b	2	0	0	0
L. May, 1b	3	0	0	0
B. Robinson, 3b	3	0	0	0
Hendricks, c	3	0	0	0
Belanger, ss	2	0	0	0
Grimsley, p	0	0	0	0
Garland, p	0	0	0	0
Total	28	0	0	0

CALIFORNIA (A.)	ab	r	h	bi
Remy, 2b	3	0	1	0
Rivers, cf	4	1	1	0
Harper, dh	4	0	1	0
Chalk, 3b	3	0	2	1
Lienes, lf	3	0	1	0
M. Nettles, lf	0	0	0	0
Stanton, rf	2	0	1	0
Bochte, 1b	3	0	1	0
El. Rdrgez, c	3	0	0	0
B. Smith, ss	2	0	1	0
Ryan, p	0	0	0	0
Total	27	1	9	1

```
Baltimore.................... 0 0 0 0 0 0 0 0 0 — 0
California.................... 0 0 1 0 0 0 0 0 x — 1
```

BALTIMORE	ip	h	r	er	bb	so
Grimsley (L, 1-7)	3⅓	8	1	1	0	1
Garland	4⅔	1	0	0	1	1

CALIFORNIA	ip	h	r	er	bb	so
Ryan (W, 9-3)	9	0	0	0	4	9

E—B. Smith. DP—Baltimore 2. LOB—Baltimore 5, California 5. SB—Belanger. S—Stanton, Remy. T—2:01. A—18,492.

August 24, 1975 New York at San Francisco

NEW YORK	ab	r	h	bi
Unser, cf	3	0	0	0
Millan, 2b	4	0	0	0
W. Garrett, 3b	4	0	0	0
Staub, rf	3	0	0	0
Kingman, 1b	3	0	0	0
Milner, lf	3	0	0	0
Phillips, ss	3	0	0	0
Stearns, c	3	0	0	0
Swan, p	1	0	0	0
Vail, ph	0	0	0	0
Baldwin, p	0	0	0	0
Alou, ph	1	0	0	0
Total	28	0	0	0

SAN FRANCISCO	ab	r	h	bi
D. Thomas, 2b	2	2	0	0
DaRader, c	3	2	1	0
Thomasn, cf	4	2	3	2
Matthews, lf	3	0	0	0
Montanez, 1b	4	0	2	2
Speier, ss	4	0	1	0
Ontiveros, rf	4	0	1	0
B. Miller, 3b	3	0	0	0
Halicki, p	4	0	0	0
Total	31	6	8	4

```
New York.................... 0 0 0 0 0 0 0 0 0 — 0
San Francisco............. 2 0 0 0 2 0 2 0 x — 6
```

NEW YORK	ip	h	r	er	bb	so
Swan (L. 1-1)	5	4	4	4	3	5
Baldwin	3	4	2	2	2	1

SAN FRANCISCO	ip	h	r	er	bb	so
Halicki (W. 8-10)	9	0	0	0	2	10

E—D. Thomas. DP—New York 1. LOB—New York 3, San Francisco 6. 2B—Speier. 3B—Thomasson. SB—D. Thomas 3, DaRader, Thomasson. WP—Baldwin. T—2·15. A—24,132.

Sept. 28, 1975 California at Oakland

CALIFORNIA	ab	r	h	bi
Remy, 2b	4	0	0	0
Chalk, 3b	2	0	0	0
Rivers, ph	1	0	0	0
Stanton, cf	3	0	0	0
Balaz, rf	3	0	0	0
Bochte, 1b	3	0	0	0
Jackson, lf	2	0	0	0
M. Nettles, lf	1	0	0	0
Dade, dh	1	0	0	0
D. Briggs, dh	1	0	0	0
Allietta, c	3	0	0	0
Hampton, ss	2	0	0	0
Collins, ph	1	0	0	0
Ross, p	0	0	0	0
Monge, p	0	0	0	0
Pactwa, p	0	0	0	0
Total	27	0	0	0

OAKLAND	ab	r	h	bi
North, cf	4	0	1	0
Washington, lf	4	2	1	0
Tenace, c	3	1	0	0
R. Jackson, rf	4	2	2	3
Bando, 3b	4	0	2	2
B. Williams, dh	4	0	0	0
Rudi, 1b	1	0	0	0
Holt, 1b	1	0	0	0
Harper, ph	1	0	0	0
Fosse, c	0	0	0	0
Cmpners, ss	3	0	1	0
Hopkins, pr	0	0	0	0
Te. Martnz, 2b	1	0	0	0
Garner, 2b	3	0	1	0
Maxvill, ss	1	0	1	0
Blue, p	0	0	0	0
Abbott, p	0	0	0	0
Lindblad, p	0	0	0	0
Fingers, p	0	0	0	0
Total	34	5	9	5

```
California......................  0 0 0 0 0 0 0 0 0 — 0
Oakland ......................  2 0 1 0 0 0 2 0 x — 5
```

CALIFORNIA	ip	h	r	er	bb	so
Ross (L, 0-1)	5	6	3	3	1	4
Monge	2	2	2	2	1	1
Pactwa	1	1	0	0	1	0

OAKLAND	ip	h	r	er	bb	so
Blue (W, 22-11)	5	0	0	0	2	2
Abbott	1	0	0	0	0	0
Lindblad	1	0	0	0	0	1
Fingers	2	0	0	0	0	32

E—Campaneris, Hampton. DP—Oakland 1. LOB—California 2, Oakland 8. 2B—Bando. HR—R. Jackson 2 (36). SB—Bando, Stanton, Hopkins. T—1:59. A—22,131.

Bibliography

Allen, Lee and Meany, Tom. *Kings of the Diamond.* New York: G. P. Putnam's Sons, 1965
Allen, Maury and Belinsky, Bo. *Bo: Pitching and Wooing.* New York: Dial Press, 1973
Allen, Maury. *Voices of Sport.* New York: Grosset & Dunlap, 1968
Alston, Walt and Burick, Si. *Alston and the Dodgers,* 1966
Angell, Roger. *The Summer Game.* New York: Viking Press, 1972
The Baseball Encyclopedia. New York: Macmillan, 1974
Best Sports Stories: 1960, 1964, 1965. Edited by Irving T. Marsh and Edward Ehre. New York: Dutton & Co., 1960, '64, '65
Book of Baseball Records. Edited and published by Seymour Siwoff, with cooperation of American and National baseball leagues, 1974
Creamer, Robert. *Babe.* New York: Simon & Schuster, 1974
Kahn, Roger. *The Boys of Summer.* New York: Harper & Row, 1973
Koufax, Sandy and Linn, Ed. *Koufax.* New York: Viking Press, 1966
Meany, Tom. *Baseball's Greatest Pitchers.* Cranbury, NJ: A. S. Barnes & Co., 1951
Neft, David S., Johnson, Roland T., Cohen, Richard M., Duetsch, Jordan A. *The Sports Encyclopedia: Baseball.* New York: Grosset & Dunlap, 1974
Pepe, Phil. *No-Hitter.* Four Winds Press, 1968.
Ritter, Lawrence S. *The Glory of Their Times.* New York: Macmillan, 1966
Sobol, Ken. *Babe Ruth··An American Life.* New York: Random House, 1974

Index